Asia–Pacific Constitutional Systems

This book describes and critically analyses the formal constitutional changes that have recently taken place in the Asia–Pacific region, embracing the countries of East and Southeast Asia and Pacific Island states. In examining the variety amongst constitutional systems operating in the region, it asks several key questions: What constitutional arrangements operate in the region and how can their fundamental differences in structure and operation be explained? How do social, political and economic factors limit the effects of the constitution in place? What lessons exist for the practice of constitutionalism elsewhere? The aim of the book is to ground the idea of constitutionalism in local and global practices, and, through examining these practices, to identify significant challenges to the workings of contemporary constitutional orders.

Graham Hassall is widely published in Pacific Studies and is an expert on the states of Melanesia in particular. He was Research Fellow and Director of the Asia–Pacific program in the Centre for Comparative Constitutional Studies at the University of Melbourne Law School, and is currently the Associate Dean of Undergraduate Studies at Landegg International University, Switzerland.

Cheryl Saunders is one of Australia's leading scholars in the fields of comparative and international law. She is the Director of the Centre for Comparative Constitutional Studies at the University of Melbourne. She has been an adviser to many governments in the region on the question of constitutional development and reform.

CAMBRIDGE ASIA–PACIFIC STUDIES

Cambridge Asia–Pacific Studies aims to provide a focus and forum for scholarly work on the Asia–Pacific region as a whole, and its component sub-regions, namely Northeast Asia, Southeast Asia and the Pacific Islands. The series is produced in association with the Research School of Pacific and Asian Studies at the Australian National University and the Australian Institute of International Affairs.

Editor: John Ravenhill

Editorial Board: James Cotton, Donald Denoon, Mark Elvin, Hal Hill, Ron May, Anthony Milner, Tessa Morris-Suzuki, Anthony Low

R. Gerard Ward and Elizabeth Kingdon (eds) *Land, Custom and Practice in the South Pacific*
0 521 47289 X hardback

Stephanie Lawson *Tradition Versus Democracy in the South Pacific*
0 521 49638 1 hardback

Walter Hatch and Kozo Yamamura *Asia in Japan's Embrace*
0 521 56176 0 hardback 0 521 56515 4 paperback

Alasdair Bowie and Daniel Unger *The Politics of Open Economies: Indonesia, Malaysia, the Philippines and Thailand*
0 521 58343 8 hardback 0 521 58683 6 paperback

David Kelly and Anthony Reid (eds) *Asian Freedoms*
0 521 62035 X hardback 0 521 63757 0 paperback

Danny Unger *Building Social Capital in Thailand*
0 521 63058 4 hardback 0 521 63931 X paperback

Yongnian Zheng *Discovering Chinese Nationalism in China: Modernization, Identity, and International Relations*
0 521 64180 2 hardback 0 521 64590 5 paperback

Doh C. Shin *Mass Politics and Culture in Democratizing Korea*
0 521 65146 8 hardback 0 521 65823 3 paperback

John A. Mathews and Dong-Sung Cho *Tiger Technology: The Creation of a Semiconductor Industry in East Asia*
0 521 66269 9 hardback

Samuel S. Kim (ed.) *Korea's Globalization*
0 521 77272 9 hardback 0 521 77559 0 paperback

Gregory W. Noble and John Ravenhill (eds), *The Asian Financial Crisis and the Architecture of Global Finance*
0 521 79091 3 hardback 0 521 79422 6 paperback

Peter Dauvergne *Loggers and Degradation in the Asia-Pacific: Corporations and Environmental Management*
0 521 80661 5 hardback 0 521 00134 X paperback

Anthony J. Langlois *The Politics of Justice and Human Rights: Southeast Asia and Universalist Theory*
0 521 80785 9 hardback 0 521 00347 4 paperback

Alan Dupont *East Asia Imperilled: Transnational Challenges to Security*
0 521 81153 8 hardback 0 521 01015 2 paperback

William T. Tow *Asia-Pacific Strategic Relations: Seeking Convergent Security*
0 521 80790 5 hardback 0 521 00368 7 paperback

John Ravenhill *APEC and the Construction of Pacific Rim Regionalism*
0 521 66094 7 hardback 0 521 66797 6 paperback

Asia–Pacific Constitutional Systems

Graham Hassall
Landegg International University

Cheryl Saunders
University of Melbourne

CAMBRIDGE UNIVERSITY PRESS
Cambridge, New York, Melbourne, Madrid, Cape Town,
Singapore, São Paulo, Delhi, Mexico City

Cambridge University Press
The Edinburgh Building, Cambridge CB2 8RU, UK

Published in the United States of America by Cambridge University Press, New York

www.cambridge.org
Information on this title: www.cambridge.org/9780521591294

© Graham Hassall and Cheryl Saunders 2002

This publication is in copyright. Subject to statutory exception
and to the provisions of relevant collective licensing agreements,
no reproduction of any part may take place without the written
permission of Cambridge University Press.

First published 2002

A catalogue record for this publication is available from the British Library

National Library of Australia Cataloguing in Publication data
Hassall, Graham.
Asia–Pacific constitutional systems.
Bibliography.
Includes index.
ISBN 0 521 59129 5
1. Constitutional law – Pacific Area. 2. Constitutional
law – Asia. I. Saunders, Cheryl. II. Title.
342.5

ISBN 978-0-521-59129-4 Hardback
ISBN 978-0-521-03341-1 Paperback

Cambridge University Press has no responsibility for the persistence or
accuracy of URLs for external or third-party internet websites referred to in
this publication, and does not guarantee that any content on such websites is,
or will remain, accurate or appropriate. Information regarding prices, travel
timetables, and other factual information given in this work is correct at
the time of first printing but Cambridge University Press does not guarantee
the accuracy of such information thereafter.

Contents

Acknowledgements	ix
Map: The Asia–Pacific Region	x
Introduction	1

Part I Modernity and Nation-States at the Dawn of the Global Era

1 Traditional states and colonisation	13
2 The modern constitution	29
3 Writing the constitution	54

Part II The Constitution of Modernity

4 The legislature	75
5 Representation	91
6 Head of state	119
7 Constitutional revision	141

Part III Democracy and the Rule of Law

8 Courts and the judiciary	169
9 The suspension of constitutional power	198
10 Devolution	222
Conclusion: Postmodernity and constitutionalism	241
Appendix: Chronology of constitutional events in the Asia Pacific	250
Bibliography	280
Index	301

Acknowledgements

This project has benefited from our collaboration with many colleagues. We owe particular thanks to the members of the Comparative Constitutional Law Committee of Lawasia, with whom we gathered on several occasions to confer on constitutional trends in the region. A number of these colleagues also contributed chapters to the Asia–Pacific Constitutional Yearbook, first published by the Centre for Comparative Constitutional Studies to cover the events of 1993, which contributed many insights to our own work.

Some of the ideas presented here were first formulated in papers presented at conferences of the Pacific History Association, the Asian Studies Association of Australia, and the International Association of Constitutional Law. We have also benefited greatly from exchanges with our colleagues at the University of Melbourne.

We were granted considerable insight into practical issues facing Pacific Islands through being allowed to observe at meetings of the Pacific Islands Law Officers Meeting (PILOM), an annual conference of attorneys-general from the Pacific region, and through association with the Constitutional Review Commission of Papua New Guinea and the Constitution Review Commission of Fiji.

The Asia–Pacific Region

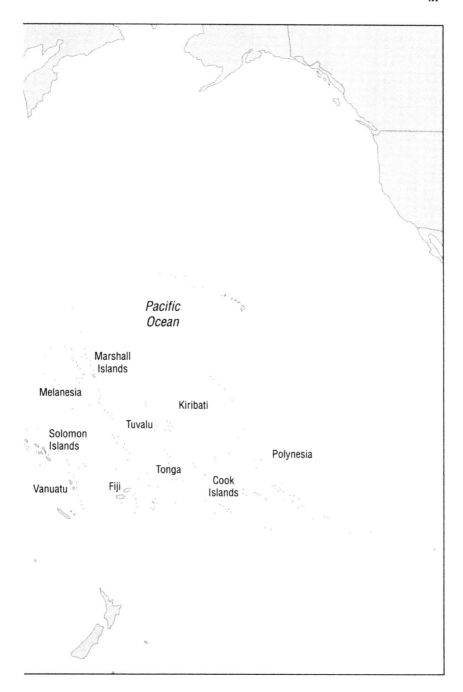

Introduction

Among the immense challenges facing states at the beginning of this new century is that of establishing a global order in which the legitimate rights of peoples and nations are balanced with the inevitable adjustments required by globalisation. The Declaration of Human Rights, adopted and acclaimed by the General Assembly of the United Nations on 10 December 1948, must surely have had more impact on thinking about law, constitutionalism and governance than any other document produced in the last century. In the twentieth century, government was based on the philosophical presuppositions of modernity: sovereignty resided in the people, and the legitimacy of states rested on adherence to the rule of law, the holding of periodic elections, and the maintenance of democratic values that maximised the freedom of the individual. While these presuppositions continue to inform the thinking of many occupants of public office, new ideas about governance are emerging from reflection on the successes and failures of statecraft in the last century.

This book provides an opportunity to reflect on the constitutional experience of the states of Asia and the Pacific during this period of transition. It consults history so as to face the future. It focuses on a unique sub-region of the world system, one with immense diversity in cultural, religious, political and social–economic traditions. Curiously, however, the constitutional arrangements of Southeast Asia and the Pacific Island countries have received relatively little attention in Western literature.[1] There are few studies of constitutionalism within anthropological literature,[2] and somewhat surprisingly, much political science literature avoids consideration of the constitutional framework. Legal literature, in turn, can tend to ignore the vital evidence supplied by social science literature.

This silence is open to a number of possible explanations. Discrepancies between what governments do and what constitutions promise may have raised questions about the nature of constitutionalism in the region and its usefulness as a subject for study by constitutionalists, as opposed to scholars in other disciplines. Yet this divergence between positive law and 'underlying legal postulates' is the very source of motivation for further inquiry.[3]

A process of constitutional development is under way, worthy of study in its own right, as nations and their peoples evaluate and refashion the colonial constitutional heritage. States in which formal constitutional change has taken place in recent years include Hong Kong, Singapore, Malaysia, Vietnam, Thailand, Taiwan, China, Nepal, Fiji, Papua New Guinea and Kiribati. Constitutional discussions continue in some of those states, as well as in others, notably the Cook Islands, Indonesia and Sri Lanka. Discussions between the leaders of North and South Korea herald the closure of hostilities that have split that nation for more than a generation. A 'civil coup' in Fiji and a 'copy-cat' coup in the Solomon Islands, on the other hand, and concern at the viability of some smaller states, point to the fragility of constitutionalism in the small states of Melanesia, and highlight the need for close study and evaluation of effective state-formation in the post-colonial Pacific.

This study also coincides with a period of constitutional reflection elsewhere (in Eastern Europe, in South Africa, and in the former Soviet Republics), since it has become increasingly evident that the established institutions and principles of government in the new democracies also need adjustment to meet the challenges of the emerging era of globalism. The method calls for both generalisations that are sufficiently explanatory and instances that bring specificity to the broader view.

This book is a contribution to the understanding of constitutional arrangements in Asia and the Pacific, as they currently operate. Its principal focus is the ASEAN group of countries and selected islands of the Pacific, including Papua New Guinea, the Solomon Islands, Vanuatu, Fiji and Tonga. Where appropriate, it also draws on countries outside that range to illustrate particular trends, approaches or challenges. Even confined in this way, the scope of the project is vast. It is not our intention, however, to deal with countries and systems in detail. Rather, the aim is to identify and explain constitutional arrangements in the region more broadly, using particular countries to illustrate their operation. For those with an interest in particular countries or systems, the book also offers a broad bibliography of the literature in the field.

By the latter part of the twentieth century, almost every independent state had a written constitution, entrenched in some way. The Asia–Pacific countries are no exception. The ostensible purpose of such instruments is to provide a framework for the allocation and exercise of state power. In the Western constitutional tradition, at least, constitutions ideally prescribe institutions and rules considered the most important for the state concerned and impose substantive or procedural restraints on state power.[4] Typically, they identify the state and create a position of head of state; specify the rights of individuals and groups which are to receive constitutional protection and, sometimes, prescribe responsibilities and duties; allocate a hierarchy to sources of law; describe the principal structures through which government is delivered; and outline the most important processes to be followed. The institutions invariably include a law-making body, an executive, and a judiciary. Other significant institutions, such as the military, the public service and an ombudsman, may be included as well. In some states the constitution also may allocate power between central and regional governments.

But, as David Sciulli suggests, successful constitutionalism does not reside in 'forms of government in and of themselves', or in the division of powers, or relations between the economy and the state, or even in the 'natural rights' and subjective interests of individuals. Success requires, rather, the emergence and growth of a *collegial form* in society, without which government will ultimately be reduced to forms of social control. In other words, without a collegial form of society – some form of bonding or networking or system of mutual interrelations – constitutionalism and the operation of government powers will do no more than prevent the pursuit of heterogeneous interests from fragmenting the body politic.[5]

Hence, the subject-matter of this book is not confined to constitutional law or theory, or to the formal institutions and other legal rules which derive their authority from constitutions. Indeed, constitutional studies cannot be confined to a single discipline, whether law, history or political science. What is required, rather, is inquiry that includes, in addition to the constitution and its associated arrangements, the operation of the system of government in practice; its historical evolution; the traditions on which it rests; and its social, political and economic context. Inevitably, these wider considerations will cast parts of the constitution in a new light and augment its bare terms significantly and substantially. They may, indeed, show that the constitution itself has limited or no effect, because it is not conceived as a binding instrument, because real power lies with people or institutions beyond the confines of the constitution, or for some other reason. Whereas the People's Republic of China has had new constitutions in 1954, 1975, 1978 and 1982, other post-war constitutions, including those of Japan and Indonesia, remain unchanged. Clearly, then, the nature and scope of constitutional change differ markedly between peoples and nations, and practices of constitutional revision are closely linked to other political and social forces.

Notwithstanding the multidisciplinary nature of the subject, the single disciplinary approach adopted by much modern scholarship tends to strip constitutional studies of its inherent complexity. If it is true, as Loughlin has recently argued, that public law in England 'is simply a sophisticated form of political discourse; that controversies within the subject are simply extended political disputes',[6] then a similar relationship exists between law and politics in the Asia Pacific.

One of the central concerns of this book is examination of the relationship between the legitimacy of the constitutional framework and its effectiveness in the delivery of good governance. In the context of Western social theory, Jurgen Habermas has suggested the inadequacies of both liberal democracy and welfare models of government, on the grounds that the former protects rights at the expense of fair distribution of wealth, while the latter delivers welfare while creating dependency and reducing individual choice. His 'third paradigm' of constitutionalism develops, instead, an approach to government which is based on the fullest exchange of the views of the people concerned. It assumes that the decisions thus reached will be the best in the circumstances, so long as the communication which takes place is not distorted. The present study is interested in how such a concept applies in the Asia Pacific. For Habermas, it 'reproduces itself only in the forms of a constitutionally regulated circulation of power, which should be nourished by the communications of an unsubverted public sphere that in turn is rooted in the associational network of a liberal civil society and gains support from the core private spheres of an undisturbed lifeworld'.[7]

It is easily conceded that no system reaches an ideal state of communication; to suggest that it be sought in the contested societies of the Asia Pacific may require even deeper apologetics. Apart from the logistical difficulties, now dwindling in the face of information technology, there are also immense practical impediments to the removal of distortions to communication which favour the more articulate, the more persuasive, the better situated, the more interested and the more affluent.[8] Yet while Habermas' views were developed principally in the context of Western, and specifically European, constitutional debate, they nevertheless suggest at a more general level an approach to constitutionalism which has universal application.

Given the incompatibility of significant Western constitutional concepts with Asian legal traditions, it is not surprising that constitutionalism has a reputation as a legal gloss for authoritarian rule.[9] This was particularly so during the period of martial law in the Philippines under President Marcos, 1972–84.[10] Marcos spoke of a 'New Society', but his manipulation of the constitution and public power came to be known as 'Constitutional Authoritarianism'.[11] Ideals of constitutional rule and the spread of democracy have at times also given in to the exercise of centralised authority elsewhere in the region. In Indonesia, Soekarno established 'Guided Democracy', in Cambodia King Sihanouk promoted 'Buddhist Socialism', and in South Vietnam Ngo Nhu Diem cultivated 'Personalism'. Recently, the 'Singapore School', led by retired prime minister Lee Kuan Yew, has advocated a state philosophy based on 'New Confucianism'.[12] Doctrines of authoritarian rule have also been established in Burma, China, Taiwan, North Korea and Brunei.

A contextual approach is particularly appropriate for the comparative study of constitutional systems which includes, for present purposes, generalisations about constitutional arrangements across a number of different states in the same region. There is little insight to be gained from the mere juxtaposition of legal principles and institutions without taking into account the historical, philosophical and human circumstances to which they respond and which affect their operation and significance. Arguably, a contextual approach is even more important, albeit more difficult, for those who seek to understand the constitutional arrangements of states with a history and culture very different from their own.[13] A useful starting-point, variously identified in legal comparative literature, is the manner in which different legal systems perform common functions or meet common problems.[14] In comparing constitutional arrangements, functions necessarily performed everywhere include community decision-making of all kinds, ranging from general rules to their day-to-day application; dispute resolution and prevention; the provision and financing of public goods; and defence against internal and external threats, however conceived. A common issue, or problem, is the basis on which these arrangements are accepted by the communities to which they apply.

Following Anderson's suggestion that nations are 'imagined communities',[15] the constitution plays an essential role in defining the nation in legal form. Where such nations bring together numerous ethnic traditions, there will be a reduction of diversity in such things as language and culture. To the nationalist movements that emerged in opposition to the colonial powers, the 'constitution' was a statement of and framework for independence. The nationalist idea was spread by the communists under Ho Chi Minh in Vietnam, by Sun Yat Sen in China, by Soekarno in Indonesia, and by Bonifacio and Rizal in the Philippines. Sun Yat Sen's constitutional framework was adopted by the Republic of China (Taiwan), which had been under Japanese occupation (1895–1945) and which established its constitution in 1947. Since such national constitutions invariably break with the received constitutional traditions, they are often guided by a manifesto or statement of guiding principles.

Despite its multidisciplinary approach, however, this study only considers developments in politics and public life to the extent that they inform a study of the constitutional framework itself. This means that the book discusses only the framework, rather than each and every subsequent development having constitutional significance. For such detail, the reader must refer to more country-specific studies.

Description and understanding is one thing: evaluation is another. It cannot entirely be avoided in constitutional study. Constitutions, whether formal or informal, exist to structure the exercise of power in accordance with particular standards. Compliance with these, both in substance and operation, is the essence of constitutionalism, which is far more important from the standpoint of the communities concerned, than the constitutions themselves. In a comparative constitutional project, there is an obvious danger of applying too narrow a framework of analysis to different systems, derived from more familiar, or dominant, constitutional cultures. Equally, however, danger lies in having no analytical framework at all and thus no standards, accepting every regime as constitutional and undermining the purpose of the distinction: constitutional scholars must steer a course between uncritical adherence to their own view of constitutionalism on the one hand and unbounded relativism on the other.

The principal characteristics we adopt for this purpose are the emphasis on procedure rather than fixed, substantive standards; the requirement for shared and structured as opposed to arbitrary exercise of public power; the need for wide involvement in public decisions, both to secure quality and as a source of legitimacy; and the underlying assumptions of human worth, which must be reflected in any constitutional arrangement. Accordingly, this study adopts four broad themes for the purpose of constitutional analysis: legitimacy, democracy, justice, and prosperity.

Legitimacy refers to the acceptance of the principles on which a state is founded and of the means for their revision. Legitimacy in this sense confers a sense of constitutional unity—or, at least, coherence—without which the state is in danger of serious internal conflict, or even collapse. The most obvious and direct means of establishing legitimacy is through the consent of the people at the time of the formation of the state. Legitimacy also can be established over time, however, if the needs of the people are met and a sense of unity of purpose develops. The source of a constitution has great bearing on its legitimacy, and the legitimacy of a constitution has bearing on its effectiveness. In numerous non-Western countries, the constitutional state is an alien creature, so there must be effort to boost constitutional legitimacy. A constitution must come from a body higher than that which subsequently enacts ordinary laws. The law of the constitution is not the source but the consequence of the rights of the individuals. This insight led to the increased significance of courts as protectors of people's rights and as determiners of the law.

Legitimacy requires effort both to establish and to maintain. In states that have multiple centres of coherence that interact, compete and clash, there is often competition from other sources of power, offering methods of social ordering which rely on control and which are not necessarily sympathetic to a return to constitutional government. Even in normal times, the ability of a state to build and maintain legitimacy is affected by the quality of its dialogue with the people. In this way, the legitimacy of a state provides a foundation for the operation of democracy.

Democracy, broadly defined, is a corollary of legitimacy. Its content is not fixed in detail but may vary within states and over time. As a minimum, however, it requires a regular choice of leaders by the people, on a basis which is fair, to make decisions which cannot or will not be made by the people themselves. Regular elections confer a degree of popular control both over the leaders and over the decisions they make. They imply that the power of government is held by the leaders on trust for the people. Necessarily, as trustees, they are accountable for its exercise. This concept of government, coupled with the right to participate, provides people in turn with an incentive to take an interest in public and community life and to be informed.

Whether the incentives on either side are sufficient is a question for the twenty-first century, recently joined in the debate on deliberative democracy. The simple majoritarian model of electoral democracy has been modified already, however, in other respects. In the second half of the last century, the experience of global war and the atrocities associated with it prompted international and national recognition of civil, political, social and economic rights on a wider scale than ever before. The protection of rights affects electoral democracy by limiting the decisions which communities may make, by identifying circumstances in which the interests of minorities or individuals are entitled to prevail, and by providing new, qualitative criteria to evaluate the decisions that are made. There has been a continuing dispute between regions of the world, not yet resolved, over the extent to which particular rights are culturally specific, and concerning the priorities which should apply between them. All constitutional states, however, accept the underlying imperative of a social and political community in which individuals are valued and are free to pursue goals of their own choosing, to fully develop their personalities, abilities and talents, and to contribute the fruits of their efforts back to society.

Justice is a response to the acceptance of equality, or equal worth. It encompasses the whole business of government: the rules which are made, their administration, the resolution of disputes, and the distribution of wealth. It requires wisdom and experience and impartiality in the governing institutions. It is both subjective and objective: decisions must not only be fair but be perceived to be fair, in the interests both of harmony and of the legitimacy of the system. Justice is antithetical to corruption, which privileges some without reason or fairness.[16]

Prosperity has its usual connotations: economic development, enhanced growth rates, improved infrastructure, broader industrial opportunities, and the spread of material benefits. It is included here for its broader goal, however: its contribution to the well-being of people and to their ability to make best use of their potential through life. Important products of prosperity include health and education in both their technical and broader senses. In industrial communities, prosperity also may be a precondition for a clean and safe environment.

A central purpose of democratic constitutions has always been protection of the concept of a 'public sphere' in which all citizens are free to discuss issues of public concern. A 'civil society' built on the values of free speech and free association provides feedback about the performance of government and a forum for discussion of alternative policy options. The capacity of civil society to discuss the constitution has also been an important factor in choosing mechanisms of constitutional design and change. Societies lacking an educated and informed public have fewer resources available for such discussion. But civil society is only possible where the constitutional order is agreed. Civil societies, whatever their form, presuppose 'a juridical structure, a constitution, that articulates the principles underlying their internal organisation'.[17]

At times and places throughout the Asia Pacific, constitutional orders have been under grave threat of disruption and even dissolution. In some cases, the threat has been state-sponsored and, in others, based in the discontents of fragmented societies. Thus, it cannot be overlooked that at the beginning of the twenty-first century armed conflicts continue to thwart aspirations for democracy and prosperity in Sri Lanka, Nepal, India, Pakistan, China, Indonesia, the Philippines, Papua New Guinea and the Solomon Islands. The constitutional order has been disrupted in Fiji by no fewer than three military and civil 'coups'.

It seems evident that colonisation has left much of the Asia Pacific a paradoxical legacy of both a strong executive and a reliance on the Westminster model of parliamentary democracy. The result has been a failure of parliaments to function well, often having their role diminished by a president or prime minister, or even by the armed forces. The accountability that parliament is meant to provide in such matters as scrutiny of public accounts, and in controlling the use of power by the executive, is often lacking. Students of governance in this region must recognise, admit and respond to the harsh reality that a large number of constitutional systems currently in operation are not delivering the justice, legitimacy, democracy and prosperity they promise.

This book pursues these themes principally through examining the functions which governments everywhere perform and the issues with which they must deal. First, however, it surveys the main underlying influences on constitutional systems in Asian and Pacific countries: the historical phases of constitutional development, each of which has left its mark, and the political and philosophical approaches derived both from history and from more recent circumstances.

Notes

1 The point is made solely for the purposes of comparison with the bodies of literature on constitutional systems elsewhere. It neither overlooks nor underestimates the important scholarship which in fact exists on the constitutional arrangements of countries in the region, individually and collectively. The scope of this literature may be gauged from the Bibliography: there is little extant literature describing the theory and practice. While there are few studies of constitutional processes in Asia, a notable contribution is that by Nasution, *The Aspiration for Constitutional Government in Indonesia*. There are gaps in the literature from the first round of constitution-making (1940s–1950s) into more recent times (e.g. Cambodia in 1993). In many constitutional studies, the processes of actual constitutional construction remain hidden, presumed, and form part of the context, rather than the rules in play (see Lane, *Constitutions and Political Theory*).
2 See Rodman, 'A Law unto Themselves'.
3 Chiba, 'Three Dichotomies of Law in Pluralism', 423.
4 Lane, *Constitutions and Political Theory*, 10.
5 Sciulli, *The Theory of Societal Constitutionalism*.
6 Loughlin, *Public Law and Political Theory*, 4.
7 Habermas, *Between Facts and Norms*, 408.
8 See, for example, the 'sceptical eye' which Stokes turns on 'deliberation and its effects': 'Pathologies of Deliberation', 123.
9 Beer, *Constitutional Systems in Late Twentieth Century Asia*.
10 Republic of the Philippines, Constitutional Commission of 1986, *The Constitution of the Republic of the Philippines*, National BookStore, 1986; Bernas, dismantling the Dictatorship.
11 Payayo, 'The rule of Law and the Decree-Making power of the President'.
12 Mahbubani, 'The Dangers of Decadence' and 'The Pacific Way'.
13 See, for example, Buxbaum, *Traditional and Modern Legal Institutions in Asia and Africa*.
14 See, for example, Zweigart and Kötz, *An Introduction to Comparative Law*.
15 Anderson, *Imagined Communities*.
16 Abas, 'Legal Perspective of the Third World'.
17 Arato and Cohen, 'Civil Society and Social Theory', 201.

Part I

Modernity and Nation-States at the Dawn of the Global Era

1 Traditional states and colonisation

The constitutions in operation in the Asia Pacific in the second half of the twentieth century, often described as statements of 'national independence', should more properly be regarded as being among the final artefacts of the colonial era. Their imposition on peoples and states was everywhere contested, albeit at different levels of intensity and in ways sometimes explicit, but also in deep-rooted, almost subterranean forms that continue to survive and manifest themselves in the conflict-laden public lives of modern times. But before telling these stories, we must review an earlier period, for the peoples of Southeast Asia and the Pacific Islands have constitutional histories considerably more extensive than those of current memory.

Knowledge of prior constitutional arrangements assists an understanding of the present in all parts of the world: in Asia and the Pacific, it is essential. Before regular European contact, political communities throughout Asia conducted their affairs according to sophisticated legal codes, as did the chiefly regimes of Polynesia and other parts of the Pacific. Relations between ruling elites and peasantry were based on patron–client relationships akin to those that existed under European feudalism. Obligations had to be observed on both sides to ensure maintenance of the political system.

As a generalisation, in the case of most former colonies and as ironic as it may appear to be, independence constitutions were greatly influenced by the legal institutions and practices of those responsible for their bondage.[1] There was some tutelage together with enslavement, and this same mixture of admiration and resentment continues to affect contemporary attitudes towards modernity in the region. Its legal form, the modern constitutional state, is at times selectively applied to meet a combination of modern and traditional aspirations, so as to produce sometimes a more autochthonous constitutionalism and at other times an apparent withdrawal – or else again, a combination of the two.

Traditional states in Southeast Asia

There were some forty kingdoms, principalities and sultanates spread across Southeast Asia prior to the colonial period. Archipelagic states were either land-based 'agrarian' societies that controlled water for the cultivation of rice, or sea-based societies that depended on navigation and commerce. The agrarian states that preceded modern Burma, Vietnam, Cambodia and China were 'organised and controlled by a centralised hierarchy of officials, and headed by a ruler who was absolute and (in some cases) regarded as semi-divine'.[2] On Java, the agrarian-based kingdoms were located in highly fertile valleys and plateaux between volcanic complexes and along rivers. Peasant populations lived as compact villages and practised wet-rice agriculture and intensive irrigation. The centre of the kingdom was the court town with its royal palace complex. Kingship was based on the notion of a close connection between the structure of the universe and the realm of man. The concept of divine kingship helped to stabilise ancient governments through religious sentiment; but it was relatively easy for a usurper to seize the capital and the divine symbols of kingship and authority. Thus, Cambodian, Burmese and Javanese histories feature successive revolts, in which the social order and even the bureaucracy remained unchanged but dynasties supplanted each other.

The sea-based kingdoms, whose rulers were often Muslim, were each centred on a port and usually had a large trading fleet but not an extensive hinterland and population. The major sea powers – Sriwijaya (a Hindu empire, based on Sumatra and Malaya around 700–1200), Malacca (on the opposite side of the strait), Bantam (on the Sunda Straits), and the port states of North Java, Brunei in North Borneo, and Macassar in the South Celebes – were governed by aristocratic elites who used naval power to control the trade of such goods as pepper, rice and spices.

Not all Southeast Asian societies had well-formed state-type models. In the archipelago now known as the Philippines, cultures were characterised by Malay kinship structures and patterns of leadership. The first settlers established autonomous *barangays* of approximately 2000 people, each headed by a *datu*, or chief, whose position could be hereditary or won through wealth or strength. Some *barangays* formed federations to enhance their security, and each had a system for making laws and for adjudication. Society was hierarchical, consisting of nobility based around the *datu* and his relatives, and there were also freemen and slaves. The *datus* promulgated laws, some of which were preserved as written codes.[3]

In reviewing pre-colonial law in Asia, Hooker refers to three 'greater' traditions based on the Indian, Islamic and Chinese legal worlds around which 'lesser' traditions were established in individual countries and among specific peoples.[4] Whereas rights may not have been given explicit attention in pre-colonial polities, sovereigns and administrators were generally bound by laws derived from religious traditions and from other lore specifying their duties towards their subjects. Social relationships in these traditional legal worlds were based on status. Law was concerned with the distribution of personal obligation between persons of different status. Obligation was thus a function of status, individual initiative was limited, and the responsibility of individuals had moral and ethical dimensions more than legal ones.

The *Indian tradition*, initially based on Hindu law, had a formative influence on Burma, Siam, Champá and Khmer, and Java between the seventh and fifteenth centuries. Rules for moral and social order referred to 'duty' and to ethics. The laws (the *Agama*) of the fourteenth-century kingdom of Majapahit, which originated in the Code of Manu, codified law in ten categories[5] and solved disputes through collective decision-making (*musawarat-mupakat*), a process that remains 'one of the most important techniques of handling administrative affairs in modern Javanese rural society', indicative of 'the continuity of a Javanese tradition'.[6] Majapahit's influence also continues in the term *nusantara*, used by modern Indonesia to recall the glory of the former Javanese empire.

Buddhist law texts, like their Hindu predecessors, provided rules of conduct for leaders and their subjects within a context of ethical behaviour based on a religious view of human nature in relation to the universe.[7] Thus, traditional Burmese law (Dhammathat) comprised the Adoration of Buddha, the story of Rishi Manu, and rules modelled on the Hindu Dharmasastras applying to, for example, marriage, gifts, divorce, and inheritance. These laws expressed sets of obligations, rather than rules.[8] The Buddhist kingdoms, notably those in Burma, Thailand and Laos, were quasi-hereditary but less highly regulated than the Vietnamese.

Thailand's history of law and constitution can be traced for almost a millennium and shows the extent to which contemporary forms of governance are influenced by ancient polities. Thailand's traditional legal order was also based on the Code of Manu (Dhammasattham), introduced from India through the Mon Kingdom some time before the Sukhothai period (1238–1350), and the Code of Manu is now part of the Thai national heritage and mythology. Classical Thai law is contained in the Legal Code of Rama I (1805), also known as the Law of the Three Great Seals. The Thai version of the Dharmasastras – Pra

Thammasat – codifies laws in three volumes,[9] and the decisions of Thai monarchs make up the Rajattham literature.

The Kingdom of Sukhothai adopted a paternalistic system of government in which the king, although possessing absolute sovereign power, tended closely to the needs of his subjects. Khmer traditions of kingship continued through the Ayuthaya period (1350–1767), until Brahmin concepts of religion and government transformed the idea of king as 'father of his people' into one of a god on earth who 'rules with righteousness'.[10] King Barommatrailokanat (1448–88) divided civil from military administration and established a strong centralised government. The Ratanakosin Kingdom established in 1767 in Bangkok continued this basic pattern, until King Rama V (Chulalongkorn the Great, 1868–1910) initiated major reforms in response to the threat posed by colonialism.

The *Islamic tradition* had its main effect in the islands of Southeast Asia. Islam appeared in what is now Indonesia around 1100–1300 and continued to spread geographically until 1900. Muslim societies now extend from southern Thailand through Malaysia to Indonesia and the southern Philippines. Islamic law, which derives from the Koran as revealed by the Prophet Muhammad, is equated with justice. It is complemented by the Shariah, comprising legal decisions on matters not considered in the Koran and defining crime, sin, obligation, duty, rights, and so on. But Islam as practised in Southeast Asia differs from its practice elsewhere, most notably through adherence to local traditions and customs ('urf). Hooker identifies four 'types' of Islamic texts that state the basic rules of Islam in accordance with local cultural patterns (*adat*) and which deal with such matters.[11] By the late twentieth century, Islam had become the central constitutional ideology in Pakistan, Brunei and Malaysia, and a significant influence on the law in Indonesia, southern Thailand and the southern Philippines.

The *Chinese tradition* comprised law codes based on Confucian principles. These supported an administrative and social system through bureaucratic regulation. In traditional China, the authority of the emperor rested on the 'mandate of heaven'. As explained by Chen:

> Although traditional Chinese thought appears to lack the concept of democracy (*minzhu*) or sovereignty of the people, there are elements in Confucianism which emphasise the ruler's need to pay attention to the well-being of the people. Scholars have termed these ideas *minben*, or 'people-as-basis', and frequently quote a statement by Mencius, a disciple of Confucius and one of the founders of Confucianism: 'The people rank the highest, the spirits of land and grain come next, and the ruler counts the least'.[12]

Laws regulated relations with the state, rather than individual behaviour. Confucianism may be characterised as an essentially secular, humanist natural law theory that emphasised adherence to such moral values as benevolence, education and harmony, but within a hierarchical social order. Government was headed by a central authority figure, governing under the 'mandate of heaven' and advised by a bureaucracy selected on academic merit. The Chinese tradition extended to Vietnam, through the *Le* Code.

Traditional states in the Pacific Islands

The second region treated in this book, the Pacific Islands, broadly comprises three ethnographic and geographic regions: Melanesia in the southwest Pacific, Polynesia in the eastern Pacific, and Micronesia in the north Pacific.

In Melanesia, societies traditionally organised themselves around strong individual leaders and within strong ties of kinship and trade with neighbours. No 'states' developed as such, although clans possessed and exercised sovereignty over their lands. The countries of Polynesia, in contrast, developed more formalised and hierarchical political structures, such that the monarchs of Tonga, Samoa, Hawaii and other kingdoms ruled over scattered island groups. The islands of the north Pacific comprise low coral limestone and sand islands and their natural resources are limited to phosphate deposits, marine products, and deep seabed minerals. The Marshall Islands, for instance, has no arable land or forests. Such a stark geographic and natural landscape inevitably impacts on how its residents organise their affairs.

Melanesia traditionally consisted of small self-contained communities of 300–3000 members, each having a distinct language and a social structure based on common affinity. Leadership seldom extended over large areas, in part because technology was based on wood, stone and bone, and there was no written literature. In contrast to Southeast Asia's written codes of law, rules in Melanesia were held in custom and in myth, conveyed through words and actions. Rules covered relations with the natural and the supernatural. Some laws were believed to originate with the ancestors. Law was not an independent discipline, but an integral part of the way of life. Leaders did not 'make' law but gave 'wise counsel of what ought to be, or be avoided'. Knowledge of law, in this sense, was transmitted by clans through dialogue at the meeting house. Law thus was part of the shared knowledge of the community, rather than a 'phenomenon which controls society'.[13]

Melanesian and Polynesian societies have been distinguished by reference to differences in scale, structure, political performance, and qualities of leadership.[14] Melanesian groups were generally smaller than

Polynesian and had autonomous kinship–residential groups rather than extensive groups under a paramount chief. As a consequence of having more effective political structures, Polynesians were better able to resist colonial intrusion. Melanesia's 'big-man' system was more capitalist, while Polynesia's extended hierarchies tended to be feudal.[15] In Melanesia, leadership was acquired (through hereditary chieftainship and investiture, through personal prowess, or through appointment by others) and each 'big-man' had constantly to work at establishing and maintaining his relationships.

In contrast with such societies where traditional status and power were *achieved*, and where modern electoral systems tend to be more egalitarian and democratic, those in the Polynesian societies of the eastern Pacific reflect a tradition in which status and power were traditionally *ascribed*.[16] Tonga, Fiji and Western Samoa are among those states that have most effectively retained traditional, chiefly (or aristocratic) constitutional principles – few of which were democratic. Highly centralised chiefly societies supported powerful monarchs, buttressed by nobility and revered and feared by the commoners and slaves. Consequently, aristocracies, or 'chiefly societies', while now somewhat constitutionally limited, checked the potential for popular democracy.

Tonga provides an illustration of traditional government arrangements in Polynesia. The king (Tui Tonga) has been accepted as both the sacred and secular ruler since the first Tui Tonga is believed to have been born to a mother and Tangaloa (The God in the Sky) in approximately AD 1000. The Tui Tonga, whose authority thus came from a divine source and who was the people's mediator with the gods, controlled a highly organised monarchical system. At one time the greater Tongan empire is thought to have included Niue, Samoa, Tokelau, Wallis and Futuna, Rotuma, and part of the Lau group of Fiji.[17]

Tonga was a class society. Beneath the kings (*ha'a tu'i*) were chiefs (*hou'eiki*), then *kau mu'a* (sons of a union between a chief and a *matapule*), *ha'a matapule* (chief's attendants), and *kau tu'a* (commoners). At the bottom were the *kau popula* (slaves). Land was divided among the principal chiefs. The different social classes were linked by a 'deep sense of obligation' which, together with severe punishments for the transgression of social taboos, 'helped to maintain stability, peace and prosperity in the land'. But absolute power lay with the village chiefs and, 'as chiefly ambitions grew, they fostered local autonomy, thus threatening the political unity of Tonga as a whole'.[18]

This brief survey of the politico-religious circumstances of peoples spread across the Asia Pacific reminds us that colonisation implies the imposition of new systems on old. Of course, the picture on the ground was far more complex and societies around the Pacific contained wide variations in patterns of leadership. In Vanuatu, for example, the ceremonial killing of pigs bestowed rank and responsibilities on men from Aoba and Malekula,[19] while on Erromango bravery was required, and on Efate, rank was hereditary. Systems of land ownership were similarly diverse and land remains a source of identity. Clan holdings were clearly known and could be temporarily, but not permanently, alienated. Land holding was patrilineal in West Ambai and matrilocal in East Ambai and North Pentecost.

In the absence of central governing institutions, people followed custom and well-established methods of settling disputes, whether through fear of shame or of removal from the community, or simply because custom was 'intertwined with the way of life of the community'.[20]

Colonisation in Southeast Asia

From the seventeenth century into the nineteenth, Europeans came to Asia and the Pacific in search of wealth and expansion of empire. The French, Portuguese, British, Dutch, Spanish and Americans exerted their influence, not only imposing colonial rule but also establishing such infrastructure as roads and railways, and elaborating new regimes of taxation and administration. Colonial rule was either direct or indirect: whereas direct rule involved the removal of existing leadership, indirect rule incorporated traditional leaders into the colonial project. This recognition or rejection of traditional authority influenced the power arrangements in later independence constitutions. In each colony, doctrines evolved to govern the new mix of Western and traditional law, and by the end of the colonial era the forty states in Southeast Asia had shrunk to approximately ten.

The Portuguese arrived first. They established a number of enclaves in the sixteenth century, in Goa, Diu, Daman, Calicut, Colombo, Malacca, Macau, Java, the Moluccas, and Timor. From early in the seventeenth century the Dutch began to establish their authority over all parts of the East Indies. By the beginning of the twentieth century the borders distinguishing the Dutch from British, Australian and German colonies were clearly defined. The Netherlands East Indies administration had been transformed from a traditional patrimonial to an authoritarian model, and its economy had been enlarged. But there were seeds of change. The colonial experience prompted national sentiment among the Malays. It aroused interest in new approaches to government based on socialism, communism or democracy.

British colonies in Southeast Asia encompassed Penang (1786) and

Singapore (1819), which together formed the Straits Settlements, the Malay states (1874 to 1930), British Borneo (1896) and Burma (1886). When nine states of the Malay peninsula and the British settlements Penang and Malacca formed the Union of Malaya in 1946, the sultans only agreed under duress. Thirty-nine Malay organisations declared that the British document was illegally obtained and established the United Malays National Organisation (UMNO) to restore Malay sovereignty. First President Dato Onn resigned as head of UMNO when the party refused to permit membership of non-Malays. His new multiracial party, IMP (Independence of Malaya Party), failed to attract a large following. A 1947 declaration of the Pan Malayan Council of Joint Action[21] demanded a United Malaya, inclusive of Singapore; a fully-elected central legislature for the whole of Malaya; equal political rights for all who regarded Malaya as their real home and as the object of their loyalty; recognition of the full sovereignty of the Malay rulers; Malay control over matters relating to custom and the Muslim religion; and special measures to advance the position of the Malays.

When the British realised the depth of Malay opposition to the Union, they agreed to discuss the possibility of a federation. When established in 1948 it included a conference of rulers (instead of a council of sultans under a British governor). Each of the nine Malay states had a state council, an executive council to advise the ruler, and a chief minister (Mentri Besar). The rulers possessed powers over citizenship rights. Unlike the Union proposal, the federal proposal was worked out through consultation.

The Malay states, apart from Brunei, gained independence as the Federation of Malaya in 1957.[22] In 1961 Malayan Prime Minister Tunku Abdul Rahman proposed a political union between the Federation of Malaya, Singapore, Sarawak, North Borneo and Brunei, with a central government responsible for defence, foreign affairs and internal security, and states responsible for education and labour. Singaporeans supported the proposal at a referendum held in September 1962 and Malaysia was formed on 16 September 1963. Brunei chose not to join, and the initiative was opposed by the Philippines and by Indonesia, whose revolutionary President Soekarno launched military action now referred to as *Confrontasi*.

Britain and Portugal leased from China the small islands of Hong Kong and Macau, respectively. Following the defeat of China by the British in the opium wars, a series of 'unequal treaties', beginning with the 1842 Peace of Nanking, transferred first Hong Kong Island and then additional Chinese territory to British control. The Crown Colony's reversion to Chinese sovereignty on 1 July 1997 was decided by China and Britain without reference to the Hong Kong people.

The French imposed their legal code on Laos in 1893, and on other regions of Indochina between 1862 and 1884. Despite several armed revolts, Laos continued as a French colony until Japanese occupation during World War II. In response to nationalist pressures, France granted Laos formal independence within the French Union in July 1949. Although the French withdrew from Indochina following defeat by the Vietnamese in 1954, North and South Vietnam remained divided and at war until 1975. Throughout the colonial era, Thailand retained its sovereign independence while at the same time experiencing considerable influence in its economy and politics from European interests.

The archipelago now known as the Philippines has been contested by the Spanish, the Portuguese, and Malay Muslims. In 1571 the Spaniards established their capital in Manila before moving into the easily accessible hinterland, securing loyalty from local chiefs by diplomacy or by force. Land was allocated among various clerical orders under a feudal-type arrangement that required geographic regions, or *haciendas,* to deliver specified produce for export. A governor-general appointed by the Spanish king had legislative and judicial power, subject only to the authority of the Supreme Court (Royal Audencia) and the Catholic Archbishop. Several times in the early 1800s, the colony sent delegates to the Spanish parliament (Cortes). Spain's colonial code of laws and its civil, penal and commercial codes were applicable.

There were numerous revolts against Spanish rule, notably the Katipunan led by Andres Bonifacio. Although the revolutionaries declared the first Philippines Republic in June 1898 on the basis of the Malalos constitution, the United States purchased the Philippines, Guam and Puerto Rico from Spain under the USA–Spanish Treaty of Paris, and the Philippines remained an American colony until gaining independence in 1946. In 1900 military administration was replaced by an elected government, and Commissioner Taft enacted 499 laws creating a civil service, municipal and provincial boundaries, a code for civil procedure, the Philippines Constabulary, bureaus for agriculture and forestry, a public school system, and government. Municipal elections were held in 1901 and provincial elections a year later. A bicameral legislature was established and the Tydings-McDuffie Act 1934, by which the Philippines attained Commonwealth status in 1935, promised full independence at 4 July 1946.

Colonisation in the Pacific Islands

The Pacific Islands were no less subject to colonial rule than the lands and peoples of Southeast Asia. After World War I some colonies were regulated as mandates of the League of Nations, while others were administered outside international scrutiny or provisions. Although the mandate system was intended to provide national administration under international supervision, pressure from the Australian and South African governments resulted in the creation of class 'C' mandates, described in paragraph 6 of article 22 of the League of Nations Covenant:

> There are Territories, such as South West Africa, and certain of the South Pacific Islands, which, owing to the sparseness of their population, or their small size, or their remoteness from the centres of civilization, and other circumstances, can best be administered under the laws of the mandatory as integral portions of its territory, subject to the safeguards above mentioned in the interests of the indigenous population.[23]

Following World War II, when the newly established United Nations considered the question of trusteeship, US interests in the north Pacific were accommodated through the creation of 'Strategic Trusts', supervised by the Security Council, in addition to 'non-Strategic Trusts', supervised by the General Assembly through its subordinate Trusteeship Council. In all trusteeship areas, colonial powers were responsible for promoting social and political advance, and training towards self-government. In the Pacific, however, impetus towards independence only followed the 1960 UN declaration on decolonisation. Subsequent decolonisation of Asian and African states finally provided the impetus to decolonisation in the Pacific, and Western Samoa was the first Pacific state to be granted full political independence, in 1962.

Apart from the phosphate-rich island of Nauru, which was placed under the joint UN Trusteeship of Australia, New Zealand and Great Britain,[24] European motives for remaining in the Pacific were more often strategic than commercial. Relationships established with small kingdoms and island communities were designed to thwart the influence of other European powers in the region, and Pacific territories also proved to be valuable as 'pawns' for trade in the global power game of imperialism.

Germany had interests in the Solomon Islands until 1898 and in Samoa, New Guinea, the Caroline Islands and the Mariana Islands until 1914. Following German annexation of New Guinea in 1884, an agreement between Germany and Great Britain at the turn of the century identified the island of Bougainville with New Guinea, rather than with the Solomon Islands. The result was a colonial border between the Bougainvilleans and the communities to the east with which they were associated, laying the foundations for an ethno-political dispute still unresolved more than a century later. At the beginning of World War I, German rule was replaced by Australian military control until 1921, when the British, on behalf of the Commonwealth of Australia, assumed a League of Nations mandate over New Guinea.

Japan occupied parts of Micronesia to secure strategic objectives and subsequently secured the Caroline Islands, Palau, Truk, and the Marshall Islands as a League of Nations trusteeship. In 1935 Japan withdrew from the League of Nations and intensified fortifications on its Pacific islands without international scrutiny. A number of smaller islands in the Pacific remain 'incorporated territories' of larger powers, and their small geographic size and population suggest this status will continue.[25]

The British and French shared control over the New Hebrides Condominium. The 1914 Protocol declared the islands a 'region of joint influence' and provided for a complicated court system, English, French and New Hebridean codes of law, and the establishment of joint services. To ni-Vanuatu, colonialism meant labour-recruitment ('blackbirding'), missionisation, and Anglo-French administration. The European impact devastated the indigenous population, which declined from an estimated 100,000 in 1892 to 45,000 in 1935. Post-war moves towards nationalism and independence were fuelled by land alienation that occurred gradually during 1888–1941, and by the clash of conflicting English and French colonial policies ('self-sufficiency' versus 'assimilation').[26] Just as the New Hebrides was the most politically divided Pacific colony after New Caledonia, the independent state of Vanuatu now guards its national sovereignty and resists the imposition of metropolitan influences on it.

The British exercised protectorates over the Solomon Islands, Fiji and Tonga. Although the 1878 Treaty of Friendship between Tonga and Britain, and its 1900 revision, placed the monarch (Tupou) under British protection, Tonga was never colonised and its constitution of 1875 continues as the most long-standing constitution in the Pacific Islands. In 1905 the British compelled Tupou to sign a supplementary treaty to the 1900 revised one, and Tonga then became a British Protectorate. The 1905 treaty required the king to rule with and through the chiefs, and to consult with and take advice from the British agent and consul. It also granted the British authority to appoint chief justices and to provide their salaries, a practice only concluded with the departure of Chief Justice Gordon Ward in 1995. In 1970 Tonga regained its full independence, under Tupou IV.

Tonga and Western Samoa both possess a high degree of ethnic homogeneity which, in Tonga especially, assists in explaining the longevity of the Tongan monarchy and its survival through the colonial period. However, in these countries, as in Fiji, an emergent middle class is supporting such untraditional values as greater accountability in spending, greater participation in government decision-making, and greater freedom of expression. Democratic aspirations in Tonga have been kindled by the apparent lack of accountability of government ministers and court officials, and what the reformers consider abuses of public office.[27]

Fijian chiefs, having established sovereignty through alliance with Chief Cakebau and eleven other chiefly signatories, acted under British authority between 1874 and 1970. Provincial councils mirrored traditional territorial and group boundaries, and chiefs were incorporated into a regime of 'indirect rule'. Labourers shipped from India with British consent to work the sugar-cane farms were allowed to stay following their period of indenture and permanently altered the Islands' demographics. Their presence also affected Fiji's subsequent constitutional history.[28] In 1987 the Fijian military, believing that Fiji Indians had usurped chiefly authority, staged two coups in an attempt to re-establish Fijian hegemony. While Fijians in favour of the coup pointed to irreconcilable differences between the Westminster system and customary distribution of power,[29] the 'pro-Fijian' constitution of 1990 was thoroughly reviewed in 1997. Although the consequent constitution espoused multiracialism while simultaneously recognising the paramountcy of Fijian interests, it was unable to withstand a civilian-led coup in 2001, once again undertaken in the name of ethnic Fijian interests.

Elsewhere in the Pacific, island populations came under French control: New Caledonia (Territoire des Nouvelle-Calédonie et Dependances), Tahiti (French Polynesia) and the Marquesas. Besides alienation of their land, the Kanaks of New Caledonia were subjugated by the *indigenat*, a 'native regulations' code common to French colonies before World War II that enforced segregation and restricted freedom of movement. Kanaks were deprived of any French common-law rights and were faced with arbitrary colonial authority. They were barred from trespassing on 'private property', or disturbing the peace of the whites. They could not enter public bars or carry traditional weapons in European residential areas and were forbidden to hold traditional feasts and festivals in 'unsocial' hours. Native crimes included 'charlatanism', witchcraft, showing a lack of respect for the authorities, and breaches of leprosy regulations. Kanaks could also be fined simply for being naked, and they faced a 9 p.m. curfew except on Wednesday and Saturday nights. Offenders risked fines and up to fifteen days in jail.[30] Although French overseas territories were granted the right of representation in the French national assembly in 1948, New Caledonia became an overseas territory only in 1956.

In the north Pacific, the colonial influence was American. The United States purchased the Marshall Islands and Guam from the Spanish, and administered a UN Trust Territory in the north Pacific after World War II. Guam remains an 'unincorporated territory' belonging to the United States. Although the US Congress gave the territory the right to frame its own constitution in 1976, the restrictive terms were rejected by the people at referendum. In 1988 Guam submitted to the US Congress a draft Act to confer Commonwealth status on the island, but the Guam Commission on Self-Determination (CSD) and the US administration have been unable to satisfactorily conclude discussions on the proposal. Whereas the CSD is seeking recognition of the application of US federal laws to Guam, and the right of the Chamorros, the indigenous people of the island, to self-determination, the US administration argues that 'mutual consent' is inconsistent with US claims to sovereignty over the island and that Chamorro self-determination would, if granted, violate US constitutional protection of the rights of all US citizens.

Another US possession, American Samoa, also has limited self-government, and its efforts to improve its status in relation to the United States have moved forward very slowly. The islands were acquired in 1899 as an 'unorganised' territory, unincorporated into the Union of the United States. A revised constitution took effect in 1967. Two official inquiries (1970 and 1979) into the territory's future political status, ranging from full incorporation with the United States to full integration with Western Samoa, produced no change.[31]

New Zealand's 'Pacific Empire' included the Cook Islands from 1901, Niue between 1901 and 1974, and Western Samoa between 1914 and 1962. The Cook Islands in 1965 and Niue in 1974 attained 'self-government in free association' with New Zealand. By 1957 the Legislative Assembly of Western Samoa had full legislative powers. Australia exercised control over Papua from 1906 and New Guinea from 1914, and subsequently both territories together under League of Nations and United Nations mandates. Post-war constitutional development commenced with the Papua and New Guinea Act of 1949, and continued with the establishment of a Legislative Council in 1951 and a Legislative Assembly in 1964. Papua New Guinea achieved independence in 1975. Other dependencies in the Pacific Islands include the Chilean province Easter Island, the Ecuadorean province Galapagos Islands, and the British Crown Colony Pitcairn Island governed by a high commissioner in New Zealand.

Pacific states, like their African and Asian counterparts, were defined by the pattern of colonial penetration and partition. Their international borders are those drawn by colonial draughtsmen and do not represent the boundaries of ancient nations. Their regional divisions (with notable exceptions) mirror geographically convenient administrative units. The territories of Papua New Guinea, Solomon Islands and Vanuatu, for instance, are products of colonial rule, and their national sovereignties are a new creation. They define regions, not peoples. Peoples (ethnic groups) are sometimes divided between states, and between constitutional systems, and territory not clearly claimed by one state may be claimed with equal legitimacy by another.

Very few of more than twenty modern Pacific Island political entities reconstitute ancient nations. Even modern Samoa and Fiji have undergone considerable alteration: Samoa, an ethnic nation divided into two states; Fiji, an ethnic nation-state now expanded into a plural ethnic state. In such states, independence did not signify the liberation of ancient polities. For this reason, the geography of some states is clearly articulated in constitutions. The constitutions of Tuvalu and Kiribati, for instance, the two micro-states that emerged from the Gilbert and Ellice Islands Colony, define their respective territories with considerable geographic and cartographic precision, and the emergence of two nations rather than one reflected perceived distinctions between Tuvaluan and Gilbertese ethnicity.[32]

The arbitrary nature of national boundaries has also led at times to proposals of amalgamation of states in addition to demands for their dismantling. In 1962–63 Philippines President Macapagal proposed a confederation of Malaysia, Philippines and Indonesia under the name 'Malphilindo'. Similarly at the time of decolonisation in Melanesia, there was discussion of some form of confederal arrangement between the Solomon Islands, the New Hebrides, and even Papua New Guinea.

Conclusion

Colonisation did not have a uniform impact on traditional states and peoples. It implied 'dominance and subordination' in some contexts, and 'confluence' of indigenous and colonial interests in others. The various metropolitan powers differed in their approach, with one factor being proximity to the centre of colonial authority. To cite an instance from Vanuatu, Rodman reports that even though the island of Aoba was formally under joint British and French authority, 'colonial rule was so indirect under ordinary circumstances as to be imperceptible'.[33] In the case of Java and Burma, Adas has pointed out that 'European conquest in both . . . was gradual and advanced by stages spread over nearly two centuries in the former and several decades in the latter area. The extension of effective control over local areas and the village populace came only decades after formal annexations in most regions.'[34]

From across the Asia Pacific come reports of divergent experiences of foreign rule. Nonetheless, a number of themes can be said to apply generally. Once it became apparent that Europeans had entered a region in force and with intent to stay, traditional leaders negotiated with them the terms of their unequal relationship. As noted, colonial authorities were quite prepared to co-opt local rulers where possible, as a means of gaining wider control over the population. Thus, while formal power accrued to the new regime, administrative powers were often delegated to this co-opted class. Matters of personal status were generally left in the realm of customary law, although individual rights and freedoms were considerably restrained by legal regimes designed to control and monitor rather than liberate and foster. Different laws applied to the indigenous population and the Europeans, and the unequal nature of these relationships planted the seeds of aspirations towards autonomy, nationalism and independence.

Notes

1 Thompson, *The U.S. Constitution and the Constitutions of Asia.*
2 Tate, *The Making of Modern South-East Asia*, vol. 1, 9.
3 The earliest extant code is the Maragtas Code, which dates to the thirteenth century. It outlawed indolence, robbery, and the procreation of more than two children within a poor family. The Kalantiaw Code of the fifteenth century outlawed such acts as the drowning of aged people, the non-payment of debts, the telling of lies, cruelty to wives, disturbing the peace, dishonesty in exchanging food, and disrespect for sacred places and trees. Penalties included flogging, being thrown to crocodiles, exposure to ants, relegation into slavery, and various forms for the infliction of death.
4 Hooker, *A Concise Legal History of Southeast Asia*. It is worth noting that, in Japan, the 1889 Meiji Constitution was one of the few exercises in constitutionalism in nineteenth-century Asia. Codified laws that existed in both the Tokugawa and Meiji periods provide the context in which modern Japanese law has evolved: see Henderson, 'Promulgation of Tokugawa Statutes'.
5 1) Eight malefactors; 2) mixed arts; 3) eight thieves; 4) agricultural misdeeds; 5) public order offences; 6) loans; 7) sale and purchase; 8) marriage and sex; 9) bondmen/women; 10) sorcerers.
6 Hooker, *The Laws of South-East Asia*, vol. 1, 260.
7 There are similarities here with Europe in the Middle Ages: see Nederman, 'Conciliarism and Constitutionalism'.
8 The distinction is drawn by Hooker,*Concise Legal History*, 47.
9 See Wenk, *The Restoration of Thailand under Rama I.*
10 Wyatt, *Thailand*, 50. See also Likhit Dhiravegin, *Demi-Democracy*, esp. chs I–IV on the Sukhothai, Ayuthaya, Thonburi and Ratanakosin periods, 1–90.
11 These are Malay-Muslim, Java-Muslim, European (secular)-Muslim, and Islamic texts written between the seventeenth and nineteenth centuries. The Malay-Muslim texts can be further identified as the Trengganu inscription,

Malacca (and Johore) laws, Pahang laws, Kedah laws, Perak laws, Minangkabau laws, Aceh laws, and Moro laws.
12 Chen, 'Civil Liberties in China', 108.
13 Narokobi, 'Law and Custom in Melanesia', 17; see also Narokobi, 'Lo Biling Yume Yet', 4, 30.
14 Sahlins, 'Poor Man, Rich Man, Big Man, Chief'.
15 Lasaqa, *The Fijian People before and after Independence*, 19.
16 Mellor, 'Traditional Leaders'.
17 See Bott, 'Power and Rank in the Kingdom of Tonga'.
18 Latukefu, *Church and State in Tonga*, 10.
19 For Aoba, see Rodman, 'A Law unto Themselves', 605.
20 Chalmers and Paliwala, *An Introduction to the Law in Papua New Guinea*, 7.
21 Established in December 1946 by the Malayan Democratic Union, Singapore Federation of Trade Unions, Clerical Union, Straits Chinese British Association, Malayan Indian Congress, Indian Chamber of Commerce, and Ceylon Tamil Association.
22 Shafruddin, 'The Constitution and the Federal Idea'.
23 Cited in Twitchett, 'The Colonial Powers', 167.
24 Weeramantry, *Nauru*.
25 Incorporated territories include Britain (Pitcairn), New Zealand (Kermadec Is), Australia (Norfolk Is), Japan (Ryukyu Is, Ogasawara Is), United States (Midway, Wake, Hawaii, Johnson, and American Samoa), Chile (Easter Island), and Mexico (Guadaloupe, Revilla Gigedo). Of these, Hawaii and American Samoa are the most likely to change in status.
26 Lini, *Beyond Pandemonium*; Van Trease, *The Politics of Land in Vanuatu*.
27 See *Matangi Tonga*, March 1992.
28 Much of the disagreement between the communities in contemporary Fiji stems from different understandings of the terms of the Deed of Cession agreed to between the chiefs and the British in 1874. See letter to editor, *Fiji Times*, 4 July 1995, and 'Race Relations', *Fiji Times*, 21 October 1995, 16; see also Macnaught, *The Fijian Colonial Experiences*; Brown, 'Ethnic Politics in Fiji'.
29 See Sanday, 'The Military in Fiji'. Few, if any, commentators have sought links between events in Fiji and the recrudescence of ethno-nationalism in South and Central Asia, and East and Central Europe, or explored the primordialist and instrumentalist approaches to ethnicity used in those contexts. A useful starting-point is Douglass, 'A Critique of Recent Trends'.
30 Robie, *Blood on Their Banner*, 88.
31 Laughlin, 'The Application of the Constitution'.
32 Macdonald, *Cinderellas of the Empire*.
33 Rodman, 'A Law unto Themselves', 605, 607–8.
34 Adas, 'From Avoidance to Confrontation', 229.

2   The modern constitution

Sociologist Anthony Giddens describes modernity as 'the institutions and modes of behaviour established first of all in post-feudal Europe, but which in the twentieth century increasingly have become world-historical in their impact'.[1] Law and the constitution have contributed as much to this 'modernist project' as have other social, political and economic forces. This chapter looks at a group of ideas central to the approach to constitutionalism that is typical of modernist thinking.

The constitution was regarded as the supreme source of law and as a founding document that specified not only the sources of law and a hierarchy of laws, but also the procedures by which laws were made and implemented and by which disputes concerning the law were to be settled. The hierarchy of laws named the constitutional document itself as the supreme source of law, followed by statutes created by parliament, the 'received laws' in place at the time of independence, and customary law and common law.

The legitimacy of the operation of the constitutional system relies on the concept of 'the rule of law': laws are 'legitimate' when they are made by a representative parliament, protected by a court and implemented by an accountable executive. They must also have been generated and issued through agreed and transparent processes. The rule of law is associated with ideas of 'due process' and 'natural justice', which suggest that all decisions must align with a generalised notion of law being applied in a just manner. The concept of the rule of law developed as part of the common-law tradition of the English. It includes the notions that no person is punishable or can lawfully be made to suffer except for a distinct breach of law, as determined by a court; and that all people, regardless of their rank or condition, are subject to the law and to the jurisdiction of the courts.

Other ideals, or values, embedded in these constitutions, included sovereignty of the people, representative government, majority rule, limited government, individual rights and freedoms (in some cases articulated in bills of rights), judicial independence, supremacy of the civilian power over military authority, specified protections for the rights of minorities and, in some cases, promotion of individual and social welfare. High expectations were placed on all branches of government, but particularly the executive, to act in the public interest, while at the same time sufficient measures were built into the constitution to ensure that government remained accountable. In addition to the holding of 'free and fair' elections at regular intervals, providing for ensuring freedom of the press and of individual expression, and a 'separation of power' between the three principal organs of state (the legislature, the executive, and the judiciary), was the presumption that the well-being of the constitutional order as a whole would be monitored by 'civil society'. Underlying the entire constitutional project were presuppositions concerning its utility in reaching the goals of modernity and in realising 'democracy'.

Although many states espouse the philosophy of democracy, there is little certainty as to what this means, and there is even less uniformity in the way that democracy is exercised. Is there only one model and standard of democracy? If so, is that standard to be the received (Western) standard? In establishing democracies in the Asia Pacific in accordance with modernist models of constitutionalism and democracy, a number of difficulties have been encountered. The first concerns some imported presuppositions about democracy. Some scholars interpret non-Western constitutional frameworks according to a singular ('universal') model of democracy. Lawson, for instance, appraises the role of Fijian chiefs in the dismantling of Fiji's post-independence constitutional order according to the doctrine of constitutional opposition, an explicitly Western doctrine. It may be correct to suggest that Fijian chiefly values are non-democratic; what is problematic is the presumption that they should be.[2]

In a second example of concern at the impact of contemporary constitutional design, the organisation of political parties has in many regional countries overlapped with ethnic identity, producing highly polarised communities in which the alignments with so-called democratic processes are based on ethnic identity rather than political ideas. This in itself has been detrimental to social harmony in such states as Malaysia and Fiji. But, whereas Lawson has written of the 'failure of democratic politics in Fiji' following the coups of 1987 (and upheld the model, which she similarly upholds in the context of Singapore), Fiji's one-time attorney-general Isikeli Mataitoga is one among others who have questioned the appropriateness of the entire constitutional order.[3]

Yet, whereas the Western tradition has provided the most familiar expressions of democratic values, the idea of democracy itself has been elaborated through the experience of diverse cultures, and no single tradition has fully embodied it:

Classifications based solely on liberal criteria, such as civil liberties and political rights, including 'the right to participate in free competitive elections,' are liable to the criticisms of those who believe in the derivation of democratic criteria from communitarian, populist, and socialist, as well as liberal, currents of thought. From this standpoint, democracy is not the property of one or another ideological camp; every country in the world is a veritable laboratory for the discovery of democratic principles and workshop for the construction of democratic machinery.[4]

This does not deny the possibility that democratic values and ideas may attain universal validity. It suggests, rather, that the form given to democratic ideals has required adaptation to the circumstances of particular times and places. Democracy has both Western and other origins. To speak of democracy is to infer an implicit relationship between freedom, right and responsibility. Democracy does not mean freedom, but freedom within limits.

Diamond has suggested that a democratic government meets three essential conditions:

meaningful and extensive *competition* among individuals and organised groups (especially political parties) for all effective positions of government power, at regular intervals and excluding the use of force; a highly inclusive level of *political participation* in the selection of leaders and policies, at least through regular and fair elections, such that no major (adult) social group is excluded; and a level of *civil and political liberties* – freedom of expression, freedom of the press, freedom to form and join organisations – sufficient to ensure the integrity of political competition and participation.[5]

Fundamental to democracy is the practice of explicitly defining the 'limits of government' in constitutions and bills of rights, which are subject to public scrutiny, parliamentary review and judicial process. Free and open societies are only made so by the existence of rules. In developed democracies, therefore, there has been an acceptance of ordered conflict as part of the process of obtaining objectives. Western states have tended to have highly developed civil societies, sufficiently strong to monitor and comment on its activities, for instance, through the media and interest groups, the activities of which work to balance any excesses of the government of the day.

In general terms, the tasks of law-making and oversight of the executive in the modern constitution are allocated to the *legislature*, a 'predominantly elected body of people that acts collegially and that has at least the formal but not necessarily the exclusive power to enact laws binding on all members of a specific geopolitical entity'.[6] The core functions of any parliament are those of legislation, overseeing of administration, passing of budget, ventilation of public grievances, and discussion of such other matters as international relations and national policies. Other functions include acting as agencies of political recruitment, representing the view of the people to non-legislative elites in the executive and the bureaucracy, educating and informing the public on major political issues, overseeing the activities of the bureaucracy, nation-building and national integration, mobilising public support for a regime, and helping to legitimate a political system. A parliament's law-making power generally includes the power to repeal, to revoke, to amend, to modify or to extend laws that the parliament has previously passed.

The second site of power under the modern constitution – the *executive* – has both political and non-political components. The 'executive' generally refers to the salaried civil service that remains in office independently of the elected leadership. This administrative executive is given direction by the 'political executive', which consists of the elected leadership – whether the president, or prime minister and cabinet. In some constitutional systems, executive power is exercised jointly by the president and prime minister. Since the executive is often regarded as the most powerful branch of government, it is frequently the most coveted by political interests, and subject also to the most scrutiny by other public bodies, particularly the legislature but also the courts, on application, and such other offices as ombudsman and auditor-general.

In most parliamentary forms of government, the executive is formed from the legislature. The chief executive is chosen by, and is accountable to, the national legislature. The position of prime minister is generally described as the office held by the person who 'commands' the confidence of the legislature. This is taken to mean that the prime minister commands the allegiance of more than 50 per cent of its members. (In most, but not all systems, the prime minister must first be a member elected to the parliament.)[7] The task of securing and maintaining this allegiance, however, has become a source of concern. Prime ministers can generally be removed mid-term, and members of government are always under enticement from opposition members seeking to form an alternative government, and the resulting action has been the cause of much constitutional instability.

In presidential systems, a chief executive is chosen for a fixed term, with significant independent authority (e.g. power of veto over legislative bills, or responsibility for initiating budgetary legislation, foreign treaties or other special policies, appointment of major executive officials, and emergency and war powers). The president is elected separately to the legislature, so as to maintain a separation of powers and to avoid abuse of power. There are generally limitations on the re-election of the president. Both presidential and parliamentary forms of executive government establish a 'cabinet' to give collective oversight to government. Constitutions generally state the number of portfolios allowed in a cabinet. This sets a limit on the ability of a government. Most often the size of cabinet varies in accordance with political need.

The third fundamental site of constitutional power is *judicial*. The judicial system of a country generally consists of a Supreme or High Court and other courts established by the constitution or by parliament, and it may have such other features as a jury. Judicial decisions determine the meaning and application of law, and the limits to the powers of various organs of the state. In the common-law tradition, courts use an adversarial approach in which representatives of conflicting parties argue their cases in front of a judge, who decides on the basis of the arguments presented. The civil-law tradition is based on an inquisitorial approach, which allows the judge to inquire into the matters presented. In recipient countries such as Thailand, judicial branches argued among themselves as to which of the two European approaches to adopt.[8] Many regard judicial independence as a more important objective than other aspects of the separation of powers. Judicial restraint on executive agencies of government is seen as essential to constitutional government.

Constitutions are necessarily premised on political ideas and philosophies, as well as on inherited legal traditions. In Westminster models, the legislature is formed to make laws and to provide a chamber for expression of the will of the people. The chief executive is chosen by, and accountable to, the national legislature. In presidential models, the legislature is formed to make laws, to provide a chamber for expression of the will of the people, and to provide checks on presidential power and on the power of executive heads presidentially appointed. The diverse approaches within 'constitutionalism' are sometimes explained as being a dichotomy between liberal approaches, which centre on rights-possessing individuals who seek equality before the law, and socialist approaches, which grant rights to the community at the expense of the individual and which allow community interest to be determined by the state.

In addition to describing the politico-legal premises of constitutional states, a word should be added concerning the limits of the use of the term 'constitutional'. The fundamental question is whether all states are, per se, *constitutional* states? Can any and all actions by the possessors of state power be regarded as 'constitutional' provided that they occur under the pretext of one or other law? Even the most controlled society in Asia, North Korea, has made efforts to conduct its state business by 'constitutional' means. Such efforts notwithstanding, we suggest that a 'constitutional' state has both a legal form and an accompanying set of public values with which the legal form is in accord. Actors in non-constitutional states dismiss the pre-political claims to legitimacy by either the individual or the community, and exercise power in their own interests rather than the interests of 'the people', however conceived. It is not beyond non-constitutional regimes to cloak their hold on power in constitutional guise, and it is for this reason that current and future analysis of constitutional practice must strengthen itself through the generation of sound theoretical grounding. In non-constitutional states, law is generally exercised according to the decisions of a single ruler.

Agpalo explains the 'authoritarian shift' as part of modernisation's 'iron logic'. New states, seeking to emulate the already industrialised states of the first world, adopted policies of rapid modernisation:

Their attempts to modernize rapidly led to the imposition of new and strange laws, roles, and expected values for the people and sudden or drastic changes in the people's environments, life-styles, and roles. These changes eventually led to social turmoil, cultural crisis, economic dislocation, and political instability. To cope with these critical problems and to avoid anarchy, their societies or polities looked to authoritarian rule through military junta, charismatic leaders, or a predominant, hegemonic, or monolithic party or similar forceful agency.[9]

The liberal-democratic state

Liberal philosophy presumes that the purpose of the state is to protect the rights of the individual through the rule of law. By protecting the rights of each individual, the rights of the community are also being preserved. The correct approach to government is therefore one that preserves the rule of law in society, allowing individuals and organisations maximum opportunity to pursue their own interests without interference from the state. To the extent that laws are necessary, they are created by representatives of the people, who are periodically elected by universal suffrage. Full freedom of expression and association is required in order that individuals may meet in civil society and form coalitions that express shared concerns. Since those who exercise public power have no inherent right to it, such power is divided among a number of state institutions to ensure that no individual or group monopolises it, and to ensure accountability. Commonwealth countries and the United States, particularly, tutored their colonies in liberal philosophy and measured their preparedness for independence in terms of their capacity to operate their systems of government according to liberal-democratic principles.

The expression of 'rights' in laws burgeoned in the twentieth century. Whether this tendency is an indication of the maturation of the idea of the individual, or a condition necessitated by the rapid expansion of state power, the fact is that more than at any time in history legal paths have been constructed for the protection of individual liberties. In theory, the rights of citizens comprise guarantees of human rights; security against arbitrary arrest and imprisonment; freedom of speech, press and assembly; freedom of petition and of association; freedom of movement; and freedom of religion and belief. In recent times, standards have been set concerning the rights of minorities, of indigenous peoples, and of children. In Asia–Pacific states, however, these rights are less often articulated and, even where they are, are more often curbed by corresponding 'savings' clauses which specify the conditions under which such freedoms may be legally constrained.

Although constitutions may recognise some rights as 'fundamental', not all do. There has been an increasing trend, however, to amend them by adding 'bills of rights' which cannot be resiled from. Delineating the rights of 'the people' in Asia–Pacific independence constitutions posed delicate issues and required balance between ideals of equality for all citizens and recognition of the special status of some citizens, whether for privileges (as in Malaysia and Fiji) or needs (as with affirmative clauses covering the untouchable classes in India). Most Pacific Islands constitutions include a bill of rights expressing the fundamental rights of citizens. Second, the rights of peoples were crafted in light of not only the new ideas of human rights, but also traditional views on the rightful role of the state, and attitudes towards relations between the individual and the community/society. The citizens of small states are less likely to enjoy the protection of international human rights law, as not all Pacific Islands states have become signatories to the major instruments, and reporting to international agencies is not easy from small and remote jurisdictions.

The socialist–democratic state

The socialist/communist approach to state power holds that the rights of individuals only exist in relation to and are subordinate to the rights of society. In the People's Republic of China, North Korea and Vietnam, states in which Western constitutional concepts contradict the Marxist–Leninist notion of the supremacy of the party, constitutions establish the guiding principles of state policy but do not seriously seek to elaborate entitlements that individuals can enforce against the executive through the judicial system.[10]

Recent constitutional reforms have focused on liberalising the economic structure rather than the political structure. The People's Republic of China, for instance, amended its 1982 Constitution in March 1993 to reduce constraints on the market economy, without significantly altering the role of the party in the decision-making process. Similarly, in Vietnam, a policy of *doi moi* (open door) has been accompanied by efforts to reform the state's structure of government and its laws for investment. Following promulgation of the revised constitution in April 1992, the election of 395 members (in 158 constituencies) to the National Assembly was held in July. Under the revised constitution, the Communist Party has given up its power to rule by fiat in favour of rule by law. It retains, however, control over policy-making and political power, and the state remains a one-party system without other forms of political pluralism. In North Korea, there has been little change to the Stalinist *juche* ideology established by President Kim Il Sung, who ruled 1948–94, under his son and successor Kim Jong Il.

A further factor in determining attitudes to the limitation of power – or lack of it – may lie in attitudes towards the impossibility of 'dividing' power, and the impossibility of distinguishing between 'law' and 'politics'. Thus, for instance, the Indonesian state philosophy (*pancasila*) suggests that state power is shared, rather than divided between branches of government. This idea, when practised, places considerable limits on a system's ability to privilege the rights of individuals. In socialist states, constitutions are not regarded as 'supreme law', above the will of the party, but as an expression of the party's state policies and directives.

The possessors of state power take responsibility for correcting the inequalities between rich and poor that emerged through histories of class struggle. Socialist constitutions thus accord the state a more extensive role than the individual in the allocation of goods in society. Communist states, which are also in a sense 'law-based', derive their law from a legislature that is not representative of the people but of the Communist Party, acting as the 'vanguard of the people'. In the People's Republic of China, for instance, the State Council is the executive body of the highest organ of state power.

Where political organisations advocating socialist and communist policies captured state power, as in China, Vietnam, Burma and Laos, the operation of the constitution and its legal institutions was subordinated to party ideology, policy and practice.[11] China's philosophy of state, as expressed in the preamble of its 1982 Constitution, recalls the nation's progress from a feudal past to semi-feudalism after the 1840s, to the end of 'feudal-monarchy' after the 1911 revolution, and the establishment of a socialist society following the victory of the Communist Party in 1949:

The basic task of the nation in the years to come is to concentrate its effort on socialist modernization. Under the leadership of the Communist Party of China and the guidance of Marxism-Leninism and Mao Zedong Thought, the Chinese people of all nationalities will continue to adhere to the people's democratic dictatorship and follow the socialist road, steadily improve socialist institutions, develop socialist democracy, improve the socialist legal system and work hard and self-reliantly to modernize industry, agriculture, national defence and science and technology step by step to turn China into a socialist country with a high level of culture and democracy.

This Constitution affirms the achievements of the struggles of the Chinese people of all nationalities and defines the basic system and basic tasks of the state in legal form; it is the fundamental law of the state and has supreme legal authority.

China's constitutional progress suffered reverses during the Cultural Revolution of 1965–75 until the authority of the People's Congresses was restored by the 1978 Constitution. In the years since, the Chinese leadership has sought to develop a 'socialist democracy and legal system with Chinese characteristics'.[12]

In Vietnam, similarly, the state works towards equality of persons by correcting the distribution of wealth that occurred in previous, unjust, regimes. The constitution and the institutions it establishes implement this reform program. It is the reform program desired by the people, but implemented on their behalf by the party.

The constitutional frameworks of some states have shifted to accommodate a change from liberal-democratic to socialist orientations. Burma's 1947 Constitution provided for a federal system of government with separate executive, legislative and judicial branches. The states under the Union were considered autonomous, and according to article 201, ethnic minorities had, in theory, the right to secede from the Union.[13] However, subsequent events resulted in a shift away from these constitutional arrangements, first towards a socialist form of government and then, for the final decade of the twentieth century, a military junta. Between 1948 and 1961, various minority ethnic groups joined an armed insurgency led by the Communist Party of Burma. General Ne Win's coup d'etat of March 1962 installed one-party (the Burma Socialist Programme Party) rule under military control and heralded a program known as the 'Burmese Way to Socialism'. In 1966–67 'Workers Councils' replaced Burma's parliamentary system, and a ruling 'State Council' of 29 members was elected by a 464-member People's Assembly (Pithu Hluttaw). The 1974 Constitution maintained one-party rule.

Laos also established a socialist government. As expressed by its 1991 Constitution:

The Lao People's Democratic Republic (LPDR) is an independent, sovereign and united country and is indivisible. The LPDR is a people's democratic state. The people's rights are exercised and ensured through the functioning of the political system, with the Lao People's Revolutionary Party as its leading organ. The people exercise power through the National Assembly, which functions in accordance with the principle of democratic centralism.

The socialist idea was taken to extremes in Cambodia (Kampuchea) during the rule of the Khmer Rouge (1975–79) and produced one of the most genocidal regimes of the century.[14] Following the collapse of this intolerable form of government, communist thought continued to be influential in Cambodia. The Cambodian Communist Party, established by the Vietnamese following their invasion in 1978, eventually came to share power in the reconstituted National Assembly.

In other countries, socialist and communist organisations did not achieve power and were legislated out of civil society. In Indonesia, Malaysia, Singapore and Thailand, communist activity was either banned or dealt with under emergency powers. The Malayan Communist Party, established in 1931, opposed the Malayan Union and in 1948 commenced a 'communist revolt', which in turn provoked a state of emergency. Citing the need to prevent conflict between social groups as well as the need for economic progress, the Malaysian executive has progressively reduced constraints on it which were written into the Westminster-style independence constitution. Controls over the press have been tightened, and the role and effectiveness of parliament have decreased. Judicial review of a widening range of government acts has been eliminated, including in relation to the use of emergency powers and decisions made under anti-sedition laws.

In Indonesia following some success under President Soekarno, the Communist Party was violently purged from power in 1965-66.[15] In the Philippines, the Communist Party opposed the state without replicating the success of the Communist Party in China. Relations between landlords and tenants deteriorated rapidly in the first decades of the twentieth century consequent to the withering of customary landlord obligations, deterioration of share-cropping terms, and increased fraudulence and forced dispossession. In this disaffected environment, the Communist Party and other movements were established, protesting inequitable property distribution and excessive taxation.[16]

In a very few countries, notably India, and more recently Nepal, communist parties have accommodated themselves to parliamentary democracy and become part of governing coalitions or members of the parliamentary opposition. Where the idea of 'democratic socialism' has prevailed, the members of a single ruling party have often been framed as the representatives of 'the people'.

There has been little if any influence of Western-style communist ideology in the Pacific Islands, although some discussion of 'Melanesian Socialism' accompanied early nationalist movements in such places as Vanuatu.[17]

The ethno-nationalist state

Ethno-nationalist philosophies comprise a third constitutional tradition. Their key distinguishing feature is their willingness to modify received constitutional doctrines to suit local conditions. For example, the notion of 'separation of powers' has in some places been modified to incorporate forms of 'consociation'.[18] Such systems grant more recognition to traditional political authority, and they frequently distinguish between the rights of citizens on the basis of ethnicity. Although ethnicity is commonly associated with race alone,[19] it is more realistically determined by an amalgam of such factors as common racial identity, culture, language, religion, kinship, history, and stable geographic contiguity. Many of these facets of ethnic identity are expressed in legal rule, some of which are found in constitutions. Constitutions that privilege a specific ethnic community uphold such rights either against the rights of other groups within the state, or in nearby states. Some claims to privilege have been premised on prior occupation of territory to which migrant communities came at a later date, as in Malaysia and Fiji.

Treaties between the British and the sultans of the Malay states between 1874 and 1914 made colonial rule a form of trusteeship on behalf of the Malay rulers and their traditional subjects. In addition to Westminster-type provisions concerning the machinery of government, parliamentary supremacy, citizenship, and the judiciary, the Malaysian Constitution thus recognised the Sultanate, the Islamic religion, the Malay language, and Malay privileges. At independence, the constitution gave the monarch the responsibility of safeguarding 'the special position of the Malays and natives of any of the States of Sabah and Sarawak' (art. 153), and power to reserve to Malays a number of privileges, from educational opportunities to the granting of licences. Such 'pro-bumiputra' policies were increased by constitutional amendments and policy initiatives in 1971 designed to strengthen the position of traditional Malay rulers and to establish a system of preferential treatment for Malays. Of the Malaysian Constitution, Zakaria states:

> The period between 1957 and 1969 may appropriately be characterized as 'democracy on trial', not because there was a conscious effort to test the democratic process but rather because the Westminster model was adopted

without much modification, in spite of the realities of the society's communal nature and the naïve understanding of freedom in a democracy, which meant few or no restrictions on the voicing of ethnic demands.[20]

In a number of Pacific Island states, the role of customary law and the authority of 'tradition' are influential forces.[21] The constitutions of American Samoa (1967), Cook Islands (1965), Federated States of Micronesia (1979), Marshall Islands (1979), Palau (1979), Tonga (1986), Vanuatu (1980), Wallis and Futuna (1961) and Western Samoa (1962) each give some degree of formal recognition to chiefly authority, whether as an advisory body or having powers to appoint offices or veto parliamentary bills, while others allow for an upper house of appointed members. In the Federated States of Micronesia (FSM), for example, a provision of the 1979 Constitution concerning 'Traditional rights' allows the congress to establish, 'when needed', a 'chamber of chiefs consisting of traditional leaders from each state having such leaders, and of elected representatives from states having no traditional leaders. The constitution of a state having traditional leaders may provide for an active, functional role for them.'[22]

In some places, traditional chiefs have entered the political process, so that the prime minister or president, who in the view of a Westerner is respected for winning popular office, may actually exercise influence in his society through traditional, chiefly, authority. In Fiji, such figures included Ratu Penaia Ganilau and Ratu Sir Kamisese Mara. In April 1992 the Fijian Great Council of Chiefs named Mara the Tui Nayau, and Ratu Sir Josaia Taivaiqia the Tui Vuda, at the same time designating them 'vice-president'. Vanuatu has recently announced a process of constitutional review and signalled its interest in strengthening chiefly authority. In New Caledonia, the French administration has established a 'Council of Chiefs'.

For the remainder, 'Pacific nationalisms' that consist of the assertion of the rights of one ethnic group over those of another within the same state will be problematic. Chiefly societies distinguish between the rights of citizens on the basis of traditional status, and responsibility for the implementation of law can be given to traditional leaders, who need not be elected. This is the case in Tonga, perhaps the only ethnic nation residing mostly in one state that both precedes and follows the colonial period – a fact which no doubt has bearing on the Tongan approach to constitutional monarchy.[23] Parliament comprises 9 people's representatives, 9 members appointed by Tonga's thirty-three nobles, and a 12-member cabinet appointed by the king. Laws and regulations are initiated by the king and the Privy Council before being debated by the Legislative Assembly. Regardless of whether the Legislative Assembly approves the bill or not, the king and the Privy Council decide whether to pass it into law.

In Fiji, chiefly authority is substantially entrenched in effective law but the importance of chiefly titles outweighs their formal description.[24] Fiji's post-independence constitutions (1970, 1990 and 1997) retained the Westminster system of government, while incorporating elements of neo-traditional Fijian political structure.[25] A Council of Chiefs (Bose Levu Vakaturaga – BLV), a neo-traditionalist body that originated as part of British colonial 'indirect rule', has a role in appointing the president and some members of the Senate, and has certain powers of review (including the power to approve and amend in the making of the constitution).[26]

Empowerment of the BLV in these ways virtually ensures chiefly retention of state power. Under the 1990 Constitution, the prime minister had to be Fijian and appointed from the Fijian members elected to parliament.[27] This provision was changed in the 1997 Constitution, but the issue remains controversial. The Fijian parliament has been mindful of the need to balance 'modern' law with continuing recognition of Fijian customary law.[28] The matter reached a tragic climax in 2000, when the government, head of state, and constitution were all removed through the intervention of a coup led by George Speight.

The House of Ariki in the Cook Islands, established by legislation in 1966, consists of 14 chiefs from the major islands who are empowered to 'Consider such matters relative to the welfare of the people of the Cook Islands as may be submitted to it by the legislative assembly' (arts. 8, 9). They are further empowered to make recommendations to the legislative assembly 'upon any question affecting the customs and traditions of the Cook Islands', but they cannot discuss the appropriation or expenditure of funds.[29]

The independence constitution of Western Samoa (now Samoa) incorporated the nation's two highest chiefs, Tupua Tamasese Mea'ole and Malietoa Tanumafili II, as joint heads of state: 'O le Ao o le Malo'. When both are deceased, the next head of state will be elected from among the members of parliament for a fixed five-year term (although this transformation will not affect the continuity of the chiefly system as such). Soon after independence, the Samoan parliament began enacting laws to accommodate and recognise chiefly authority.[30]

Where chiefly authority is not constitutionally recognised, such authority was sometimes nonetheless recognised through political practices. The country's first and second prime ministers held the highest possible title, that of Tama-a-aiga.[31] Tupuola Efi, the first non-Tama-a-aiga to become prime minister, subsequently rose to that title.

In American Samoa, there are provisions restricting the ownership of land to citizens who are ethnically Samoan.[32] In Vanuatu, the Council of Chiefs (Malvatu Mauri) is influential and, although it is not constitutionally recognised, its members are elected every four years under Electoral Commission supervision. Custom chiefs have been appointed to local government councils on the instruction of the Minister for Home Affairs.

In some parts of the Pacific, customary leaders have taken matters into their own hands. Custom chiefs from four villages in Ambae in Vanuatu announced in February 1997 that they had established their own constitution. The 16-page document states that chiefs of certain villages in the area are to protect and safeguard the general welfare of their people, protect and promote traditional values, resolve disputes and disagreements, and assist the police and other authorities, including churches, schools and other social welfare institutions for the benefit of their people. The national constitution recognises custom chiefs but does not define their role in decision-making about non-traditional matters. Although chiefs traditionally had a role in what are now demarcated as penal and civil jurisdictions, they now possess only an advisory role and need specific rules to guide them. In some instances, chiefs are sitting as a court at village level and hearing cases beyond their jurisdiction.

Law and values

Constitutionalism and the rule of law are not ideas that have built-in value systems. Whereas, for example, 'the rule of law' implies a sense of procedural fairness, any concept of fairness derives from elsewhere in society, generally from a religious or ethical system. Indeed, it can be suggested that failure to identify the values that accompany a set of laws renders those laws ineffective. There is a distinction, for instance, between a rule or a ruling being constitutional, and a rule or ruling complying with a notion of constitutionalism. For such commentators as Baxi, furthermore, the rule of law is 'a heavily over-worked notion which performs certain legitimation functions for those who hold power in any society. In one sense, it simply means conformity with the lawyer's law, that is due observance of the procedures prescribed. This is not the most significant aspect of the notion as such conformity is consistent with the grossest inequity.'[33]

Constitutionalism in the West is mostly identified with secular thought, but this is in turn premised on the ethical principles of the Christian tradition. Elsewhere in the Asia Pacific, legal systems continue to draw on other religious traditions, notably Hindu, Buddhist and Islamic. Similarly, the Chinese legal systems continue to reflect the ethical systems of Confucian thought.

While the role of religious beliefs, laws, and authorities in the operation of regional constitutions is often understated, it nevertheless remains ever present. Santri Muslims sought throughout the twentieth century to make Islam the state religion in Indonesia, and Islamic movements continue to work towards the formation of Islamic states in Indonesia and Malaysia.[34] In Singapore, Muslim law governs the Muslim community in religious, matrimonial and related matters, and is administered by a separate system of courts and judicial officers. The Malaysian Constitution holds that Islam is the 'religion of the Federation', but that other religions may be practised in 'peace and harmony'.[35] Religious belief continues to be influential in China, despite half a century of suppression by communist authorities. In the Pacific Islands, the early influence of Christianity produced a desire to establish 'Christian nations', which some have sought to ensure through the banning of all non-Christian religions. This may be a response to the rapid spread of Baha'i communities, and to a lesser extent of Islam, within the Pacific.

Realities

The extent to which the modern constitution, as outlined above, has operated effectively in the Asia Pacific is problematic. Examination of its specific features, as enacted in the region, points to the model as a form of 'myth' which may have been necessary, but which remains far removed from historical experience. The idea that constitutions derive from 'the people', and that sovereignty is somehow vested in them, must be examined in the context of the extent to which 'the people' were actually involved in constitutional design. A number of protracted and continuing political conflicts in the region are based on the grievances of ethnic groups claiming that their views on inclusion in the polity were never sought.[36] For a variety of reasons, modern constitutions have not been able to claim legitimacy on the basis of the voiced 'consent' of all the people.

In recent times scholars have expressed ambivalence about executive power, realising the need for the concentration of effective public power, yet ruing the extent of its misuse.[37] There has been a concern that 'strong executive' power has been exercised at the expense of an effective parliament and that judicial power has also been weakened.

Executives have diminished the role of parliaments in order to take more decisive and untrammelled executive action, such that a number of parliaments in the region are regarded as little more than 'rubber stamps'. In the Philippines, for instance, the Supreme Court's upholding of the 1973 Constitution which gave the dictatorship the cloak of legality was crucial. Marcos had a strong legal background, and the issuance of some 3000 letters of instruction and presidential decrees during his fourteen-year dictatorship showed his understanding of the need to provide a clear set of basic rules in the absence of any other lawmaking body.[38]

Domination of the operation of the constitution by the executive branch has raised issues concerning the viability of constitutionalism. In theory, as stated above, executive government is checked by the parliament, and the laws of parliament are restrained by the constitution, as judged by an impartial court. In practice, the executive has come to dominate the other branches of government, delivering 'strong government' in accordance with the arguments that national development requires decisive, not weak and divided, government.

There is a perception that some courts in the region do not restrain the executive to the extent required or intended, and few judicial institutions in the region are renowned for their diligence in protecting and upholding justice. The Indian Supreme Court has been active in enforcing judgments against sometimes petulant executive agencies, but recent judicial practice in Malaysia, Indonesia and Pakistan, for example, has drawn attention to concerns at the lack of judicial autonomy and of judicial integrity. The Indian Supreme Court has gone so far as to restrict the right of the legislature to alter the constitution under a 'fundamental framework' doctrine. In 1973 it decided that parliament had no power to amend the basic structure of the constitution. This was held to be an inherent limitation on the power of amendment, in spite of the manner and form having been adhered to by parliament.[39]

Whereas courts derived from Western legal thought are based on the 'separation of powers' doctrine, those of other states sometimes appear to be treated as instruments of political power with which to protect the interests of the state rather than the rights of individuals. In such constitutional frameworks, there is often close contact between personnel in the ruling party and in the judiciary.[40] Indonesia's judicial ideology, at least during the Soekarno and Soeharto presidencies, viewed courts as part of a 'division of labour' among government branches, rather than as a safeguard for the separation of powers, or the protection of individual rights and freedoms. As the judiciary was not seen as representing the people, it did not seek authority to strike down legislation for being unconstitutional.

In the case of Papua New Guinea, Deklin has argued that the Constitutional Planning Committee envisaged a modified form of the separation of powers, in which the legislature and the executive are partners rather than rivals in governing in the nation.[41] The Organic Law on Local and Provincial Level Government (1997) blurs the distinction commonly made in constitutions between executive and legislative powers. It allows provincial MPs (i.e. those who are elected to represent an entire region) to become, at the same time, governor and chief executive in their province. Similarly, MPs for Open electorates have significant authority over local-level government. They can decide upon and execute large development projects funded by an Electoral Development Fund allocated to each MP, money that in other places would be administered through one or other branch of executive government.

The involvement of military authorities in the operation of the state, as opposed to merely defending it, marks a further problematic shift away from the ideal of military–civil relations under the modern constitution. In Indonesia, for example, military involvement relied on its own doctrine (*dwifungsi*):

The position of the military in the MPR, and in the DPR, is in accordance with the idea of dwifungsi: that is, that ABRI is both a defence and security force and a socio-political force. As a defence and security force, it is a state apparatus and forms the nucleus of the 'total people's defence and security system'; and in this regard it is an instrument of the government. As a socio-political force, it is one of a number of legitimate socio-political forces in Indonesia's plural society. In this mode it is not 'government oriented' but 'people oriented'.[42]

In Burma, the role of the military has been similarly premised on belief in the centrality of the military to the existence of the state. Elsewhere, as in Bangladesh, Pakistan, Thailand, and most recently Fiji, it has resulted at various times in breakdowns in democratic rule, which the military has responded to by 'coming out of the barracks'.

Given the uneven and unequal social relations that figured in traditional and colonial societies, the expectation that societies would rapidly emerge on the basis of equal and autonomous individuals was perhaps too great. Nonetheless, much of the constitutional machinery of the modern state is premised on the fulfilment of such social roles: the voters, whose rational choices will identify the best representatives to rule democratically; the minorities, who will abide by the will of the majority knowing that they, in turn, may constitute a majority next time round; and the elected leaders, whose behaviour respects the ideals of representative government, freedom of speech and assembly, and the separation of powers, and whose primary focus is attaining the interests of all rather than the desires of special interest groups. However idealistic this scenario seems, it nonetheless describes the presuppositions of modern constitutionalism. Most would agree that in a great many states in the region there is wide variation between the law as stated and the extent to which it is complied with. For Habermas, this is the distinction between 'facts' and norms.[43]

One of the major obstacles confronting the establishment of democracy in Asia is the lack of education in the principles of civil society. Democracy is often taken to be based on skills of group reciprocity and adjustment. It is based on the sharing of power and responsibility. It requires an educated electorate, able to make informed decisions and to choose between alternative social values and objectives. Where these ideas and capacities are not deeply ingrained in a society – for example, because strong patterns of patron–client relations continue – the implementation of democracy has been unpredictable. In Siam, for instance (as Thailand was known until 1939), the monarchs of the Chakri dynasty realised the value of a more open system of government but felt their people were not ready. This argument has at times and places been genuine; at others, it has provided a ready excuse for authoritarian rule. At the present time, the argument is continued as a justification for the suppression of free speech. Thailand has only slowly developed the body of laws required for the effective functioning of modern states. During some periods of parliamentary stability, progressive laws have been enacted.[44]

Equally problematic are notions of equality of citizens before the law. Whereas the modern constitution presumes that the legal equality of persons is an uncontested value, it is associated in many Asia–Pacific states with the granting of equal rights to groups that may have been rivals in former times. 'Equality' is in this case an ideal to which conflicting social or ethnic groups have not yet consented. The status of 'citizenship' is similarly troubled, since conditions for inclusion also imply conditions for exclusion, and the Asia Pacific is nothing if not a region in which lands have been contested by peoples for untold generations. For many, social relations have depended on networks of patronage between landlords and peasants, on affiliation with an ethnic or religious group, or on allegiance to a semi-divine ruler, rather than on contracts with the state of a type that all others are similarly contracted to.

One of the characteristics of many East Asian societies in recent years has been the development of a prosperous, well-educated middle class. If indeed there is a connection between education and democracy, it might be expected that these societies would be strengthening their democratic institutions. In three instances, it would seem that the development of a sophisticated population has led to diffusion of decision-making power between governmental institutions, and to greater accountability of those institutions. In Thailand, where constitutional governments have been periodically and routinely dismantled by military coups since the establishment of parliamentary democracy in 1932, there are indications that an emerging middle class will assist in stabilising regime behaviour and performance.[45] One of the rationales for military intervention in that country – the failure of liberal-democratic governments to achieve stability or effectiveness – is thus losing its legitimacy. Evidence of this change was recently expressed in the popular resistance to the selection of a non-elected prime minister by the military following general elections in 1991.

Similarly, both South Korea and Taiwan had before 1987 been subject to authoritarian governments closely linked to the military. In both states,[46] opposition parties were regularly banned under anti-sedition laws and judicial review remained minimal. In South Korea, successive regimes regularly amended the constitution to legitimise their exercise of power.[47] Change of government was effected by coup rather than through constitutional processes. On Taiwan, the operation of the 1947 Constitution had been heavily qualified by the declaration of a national emergency in 1948.[48] Popular representation in Taiwan's legislative bodies was distorted as many seats were held by members representing constituencies on the mainland, who could not be removed because elections in communist-controlled areas were impossible.

In both Taiwan and South Korea, the years since 1987 have been marked by rapid political and constitutional changes. In South Korea, unrest from the prosperous and well educated classes as well as more traditional opponents of the regime led to the fall of the Chun regime in mid-1987. Later that year, substantial revisions to the 1948 Constitution strongly endorsed at referendum provided for the election of the president by direct vote, increased powers for the legislature, and the creation of a Constitutional Court empowered to review the constitutionality of legislation.[49] Despite these changes, the transition from military rule proceeded cautiously,[50] and the direct election of former general Roh Tae Woo as president in December 1987 implied the continuation of some military influence over government. The subsequent merger of two opposition parties with Roh's ruling DJP to form the Democratic Liberal Party in 1990 ensured control over the legislature. The DLP's candidate, Kim Young Sam, won the 1992 presidential elections. However, in contrast with the past, all of these events occurred within the framework of the constitution. Further, Kim, a civilian and former dissident detainee, asserted strong civilian control over the military.[51]

Constitutional and political change in Taiwan has been as significant.

Martial law was lifted in 1987. In May 1991 President Lee Teng-hui announced the end of the period of communist rebellion and the restoration of the suspended provisions of the 1947 Constitution. The most severe of the anti-sedition laws were repealed. The National Assembly, the body responsible for constitutional reforms, passed amendments allowing for the direct election of local government officials. Provisions have also been introduced concerning equal treatment for women, and protection for disabled and indigenous people and for the environment.

The articulation of rights, and their enforcement, are to some extent dependent on the capabilities of the state, and of civil society. Most, perhaps, Asia–Pacific states lack human rights traditions. As suggested above, traditional states were less intrusive in village-level life. The well-being of communities was protected through networks of patron–client relations rather than through articulated state laws. Patronage networks established patterns of mutual obligation tying tenant to landlord, master to servant or to slave. Patronage systems have a variety of names, and permutations, such as 'patron–client relations' and 'peasant–landlord relations'. These can be regarded as feudal in type, in the sense that the parties are unequal but exist symbiotically: they require and rely on each other's services. In the Philippines, for instance, patronage pervaded pre-colonial Malay societies, adapted itself to Spanish and then American colonial rule, and has reasserted itself in the independent state, despite the introduction of an American-influenced system of government, complete with president and congress.

Furthermore, whereas rights may not have been given explicit attention in pre-colonial polities, sovereigns and administrators were generally bound by laws derived from religious traditions and from other lore specifying their duties towards their subjects. There was thus more emphasis on the performance of duties, and the meeting of obligations, than on the acquisition and satisfaction of (individual or group) rights.

This analysis of modernisation from a political science perspective can be supported with a range of theoretical models of constitutional law. Its main thesis is that 'Modernization and integration means the expansion of the power of bigger groups and the state' and that, furthermore, 'The polity or society that adopts and carries out a policy or attains very high levels of rapid modernization will tend to fall into the grip of authoritarian or even totalitarian rule'.[52]

Law's reason was to facilitate development, and the choice of constitutional form followed these imperatives. The colonies of the Asia Pacific viewed the attainment of independence as a necessary first step on the path to modernisation. With the emergence of notions of 'development' and comparative statistics, the states of Asia and the Pacific had become identified with the 'third world'. There was a strong feeling that the influence of the West had to be countered by identifying and reviving 'traditional' values and institutions. In regions affected by World War II, the tasks included national development and reconstruction. In such contexts, the role of the state was to identify the appropriate policies, and that of law was to give these aspirations legal form. Intense debates occurred among elites during the transitions to independence concerning which model would best facilitate this eagerly awaited modernisation. Tensions emerged between advocates of modernisation through development of a liberal state and the rule of law, as applied generally in the West, and those who advocated suppression of individualism in favour of a corporate, nationalistic, identity. These two ideological positions were still in conflict at the turn of the twenty-first century. If the introduced forms of law and constitution were perceived as inhibiting this road to development, they were subject to rapid change, or even overthrown.[53]

An ironic feature of post-colonial legal cultures is the extent to which laws enacted in the colonial era continued in force following independence. In Indonesia, where the Dutch had used law to protect their own rather than Indonesian interests (and despite the revolutionary approach instigated by President Soekarno in 1959 that resulted in Justice Minister Sahardo's directive in 1962 that Dutch-era civil and commercial codes were to be regarded as mere 'commentaries' rather than as codes of law, and despite the Supreme Court's subsequent questioning of the validity of colonial law),[54] Indonesian law remained indebted to Dutch law for the remainder of the century.

In the Pacific, similarly, there was a vision at independence of national parliaments replacing the foreign 'received' law with more relevant enactments, and of national courts contributing law based more firmly on custom. Ratu Sir Kamisese Mara made the suggestion during preparation of Fiji's independence constitution that executive power be exercised through a committee system, but after a half-hearted experiment with it was advised to incorporate an executive similar to Westminster.[55] In 1992 Prime Minister Sitiveni Rabuka, who had been responsible for Fiji's coups in 1987, called for adoption of a 'government of national unity' in which the executive drew on the best members of parliament, irrespective of party affiliation. He outlined some possible mechanisms for such a government in January 1993: a parliament with no opposition parties, the co-option of capable opposition members into the cabinet and their involvement in the formulation of national policies – all of which were opposed by the Fijian Nationalist Party, the Taukei movement, and his own Fijian Political Party.[56] The idea of a 'government of national unity' has also been used elsewhere, although from other motivations.[57]

The Papua New Guinea Constitution expounds the doctrine of the 'underlying law', an 'indigenous common law' that parliament and judiciary were to create. However, this has not been the post-colonial experience, with programs of law reform faltering and with courts explaining that judgments based on custom were dependent on the quality of arguments placed before the courts that relied on such custom.

Why has transformation of law proven so difficult? If it were merely the replacement of one set of rules by another, more results may have been forthcoming. More likely, law reform is a more complex exercise that requires mediation between modernity and a condition of law that is beyond the modern. It recalls the diversity that marked the pre-colonial, but which is required in a social and legal environment that is now global. Custom varies between regions and peoples, so traditional sanctions, moral codes, and so on, differ widely and make their universal application or transferability between cases problematic; and custom remains mostly uncodified and inaccessible. Paradoxically, when it is codified, its rigidity and inflexibility strip it of its major definitional characteristic.

Whereas 'the law' has historic religious origins that seek to outline legal norms as 'values', its modern counterpart emphasises law's utility for material progress, social control and the imposition of order. Much 'modern law' thus aspires to standardisation of behaviour and suppression of difference. Given the highly differentiated conditions of peoples throughout the Asia Pacific prior to colonisation, modern law has been widely interpreted at the level of culture as a repressive rather than liberating order. Herein lies the fundamental irony of modern Asia–Pacific constitutionalism: that the legal norms of constitutionalism, which speak of protection of human rights and interests, work systematically at the same time against diversity in the quest for social and political order, described as 'national unity'. States in the Asia Pacific used modern law and constitutions to strengthen nations at the same time that broader social, political, cultural and economic forces were laying the foundations of globalisation.

Notes

1 Giddens, *Modernity and Self-Identity*, 14–15.
2 Lawson, *The Failure of Democratic Politics in Fiji*.
3 Mataitoga, 'The Failure of Westminster Model Government'.
4 Sklar, 'Developmental Democracy', 691.
5 Diamond et al., 'Preface', in *Democracy in Developing Countries*, xvi.
6 Mezey, *Comparative Legislatures*, 6, see also 4.

7 Not all Thai constitutions have required the prime minister to be a member of parliament, and desire for such a reform was part of the pro-democracy and pro-accountability push of the late 1990s.
8 Thana Poopat, 'Disorder in the Courts', *Nation*, 13 November 1994; Vitit Muntarbhorn, 'Birth Pains of an Administrative Court', *Nation*, 16 November 1994.
9 Agpalo, *Modernization, Development, and Civilization*, 86.
10 For example, Chapter 2 of the PRC Constitution prescribes a number of rights for citizens which are not justiciable.
11 Hsia and Johnson, 'The Chinese Communist Party Constitution of 1982'; Kim, 'Recent Developments in the Constitutions of Asian Marxist-Socialist States'; Kutlesic, 'The New Constitution in the Former Socialist Countries of Eastern Europe'.
12 Wang De-Xiang and Wang Zhen-Min, 'Development of the Concept of Government', 94–6. .
13 Although, under art. 202, this right was not to be exercised until ten years from the date of entry into force of the constitution.
14 See Chandler, *Brother Number One*; Corfield, *Khmers Stand Up!*; Jackson, *Cambodia 1975–1978*; O'Kane, 'Cambodia in the Zero Years'.
15 Bass, 'The PKI and the Attempted Coup'; see also Feith, *The Decline of Constitutional Democracy*, and Nasution, *The Aspiration for Constitutional Government*.
16 Among them the AMT (League of Poor Labourers) and the Sakdal (Accusation) movement. The Huk rebellion, New People's Army, and Muslim separatists in the southern islands emerged in the post-war years.
17 Premdas, 'Melanesian Socialism'.
18 Brown, 'The State of Ethnicity and the Ethnicity of the State'.
19 Race defines ethnic groups biologically and explains interracial relations in hereditary–physical terms, but is not immutable and can change through intermarriage: Anthony Smith, *Nationalism in the Twentieth Century*, 88–9.
20 Zakaria, 'Malaysia', 352.
21 Shuster, 'Custom versus a New Elite'; Gouttes, *Custom and the Napoleonic Code*; Paterson, *South Pacific Customary Law and Common Law*; Powles, *Transformations of Customary Law*; Lawson, *Tradition versus Democracy in the Kingdom of Tonga*; Powles, 'Traditional Authority in the Contemporary Pacific'. Not all Pacific aristocracies lasted, however: those of Hawaii, the Marquesas and Tahiti wilted before, and were swept away by, colonial might.
22 Art. V, s. 3. Further, a state could assign one of its seats for a traditional leader for a two-year term, in lieu of an elected leader (art. IX, s. 11).
23 On the relationship between ethnic nations and states, see Nielsson, 'States and "Nation-Groups"', 27.
24 Competition for chiefly titles is intense in Fiji and elsewhere in the Pacific. On the Fijian island of Waya, for instance, competing clans installed rival leaders as the island's high chief (Tui Waya): 'Ratu Naivalu Installed as the New Tui Way', *Fiji Times*, 20 September 1995; 'FAP to Probe Ratu Manasa's Eligibility for Tailevu Election', *Fiji Times*, 21 September 1995; 'Power Struggle on Waya Island', *Daily Post*, 14 October 1995.

25 Macnaught, *The Fijian Colonial Experience*. When Fijian constitution-makers were looking for ideas in the late 1960s, they turned to Malaysia for an example of constitution-making for a multi-ethnic society. Powles suggests that, had the provisions of the 1970 Constitution been better understood by Fijians in 1987, there may have been 'less enthusiasm for the coup': 'Traditional Authority in the Contemporary Pacific', 574.
26 Ghai and Cottrell, *Heads of State in the Pacific*, 227. The July 1990 Constitution (s. 31) provides that the BLV appoints the president, and (s. 55) provides that it may appoint 24 Fijian members to a 34-member Senate.
27 The constitution does not stipulate that the president be Fijian: since the office is filled by appointment by the BLV, the issue must have seemed too obvious to state.
28 See, for example, Report of the Senate Select Committee on the Protection of Fijian Fishing Grounds, Parliamentary Paper 10 of 1994.
29 Cook Islands Legislative Assembly. House of Ariki, 1966, No. 4.
30 Mellor, 'Traditional Leaders and Modern Pacific Island Governance'.
31 Mataafa Fiame Faumuina in 1962, and Tupua Tamasese.
32 The 1998 law revises the definition of 'native' and 'non-native' so as to exclude non-American Samoans, including citizens of Samoa, from being considered as Samoan natives for the purposes of American Samoa land law. It changes the definition of 'native' from 'a full-blooded Samoan' to 'a full-blooded Samoan person of Tutuila, Manu'a, Aunu'u or Swains Island'. Under the new law, a non-native is 'any person who is not a native (as defined above)': *Samoa News*, 27 January 1998.
33 Baxi, 'People's Law, Development, Justice', 99–100.
34 Ibrahim, 'The Administration of Muslim Law in Sabah'; Rasul, 'Muslim Personal Law'.
35 Ibrahim, 'Towards an Islamic Law for Muslims in Malaysia'.
36 Indonesia (Darul Islam in Aceh; Kahar Muzakkar in South Sulawesi, Gerakan Papua Merdeka in Irian Jaya); Philippines (Huk Balahap, MILF); Papua New Guinea (Bougainville); Vanuatu (Santo).
37 Mansfield, *Taming the Prince*.
38 Tiglao, 'The Consolidation of the Dictatorship', 29.
39 *Keshavananda Bharati v. State of Kerala* (1973 [Supp.] SCR 1), popularly known as the Fundamental Rights case, was decided 7 for and 6 against.
40 Oda, 'The Procuracy and the Regular Courts'.
41 Deklin, 'In Search of a Home-Grown Constitution'.
42 Hasnan, 'The Role of the Armed Forces', 88.
43 Habermas, *Between Facts and Norms*.
44 The 1956 Labour Law, for instance, included labour protection measures, procedures for establishing labour unions or federations, and rules governing industrial relations. That law was not satisfactorily reinstated until Prime Minister Thanom Kittikachorn promulgated a new one in April 1971: Prizzia, *Thailand in Transition*, 27, 28.
45 Wright, *The Balancing Act*, 310.
46 For the purposes of this article Taiwan is described as a state. However, the governments both on Taiwan and on the Chinese mainland consider Taiwan to be part of the Chinese nation-state.
47 Yoon, 'Constitutional Amendment in Korea'.

48 Provisional Clause during the Period of Mobilisation and Suppression of Rebellion.
49 West and Baker, 'The 1987 Constitutional Reforms in South Korea'. The court's precise jurisdiction remains uncertain and is contested at least in part by the Supreme Court.
50 See, generally, Yoon, *Law and Political Authority in South Korea*.
51 *Far Eastern Economic Review*, 1 April 1993, 25.
52 Agpalo, *Modernization, Development, and Civilization*, 86.
53 In the context of the urban terror and economic instability that faced the Philippines in the 1970s, for instance, President Marcos assisted the legitimacy of martial law by tying it to the need for land reform. Presidential Decree No. 27, which declared the entire country a 'land reform area', dramatised the sweeping changes that had been sought during his presidency and that of every other Philippines president, before and after.
54 The 'circular No. 3' of 1963 listed eight codes that were no longer valid. In *An Introduction to Indonesian Law*, Guatama argues that only 4 of the 8 were contrary to the constitution, or related to it at all.
55 Mara, *The Pacific Way*.
56 Rabuka again referred to the possibility of forming a 'government of national unity' with Indian members of parliament after winning the 1994 election: *Pacific News Bulletin*, February 1994.
57 On 9 October 1990 Prime Minister Solomon Mamaloni resigned from his ruling People's Alliance Party (PAP), and formed a 'government of national unity' in order to retain control over the 38-member legislature. He replaced 5 PAP cabinet ministers with 4 from opposition party ranks and 1 independent member.

3   Writing the constitution

If we focus our attention on the post-independence history of most ex-colonial countries we see that democracy, which is planted with a great expectation to bloom to fruition as it would after the manner of the mother countries, has failed to fulfil the wishes of its founding fathers. There are, of course, many reasons for this failure but one thing is clear – that justice and democratic values can only be maintained if there is a spirit of general consensus and tolerance amongst the populace.[1]

The previous chapter detailed how almost every state in the Asia–Pacific region was subject to colonisation by a European power. In the second half of the twentieth century the vast majority of these colonies engaged in constitutional dialogue, most anticipating nothing less than joining the community of nations as sovereign, independent states. For others, the dialogue led to an act of self-determination which offered the people a choice of constitutional alternatives, from sovereign independence to forms of association within an existing political and constitutional order.

Following independence (or, in other places, during negotiations toward self-determination), laws – determining citizenship, land ownership, chiefly status and representation in the state, the structure of government, political organisation, electoral representation, freedom of speech, religion, custom, and human rights – were drafted to please departing European powers and were agreed to by signatories prepared to assent to most constitutional provisions in order to facilitate the speedy demise of colonial rule. The rules of truly indigenous modern government have been more slowly defined, if at all. Departing colonial powers sought to ensure that their tutelage resulted in the creation of viable and stable states. They had been responsible for the establishment of the colonial state, and after independence were open to criticism for past excessive and/or repressive modes of government.[2] Of course, the shape of the new state also mattered to the decolonised.

Thailand was not subject to colonisation, but the changes occurring in neighbouring states, particularly the elaboration of systematic approaches to law and administration, had begun to influence the Thai elite. In June 1932 the 700-year-old absolute monarchy was replaced by a constitutional one in a bloodless coup. Apologists of the king suggest he was already contemplating such change and hence readily complied by presenting a 'first charter', just three days later, that contained for the first time a declaration that sovereignty belonged to the people. On 10 December a fuller constitution was proclaimed, one that established a parliamentary system with the monarch as head of state but holding no political responsibilities. Since 1932, Thailand has promulgated more than twenty constitutions, with half this number being the more significant.[3]

Because modern elites emerged in Pacific countries more often within the context of co-operation with colonial authorities than in the adversarial circumstances which often accompanied elite formation in African and Asian colonies,[4] it was to these elites that the departing European authorities turned when seeking nationalist leaders, bureaucrats and technocrats to lead the new Pacific states.[5] For yet other colonies, however, independence came through military struggle rather than constitutional dialogue, and independence constitutions were 'declared' as part of the violent overthrow of colonial rule. In the case of French and Dutch territories, independence documents were drafted in haste by nationalists who were, at the same time, revolutionaries.

These two constitutional paths – 'negotiated' and 'declared' – were markedly different, not only in their drafting but also in their efforts to establish legitimacy as the ground of all subsequent legal authority in the new state. There were, too, colonies that experienced both negotiated and declared constitutions, as part of their quest for independence as sovereign nation-states. These included Indonesia, with the 'Pancasila' constitution of 1945, and Vanuatu, where independence was 'negotiated' while separatist rebellions were suppressed in the northern island of Santo, where the Nagriamel movement attempted to declare the Republic of Vemarana. The Philippines' Malalos Constitution of 1899 was drafted by a convention of nationalist revolutionaries and proclaimed in the face of Spanish/American colonial rule.

Constitutional designers are required to clothe the essence of constitutionalism in a political and legal form that is neither slavish to tradition, on the one hand, nor a copy of Western models, on the other. If one considers the anti-colonial and anti-imperialist sentiments that accompanied most nationalist movements, it is somewhat surprising to note the extent to which post-colonial states continued to use the constitutional foundations laid prior to independence.

Negotiated independence constitutions

Former British colonies such as India, Malaysia and Singapore adopted parliaments of the Westminster tradition, and the Philippines and the smaller Pacific Island states formerly under US trusteeship adopted presidential systems. Other states, including Bangladesh, Pakistan and Sri Lanka, have alternated between the two in search of the most effective system.[6]

Irrespective of what constitutional path was available or taken, the constitutions produced almost always addressed a common set of key questions. A preamble served as a rationale for the document, often offering an account of the state's history. Definitions were given for both the people and the territory. A section on state principles clarified where sovereignty resided, the political form of the state (i.e. whether it was a democracy, a republic, a monarchy, a federation), and relations between 'centre' and 'periphery' (e.g. whether the state was unitary or federal, and the administrative and fiscal measures required by this relationship). Some but not all constitutions defined rights to property. Other significant sections clarified the rights and duties of citizenship and set out the state structure: the powers of the head of state, the legislature, executive, judiciary, and other constitutional offices. Also important were sections defining how these offices were filled and dismissed. Wise constitutional authors included sections on how the constitution was to be suspended in times of emergency, on how the suspension was removed, and on when and how the constitution itself was to be revised.

The process of constitution-writing took one of several forms, depending on circumstances. The most participatory method of writing or reforming a constitution requires the establishment of a representative body – often known as an assembly or a convention – to investigate and make recommendations. This model usually involved parliaments sitting briefly as constituent assemblies to amend and approve constitutions drafted for them by expert commissions and technical advisers.

Constituent assemblies in Southeast Asia

India convened one of the most successful constituent assemblies in modern times. The resulting independence constitution of 1947 included such revolutionary laws as the banning of untouchability. But constituent assemblies have either failed to complete their term or failed to provide a viable constitution in Indonesia, Bangladesh, Burma and the Philippines. In Burma, a 1947 constituent assembly resolved to establish an independent republic. After independence in 1948, the first constitution operated until a 1962 military coup led to a socialist government. A revised constitution of 1974 operated until 1988, when the Tatmadaw (Armed Forces) responded to civil unrest by creating a 21-member State Law and Order Restoration Council (SLORC). At this time also, those in power changed the name of the country to 'The Union of Myanmar'.

The experience of India's neighbours, Bangladesh and Pakistan, similarly exemplifies the failure of constitutional aspirations to counter strategic interests. A 1953 constituent assembly was dissolved and the elected prime minister dismissed by the governor-general. A second (Pakistan) constituent convention in 1956 adopted a parliamentary form of government. In 1970 an election was held to elect a constituent assembly to adopt a new constitution for Pakistan. The session which was to convene on 3 March 1971 was postponed by the military head of state, who opposed the federal model favoured by East Pakistan. This provoked civil protests that the military attempted to suppress, and the use of force prompted the elected members of the eastern wing to declare themselves members of a sovereign constituent assembly. They met as the Constituent Assembly of Bangladesh from 10 April 1971 and adopted a constitution based on a parliamentary model on 4 November 1972. In January 1975 the parliamentary model was replaced by a presidential one. The assassination of the president in August led to suspension of the constitution and imposition of military rule. The general elected in April 1978 was assassinated on 29 May 1981. Two presidents have been assassinated; coups have succeeded three times and failed on almost twenty other occasions. Bangladesh's constitutional system has remained in disarray, and the country has suffered greatly through its inability to found a constitutional order acceptable to all strategic interests.

The Philippines is another colony that came to independence with a constitution drafted by a constitutional convention. Following passage of the Philippine Independence Act of 1934, a constitutional convention of elected delegates framed the 1935 Constitution, based on the American model, which was to come into effect after ten years. 'The best minds of the country', asserts Corte's, 'worked on that constitution, which served as the basic law for the ten-year period of transition and for the independent Republic of the Philippines'.[7] According to Abueva, the inferior status of the Filipinos as a colonised people at that time, and the subsequent devastation and economic dislocation caused by World War II, enabled the US government to impose restrictions on Philippine sovereignty – as exemplified by clauses concerning free trade, which benefited North America more than the Philippines and allowed foreign exploitation of natural resources and control over public utilities, as well as the retention of military bases.[8]

Indonesia's constitution was drafted and declared by the Nationalists in 1945, as discussed below. In 1950 a liberal constitution was adopted, and a period of parliamentary democracy commenced. It was regarded as an 'interim constitution', subject to the work of a constituent assembly. Although this assembly was elected in 1955, it was dissolved by Soekarno by presidential decree in 1959, and the 1945 Constitution was reinstated.[9] Although this too was intended as only provisional, it remained in effect unrevised until changes occurred under the presidency of Abdurrahman Wahid.

The expert commission

A less participatory method, but one often thought more expedient, engages a group of experts to undertake the process of constitutional design. The extent to which an exercise in constitution-writing was shared across a population, or kept within a political and technical elite, was subject to both political and practical considerations. Certainly, a widespread exercise in consultation and participation in dialogue and drafting is more costly and requires the participants to possess some threshold of knowledge of the constitutional project. It was often presumed that the colonies were lacking in both.[10]

An independence constitution was provided for Sri Lanka by the British under the Soulbury Commission. In the years since, however, a struggle for constitutional revision has been waged in the context of strategic plays by parties within the system and outside it. In August 1995 President Kumaratunga initiated constitutional changes based on federal principles, divesting the central government of a range of powers and establishing a clearer division of powers between the centre and the regions.[11] Debate on draft proposals continued without resolution into the new century.

From the 1950s Singapore's leadership conducted talks with the British on attaining full internal self-government. The main terms of a new constitution were negotiated by Chief Minister Lim Yew Hock during talks in London in March 1957 and the Constitutional Agreement was signed on 28 May 1958. In September 1963 Singapore became part of the Federation of Malaysia, but this arrangement fell apart in August 1965.

Constituent assemblies in the Pacific Islands

In the Pacific, there was little constitution-making by independent states prior to the decolonisation movements following World War II. The Tongan Constitution of 1875 was created by Tupou I, partly to avoid colonisation by foreign powers and partly to limit the power of the chiefs. Under the terms of the trust territories established by the UN Trusteeship Council in 1946, colonial authorities were responsible for promoting social and political advance and for training towards self-government.

Almost all Pacific Island states chose at independence a constitutional form familiar to them from the colonial era. Hence, those associated with Britain, Australia and New Zealand now have parliamentary systems, while those associated with France and the United States, presidential. Western Samoa was first, gaining independence from New Zealand (which had exercised a UN trusteeship) in 1962.[12] A series of small nations followed: Nauru in 1968, Tonga and Fiji in 1970, Papua New Guinea in 1975, Solomon Islands in 1978, Tuvalu in 1978, Kiribati in 1979, and Vanuatu in 1980.

Only the Marshall Islands, formerly part of the US Trust Territory of Micronesia, made the transition from presidential to parliamentary form of government. Kiribati, once part of a British colony, elects from the members of parliament a head of the executive who is also head of state.

A number of small Pacific Island states chose, in their moment of self-determination, to limit their sovereignty by aligning themselves with a metropolitan power.[13] For each of these states, 'the constitution' in practical terms refers to the combined effect of the constitution and the terms of association with the relevant metropolitan power.

By 1975 the Northern Marianas had entered into a 'Covenant to Establish a Commonwealth of the Northern Mariana Islands in Political Union with the United States'. It was concluded by the Marianas Political State Commission on 15 February 1975 and approved by Congress on 24 March 1976. The constitution was ratified on 6 March 1977 by a 93 per cent vote, and the covenant was brought into full force by proclamation 5564 on 3 November 1986.[14] In the Marshall Islands, a constitutional convention adopted the nation's first constitution in 1978. In 1986 the Marshall Islands and the Federated States of Micronesia (FSM) entered Compacts of Free Association (COFA) with the United States, approved by Congress on 14 January and brought into full force by proclamation 5564 of 3 November. Their governments have full control over internal affairs and ability to conduct foreign affairs and join regional organisations, but they are subject to full US authority in security and defence matters. The COFA gives the United States the right to use territory for military purposes.[15]

Anglim and others assert that, in the case of Palau, whereas the United States expressed its intention of preparing the region for an act of self-determination, its real intention was to incorporate Palau as US territory, subject to US law. Evidence for this mounted during the extensive legal battle subsequent to the passing by Palauans of their constitution in 1979. Because the constitution includes clauses preventing the use of several types of weaponry and hazardous substances, including nuclear weaponry, the Palauans were unable to ratify a COFA with the United States, which insisted on full military access to Palauan territory as a precondition to its signing.[16] A 7 February 1990 vote failed to pass the COFA: 60.5 per cent (4250) voted in favour but 75 per cent was required. President Etpison wanted the island legislature to amend the constitution to allow acceptance of nuclear arms by a majority (not 75 per cent). Palau's eighth plebiscite on its constitutional status was passed on 9 November 1993 by a majority of 68 per cent (following passage of a constitutional amendment, only a simple majority was required). Passage of the COFA brought to a close the work of the UN Trusteeship Council and gave Palau the status of a sovereign state. Under the COFA terms, Palau delegates responsibility for all defence and regional security responsibilities to the United States.

Tokelau, the Cook Islands and Niue established free association with New Zealand. Tokelau was transferred to New Zealand administration in 1925. The 1948 Tokelau Islands Act included islands within the boundaries of New Zealand from 1 January 1949. In September 1980 New Zealand's Minister for Foreign Affairs was empowered to appoint the Administrator of Tokelau. By 1980 the Cook Islands parliament felt that it was no longer desirable for the New Zealand parliament to pass laws for the Cook Islands.[17] A report by Niue's constitutional review committee, tabled in April 1985, recommended maintaining its status of self-government in free association with New Zealand.[18]

In the British colonies, the process of decolonisation and self-determination generally occurred across a number of years. Inquiries and reports were followed by discussions held in London, and the pace of change was often dictated by the English rather than by Pacific Island leaders. In the case of the Gilbert and Ellice Islands Colony, for example, there was little demand for political change in the 1950s. Parliamentarians discovered through meetings with Anthony Kershaw, Britain's parliamentary under-secretary for foreign and commonwealth affairs, that Britain intended the colony to become independent rather than to attain some form of self-government in free association with Britain. In 1974, 92 per cent of Ellice Islanders decided at referendum to break with the Gilbertese.[19] Administrative separation was implemented at the beginning of 1976, and full independence was achieved on 1 October 1978. Tuvalu became a constitutional monarchy with Queen Elizabeth as head of state, represented by a Tuvaluan governor-general. The Gilbertese Constitutional Convention of 1977 decided to create a single legislature, with provision for run-off elections when candidates failed to win a majority of all votes in a general election.

In the case of Fiji, Sir Ratu Mara has admitted that the 1970 Constitution was not 'developed and adopted by the people of Fiji as a whole' and was not 'put to a plebiscite'.[20] Indian and Fijian delegates attended a constitutional conference in London at which the Indian delegates accepted a communal voting system, and agreed to postpone their campaign for 'one man, one vote' until a future date. Communal voting included a 'cross-vote' which allowed members of one race to vote for a representative from the other, and the intention was that this left the way open for further cross-voting in the future.

Papua New Guinea

In the 1960s Australian experts consulted on whether the Territory of Papua and New Guinea should adopt a federal or unitary system of government. For at least eight years prior to independence, the issue of establishing a constitution for the future independent state was discussed to greater and lesser extents by specially nominated bodies. In the year following the election of the second House of Assembly (1968), a constitutional planning committee (CPC) was established. John Momis was the chairman during 1972–74, when its members traversed the country to consult with representatives of each region in an effort to supply the drafters of the constitution with comprehensive deliberations by which a truly 'autochthonous' charter could be written. The CPC reported in August 1974, and lengthy debates occurred in the House of Assembly before provision for provincial governments was, in March 1975, secured in the draft constitution (although details were left for inclusion in an organic law, to be drafted later).

The views of outside experts were also sought. Professors Tordoff and Watt presented their Report on Central–Provincial Government Relations in April 1974, and the Kilage Committee its Public Services Structure Review Committee Report in December 1974. Both recommended the establishment of provincial government. The Kilage report recommended the creation of a Department of Provincial Affairs: the idea was 'one nation, one public service'. Professor Watt and Dr Lederman reported in July 1975 as consultants to the constitutional drafting committee.

Prior to independence, however, the draft provisions regarding provincial government were withdrawn. Despite the merits of political and administrative devolution, the fear that federalism would open the way to outright secession – a fear articulated by Somare and others – resulted in the creation of a unitary form of government (discussed in the chapter on devolution). The 1975 Constitution, amounting to 275 sections and five schedules, was directed by the weighty findings of the CPC. Although the Papua New Guinea legal system was much influenced by the Australian system, the problem of establishing 'autochthony' was solved by having Australia repeal the Papua New Guinea Act, under which the Territory had been administered, to ensure that the constituent assembly was a 'creature of its own authority' rather than a body deriving its authority from somewhere outside the country.

The constituent assembly, which included all members of the House of Assembly, adopted the independence constitution on 15 August 1975. It provided for the Queen of England as head of state, represented in Papua New Guinea by a governor-general, and a unicameral chamber from which a prime minister was elected. The prime minister then appointed a National Executive Council. Thus, despite the efforts attached to finding the will of the Papua New Guinean people, the constitution basically replicates Western models. As one Papua New Guinean wrote in a letter to a local newspaper in 1991:

I vehemently believe that the Constitution of PNG is dominated by Western ideas which were written by the colonial masters . . . The Constitution does not seem able to solve our problems. As I have mentioned, a constitution is set by the natives of a country itself. Our constitution must correspond with traditional customs and regulations that suit our society in every aspect.[21]

Solomon Islands

The constitutional structure for an independent Solomon Islands was outlined by a committee in 1975–76. It broadly followed the Westminster model but made modifications for local circumstances, incorporating a parliamentary democracy with the Queen of England as head of state and her representative, the governor-general, elected by parliament; a single chamber legislature and a prime minister, elected by and from the members of parliament, who could be removed only by a motion of no confidence.[22]

The American colonies

The constitutions of the Pacific Island nations that emerged from the US Trust Territory evolved over an extended period of time. In 1946 a three-point formula for self-determination was established, and between 1947 and 1963 legislatures were established in the six administrative districts that had existed since the time of German rule.[23] The Congress of Micronesia was established in 1965 and the first Political Status Commission in 1967. A Micronesian political status delegation was established in 1969 to confer with the US government on early resolution of the future political status of Micronesia.[24] In 1970 this became the joint committee on future status regime legitimation. Subsequent resolutions passed by the US Senate requested the 'President and Congress of the United States to consider seriously the future political status of Micronesia', and a responsibility to 'identify the major political, legal and administrative questions which will have to be decided in the event that Micronesia chooses to enter into Free Association with the US, and likewise those which will have to be decided if Micronesia chooses to become an independent state, together with information which will facilitate decisions on all these questions'.[25]

In 1975 the Micronesian Constitutional Convention convened for 90 days between July and November, and the resulting Constitution of the Federated States of Micronesia was ratified by the people of four of the six states that participated (Yap, Pohnpei, Truk and Kosrae).[26] The two states that rejected the constitution – Marshall Islands and Palau – established their own agreements.

In 1976 the US Congress gave Guam the right to frame its own constitution, but terms were restricted such that the people rejected it at referendum. In December 1989 Guamanian leaders presented their grievances on Guam's political status to a US Congressional Committee in Hawaii. The US Department of Interior assistant secretary said that giving Guam veto power over all US federal laws was 'constitutionally unfeasible' and that it could lead to regulatory and legislative chaos.[27]

In the 1990s a push for 'Hawaiian sovereignty' emerged which included proposals for a constituent assembly. Hawaii has been administered, in accordance with article 73 of the UN Charter, under the administering authority of the United States. A 1959 plebiscite offered Hawaiians the choices of statehood or continuation of territorial status (but not of independence as required by international law); they chose statehood. In 1978 a state constitutional convention created the Office of Hawaiian Affairs to administer to the needs of Native Hawaiians and get them a share of the proceeds from the use of 1.7 million acres of public land that once belonged to the Kingdom of Hawaii.

In 1993, on the occasion of the 100th anniversary of the overthrow of Queen Lili'uokalani and the Kingdom of Hawaii, the US Congress passed a Joint Resolution acknowledging the 'historical significance' of that event, 'which resulted in the suppression of the inherent sovereignty of the Native Hawaiian people', and apologised to Native Hawaiians.[28] This conciliatory gesture fuelled the Hawaiian sovereignty movement. In a 1996 ballot of 80,000 Native Hawaiians (including many residing outside Hawaii), 73 per cent agreed to the formation of a 'Native Hawaiian Government'.[29] Divisions remain, however, on the constitutional form of any future Hawaiian government.

French Overseas Territories

In the French Overseas Territories (French Polynesia and New Caledonia), where the French idea of an indivisible republic clashed with indigenous aspirations for greater autonomy and even full sovereignty, the path to constitutional reform has been extremely difficult. Until the 1990s these opposing positions resulted in social and political conflict rather than constitutional innovation.

In New Caledonia in June 1988, the Matignon Accord was signed by Melanesian nationalists, their non-indigenous, pro-France opponents, and the French government. Although not a document of independence, the Accord replaced a cycle of violence with an agreement to develop the Territory and to defer the issue of independence for at least ten years. France agreed to finance improvements in infrastructure, educational standards and employment prospects for the Melanesian population, and all parties agreed to the holding of a referendum in 1998.[30] In 1999 the French parliament amended the constitution to clarify issues concerning the definition of New Caledonian citizenship and the voting rights of citizens that emerged from the Noumea Accords signed on 5 May 1998. The amendments define eligible voters as those 'already on the electoral roll . . . November 8, 1998' who had already been resident in New Caledonia for at least ten years. The names of additional French voters not qualified to vote in provincial, congress and referendum polls, but eligible to vote on 'strictly French matters', are to be kept on a separate 'register'.

In 1999 the French parliament approved constitutional amendments changing French Polynesia's political status from overseas territory to 'overseas country',[31] establishing French Polynesian citizenship and empowering the government to negotiate and sign international treaties, but maintaining French control over law and order, public liberties, civic rights, the judiciary, defence, and monetary matters.

Table 3.1 *Constituent assemblies in the Asia Pacific*

Country	Year(s)
Bangladesh	1970–71
Bougainville	1999
Burma	1947, 1971, 1993–97
Cambodia	1993
Commonwealth of Northern Mariana Islands	1973, 1984, 1995
Federated States of Micronesia	1975, 1982, 1990
India	1947–48
Indonesia	1955–59
Kiribati	1977, 1998
Marshall Islands	1978
Pakistan	1953, 1956, 1970
Papua New Guinea	1975
Philippines	1934, 1971–72
Sri Lanka	1971–72
Taiwan	1946
Thailand	1997
Western Samoa	1960

Declared independence constitutions

In some places, colonial powers sought to resist the forces of nationalism and were not prepared to transfer sovereignty or to negotiate the terms of independence constitutions, so these documents were 'declared'. Indonesia had three constitutions during the period of achieving national sovereignty. Its 1945 Constitution was drafted shortly before the Japanese surrender, and in the face of Dutch efforts to re-establish their control over the Netherlands East Indies. Between May and July 1945 a 62-member 'Investigating Committee for the Preparation of Independence' reached agreement on constitutional and economic questions, and Soekarno articulated five basic principles that he felt should provide the new state's philosophical foundation, known as 'Pancasila': Nationalism, Humanitarianism (internationalism), Democracy, Social Justice, and Belief in One God. As expressed by Roeslan Abdulgani, 'For us, the idea of construction is based on our ideals of Pantja Sila, a political and philosophical group of concepts which aim at the building of a just and prosperous society. We regard the two factors as inseparable. Justice without prosperity, or prosperity without justice, would be unacceptable because incomplete.'[32]

On 17 August, two days after the Japanese surrender, the Indonesians proclaimed their republic. The constitution comprised a preamble, thirty-seven articles, four transitional clauses and two additional provisions. The transitional clauses, intended as a temporary measure, stated that Dutch legal codes continued in force until superseded by new statutes. The constitution conferred broad discretionary powers on the president, and contained few provisions for executive accountability or for the protection of fundamental freedoms.

The constitutional founders' idea of 'integralism', forerunner of later ideas of 'corporatism' advanced in the region, viewed Indonesian culture and social organisation as reflecting an underlying harmony between nature and humankind. Conflict and exploitation are viewed as products of Western individualism and as having no legitimate place in Indonesian society. Article 33 states that the economy shall be organised co-operatively, that important branches of production affecting the lives of most people shall be controlled by the state, and that the state shall control natural resources for exploitation for the general welfare of the people. Society was viewed as a whole, and the relationship between the ruler and the ruled similar to that of parent and child. Such patrimonial conceptions of state authority and legitimacy have resisted movements seeking democratic reform and resulted in tensions in Indonesia and elsewhere. Conversely, the patronising approach to the Pancasila adopted during the Soeharto presidency provoked protests from the grassroots to the intelligentsia.[33]

Unfortunately for the Indonesians, the Dutch attempted to reclaim the colony and a period of conflict ensued that featured both battle and constitutional negotiations. Eventually, on 27 December 1949, the Republic of the United States of Indonesia received complete and unconditional sovereignty (with the exception of the western part of New Guinea). During 1950, the federal government system was abolished and Indonesia became a unitary state. The new provisional constitution was approved by the House of Representatives and came into force on 17 August 1950.

Defining 'the people'

For virtually all of North and South Asia, and every island throughout the Pacific, the process of establishing 'sovereign independence' was a drawn-out process laden with contention and dispute. In fact, it was a double conflict. Externally, there was struggle to negotiate the terms, using metropolitan languages, by which the metropolitan powers would agree to withdraw. Internally, struggle focused on the contest between competing traditions to provide the ethical, spiritual and social bases on which the newly independent states should grow. This conflict had at stake the philosophical foundations of the state.

Another dimension to constitutional conflict resulted from the desire of distinct ethnic groups to gain separate sovereign status at the time of independence. Although citizens are empowered to reorder their constitutional arrangements, they cannot similarly determine their external boundaries, and thus efforts to break existing (colonial) states into smaller (independent) ones gained little support. The creation of new states depends on the presence of necessary conditions within the prospective state and acceptance of the new state by the international community. International law recognises the rights of 'peoples' to self-determination, but no legal instrument as yet defines the rights of minorities, except when defining human rights, which are intended to be universal. A 'desire for succession' is not sufficient, and ethnic distinctiveness is not of itself a sufficient cause.[34] Political unity and integral statehood have rarely been matched by national unity and ethnic homogeneity at the time that a colony or subject people has acceded to independence in the name of self-determination.[35]

By defining 'peoples' as the inhabitants of whole territories, and not as minority groups within such territories, the UN Charter and subsequent UN resolutions, as well as the Covenant on Civil and Political Rights, circumvent the assertion of independent status by ethnic minorities within states, except in the most extreme circumstances.[36] According to art. 27 of the Covenant on Civil and Political Rights: 'In those states in which ethnic, religious or linguistic minorities exist, persons belonging to such minorities shall not be denied the right, in community with the other members of their group, to enjoy their own culture, to profess and practise their own religion, or to use their own language'.[37] Such articles, however, fall short of recognising the sovereignty of a minority within a people. Groups have the right to their own culture, religion and language, but they may at the same time be required to adapt to another culture and language more dominantly expressed in the structure of the state.

Bougainvillean advocates of secession from Papua New Guinea had little or no knowledge of international law and their efforts to achieve independence failed in 1975–76, as they did again in 1990–97. In the second week of September 1975 the young Catholic priest John Momis rushed to petition the Trusteeship Council of the United Nations about Bougainville's desire to secede on the basis of ethnic and cultural separateness. But he was beaten to New York by Papua New Guinean representatives[38] who argued that, on the basis of ethnic distinctiveness, all Papua New Guinea's distinctive groups could petition to become independent countries. In 1976 Fr Momis sought once more to argue the Bougainvillean case at the United Nations, this time accompanied by Hahalis Welfare Society leader John Teosin. He was again unsuccessful.

An attempt by the people of Banaba Island to secede from Kiribati and come under Fijian protection also failed. In that case, the government's attempts to placate the Banabans included specific provisions in the constitution, such as giving them a seat in the House of Assembly and returning to them land on Banaba acquired by the government for phosphate mining. In Fiji, a series of efforts to secede by the people of Rotuma have similarly failed. The Papua Besena in Papua New Guinea and the Western Breakaway Movement in the Solomon Islands are among the more prominent of many failed separatist movements in Melanesia.

These examples illustrate the tendency for multi-ethnic colonial states to transform, at the time of independence, into nation-states having the same boundaries, with few peoples within states satisfying the rigorous conditions identified in international law as being the exceptions that would allow for the formation of separate states. The rare exceptions include the evolution of the Gilbert and Ellice Islands Colony into Kiribati and Tuvalu, and the dissolution of the US Trust Territory into several separate polities.

Regardless of whether independence constitutions were viewed as legal instruments, political manifestos or social contracts, their drafting played a vital role in defining the new states for the benefit of both external and internal consumption. The definition of a 'state' in twentieth-century international law contributed to the method by which colonial states negotiated their way to independence.

The public sphere

We have noted the extent to which constitutions in the Asia Pacific evolved outside the 'public sphere', principally through those holding executive power or through the nationalist elites who succeeded in obtaining it. There are few instances in which 'the people' participated in any genuine sense in creating the independence constitution. This then poses a question concerning the extent to which such constitutions are 'of the people'.

It has also been pointed out that, because of social and historical circumstances, the establishment of national constitutions by the elites, whether in or out of power, is quite understandable given the lack of mass education when the wave of independence came to Southeast Asia and to the Pacific Islands. Nationalism was, in a sense, an avante garde ideology that the masses learnt about after the fact. It can also be argued that, in some countries in the region, nationalist ideals have not entirely replaced traditional loyalties based on ethnicity and locality. While it is clear that their emerging middle classes and articulate educated groups desire the operation of liberal societies, their aspirations have faced a number of obstacles, including lack of education in such matters among the masses. It is difficult to define 'the people' in states whose residents have had no constitutional voice. Can a state whose people have not been consulted fully on their constitution be said to have done their own constitutional thinking?

Notes

1 Abas, 'Legal Perspective of the Third World', 252.
2 This is the theme, for example, of several publications that accompanied Vanuatuan independence: Weightman and Lini, *Vanuatu*; Kele-Kele, 'The Emergence of Political Parties'; Lini, *Beyond Pandemonium*; Molisa et al., 'Vanuatu'.
3 The most noted are those of 1932, 1946, 1947, 1949, 1952, 1959, 1968, 1972, 1974, 1976, 1977, 1978 and 1991.
4 See, generally, Kedourie, *Nationalism in Asia and Africa*.
5 Macdonald, 'Decolonization and Beyond'; Ghai, 'Constitution Making and Decolonisation'. Concerning Pacific colonies about which my statement does not hold, see Robie, *Blood on Their Banner*.
6 It could be argued that the shifts were 'instrumental' rather than 'constitutional': Sri Lanka's 1972 Constitution established a model of parliamentary sovereignty that the party then in power believed most suited its program of socialist reform. Sri Lanka's second Republican Constitution of 1978 was designed by J. R. Jayawardene to facilitate his vision of 'stability for development' and the need for a strong leader. On winning general elections and becoming prime minister in 1994, Chandrika Kumaratunga abolished the existing executive presidency and re-established a Westminster form of government. In November of the same year she contested and won the newly established position as president.
7 Corte's, 'Constitutionalism in the Philippines', 340.
8 Abueva, 'Filipino Constitutional Democracy'.
9 Nasution, *The Aspiration for Constitutional Government in Indonesia*.
10 For theoretical analysis of these variables, see Vanberg and Buchanan, 'Constitutional Choice', 43.
11 See, for example, Jayadeva Uyangoda, 'A Bold Step in Sri Lanka', *Hindu*, 17 August 1995.
12 See Davidson, *Samoa Mo Samoa*, esp. ch. 11.

13 Leibowitz, *Defining Status*; Sack, 'Constitutionalism and "Homegrown" Constitutions'; Hirayasu, 'The Process of Self-Determination'; Hills, 'Compact of Free Association for Micronesia'. UN General Assembly resolution 1541 (XV) recognised that a non-self-governing territory (and, by implication, a trust territory) could attain the charter goal of self-determination through: (a) emergence as a sovereign independent state; (b) free association with an independent state; or (c) integration with an independent state.
14 Branch, 'The Constitution of the Northern Mariana Islands'.
15 Burdick, 'The Constitution of the Federated States of Micronesia'.
16 Anglim, 'Palau's Strategic Position Places Palauan Democracy at Risk'.
17 Frame, 'The External Affairs and Defence of the Cook Islands'. Constitution Amendment (No. 9) Act 1980–81 amended art. 46 of the Cook Islands Constitution to read: 'except as provided by Act of Parliament of the Cook Islands, no Act, and no provision of any Act, of the Parliament of New Zealand passed after the commencement of this Article [5 June 1981] shall extend or be deemed to extend to the Cook Islands as part of the law of the Cook Islands'.
18 *Commonwealth Law Bulletin*, January 1986.
19 Howe et al., *Tides of History*, 184, 186–7.
20 McLachlan, 'The Fiji Constitutional Crisis of May 1987', 176.
21 Allan Renagi of Lae, *Post Courier*, 19 August 1991.
22 Solomon Islands Independence Order 1978, Supplement to the Solomon Islands Gazette, Friday 7 July 1978.
23 Legislatures were established in Truk (1947), Palau (1949), the Marshall Islands (1949), Yap (1951), Pohnpei (1952), and Mariana Islands (1963). The United States first reported to the UN Trusteeship Council in 1949.
24 Public Law No. 3c-15 (SB55) of 1969, Trust Territory of the Pacific Islands. Laws and Resolutions, Congress of Micronesia, 3rd Congress, 2nd regular session: 14 July – 27 August 1969.
25 Senate Joint Resolutions, no. 31 of 1969 and no. 63 of 25 August 1969.
26 Burdick, 1988, 'The Constitution of the Federated States of Micronesia', 256; also Burdick, 1986, 'The Constitution of the Federated States of Micronesia'.
27 *Pacific Islands Monthly*, February 1990, 20.
28 US Public Law 103–150, 103rd Congress, Joint Resolution 19, 23 November 1993.
29 The ballot asked: 'Shall the Hawaiian People Elect Delegates To Propose a Native Hawaiian Government?': Carey Goldberg, 'Native Hawaiians Vote in Ethnic Referendum', *New York Times*, 23 July 1996; Ellen Nakashima, 'Native Hawaiians Consider Asking for Their Islands Back', *Washington Post*, 27 August 1996. Less than 40 per cent of eligible voters turned out, and of 30,423 valid ballots, 73 per cent (22,294) approved the election of delegates to a convention to propose a Native Hawaiian government. However, despite the success of the vote, it was not clear who would fund the assembly, as the State of Hawaii stated that it could not afford the estimated costs of US$6–12 million (*Honolulu Star-Bulletin*, 11 September 1996), and there was an appeal of invalidity on the grounds that it did not include non-Hawaiians.

30 Henningham, 'The Uneasy Peace'.
31 Art. 78 of the French Constitution was to be modified to read: 'French Polynesia governs itself freely and democratically within the French Republic. Its autonomy and own interests as an overseas country are guaranteed through a status which is defined by an organic law.'
32 Abdulgani, 'Indonesia's National Council', 98.
33 According to Thoolen (*Indonesia and the Rule of Law*, 28), the 1980 'statement of concern' by the 'Group of 50' followed a speech by Soeharto in which he suggested that he was the personification of Pancasila.
34 Thornberry, 'Self-Determination, Minorities, Human Rights'.
35 Minority Rights Group, Minorities and Human Rights Law, Report No. 73 (1987), cited in Thornberry, 'Self-Determination', 867.
36 For a dissenting analysis of ILO Convention 169 Concerning Indigenous and Tribal Peoples in Independent Countries, see Syd Jackson, 'Indigenous Rights'. On self-determination, see Sureda, *The Evolution of the Right*; Crawford, 'Outside the Colonial Context'.
37 Henkin, *The International Bill of Rights*.
38 Ebia Olewale and Toni Siaguru (later Sir Toni, secretary-general of the Commonwealth Organisation.

Part II

The Constitution of Modernity

4 The legislature

The Constitution makers opted for a parliamentary system of government with the pious hope that only people of unimpeachable conduct and impeccable character, inspired with a deep-seated commitment to do selfless service to the people would enter the portals of Parliament and State legislatures. But, alas, it has not taken much time for the expectations of the architects of the Constitution as well as the people who have entertained high hopes about their elected representatives to be belied. The legislative bodies have lost their lustre, what with people of proven record of crime trooping in through abuse of money, muscle and liquor, thus making a mockery of the august institutions they happen to be members of.[1]

It appears to be far easier to pass a new law rather than to enforce an existing one. So it is easier for a politician to seek to meet a problem by announcing that his Ministry is preparing the draft of a bill to overcome the very problem. Thus each new problem brings about a committee to study it, a Report on the problem, a committee to study the report, a committee to prepare a Bill, a committee to consider the Bill and so on ad infinitum. Meanwhile perfectly good laws remain on the statute book which, if enforced properly, are perfectly capable of solving the problem.[2]

Legislative and parliamentary processes are at the heart of democratic constitutionalism. The parliament is the body that makes laws and oversees the implementation of government programs. In practice, however, the inability of many parliaments to fulfil their constitutional mandate has been a cause for concern in Asia–Pacific constitutional systems as much as it has caused concern elsewhere. Many of the initial challenges facing the region's legislatures have related to institution-building. For instance, such large states as India, China and Indonesia have had to establish procedures for the operation of very large consultative bodies. The Indian parliament has 543 seats (the constitution allows up to 552). Four hundred members of the Indonesian House of Representatives (Dewan Perwakilan Rakyat, or DPR) are elected and a further 100 are appointed.[3]

The smaller states have faced similar challenges on a correspondingly smaller scale. Pacific Island legislatures range in size from 12 members

(Tuvalu) to 109 (Papua New Guinea). The Kiribati legislature (Maneaba Ni Maungatabu) consists of 40 elected members, including a representative of the Banaban (Ocean Island) people. As it is highly improbable that each parliament will include members who are qualified in the law, the constitution allows for the attorney-general, who is a public servant, to sit in and take part in cabinet and legislature. His position is unique, in that he is appointed by the president and is responsible to no electorate. Fiji's 1970 Constitution had a similar provision. Despite provisions of this kind to ensure the inclusion of expertise in small parliaments, Powles has questioned whether the Pacific Island states possess 'sufficient techniques to assist ministers in the formulation and supervision of policy'.[4] In Tonga, parliamentarians have called for seminars to educate MPs about such terms as 'Resolution, Ordinance, Regulation, and so forth'.[5]

Most parliaments have a committee system to undertake the various tasks of the legislature. They usually conduct supervisory, advisory, and audit roles. The most significant committees scrutinise public accounts, public works, and legislation. Whereas committees are theoretically vitally important parliamentary instruments, they are often placed at the service of political rather than parliamentary interests, of strategic rather than communicative action. Committees often play an effective role in parliament without touching issues that are most sensitive to the executive, and which would place their existence in jeopardy. They thus engage with the less volatile issues confronting the parliament.

Effective legislative and parliamentary practices also require the allocation of sufficient resources in such areas as legislative research and drafting, and in the operation of committee systems. These challenges have been common to all parliamentary systems, whether single-party or multi-party. The Indonesian DPR provides an example of a legislature whose ability to function has been determined by both political and logistical factors. During the rule of presidents Soekarno and Soeharto, the parliament's reputation gradually waned. In the post–Soeharto period, however, its officers sought to improve the quality of legislation, and the scrutiny of government activities, through the employment of experts to assist its eleven commissions and its members of parliament.

The size of a legislature is not necessarily a measure of its importance, and the effective powers of some bodies are so limited as to render them little more than 'rubber stamps' for executive power. The proportion of appointed representatives to the Indonesian parliament is criticised by Hartono, a constitutional scholar in Bandung, who suggests that 'out of fear to be recalled or replaced, many members tend to blindly support the government, instead of really considering the wishes and thoughts of the people'.[6] Another Indonesian scholar, Muhammad Ridwan

Indra, argues that there are too many appointees to the DPR and that some among them may not function vigorously for fear of being recalled.[7]

But perhaps greater challenges than those presented by the requirements of institution-building and resource allocation have been in conducting parliamentary procedures in the context of unpredictable political conditions. In assessing the impact of politics on parliamentary processes, one must ask whether or not constitutional design has itself been a contributing factor. In the United Kingdom, over centuries, the power of monarchs was gradually made subservient to that of parliament. Within the parliament, members were free to express their views candidly, irrespective of how these might be viewed by the monarch, the church, or the majority in the parliament. Differences of opinion were referred to a court which existed outside the main deliberating chamber, and which over a lengthy period of time established its impartiality and independence. As these capacities to express individual ideas, to allow the discussion of divergent views, and to have arguments settled before an impartial court are at the heart of the British contribution to modern parliamentary democracy, their transplantation to the colonies was something 'natural'. In Western democracies, therefore, political instability resulting from the dynamics of partisan politics has become part of an accepted mindset: in the emergence of democratic governments in non-Western contexts, no better method of political organisation was adopted, and the divisive practices of the West were added to those already present. It has also been argued that alternative models of parliament, such as Indonesia's use of *mufakat* (consensus), show the inadequacy of trying to please every interest in society.[8]

However, experience with the Westminster model in the Asia Pacific suggests that transplantation is not without side effects. While invoking the advantages of determining the executive, legislative and judicial powers using this model, those subject to its implementation in new social and political contexts experienced varying degrees of divergence from the ideal.

The executive

A key presumption in the Westminster system of parliament is that the best 'check and balance' on the allocation and use of public power is to place executive power in the hands of those who constitute 'the majority' of the elected members of parliament, and to make this executive responsible to the whole of parliament. The rules of parliament –

whether for the making of new legislation, for the revision of existing legislation or for the scrutiny of the performance of government – are all designed to provide for accountability of the government in its use of executive power.

While this model provides a sound theoretic basis for parliamentary accountability, its success or otherwise should be measured in terms of its practical operation in diverse social and political contexts. Given that few, if any, political societies in the Asia Pacific generated ideal 'two-party' systems on which the Westminster system best operates, an impartial analysis of the constitutional experience of states in the region must investigate whether it contributes to establishing stable and effective governments. In some states, the contest between political forces for control of government has extended far beyond the rules of political debate and resulted in instability and dislocation rather than, as theoretically intended, preparation of an 'alternative government' and accountability within the legislature.

The function played by parliaments in legitimating a majority as 'the government' continues to see pressure placed on constitutional processes by political actors, generally represented in the activities of the party system. It would be hard to find a parliament anywhere in the Asia Pacific that has earned the respect of its citizens for its commitment to democratic practices. More frequently, the politics of parliaments earns the derision of cartoonists, and the appeasing comments of political scientists unable or unwilling to envision more responsible constitutive dialogues.

In Papua New Guinea during the 1990s, for instance, the popular press constantly alluded to the failure of parliamentarians to answer questions placed on notice, failure to divulge details concerning expenditure of 'electoral development funds', extensive absenteeism from parliamentary sessions, and the appointment of 'parliamentary undersecretaries' to satisfy the demand for political offices, albeit in the guise of appointments to improve executive efficiency.[9]

Other instances come from Southeast Asia. The functioning of the Philippines Congress in the 1990s provides an instance of problematic performance by a legislature. Its failure to pass an appropriations bill early in 1991 created fiscal problems throughout the country. Bills of national importance (128 of them, some dating to 1987) were stuck in the Senate, in addition to some 200 bills of local application. MPs expressed their displeasure with initiatives with which they disagreed by 'filibustering' debate, using rules of procedure to ensure its delay and prolongation.[10] South Korean parliamentarians are renowned for violent outbursts.[11]

The Cambodian parliament gained a reputation for low work rate and incapacity to obtain a quorum to enable the passage of legislation. A 1990 press report observed:

Over a fortnight from June 24 when the draft law [on Nationality] became available for discussion, three articles – consisting of exactly 106 words (in the English draft) – were adopted. Just the first article got through on June 24, as CPP members had to attend their party's plenum and anniversary for the rest of the week. The session was expected to resume on July 1 but a quorum couldn't be found until July 4 when MPs were able to get two more articles approved. Between July 8–9, MPs just couldn't seem to get beyond Article 4. Why should this be? The reasons are many: There is no Wednesday meeting, because that's when the Cabinet also meets; some MPs are busy with their ministerial portfolios; some are out accompanying the Prime Ministers on trips; some are overseas; others are simply absent without leave.[2]

In Bangladesh, the legitimacy of democracy has been eroded by conflict between the political parties played out within and beyond the constitutional system. In March 1994 the three main opposition parties commenced a boycott of parliament as part of a campaign to amend the constitution and to bring down the government of Prime Minister Khaleda Zia. The MPs' actions were reinforced by widespread strikes and anti-government protests, and were undeterred by a High Court ruling that the 153 MPs join the next session of national parliament,[13] or by the efforts of Commonwealth-sponsored mediator Sir Ninian Stephen. The MPs, led by Sheikh Hasina Wajed's Awami League, accused Prime Minister Khaleda Zia's government of vote fraud, corruption and incompetence. They threatened to resign en masse unless President Abdur Rahman Biswas dissolved parliament and appointed a caretaker and a neutral prime minister and neutral board of advisers, and unless the government agreed to table an opposition-backed bill to amend the constitution. As new general elections were not due until 1996, the prime minister labelled the opposition demands as unconstitutional. However, on 25 November 1995, the prime minister asked the president to dissolve the parliament.

Executive government in socialist states

In socialist states, such as China, Laos and Vietnam, the government is derived from a standing committee, given powers of 'supervision and control' over other branches of government. In Laos, the National Assembly elects a standing committee that holds extensive powers over the National Assembly, the government and even, ultimately, the judiciary. The Laotian National Assembly is empowered to amend the constitution, to endorse, amend or abrogate laws, to elect or remove the President of State and Vice-President of State, as proposed by the standing committee, to adopt motions expressing no confidence in the government, and to elect or remove the President of the People's Supreme Court, on the recommendation of the standing committee. In Vietnam, the standing committee, which is the permanent Committee of the National Assembly, presides over the election of the National Assembly, prepares for and convenes its sessions, interprets the constitution, laws and decrees, and enacts decrees on matters entrusted to it by the National Assembly. The committee's power to supervise and control other branches of government is extensive.

Bicameral legislatures

Legislatures are either unicameral or bicameral. In bicameral systems, the lower house is usually considered the 'people's house', whose representatives appear in proportion to population distribution. Upper houses are sometimes referred to as 'states' houses' and may have equal numbers of representatives of states, regardless of the numbers of people living in those states. Upper houses can also be used to ensure representation of ethnic interests. States with bicameral legislatures include Japan, India, Malaysia, Fiji, Nepal, Thailand, Commonwealth of the Northern Mariana Islands, and Federated States of Micronesia. Fiji's parliament allocates seats according to ethnicity as well as constituency. The 1990 Constitution granted the Great Council of Chiefs power to appoint 24 of 34 members of the Senate.[14] Elsewhere, ethnicity is a significant issue in elections and politics without being entrenched within the constitutional framework.

In some cases, the members of an upper house are elected, while in others they are appointed. The Malaysian parliament (Majlis) consists of the king and the two majlis (councils): the Dewan Negara (Senate) and the Dewan Rakyat (House of Representatives). The House of Representatives comprises 177 members, including 133 from the Peninsula, 20 from Sabah, and 24 from Sarawak.[15] Some members also hold seats in state legislatures. The Senate, the less powerful of the two houses, has 68 members, 26 of whom are elected by thirteen state legislatures (2 members by each) and a further 42 appointed by the king on the advice of the prime minister. Ethnicity is a significant factor in representation, even though it is operative in the country's communal politics rather than formally stated in its electoral provisions.

Constitutional provisions protecting and enhancing the position of the Malays do not extent to electoral provisions, although 'rurally weighted constituencies in Malaysia benefit parties which depend on rural voters, who are mostly Malay'.[16]

In Thailand, leadership is partly elected, partly appointed, and partly hereditary. Since 1932 Thailand's National Assembly (Rathasatha) has comprised a Senate (Vuthisatha) and a House of Representatives (Saphaphoothan-Rajsadhorn). Until the 1997 Constitution, the lower house was elected and the upper house appointed by the king on the recommendation of the Council of Ministers, with a considerable proportion of those appointed being from the military or the police. The 1992 Constitution provided for 270 senators (i.e. two-thirds of the 360-member House of Representatives), comprising 'qualified persons' from various professions.[17] The Senate screens legislation passed by the lower house and can supervise the functions of the executive branch by submitting interpellations.

The Thai military had traditionally exercised great influence over appointments to the upper house, until strong polling results in the March 1992 elections in favour of an anti-military alliance pressured it to allow an elected member to become prime minister. Unrest followed the appointment of General Suchinda Kraprayoon as prime minister, resulting in his resignation and the appointment of a second Anand government. The fact that the Thai people insisted on having an elected representative take the post of prime minister, while making no comment about a fully appointed upper house and giving allegiance to a still powerful hereditary monarch, suggests a particular attitude towards representation is in place.

However constituted, an upper house is generally premised on the need to 'check' the use of power in the lower house. Hence there is invariably a division between the interests of the two houses, except in situations where a dominant political party or coalition of parties has secured a majority in both. Another factor determining the balance of power between upper and lower houses emerges from their methods of appointment and dissolution. In Malaysia, for instance, the Senate cannot be dissolved, whereas the House of Representatives is subject to dissolution.

Minorities in a majoritarian democracy

One of the first difficulties presented by the Westminster model of parliament is its application in societies that are culturally diverse and in which factors such as ethnicity give the electorate enduring, as opposed to shifting, values and interests. The model thus suited social groups who were numerically superior, through its application of majoritarian democracy, but it soon frustrated permanent minorities, whose interests could never 'democratically' conquer in the constitutional order.

Studies have demonstrated how minority views on some matters remain in the minority.[18] The implication is that in a pluralist society, in which citizens are identified by difference rather than homogeneity, majoritarian principles will create permanent minorities on some issues – and these issues are generally ontological matters about which change is barely possible. This model is hardly adequate for the governance of plural societies, where the presence of different ethnic groups in different proportions creates 'permanent minorities' who can never express a majority view. This division between the relative constitutional strengths of majorities and minorities is exacerbated by the emphasis in the Westminster parliamentary model on dividing parliament between 'the government', which exercises executive powers, and 'the opposition', possessing only non-executive powers as members of the legislature. Parliamentary minorities become identified in plural societies with subordinate ethnic communities, rather than with government and a 'loyal opposition'.

Coalitions and the challenge of creating stable government

The problem of stabilising political party systems is linked to two processes at the heart of constitutionalism: the performance of the legislative and executive branches of government. The absence of stable two-party systems has been noted. Given the complex nature of political interests in the majority of countries in the region, executive governments are formed through coalitions of parties more often than not. The necessity of coalitions – sometimes resulting in coalitions between numbers of parties – has a significant impact on the capacity of parliaments and governments to carry out their duties.

No-confidence motions

The constitutional device that most affects the life of Westminster parliaments in the Asia Pacific is the no-confidence motion. Derived from a practice that allowed for the changing of governments prior to the conclusion of their electoral term, in instances where 'a majority of the house' lost its confidence in the ability of the government to properly exercise its powers and duties, the confidence vote has become an effective mechanism used by parties in opposition to wrest executive power from the incumbent government.

The problem exists throughout the Asia Pacific. In the worst case of recent years, strategic action by political parties in Bangladesh led to a complete paralysis of the legislature.[19] Prime Minister Khaleda's victory in the nation's first free polls (1991) provoked opposition parties to orchestrate civil disruption and to boycott parliament in a campaign for a new election.[20] Although not required to call a general election until 1996, Khaleda was obliged to bow to the political climate.

Similar instabilities have hampered the Indian legislature. After the incumbency of India's first prime minister, Jawaharlal Nehru (August 1947 – May 1964), there were a further eleven leaders of government up to and including P. V. Narasimha Rao, some of whom were in office for less than a year. Following general elections in India in May 1996, H. D. Deve Gowda became prime minister, heading a thirteen-party United Front coalition government. Although the Bharatiya Janata Party (BJP) and its allies emerged as the single largest group in parliament (194 seats), and party leader Atal Behari Vajpayee became prime minister, his government resigned after just thirteen days in the face of certain defeat at a mandatory parliamentary vote of confidence.

The no-confidence motion has been put frequently before the parliament of Nepal. In September 1995 the Nepali Congress tabled a no-confidence motion and the nine-month tenure of Prime Minister Manmohan Adhikari (UML) ended five days later.[21] The struggle had commenced in June with an attempt by the opposition to put a motion of no confidence. Seventy Nepali Congress MPs requested King Birenda to call a special session of parliament.[22] The king granted a special parliamentary session but also met with the prime minister and agreed to his request that the parliament be dissolved and elections held.[23] The opposition parties, seeking to form a coalition government rather than a fresh election, appealed to the Supreme Court, which upheld their case and permitted them a second chance to put their confidence motion in parliament.

In Thailand, in 1996, the National Action Party (NAP) agreed to support the Banharn government (of which it was a coalition member) in a vote of no confidence, on condition that he subsequently resign! Banharn responded by dissolving parliament and calling for new elections on 17 November and a six-party coalition government was subsequently formed by Chavalit Yongchaiyudh, leader of the NAP.

Papua New Guinea

In Papua New Guinea, the no-confidence motion has removed no fewer than four governments since independence and has had considerable impact on others. Michael Somare, chief minister from 1972 and first prime minister in 1975, was defeated in March 1980. He returned to power in the 1982 elections and in November 1985 was again defeated in a no-confidence motion, this time led by Paias Wingti. In 1987–88 the Wingti government sat for just one day in seven months in an effort to avoid the filing of a confidence vote – yet this came to pass in July, and Rabbie Namaliu became prime minister at the head of a six-party coalition. In November 1990, now himself facing a confidence vote, Namaliu prorogued parliament until 16 July 1991. As the constitution stipulates that a no-confidence motion in a parliament's last year automatically triggers a general election, Namaliu reasoned that his opponents would rather see the parliamentary session through. However, the opposition parties contested the government's action in the Supreme Court, claiming that section 124 of the constitution obliged the parliament to sit a minimum of three times, and for a total minimum period of nine weeks, in each twelve-month period – a view with which the court concurred in its 11 January 1991 decision. Following this ruling, the National Executive Council reconvened parliament on 7 May.

In 1994 Sir Julius Chan replaced Wingti as prime minister, following elections for the premiership ordered by the Supreme Court. Following a constitutional amendment which prohibits a new government from facing a no-confidence motion in the first eighteen months of its term, Wingti had resigned and re-entered the position in September 1993 in a tactical manoeuvre designed to establish a 'new government' and hence recommence an eighteen-month period of insulation from no-confidence votes. He handed his letter of resignation to the governor-general while at dinner on 23 September.

For almost a day, few were aware of the prime minister's resignation (a number of politicians had left to attend the Rugby League grand final in Sydney and Wingti's most likely challenger, Finance Minister Sir Julius Chan, was in Washington for discussions with the IMF and World Bank). Parliamentarians only became aware of the resignation the following morning in parliament when the Speaker declared the election of prime minister the first order of business, catching both opposition and coalition members by surprise. After Wingti was elected unopposed, six government MPs joined the opposition, while the opposition announced it would protest by withdrawing its members from all bipartisan committees.

An opposition party challenge to the legality of Wingti's tactics failed in the National Court in November 1993,[24] but was upheld on appeal by the Supreme Court. The court considered whether or not Wingti's re-election was valid in the circumstances where he signed the letter of resignation to the governor-general; whether the constitution permitted the occasional reappointment of the prime minister; whether the prime minister was duly elected on 24 September, following his snap resignation the previous day; and whether the constitution permitted the Speaker to usurp the powers of the national parliament. Chief Justice Amet led a ruling that Wingti's resignation was valid but his re-election was not, as it had not taken place on the 'next sitting day following the resignation'. The court ordered the prime minister's position to be recontested and in August 1994 Sir Julius Chan was elected in place of Wingti.

In March 1997 Chan survived a confidence vote over his decision to hire foreign mercenaries to combat the secessionists of Bougainville Province, but lost power at the next elections:

. . . far from confirming the Prime Minister in power, the vote sparked extraordinary scenes in and around Papua New Guinea's National Parliament. As soon as the result was announced, gangs started stoning cars and small bands of soldiers set up road-blocks preventing MPs from leaving the Parliament. The MPs were held captive for hours before more senior military officers, loyal to the rebel commander, Brigadier-General Jerry Singirok, restored order and assured the members of their safety. Sir Julius however was not trapped in the Parliament, he fled the building as soon as the vote was cast, reportedly disguised as a policeman. Since then, the Prime Minister has not been seen.[25]

In 1999 the Skate government fell in a dramatic no-confidence vote that brought Sir Mekere Morauta to the post. Yet each prime minister removed from office through a no-confidence vote remained in the legislature, and invariably resumed executive office at a later date, suggesting that the reasons for their removal were strategic rather than related to their incapacity to govern.

Vanuatu

In Vanuatu, several governments have fallen through use of the no-confidence option. After the general elections in November 1995,[26] President Jean-Marie Leye considered dissolving parliament in February, but the conflict was resolved according to constitutional rules. When, in early February 1996, eight members of the ruling Union of Moderate Parties (UMP) sided with the opposition Unity Front, Prime Minister Serge Vohor resigned forty-eight days after taking office to avoid facing a motion of confidence filed by an opposition party and eight dissident members of his own party. Vohor subsequently revoked his resignation, however, arguing that parliament had not met to endorse his decision and neither the constitution nor standing orders were specific on such details pertaining to the resignation of prime ministers. Vohor's party boycotted an extraordinary session of parliament scheduled for 20 February and the session was adjourned until Friday 23 February, when the opposition, with 31 of the 50 seats in parliament, was expected to elect their candidate to the top job. In this extraordinary parliamentary session, Vohor's predecessor, Maxime Carlot Korman regained the premiership.

In August 1996 Willie Jimmy simultaneously submitted a no-confidence motion, signed by 27 of the 50 MPs, and called for it to be debated at a special session on 6 September. Korman's government boycotted this extraordinary meeting of parliament and invited leaders of opposition groups to join the government. The Supreme Court, however, accepted a petition from the opposition ordering that parliament sit, and Korman was defeated in a no-confidence motion (27 votes to 22) on 25 September. In early October, Serge Vohor became prime minister.[27]

Vohor reclaimed the prime ministership on 20 May 1997 after forming a new coalition when rival factions of his UMP reunited.[28] In this instance, Vohor agreed to the new coalition rather than face a no-confidence motion. The Vohor government, now with a 10-seat majority in parliament, dispensed with coalition partner the Vanua'aku Pati, which lodged a no-confidence motion the following week. Vohor's was the fourth government in just over a year. One wonders how such political struggles benefit the people of Vanuatu, who ostensibly elect members to parliament to make and implement the laws of governance.

Other Pacific Island parliaments

The one attempt, in August 1993, to put a no-confidence vote to the Tongan parliament failed for lack of recognition of such a procedure. The parliament comprises 12 cabinet ministers appointed by the king, plus 9 nobles' representatives elected by some 20 nobles who are themselves nominated by the king, and 9 'people's representatives' elected by the population of commoners. The king has held the prerogative to appoint and dismiss his appointees, and neither the courts nor the parliament have attempted to remove an elected or appointed member of the legislature.[29]

In May 1997 Solomon Islands Deputy Speaker Benedict Kinika gave notice of a parliamentary motion of no confidence in Prime Minister Solomon Mamaloni. The motion referred to Mamaloni's poor leadership, evidenced by the state of the economy and government finances.

When opposition members put the first no-confidence motion in the Marshall Islands parliament in September 1998, the parliament ceased to function for some six weeks while the government sought to avoid it. Although the courts instructed the parliament to resume, the matter was not finally settled until the Supreme Court upheld the lower court's ruling one year later.

Governments may fall in one of several additional ways. When a parliament fails to agree on renewing supply of money, or does not approve of the budget, a government can fall. This happened to Fijian Prime Minister Sitiveni Rabuka at the end of November 1993, when parliament failed to pass the 1994 budget. President Ratu Sir Kamisese Mara granted the prime minister's request for a dissolution of parliament and elections were held the following February. The people returned the Rabuka government to power (37 of 70 parliamentary seats), albeit in a coalition with the General Voters Party (4 seats) and 2 independents.

Conclusion

This chapter has shown how the constitutional means most frequently used to obtain government, other than through scheduled elections, has been through votes of no confidence and house dissolutions. The manner in which no-confidence motions have come to be used shows their susceptibility to strategic action. Whereas their constitutional intent is to ensure that a parliament is constantly guided by a competent government, they are now commonly used as a strategic device to wrest control of executive power.

The Westminster system has strengths and weaknesses as a system of government. One persistent weakness has been the instability brought into the system by competition among political actors to obtain executive power. Whereas the 'tradition' in Westminster was for governments to be formed following elections, or following confidence votes in which a majority voted against the prime minister, the practice in most Asia–Pacific states has been for parties to pursue executive power at any opportunity. A lack of party traditions has fuelled the movement of MPs between parties, and from government to opposition and vice versa.

The absence of firm party loyalties and clear ideological commitments by MPs in the Pacific states has driven successive prime ministers to the distribution of political patronage in their effort to win and retain their parliamentary majorities. The principal mechanism used by governments to defend their majorities has been the allocation of posts and benefits within the parliament and within the executive. In 1995, for instance, Thailand's Prime Minister Banharn Silpa-archa held together a seven-party coalition government by including 6 deputy prime ministers and a total of 49 members – the maximum size of cabinet under the law. Much of such activity rehearsed the distasteful allocation of favours familiar to political systems elsewhere; and some of it breached laws on corruption, clearly established in Leadership Codes.

The task of defining the purposes and powers of parliament in relation to the individual, and in relation to other state and societal structures (such as the bureaucracy, economy, military, civil society), is in some cases incomplete, and in others, simply differently configured. In the representation of individual interests and of functional interests in the state, the difference between Western practice and Asia–Pacific practice is institutional. In the West, functional interests – and public interest groups – put their views to parliamentarians informally, through sophisticated lobbying. In the Asia Pacific, interests representation can take a more corporate form, with the state playing a role in defining them and assisting in their articulation.

The challenge for parliaments in relatively new democracies includes finding ways to improve the practice of consultation and decision-making at national level, without losing the democratic nature of representation. In summary, the instability of executive governments in many regional countries can be traced to the problem of trying to form and hold together majorities in legislatures, where no single party or stable coalition has a majority.

Notes

1 P. L. Prasada Rao, 'Shadow of Crime', *Hindu*, 15 August 1995, 25.
2 Abdullah, 'Citizens' Rights and Enforcement of Conservation Laws', 37.
3 The 1945 Constitution is silent on matters of form and structure, and the number of members of the MPR and DPR was left for determination by subsidiary legislation. Article 19 states that the composition of the House of People's Representatives 'shall be established by legislation'; and that it will 'convene at least once annually'. This structure did not form part of the 1949 and 1950 constitutions, and was only implemented through Presidential Decree 2 of 1959, which regulated establishment of a Provisional People's Consultative Assembly, and reinstated the 1945 Constitution as of 5 July 1959. Law 16 of 1969 stipulated that the MPRS was to be composed of members of the DPR, augmented by representatives from the regions, political groups, and functional sectors. The total number, in 1969, double that of the DPR, was $2 \times 460 = 920$. The numbers have subsequently increased. The DPR now comprises 400 directly elected members and 100 presidential appointees (about 22 per cent, including 75 appointed from the

Armed Forces). When Act No. 5 of 1975 was amended by Act No. 2 of 1985, the membership of the house grew to 500 and that of the assembly to 1000.
4 Powles, 'The Relationship between the Executive and the Public Service', 146; see also *Pacific Islands Monthly*, September 1990, 35, 51.
5 *Matangi Tonga*, July–September 1993, 34.
6 Hartono, *In Search of New Legal Principles*, 16.
7 Indra, *The President's Position*; Indra, *The 1945 Constitution*.
8 In Indonesia, deliberations aim to reach consensus (*mufakat*) on any question. In the event a consensus is not achieved, the matter is referred to the steering committee. Should this committee arrive at a consensus, all members are duly informed. In case of failure, the matter is submitted to the plenary session of the house, which must then decide whether the matter is to be put to a vote, postponed or dropped altogether. Voting requires the presence of all factions and a quorum of two-thirds of the total membership of the house. Resolutions or decisions are adopted by majority votes. Voting on nominations and appointments is done by secret ballot; on any other matters, by a show of hands. If a vote cannot be accomplished because a two-thirds quorum cannot be reached or because all factions are not present, the matter is returned to the steering committee.
9 Most of this legislation was enacted during 1992.
10 *Manilla Bulletin*, 31 March 1991.
11 Chan Wook Park, 'The National Assembly in the Consolidation Process of Korean Democracy'.
12 Ker Munthit, 'MPs Busy Passing 106 Words a Fortnight', *Phnom Penh Post*, 5:14, 12–25 July 1996.
13 The home of High Court Judge Kazi A. T. Monwarddin was bombed after the ruling. The court did not rule on a separate petition asking that opposition members return the allowances paid to them while they boycotted parliament.
14 Chapter 6, part 3.
15 A summary of electoral facts and figures for the period 1955–86 can be found in NSTP Research and Information Services, *Elections in Malaysia*, Kuala Lumpur, 1990.
16 Milne, 'Bicommunal Systems', 105. See also Zakaria, 'Malaysia', 370.
17 The provisions did not prohibit government officials from becoming senators, and some 25 per cent of nominees submitted to the king by the prime minister had been close to the National Peace-Keeping Council and appointed by the previous military government.
18 Carens, 'Democracy and Respect for Difference'; Lijphart and Grofman, *Choosing an Electoral System*; Rosenfeld, 'Modern Constitutionalism'.
19 See Ahmed, 'Reforming the Parliament in Bangladesh'.
20 Awami League of main opposition leader Sheikh Hasina Wajed, the Jatiya Party of deposed president Hussain Muhammad Ershad and the Moslem fundamentalist Jamaat-e-Islami Party.
21 The Nepali Congress (82 seats), Rastriya Prajatantra Party (19), and Nepal Sadbhavana Party voted as a block in favour of the motion and were supported by a number of independent MPs. To add to the climate of drama, Prime Minister Adhikari made his defence via video, while recovering from a helicopter crash.

22 In accordance with constitutional art. 53(3), which provides for recall if requested by one-fourth of the 205-member house.
23 King Birendra dissolved the House of Representatives on 13 June, and general elections were called for 23 November.
24 *Financial Review*, 27 September 1993; *Times of Papua New Guinea*, 30 September, 7 October 1993; *Pacific Islands Monthly*, November 1993, 18–19. Justice Maurice Sheehan found that the time for appointment of a prime minister arises when the vacancy occurs, and that there was nothing in the constitution stating that the vacancy arises only when parliament is told of it.
25 [ABC International News] 'PNG Crisis Deepens Despite Confidence Vote', Wednesday 26 March 1997.
26 Ambrose, 'A Coup That Failed?'. The Union of Moderate Parties was divided in the lead-up to elections, with factions lodging differing lists of UMP candidates to the electoral office on the last day for registration of candidates. Following the election, the two UMP groups manoeuvred separately to form coalitions with other parties. Incumbent Prime Minister Serge Vohor declared himself prime minister again, with the support of some UMP members and Walter Lini's National United Party MPs. Six other UMP members, however, allied with Donald Kalpokas' Unity Front and gained office, with Carlot Korman as prime minister (Kalpokas' group obtained seven ministries and the deputy prime ministership in the 22-member government). A petition against the government's legitimacy failed in the Supreme Court.
27 'Premier Serge Vohor Revokes Resignation', Radio Australia external service, Melbourne, 20 February 1996; Pauline Swain, 'Vanuatu Politicians Revel in Power Games', *Dominion*, 29 August 1996, 8; 'Vanuatu – Turmoil Endemic', *New Zealand Herald*, 2 October 1996; 'Vanuatu Turmoil', *Courier-Mail*, 26 October 1996, 33; 'Sope, Three Allies Sacked', *Courier-Mail*, 28 October 1996.
28 His 29-member coalition government comprised 20 members of the UMP, 5 from the Melanesian Progressive Party, 3 National United Party members and 1 from the Free Melanesian Party.
29 *Matangi Tonga*, July–September 1993, 7.

5 Representation

Representation functions as an 'intermediary principle' by which democratic systems can be created. Representative government ensures that nobody is in a position to exercise absolute power, and control over their representatives through elections is one way in which the people exercise their political power. The concept of what is represented changes between countries: the representatives of different segments of the population, such as ethnic communities, distinct regions, powerful ideologies, class interests, and economic and resource interests, can be judicially mixed in a successful legislature so as to preserve the viability of the system as a whole. All constitutional systems, regardless of the extent of their democratic nature, include a system of representation. Not all constitutions aim at being democratic, although democracies should be constitutional. Systems of representation, similarly, are not necessarily democratic, whereas a democracy *requires* a system of representation.

The choosing of representatives through elections is an idea that is new to Asia–Pacific states. Local-level leaders and sovereigns alike were traditionally selected either through lineage, through proven ability, or by the imposition of their leadership on the group. Limited franchise came to Asia–Pacific states during the colonial period. Elections were usually for petty government officials, and franchise restricted to elites co-opted into the colonial system. Where universal franchise was generally introduced at the approach to independence or after, electoral processes manifest a number of deficiencies: lack of monitoring agencies, lack of public awareness and education, and general immaturity in the various components of civil society. Consequently, Asia–Pacific elections were characterised by maladministration and vote-buying, to the extent of the marshalling of state resources by incumbents to purchase their return to office. In some cases, those in power used evidence of civil instability to impose martial law, as occurred in the Philippines under President Marcos (1972–84), and in Indonesia under President Soekarno. These and other leaders argued that the attempt to establish 'liberal' democracies based on Western models (both presidential and parliamentary) had failed.

As well as being at the heart of democratic and representative government, elections can play a crucial role in establishing and maintaining peace in divided societies. In Fiji, for instance, a complex electoral formula facilitated the transition to independence in 1970. Similarly, agreement on an electoral formula was part of the Matignon Accord signed in New Caledonia in 1988, which allowed parties in conflict to agree to the freezing of electoral roles between 1988 and elections in 1998: 'For all its limitations in terms of social divisiveness, the formal conflict of elections here emerges as not merely preferable to but also more effective than the informal conflict of civil disruption, political extremism, and violence'.[1]

Elections are the most well known but not the only means of citizen involvement in democratic processes. Other powers open to them in some constitutional systems include the right of recall and petition. In some countries, an ancient right of people to petition their rulers has been retained in modern constitutional practice. The Philippines Constitution grants to citizens the right to initiate petitions.[2] Another technique for distributing democratic responsibility with citizens is the referendum. In Singapore, for instance, some laws can only be changed if at least two-thirds of the population approve through a vote at referendum.[3] In the Marshall Islands, 29 of 30 government-proposed constitutional amendments failed to achieve the support of two-thirds of the registered voters (about 7000) at a 1995 referendum (the one successful amendment states that the Marshallese language will be followed when a dispute arises between English- and Marshallese-language versions of the constitution).[4] In the Federated States of Micronesia, a referendum held at the same time as Senate elections in March 1995 failed to approve an extension of the term of office for senators from two to four years.[5] In the Asia Pacific, therefore, a region in which constitutional arrangements play an essential role in establishing the preconditions for peace and democracy, there has been considerable experimentation with electoral processes.

Are members of parliament 'delegates' or 'representatives'? Must they 'do' as they are told by their constituency (if that can be determined) – or are they free to decide issues on their constituency's behalf? Should candidates be held accountable for their electoral promises? Should political parties gain constitutional recognition – or remain loosely organised bodies as part of 'civil society'? Who should be allowed to vote, and who is eligible to stand for election? Are 'functional constituencies' legitimate in democratic societies? What standards of accountability should apply to 'public' leaders?

These are just some of the questions that have dominated thinking about electoral systems in the region. Answers to them determine the basis of candidacy, whether an electoral system has single- or multi-member electorates, and whether a system is to be 'first past the post', preferential, proportional, or STV ('single transferable vote'). It also determines whether voters vote for candidates or parties, and whether 'special interest groups' or functional groups can have separate representation.[6]

Most electoral systems implemented in the region have single-member constituencies, although there is a trend towards the use of multi-member constituencies and forms of proportional representation. Elections may be held for either or both houses of a legislature, for the head of state, and even for judicial and other offices. In this chapter, however, we focus on general elections.

Overview of electoral systems

Simple plurality

In 'simple plurality' electoral systems, the candidate who attracts more votes than any other candidate is declared the winner, irrespective of whether the winner obtains more than 50 per cent of the votes cast. It is perhaps the easiest electoral system to understand, and to administer. Countries which use simple majority voting include Malaysia, Palau and Papua New Guinea. There are, however, problems associated with simple plurality or 'first past the post' systems, particularly when votes are spread among numerous candidates, and the winning candidate gathers a smaller number of votes than are cast for all other (losing) candidates.

These problems were graphically illustrated in presidential elections in the small Pacific state of Palau. In 1988, under a plurality system, Ngiratkel Etpison won office as president by capturing 26 per cent of the vote, and a mere 31 votes more than his opponent, Roman Tmetuchel. This experience led to a change in the electoral law, and in September 1992, using a majority system, an estimated 85 per cent of registered voters participated in primary elections. The incumbent President Etpison attracted just 2084 votes to his rivals' 3188 (Johnson Toribong) and 3125 (Kuniwo Nakamura). As no candidate attracted more than 50 per cent of the votes cast, Toribong and Nakamura contested a second ballot on 4 November 1992, which Nakamura won.

In Papua New Guinea, there are two types of constituencies: local and regional. The voter casts one ballot for a local member of parliament and another for a provincial representative. The national parliament thus comprises 89 members from 'open' or single-member constituencies, and 20 from provincial constituencies. The simple plurality system, combined with large numbers of candidates for most seats, has brought many members to parliament with small percentages of the total vote in their constituency. In 1987 elections, 49 of 109 members were elected by less than 25 per cent of the voters in their electorates. The member for Kerowagi, for example, beat 44 candidates in obtaining 7.9 per cent of the vote.

In preparation for the 1992 elections, the Organic Law on Provincial Government (Elections) and the Constitutional Amendment (Elections) Law, 1991, were amended to state that: national and provincial elections be held simultaneously at five-yearly intervals, voter identification cards be issued, the minimum age for entry to parliament be increased from 25 to 30 years, a 'first past the post' voting system be introduced, and the use of loud hailers be banned during polling periods. The changes also lifted the nomination fee for candidates from Kina 100 to Kina 1000, an amount refundable only to those gaining office.

In its report on general elections in 1997, the Electoral Commission proposed that intending candidates first furnish a list of a minimum of 1000 supporters, to counteract the tendency for most candidates to receive fewer than 500 votes. The numbers of candidates increased from 298 in 1964 to 2371 in 1997. Extensive candidate numbers have other consequences for the administration of elections, including the increase in costs required in printing ballot papers bearing more than a few names.

Similar trends occurred elsewhere in the region. In the Solomon Islands, six parties contested general elections in May 1993,[7] while 332 candidates representing ten political parties contested the 50-seat parliament in 1997.

Proportional systems

States generally adopt an electoral system based on proportional representation when seeking to accommodate and ensure the representation of minority interests, whether of thought, territory or ethnicity. In proportional representation systems, voters select parties rather than individual representatives. Their representatives are then selected by the parties in proportion to the percentage of votes won. The simplest calculation of proportional representation divides an electorate into large constituencies, each returning several members. Those candidates are elected who obtain more than a certain fraction of the vote, and their surplus votes over that fraction are distributed among the other candidates according to the second and later choices indicated on the ballot papers. As a result of this, other candidates, whose votes then reach the required quota, are also elected. This is the method of the transferable vote.

Countries that use proportional representation include Indonesia, Cambodia, Thailand, the Philippines, Taiwan (for 36 seats in addition to local constituencies), and Vanuatu. Vanuatu's electoral system includes an element of proportional representation 'so as to ensure fair representation of different political groups and opinions'.[8] Thailand's new system combines representatives from single-member constituencies with those from party lists.

Arguments in favour of proportional systems, compared to 'first past the post' systems, are that 'no votes are wasted', they can better represent the various ideologies existing in a society, and they allow for the participation of qualified individuals on party lists who would not participate if subject to individual campaigning. In a 'first past the post' system, only those votes that go towards the candidate with the highest number of votes 'count'; that is, all other votes, even if they constitute a majority of the electorate, are 'wasted'. In a proportional system, on the other hand, each vote counts, in that a party obtaining perhaps just 20 per cent of the votes will stand a chance of obtaining a similar percentage of seats.

There is discussion of combining the majority system with the proportional representation system, so that the elector casts votes for both their favourite party and their preferred candidate. In such a system, the party votes could be tallied at national level and the individual votes at local level.

A new electoral law was passed in Indonesia prior to the 1999 general election. Voting is by party list. Each voter is given three ballot papers containing the parties' names and ballot symbols, one ballot for each legislative level (national, provincial, regency). The provinces are multi-member districts for parliament and the provincial legislatures, with the province constituted as a single multi-member district for its own legislature. In the polling booth, the voter marks the symbol of the preferred party. Seats in the national and provincial legislatures are distributed according to the percentage of votes each party receives, in a simple system of proportional representation. For the first time since the lifting of many political controls, an unlimited number of political parties were allowed to participate, and political parties had representation on both the National Election Commission (KPU) and the Indonesian Election Committee (PPI).

Multi-member systems

In multi-member constituencies, constituents are represented by more than one representative. Countries that have multi-member constituencies include Singapore, Japan and Thailand. In Singapore, multi-member Group Representational Constituencies (GRCs) were created by a 1988 constitutional amendment to ensure the representation of minority races. Candidates for election in a GRC contest in groups of four. They can belong to a single political party or be independents, and each GRC must have at least one candidate belonging to a minority racial community. Nine GRCs have at least one member from the Malay community, and six have at least one member from the Indian or other minority communities. In 1996 the number of GRCs was increased, and the number of representatives eligible for election from each constituency raised from four to six – developments the government said prepared for the establishment of Community Development Councils, but which the opposition said favoured the government's position in parliament, where it held 77 of 81 seats.

Other issues

The basis of constituencies

Voting populations are generally divided into constituencies to facilitate the representative process. The basis on which constituencies are decided is generally a sensitive issue. While geography and terrain can suggest natural constituencies, ethnicity and other traditional affiliations can also become factors. Ideally, the definition of constituencies should not be influenced by political factors, but in reality constituency design can be influenced in many ways. In Papua New Guinea, despite the fact that an independent Electoral Commission has prepared a number of submissions for the parliament recommending changes to constituency boundaries to take account of demographic shifts, these have been ignored by a legislature which can, in accordance with the law, accept or reject recommendations.[9]

The 42nd Amendment to the Indian Constitution (1976) based the allocation of seats in the Indian parliament on 1971 census figures until new figures are established by the first census taken after the year 2000. The parliament's membership is determined by dividing the number of seats allotted to each state by its population, seeking equity between the states to the greatest extent possible.

In Indonesia, each elected MP represents approximately 400,000 citizens. Hence, if the population is estimated at 180 million people, the total number of elected members is 400. During general elections, the provinces form constituencies and are entitled to representation by elected members, the number being derived from the division of the provincial population by 400,000. Provinces with very small populations are represented by a number of elected members not less than the number of districts in the province and each district shall have not less than one representative.

In Fiji, constituencies for Fijians and Indo-Fijians are established according to different criteria: representatives are not assigned in equitable proportions according to population size across the fourteen Fijian provinces; and constituencies are not equally distributed between rural and urban populations. The eastern provinces of Lau, Cakadrove and Tailevu were allocated proportionally more seats than the western provinces, and the 110,000 Fijians in urban areas were allocated 5 seats in contrast to 42,000 rural Fijians.

Geography

States can define constituencies in their constitutions or in legislation. Obviously, constitutional definition provides the most entrenchment, and this has been used where the identities of constituencies have been important in defining the constitutional state. The Marshall Islands Constitution provides for the election of 33 members from twenty-four electoral districts.[10] The Northern Mariana Islands constitution apportions a 9-member Senate between Rota, Tinian and Aguiguan, Saipan and the northern islands (which were to get their own senator when the population of the islands exceeded 1000); and apportions a 12-member House of Representatives between Saipan, Rota, and Tinian and Aguiguan. Reapportionment can occur after a ten-year period.[11] In the Philippines, the 24 members of the Senate are elected nationwide, regardless of what region they represent.

Nauru's constitution divides the republic into eight constituencies which return prescribed numbers of parliamentary members.[12] On Niue, there is a constituency for each of fourteen traditional villages. Each village returns 1 member to the Legislative Assembly, and a further 6 members, elected from a national roll, assist in balancing representation.[13] However, this level of entrenchment can be a burden as the population becomes redistributed between the constituencies.

Pacific Island territories under French and American sovereignty elect representatives to metropolitan legislatures as well as domestic. In some cases, however, these representatives cannot vote. Even where they can, their voice is a small one. The 5 seats in the French Pacific – New Caledonia (2), Wallis and Futuna Islands (1), and French Polynesia (2) – are among 22 seats in the French parliament allocated among France's Overseas Territories. This presence among the 577 members of the French parliament prompts one to ask what such representatives are able to achieve on their constituents' behalf. Representatives of American territories, unincorporated and incorporated, face the same challenge in the US Senate and Congress.

Ethnicity

Some electoral systems determine suffrage on the basis of ethnicity. The fact that parliamentary seats are allocated in this manner in India has not proven controversial, at least in the international arena.[14] In Malaysia, on the other hand, the fact that voting is weighted in favour of Malay rural areas has caused considerable discussion. Malaysian political parties are communally based but then practise consociation and coalition. Numerous political parties form the Barisan National Front coalition (the major ones being United Malays National Organisation, Malaysian Chinese Association, and Indian National Congress). The major party, UMNO, has been in power since 1957. Malaya's first national elections in 1955, through which the Malays sought to show the British that the country was ready for independence, included 52 single-member constituencies and 46 nominated seats for functional and racial groupings.[15] The system was a compromise between democracy (a fully elected house) and the demands of immediate Malayan consensus.

In the Kingdom of Tonga, constituencies continue to be based on class and what are essentially feudal obligations and relations. The Tongan Constitution states that the Legislative Assembly is to be composed of Privy Councillors and Cabinet Ministers, who are to be nobles, seven representatives of the nobles and seven representatives of the people.[16]

In the Pacific, the Fijian constitutions have determined franchise on the basis of race. Fiji's independence (1970) constitution gave each elector two votes: one for a 'communal' (e.g. Fijian) candidate, and the other for a candidate of any race. In this way, members of one ethnic community were free to vote for candidates of a different ethnic community (the 'cross-vote'). In 1987 this complex electoral formula returned a Labor Party government that polled 46.2 per cent of all votes cast (compared to the Alliance's 48.55 per cent), but just 9.6 per cent of all ethnic Fijian votes. Subsequent military intervention in the constitutional process demonstrated the depth of ethno-nationalist feeling in what had until then been regarded, whatever the shortcomings of the 1970 Constitution, as a model multiracial Pacific Island state. After a period of military rule, a new constitution (1990) was promulgated which again provided for a communal system of representation, although without the opportunity for voters from one ethnic community to vote for candidates from another. The lower house consisted of 22 Indians, 37 Fijians, 1 Rotuman, and 5 'general' members.

The Kiribati Constitution designates twenty-one constituencies, and special representation for 2 Banabans: 1 from Ocean Island (Banaba) and 1 nominated by Rabi Council.[17]

Functional constituencies

Functional constituencies exist in Hong Kong, Indonesia and the Philippines. While Hong Kong was under British rule, representatives to the Legislative Council were elected by colleges for industrial, welfare, professional and commercial groups.[18] Functional constituencies are referred to in Indonesia's constitution and also played a role in the 'National Council' that operated in the early period of Guided Democracy.[19] The legal basis of functional groups was established in Law 80, 1958 – Law of the National Planning Board – which listed seven functional labour forces: labour and employees; farmers; national entrepreneurs; armed forces; religious scholars; the Proclamation of August 17, 1945 Generation; and services. The president's message of 22 April 1959 to the Constitutional Assembly said the government interpreted article 22 as being those groups known as 'functional or labour groups, that is tools of democracy in the form of categorisation of Indonesian citizens by type of work in the fields of production and services in implementing the development of a just and prosperous society concordant with the aspirations of the Indonesian nation'.

In 1994 the Philippines legislature passed the Party-List System Act to establish representation for such sectors as the elderly, handicapped, women, youth, veterans, overseas workers, and professionals. During Marcos' rule, 25 of the 190 members of the unicameral National Assembly (Batasang Pambansa) were appointed.

Appointed members

The constitutions of India, Thailand, Indonesia, Malaysia, Macau,[20] Singapore and Tonga provide for the nomination or appointment of members to parliament. India's Council of States (Rajya Sabha) includes 12 members nominated by the president. The Lok Sabha (House of the People) includes 2 members nominated by the president to represent the Anglo-Indian community. In Malaysia, 40 of the Senate's 58 members are appointed. Indonesia's 500-seat House of Representatives included up to 100 appointed members, some from functional constituencies but most from the military. As the push for democracy increased in the 1990s, the number of military appointees declined.[21]

Representatives to India's two houses of parliament are found through a combination of direct and indirect elections, as well as by appointment. Some members of the upper houses of the state parliaments are elected by the lower house or by special electorates (such as municipalities, district boards and other local authorities), or by teachers or registered graduates; while others distinguished in literature, science, art, co-operative movement and social service may be nominated by the governor.

Since 1990 Singapore's parliament has included up to 6 nominated MPs (1 academic, 2 medical doctors, 1 technician, and 2 business executives). These members can be appointed to cabinet and have full voting rights, except on bills concerning constitutional amendments, and finance. While the People's Action Party (PAP) government argued that appointments were necessary to bring some opposition voices into a legislature it had dominated through elections since 1959, the initiative was viewed by others as a deliberate dilution of the democratic nature of parliament.[22] A second amendment to Singapore's Parliamentary Elections (Amendment) Act 1991 allows a group representation constituency to elect a group of 3 or 4 MPs (rather than the previous number which was fixed at 3).[23]

In Thailand's national elections in March 1992, held under an interim constitution, the military appointed all 270 members of the upper house, but strong polling results in elections for the 360-seat legislature in favour of an anti-military alliance put the military under pressure to allow an elected member to become prime minister.

In Papua New Guinea, the provision for nomination of 3 additional members by a two-thirds majority of parliament remains unused.

Suffrage

The age at which a citizen attains maturity and can vote varies from 17 (Indonesia), to 20 (Taiwan), to 21 (most states). For elections in Indonesia in 1971, the franchise was extended to all citizens aged 18 and over, excepting army personnel, who were represented in parliament by ABRI appointees. All voters were registered and required an authorisation card allowing them to vote. For the 1999 elections, suffrage commenced at 17, or an even younger age for those who were married. In 1988 India lowered the voting age from 21 to 18.[24] These are generally political decisions – between older and younger generations of politicians.

While it is generally accepted that candidates must hold citizenship of the state in whose elections they intend standing, a complication emerges over 'dual citizenship'. Should a citizen who also holds citizenship in another country be allowed to stand? This question faced legislators in Cambodia as they addressed a new Citizenship Law, since up to 20 members of parliament held dual citizenship.[25]

In the Tongan constitutional system, only nobles vote for 'nobles' representatives', and commoners vote for 'people's representatives'. Suffrage is granted to all literate, tax-paying males and all literate females over 21. In Western Samoa from independence in 1962 until 1990, suffrage was limited to adults holding Matai (chiefly) titles. In a 1961 referendum, 83 per cent of the people had chosen to restrict the franchise to chiefs. A 1990 referendum agreed to extend suffrage beyond the 20,000 Matai to approximately 70,000 adults aged 21 and older.[26]

In Fiji, the ability to vote as a Fijian depended on registration in the Vola ni Kawa Bula (the register of native land-owning units kept under the Native Lands Act by the Native Lands Commission). Restrictions are placed on voting according to race. Constituency boundaries are protected in the constitution rather than in subsidiary legislation.

Women

Consideration of the constitutional position of women in the Asia Pacific requires a separate study. Throughout the region, women have struggled for gender equality but their legal rights remain inferior to those pertaining to males. Legal reform is assisting to eliminate discrimination in such matters as divorce, polygamy, abortion, underage marriage, property ownership, and participation in public life and the economy.²⁷

In India, the seventy-third and seventy-fourth constitutional amendments of 1993 reserved a third of the total seats for women in all elected local bodies in rural and urban areas. In Taiwan since 1997, 10 per cent of elected seats and 25 per cent of non-elected, party-appointed seats in the legislature have been reserved for women. Thirty of Bangladesh's parliamentary seats are reserved for women. Women could not vote in Laos until a constitutional amendment in 1956.

Party systems and elections

Whereas the elaboration of legislatures along Westminster lines has encouraged the formation of political parties in most, but not all, modern Asia–Pacific states, political parties are not uniformly strong in the region.

In the Pacific Islands, where 'national politics' is not necessarily a significant factor at village level, candidates are more likely chosen on the basis of clan or religious affiliation than party affiliation. Colonies such as Kiribati and Tuvalu came to independence without the formation of any political parties. Similarly in American Samoa, the legislature (Fono) is not divided into parties. One clear trend in post-independence politics, however, has been the fragility of party systems and the continued significance of independent MPs.

In some states, governments more often fail than succeed in running a full term in office, due to shifts in party and MP allegiances. In the Solomon Islands, approximately half of the sitting members have been returned at succeeding national elections (1976, 1980, 1984, 1989 and 1993). A similar situation has prevailed in Papua New Guinea. Such a high turn-over of parliamentarians has been associated with low levels of loyalty between voters and political parties.²⁸ Politicians, too, treat party loyalty lightly. When Solomon Islands Prime Minister Solomon Mamaloni was under pressure from his own ruling party in October 1990, he resigned from it, rather than from the office of prime minister, and formed a 'government of national unity' for which he picked from both 'government' and 'opposition' members. When recontesting his seat at general elections in May 1993, Mamaloni ran as an independent. A similar pattern exists in Papua New Guinea. In March 1993 Sir Michael Somare resigned from the Pangu Party, which he had been instrumental in forming twenty-seven years earlier, in order to be free of party restrictions.[29] In larger states, however, electoral campaigns have become a major periodic feature of public life, and the stability of any parliamentary majority is now dependent on political relationships.

Not all states have multi-party democracies. Some have experimented with legislating for single-party rule but have then reverted to open party systems; while others retain single-party systems as an ideological principle. Such small states as Tuvalu and Nauru, however, do not sustain party systems at all. Burma's 1974 Constitution provided for a one-party state under the leadership of the BSPP, an elected legislative People's Assembly, which met for a limited period, and a State Council, which elected a president who presided over it. The fourth amendment (1975) to the Constitution of Bangladesh, which changed the form of government from parliamentary to presidential, also established a one-party system.

The communist states, notably Laos, China, North Korea and Vietnam, provide for a single party, namely, the Communist Party.[30] In Vietnam, more than in China, recent reforms have altered government structures: under the *doi moi* (open door) policies, the Communist Party has given up its power to rule by fiat in favour of rule by law but retains control over policy-making and political power. But, while the state remains a one-party system without other forms of political pluralism, electoral reforms have made the National Assembly more representative and effective.[31] Seats in the 450-member National Assembly are contested either by members of the Vietnamese Communist Party or by non-party candidates the party approves of.[32] Candidates for general elections in the 1990s required approval from the 'Fatherland Front'. Membership of the Communist Party was not obligatory and 112 of 663 candidates ran as 'independents'.[33] The communist states always announce high voter turnouts at general elections. Vietnam claimed 99.9 per cent of eligible voters turned out for National Assembly elections in 1997.

Single-party domination

In Malaysia, Taiwan and Singapore, a single party (or coalition) dominates. In other states, multiple parties have at times caused instability and provoked the involvement of the military, including India, Pakistan, Nepal, Bangladesh, Sri Lanka, Thailand, South Korea and the Philippines. In Indonesia, the number of parties was limited between 1957 and 1999, and during this time the military played a central role in government.

104 The Constitution of Modernity

President Soekarno . . . saw the Republic being eroded by party political dissension, cabinets overthrown by political ambition and hampered by the actions of some elements of the Army in the political and economic fields, the State used as a means to personal power. The President also realized that the pattern of political organization we had adopted did not, in fact, release all the vital energies of the people. There were, he pointed out, important elements of society which had found no political outlet. Most parties were organized in such a way that they cut across the grain of society. They often represented circles of self-interest, and not national interests.[34]

Until the late 1980s, popular representation in Taiwan's legislative bodies was distorted because many seats were held by members representing constituencies on the mainland, who could not be removed on the argument that elections in communist-controlled areas were impossible. General elections were held in December 1992 for a legislature comprising 125 district seats, and an additional 36 members appointed from lists of 'at large' candidates, on a proportional representation basis among the major parties. For the first time, the legislature (Yuan) does

---

Box 5.1 *The merging of Indonesia's political parties*

1955   First general election contested by 36 political parties, 27 gaining seats. Political instability continues.
1956   President Soekarno orders the formation of a constituent assembly to draft a new constitution.
1959   Constituent assembly suspended by Soekarno.
1960   Soekarno bans all but ten political parties. Asks Masyumi, the main Muslim Party, to dissolve itself or be banned. Masyumi originally consisted of four organisations (Muhammadiyih, Nahdlatul Ulama (NU), Perikatan Umat Islam and Persatuan Umat Islam).
1964   Formation of Golkar (Golongan Karya – functional group, or 'Joint Secretariat of Functional Groups'), a federation of 260 trade, professional and regional organisations (farmers, fishermen, professionals, factory workers, and so on) formed by senior army officers to counter growing communist influence.
1965   Attempted coup. Communist Party banned and members detained or murdered.
1967   Soeharto becomes president of New Order government.
1968   Golkar brought under government control.
1971   Government bans politics at village and sub-district level, and rationalises the party system.

not include members elected more than forty years ago in constituencies in mainland China.

In Myanmar, the military remains in control of the state. In 1988, nationwide demonstrations against the Ne Win government resulted in his resignation. The National Assembly (Pyithu Hluttaw), the Council of State and other governmental bodies were dissolved and the army established the State Law and Order Restoration Council (SLORC) through which to exercise full control. At general elections in May 1990, the main opposition party (NLD) won 81 per cent of the seats (392 seats out of 485 in total) and 60 per cent of the votes. However, SLORC postponed declaration of the results and prevented formation of a new government. Cambodia has similarly been dominated by the military.

Indonesia

The Indonesian Constitution does not specify the basis of representation in the parliament, and a series of laws on elections frame a consid-

1972	PPP formed from Nahdlatul Ulama (Muslim Scholars Party), Parmusi (Muslim Party), PSII (Islamic Confederation) and Perti (Islamic Union) – these become Partai Persatuan Pembangunan (United Development Party, or Partai Persatuan).
1973	PDI formed. PNI (Nationalist Party), Catholic Party, Christian (Protestant) Party, Indonesian Independence Party, and Partai Murba (People's Party) obliged to merge as Partai Demokrasi Indonesia (Indonesian Democracy Party, or PDI).
	The principles of the new political system: • to keep villages free of activities of political organisations – originates in opposition to communist activities at village level. • to reduce the large number of organisations.
1983	Guidelines of State Policy and Act No. 3 become basic electoral laws for 'Pancasila democracy'.
1985	The law on social organisations requires all non-government organisations (NGOs) to adopt Pancasila as their 'sole foundation'; gives government power to control all NGOs (art. 12); gives government power to disband NGOs (art. 15); bans NGOs from receiving funds from overseas without government approval.

erably constrained electoral system. A multi-party system was established from 1945.[35] Parties were established promoting a range of ideologies, principally nationalism, socialism, Islam, Christianity, and Marxism/Leninism. In such an environment, attempts to form cabinets were made difficult by the operation of twenty-four political parties and their factions, and coalition cabinets were formed and dissolved frequently. Thirty-six political parties contested general elections in 1955, twenty-seven gaining seats.[36] The resulting government proved unstable, prompting President Soekarno to progressively ban some political parties and to group the remainder into parties of Islam, the left, and the nationalists, so that by 1960 only ten parties remained.

In 1971 the New Order government banned politics at village and sub-district level. The number of political parties was 'simplified' through laws that imposed their amalgamation into the Partai Persatuan Pembangunan (United Development Party, or Partai Persatuan) and Partai Demokrasi Indonesia (Indonesian Democracy Party, or PDI), and one functional group or Golongan Karya (Golkar). All Muslim parties – NU, Parmusi, PSII and Perti – were placed together in the PPP (Development Unity Party). The PPP remained united as it prepared to campaign for the 1977 elections.

The 'non-party' organisation, Golkar, was established to marshal people's interests.[37] Politics was banned at village and sub-district level, ostensibly to prevent the formation of narrowly regional based groupings. Parties had to subscribe to the state philosophy of Pancasila and have a membership covering more than a quarter of Indonesia in order to obtain registration. The state financed the administration, campaign and leadership expenses of these parties. Under new electoral laws, the executive appointed one-third of the MPRs, and appointed 22 per cent of parliament. The security forces were given the right to reject 'unsuitable' candidates. At elections in 1992, Golkar won 68 per cent of the vote.

In June 1995 a controversial congress of the PDI replaced its leader, Megawati Sukarnoputri, with Surjadi, Deputy Speaker of the parliament. At general elections in 1997 Golkar's vote fell to 73.4 per cent, that of the Islamic Party (PPP) rose to 23.7 per cent and the PDI, which was in disarray, captured just 2.8 per cent. The electoral law requirement that parties win at least 11 seats in order to have a position in parliament provoked concern for the continued viability of the 'three party' system, as the PDI obtained only 10 seats.

During the Soeharto period, the Indonesian parliament comprised five factions (Armed Forces, Golkar, United Development Party, Indonesian Democracy Party, and regional delegates), but since general elections in 1999 it has housed many more political parties.

Nominations

In recent years, increasing numbers of candidates are standing for election. At general elections in Papua New Guinea in 1992, for instance, there were more than 1500 candidates for 109 seats, and numerous seats were won with less than 10 per cent of the vote. At national elections in the Solomon Islands in May 1993, seven political groups put forward 280 contestants for the 47 seats. In Nepal, 69 political parties registered with the election commission for the 1994 elections.

In India, candidates must be aged at least 25 to stand for election to the lower house and at least 30 if seeking a seat in the Rajya Sabha. The Papua New Guinea parliament raised the age of eligibility for candidature to 30 years in an effort to reduce the number and improve the quality of candidates.[38] In Samoa, the right to stand for election is limited to citizens holding Matai (chiefly) titles: 45 of 47 parliamentary seats are reserved for Matai and the other 2 are allocated to citizens of non-Samoan ancestry.[39]

Campaigns

Parties generally 'pre-select' candidates, who are offered to voters on a party ticket. Where literacy rates are low, party symbols and insignia become all-important, and in many countries fierce contests occur for the rights to display familiar icons on party emblems. But the party system comes at a cost to democracy: the possibility of voting for the candidate whom the voter feels most suited for the office has all but been removed.

In preparation for general elections in Indonesia in 1992, the government allowed the most open electoral campaigns since 1955. Debates were televised, with journalists acting as moderators. Electoral guidelines were established by the National Election Commission. Campaigning covered a 25-day period starting on 10 May (followed by a five-day cooling-off period before the election); car rallies and political posters were banned; parties were urged to use radio and television to convey their messages; and all political statements had to be cleared by the election commission. The commission sought from the public objections to any of the registered candidates. Notice of these objections was given to the heads of the three political parties who then had until 8 March to defend their candidates.[40]

In theory, people elect representatives to a national chamber to confer–debate–consult on matters of importance to the entire country. In practice, voters more often elect members on the basis of promises to procure as much tangible/material benefit as possible for their electorate.[41] As part of South Korea's effort to hold clean and fair elections, the Central Election Management Committee monitored 1996 campaign speeches and promises, under a mandate to prosecute candidates whose promises fell beyond their capacity to deliver, if elected. It also monitored instances of members of government using the electoral period to announce policies and to promise budgetary allocations for local projects.

Independents

In India, independent candidates have been subject to severe intimidation and violence, to the extent that government amended the Representation of the People Act 1951 so that elections are not countermanded in the event of the death of an independent candidate. In the 1992 Papua New Guinea elections, 74 per cent of candidates stood as independents and 22 (20.2 per cent) seats were won with less than 10 per cent of the vote. In 1997, 14 candidates (12.8 per cent) won with 30 per cent or more of the formal vote. The number of candidates winning with less than 10 per cent of the formal votes cast rose from 9 in 1992 (8.2 per cent) to 15 (13.8 per cent), with 3 successful candidates obtaining less than 7 per cent of the votes.

Electoral administration

The impartial administration of elections is an essential component of democratic governance and the number of independent agencies to undertake this task, commonly referred to as 'electoral commissions', is increasing. Challenges in electoral administration include accurate voter registration and vote-counting. Vote-counting requires transparency, but the levels at which counting takes place can be significant. For instance, if votes are counted at village level, the trends in that village are visible to all and in some instances have resulted in recriminations on the village from disgruntled candidates or their followers. Recrimination can also come from victorious candidates who use knowledge of voting patterns to punish those who did not support them.

Electoral laws

Electoral laws play an essential role in shaping electoral contests. They prescribe the requirements for recognition of parties, for conducting elections and for resolution of electoral disputes. The proper conducting of elections has also been encouraged through the emergence of election monitoring. In Indonesia, for instance, a group of fifty prominent activists launched the Independent Election Monitoring Committee (KIPP) to monitor the 1997 general election,[42] and this became a precursor to the monitoring efforts at general elections that followed the downfall of President Soeharto. Similar bodies have been established to monitor elections elsewhere in Southeast Asia: Namfrel, in the Philippines in 1986, to monitor the last elections held prior to the removal from office of President Marcos; and Pollwatch, in Thailand in 1992, following repression of civilians by the military.[43]

In India, parties must register with the Electoral Commission as either a national party or a state party (one recognised in less than four states).[44] In the early 1990s there were some twelve national parties and more than forty state parties. The Election Symbols (Reservation and Allotment) Order 1968 requires parties to register their symbols. At general elections for the Indian parliament in 1996, approximately 590 million voters chose from some 14,000 candidates to fill 543 seats.

The Malaysian Constitution makes no reference to political parties, but all parties must be registered according to the Societies Act 1966. This has given the government the opportunity to refuse registration to some political groups. A 1981 amendment requires all societies, clubs and associations to register as either political or non-political, a move which controls the ability of many organisations to campaign and lobby.

In the lead-up to elections in 1998, Cambodia's lack of legal and institutional infrastructure led a number of international NGOs to call for postponement. The parliament was slow to pass the Citizenship Law, Electoral Law, Parliamentary Law and Political Parties Law. By the time of the elections, however, these laws were in place and polling proceeded efficiently.

The Papua New Guinea Constitution requires passage of 'organic laws' relating to the integrity of political parties and candidates.[45] In the late 1990s the Constitutional Development Commission drafted the required laws, and although a desire for political integrity was professed widely, the path towards the law's enactment proved rough, and progress along it, slow.[46]

Small yet significant steps in improving electoral procedures were taken in even the smallest states. In 1995 an Electoral Review Committee in the Solomon Islands submitted to government a report recommending changes in ballot box arrangements (to use a single box, rather than a box for each candidate) and the establishment of a permanent national electoral office.[47]

Electoral commissions

The consolidation of competent electoral authorities in the Asia Pacific counts as one of the most positive advances in constitutional governance during the last two decades. Countries in which electoral law was strengthened include Bangladesh, Papua New Guinea, South Korea, Cambodia and Thailand. Advances include the passage of effective laws, the establishment of competent personnel, and support for these electoral rules and agencies by other branches of government and within society as a whole.

One of the most powerful electoral commissions in the region is in India. Article 324(1) of the Indian Constitution provides that superintendence, direction and control of preparation of the electoral roll for, and conducting elections to, parliament and state legislatures and to offices of president and vice-president are vested in the Election Commission. Clause (2) of art. 324 provides that it shall consist of the 'Chief Election Commissioner and such number of other Election Commissioners, if any, as the President may from time to time appoint'. The independence of the commission is protected by a specific provision (art. 324(5)) which states that the Chief Election Commissioner shall not be removed from office except in the manner and on the grounds that a judge of the Supreme Court can be removed. The commissioner's term is six years, and his or her powers under the constitution are supplemented by a number of Acts of Parliament.[48]

There are, of course, some jurisdictions in which electoral officials face social and political conditions barely conducive to such regulation of the acquisition of public power. In Bangladesh, where the electoral law was passed in 1972,[49] a 1994 amendment widened the Election Commission's authority to ensure 'fairer and impartial elections of parliament' by giving it the authority to issue identity cards to voters, and to refuse to hand a ballot paper to a voter who does not possess an identity card. The Act also allowed the commission to stop polling at any station at any stage of the election if convinced that it could not ensure a just conduct of the election due to malpractice, coercion, intimidation, or other pressures.[50]

Shortly before general elections in June 1996, the Bangladesh Election Commission published a code of conduct covering parties and candidates. The code regulated political donations, the use of government housing, the convening of public meetings, rallies and campaigns, the use of government resources during campaigns, the size, placing and distribution of posters and leaflets, the tenor of campaign speeches, and the size of campaign expenditure. It also sought to keep the election free of undemocratic influences (elections could not be 'influenced by money, weapons, muscle power or local influence'), to regulate the conduct of polling stations, and to settle electoral disputes.

Section 126 of the Papua New Guinea Constitution states that the Electoral Commission is not subject to the direction or control of any authority. However, in practice, the power of the commissioner to appoint, discipline and control returning officers depends on the levels of support forthcoming at election time from the Department of Personnel Management, which frees up public servants to take part in administration of the election.

South Korea strengthened its supervision of electoral practices in the mid-1990s. Three electoral reform bills passed by the National Assembly in 1994 reduced the period for national and local elections to a maximum of twenty-six days; lowered the limit for spending on presidential election campaigns from Won 36 billion (US$44.6 million) to Won 16 billion; reduced the limit for parliamentary elections from Won 120 million to Won 53 million; reduced the number of campaign workers each candidate could employ from 200 to 20; required candidates to pay all campaign-related expenses with officially registered cheques; and required them also to follow a strict accounting system supervised by the Central Election Management Committee. Candidates who exceeded the legal ceiling by 0.5 per cent or more faced up to five years in jail or up to Won 20 million in fines. Those who were successful in winning seats but who were subsequently found to have broken the electoral laws faced fines exceeding Won 1 million and the loss of their seat. The effect of the law, however, was that candidates spent large sums in 'preelection preparation', thus nullifying the goal of ensuring fair and inexpensive elections.[51]

Current issues

Anti-defection measures

Some aspects of political party operations cannot be easily reconciled with constitutional processes. For instance, there are different ideas concerning whether parliamentarians should or should not be allowed to remain in parliament if they leave their political party. To deny them the capacity to leave the party is a denial of free speech, but to allow them to do so, and to remain in parliament, some suggest, is to deny the will of the electorate who voted for them knowing their political affiliation. One view is that in proportional representation systems, voters actually vote for a party rather than any particular representative, and that in such a situation a representative should not be allowed to remain in parliament. This debate has taken place in many countries, including India, Sri Lanka, Malaysia and Cambodia.

Of Malaysia, where the National Front alliance has ruled since independence, the *Bangkok Post* reported in 1994: 'Party defections are so common – and financial inducements to do so are widely acknowledged – that the Sabah government has tried several times over the years with little success to curb the practice with "anti-hopping" laws. Sabah, rich in oil and timber, is known as the "Wild East" for its free-wheeling politics.'[52]

Singapore followed the British convention that an MP could change political parties with impunity, until the defection of 13 PAP MPs to the Barisian Socialis in 1963 prompted the government to amend the constitution. The Barisian Socialis MPs who had ridden into parliament on the PAP ticket in the 1959 elections constituted the largest opposition party in Singapore. Their defection reduced the comfortable PAP majority of 39 seats out of 59 to a majority of just 1. From 1968 to 1981 Singapore had a de facto one-party state.

Where the philosophy of governance privileges the role of political parties, the position of independent members of parliament is marginalised and in some instances, outlawed. In India, the Law Commission has recommended that independent candidates be banned, although the law and constitution give little direct recognition to political parties. India passed 'anti-defection' constitutional amendments in 1985, but these are relatively weak, as they do not apply during the electoral process, are powerless against subversive activity outside parliament and ineffective against 'toppling' governments. When at least one-third of the members of a party defect, they escape disqualification under the Anti-Defection Law. A provision of the Bangladesh Constitution of 1972 (art. 70) to inhibit the defection of MPs from one party to another requires them to vacate their seats. In 1996 general elections, a record number of nominees switched political allegiance ahead of the deadline, with the Jatiya Party losing the most candidates.

In the Pacific, active measures have been attempted in Papua New Guinea and Vanuatu to counter the effects of party-hopping. Papua New Guinea has attempted to restrain post-election negotiations by altering the organic law on the calling of meetings of the parliament, so as to require the first meeting following a general election to be called within seven, rather than twenty-one, days (to minimise the period available for 'horse-trading'), a measure that merely obliged politicians to conduct their negotiations more efficiently, or at a different point in time.

Vanuatu's Members of Parliament (Vacation of Seats) Act 33 of 1983 says that an MP vacates his seat if 'having been a candidate of a party and elected to parliament he resigns from that party' (s. 2(f)). The Act also requires parliament's standing orders to 'make provision for the identification and recognition of the leader in parliament of every political party and for otherwise giving effect to this section' (s. 4(5)).

Ironically, anti-defection measures, while aimed principally at the stability of the executive, have at times unduly strengthened its position. In Pakistan, for instance, the prime minister's knowledge that party members cannot show dissent by defection has at times resulted in a disregard for parliamentary interests once the post of prime minister has been secured.

Vote-buying and party corruption

Asia–Pacific states are still establishing educated electorates. Without this facilitating condition, elections that in theory are based on competition between ideas and aspirations as voiced by individual candidates become exercises in wooing unsophisticated voters with increasingly sophisticated techniques of mass persuasion. In theory, representatives are chosen among rival candidates, by election, on the basis of their abilities in open debate, and on the basis of proven capacity to assist the people address their needs and concerns. In practice, representatives often win office through the distribution of largesse, pampering to the prejudices of the people, and making promises regardless of their ability to fulfil them. The problems of 'vote-buying' and other forms of electoral manipulation have been widespread in the Asia Pacific. In the absence of firm party loyalties and clear ideological commitments, prime ministers have been driven to the distribution of political patronage in order to win, and retain, their majorities.

Interference with the polls by those in power in Bangladesh in the 1980s, for instance, quickly diminished any semblance of moral authority and succeeded only in uniting opposition groups. Given the massive rigging and use of force to undermine parliamentary elections, the opposition political parties boycotted the presidential election, and the incumbent was left to run against an array of persons who were in effect essentially 'non-candidates'. In Thailand, respect for such processes as democratic elections is only slowly emerging, and the common attitude towards voting, and towards parliamentarians, remains sceptical.

Electoral violence

Another major challenge for electoral authorities has been countering electoral violence. Partisan political processes are inherently destabilising. Western societies are generally able to meet this source of instability through the presence of compensatory stabilising factors (historically, a homogeneous electorate, and a cultural acceptance of the rules limiting permissible actions within political life). The absence of this 'culture of political restraint' in Asia–Pacific societies results in a willingness by actors to transgress the stabilising rules, and to push political games into destabilising patterns.

In Indonesia, sixty deaths occurred during the 1982 elections, and eight in the 1987 election campaign. In preparation for national elections in Papua New Guinea in 1992, the electoral commissioner worked with police to secure polling stations against electoral violence. Provincial politicians advocated prolongation of a curfew which was already in place to combat a deteriorating law and order situation. In 1997 electoral officials were dismayed that local council elections were to be held soon after national elections, as the election-related violence in some districts had not ended.[53] In India, the practice of 'booth-capturing' during elections prompted amendment in 1989 of the Representation of the People Act 1951 to provide for the adjournment of polling or the countermanding of elections in such instances.

Conclusion

Democracies require (or 'imagine') communicative action, but through the formalisation, legalisation and, increasingly, the constitutional recognition of party systems, democracies are increasingly beholden to strategic action. Political parties (or interest groups) are established to marshal numbers in a bid to acquire more than 50 per cent of the seats and therefore capture the executive (in some places, in a bid to obtain the percentage of seats required to gain control over constitutional change). In the breakdown of ideological certainty that is part of the post-modern condition, loyalty to party is premised on non-ideological factors and is increasingly liable to the fluid movement of parliamentarians between parties. In an effort to 'promote executive stability', laws are being enacted to prevent 'party-hopping' or 'defection'. Paradoxically, laws designed to promote political stability strike at the 'freedom of association' which is at the heart of democratic societies. Paradoxically, too, the more that political practice is regulated by law, the more constrained the democratic process becomes. Although Indonesia, for example, has recently undergone regime change and electoral law reform, the complexity of the new procedures poses a genuine challenge to securing further democratic reform.

Notes

1 Clark, 'Conflict Formal and Informal', 92.
2 A tradition of suspicion surrounds the use of referendums in some countries, due to the prevalence of manipulation of results. In July 1973 President Marcos asked Filipinos at referendum whether they wanted him 'to continue the reforms started under martial law', and in another referendum in December 1977 asked if they agreed that he continue as president and prime minister: both passed with up to 99 per cent approval. More recently, an organisation called Pirma mounted a 'people's initiative' aimed at amending the constitution. Because it was widely perceived as nothing other than an attempt by Ramos to find an avenue for him to win a second presidential term, the initiative met with strong opposition and ultimately failed: Abad, 'Initiative and Referendum'.
3 'Article 8: (1) A Bill for making an amendment to this Part shall not be passed by Parliament unless it has been supported, at a national referendum, by not less than two-thirds of the total number of votes cast by the electors registered under the Parliamentary Elections Act. (2) In this Article, "amendment" includes addition and repeal.'
4 'Voters Turn Down All but One Constitutional Change', *Pacific Magazine*, July–August 1995, 8.
5 'FSM Voters Again Reject Longer Senate Terms', *Pacific Magazine*, July–August 1995, 10.
6 In the 1990s the Thai parliament established the Democracy Development Institute to research politics and government and to disseminate that knowledge to parliamentarians, politicians, bureaucrats, other professions and trades and to the general public; and to offer education to leaders and members of society who need to know how to facilitate the growth of a fully-fledged democracy.
7 These were the National Front for Progress, headed by Andrew Nori; the National Action Party of Solomon Islands (NAPSI), led by Frances Saemala; the People's Alliance Party (PAP), led by PM Solomon Mamaloni; the Labour Party, led by Joses Tuhanuku; the Liberal Party, led by Bartholomew Ulufa'alu; and the United Party.
8 Constitution of Vanuatu (s. 17.1).
9 Following the first review, the commission sought abolition of provincial seats (which it described as wasteful), the creation of additional regional

seats (presumably in areas of rapid population growth), and the transfer of Lumusa district into the Mul Baiyer electorate (Western Highlands Province) rather than in Wapenamanda in the Enga Province, where they had been obliged to vote since 1964.

10 Majuro (5), Kwajalein (3); Arlinglaplap, Arno, Jaluit (2 each); Jabat, Mili, Ebon, Lib, Nambrick, Maloelap, Wotje, Likiep, Ailuk, Aur, Namu, Wotho, Enewetak and Ujelang, Bikini and Kili, Rongelap, Mejit, Utrik, Lae and Ujae (1 each). The districts of Narikrik, Erikub, Jemo, Taka, Bikar, Bokak, Rongrik and Ailinginae were to be included in 'the electoral district with which it is most closely associated, pursuant to the customary law or any traditional practice'.

11 Constitution of the Northern Mariana Islands (s. 2).

12 2nd Schedule, relating to art. 28. The constituencies, and the prescribed number of representatives, are Aiwo (2), Anabar (2), Anetan (2), Boe (2), Buada (2), Meneng (2), Ubenide (4), and Yaren (2).

13 Lamour, 'Niue'.

14 The Constitution (Fifty-Seventh Amendment) Act 1987 provides for the determination of seats reserved for scheduled tribes in Arunachal Pradesh, Meghalaya, Mizoram and Nagaland by amending art. 332 of the constitution. Under the Representation of the People (Amendment) Act 1987, 59 out of 60 seats in Arunachal Pradesh, 55 out of 60 in Meghalaya, 30 out of 40 in Mizoram, and 59 out of 60 in Nagaland were reserved for scheduled tribes.

15 These seats were allocated to representatives of Ceylonese, Eurasian and Aboriginal minorities, commerce, planting, mining, agriculture and husbandry, trade unions, 'nominated reserved seats', and state and settlement members.

16 Sections 59–60.

17 Between 1900 and 1979 Banaba (Ocean Island) was the site of extensive phosphate mining. Most Banabans now live on Rabi Island in Fiji. Their efforts to become independent of Kiribati have proved unsuccessful.

18 Prior to Hong Kong's reversion to Chinese sovereignty in 1997, the Patten administration added functional constituencies for primary production, power and construction; textiles and garments; manufacturing; import and export; wholesale and retail; hotels and catering; transport and communication; financing, insurance, real estate and business services; and community, social and personal services: Patten, 'Our Next Five Years'.

19 Abdulgani, 'Indonesia's National Council'.

20 Before Macau's return to Chinese sovereignty, its 23-seat Legislative Assembly included 8 members elected by indirect suffrage and 7 appointed by the governor, in addition to 8 elected by universal suffrage.

21 A 1995 presidential decree reduced the number of elected members of the DPR from 400 to 425, and a consequent reduction in the number of Armed Forces appointees from 100 to 75.

22 There are 23 political parties registered in Singapore, three of which are represented in parliament: PAP (77 MPs), Singapore Democratic Party (3), and Workers Party (1). Three other parties (Pertubohan Kebangsaan Melayu Singapura, Singapore Justice Party, and National Solidarity Party) contested the 1991 general elections without success.

23 *Commonwealth Law Bulletin*, 18:2, April 1992, 415.
24 The Constitution (Sixty-first Amendment) Act 1988 amends art. 326 by substituting the words 'eighteen years' for 'twenty one years'. This came into force on 28 March 1989.
25 *Cambodia Times*, 9–15 June 1996.
26 No. 6. Plebiscite Act 1990. The 32-clause Electoral Amendment Bill was passed in 1990 prior to the 1991 elections.
27 Hence reform in the 1990s to Nepal's Muluki Ain (Civil Code) of 1963.
28 Jennings, 'Political and Constitutional Change'.
29 *Pacific Islands Monthly*, May 1993, 22.
30 Article 66 of ch. 5 of the socialist constitution of the Democratic People's Republic of Korea stipulates that all citizens aged above 17 have the right to elect or to be elected irrespective of sex, nationality, occupation, length of residence, property status, level of knowledge, party affiliation, political view and religious belief. Authorities in North Korea recorded a 99.9 per cent turnout for regional elections held on 7 March 1999, the first since November 1993: 29,442 'workers, farmers, military staff and intellectuals' were elected to local people's assemblies for a four-year term. Only one candidate was fielded in each constituency. The regional elections were also the first since amendments to North Korea's Constitution were adopted during the 10th Supreme People's Assembly, September 1998.
31 Thayer, 'Renovation and Vietnamese Society', 27.
32 At National Assembly elections in 1997, 80 per cent of 663 candidates were members of the Communist Party.
33 Jeong, 'The Rise of State Corporatism in Vietnam'.
34 Abdulgani, 'Indonesia's National Council', 99.
35 See Government Manifesto of 3 November 1945.
36 Bone, 'Organization of the Indonesian Elections'.
37 Reeve, *Golkar of Indonesia*, ch. 1; Thoolen, *Indonesia and the Rule of Law*, 44.
38 Through the Constitutional Amendment (Elections) Law 1991, parliament also attempted to raise the nomination fee to Kina 2500, but this law was appealed by the Ombudsman Commission and held by the Supreme Court to be unconstitutional, as it put the possibility of nomination beyond the reach of the majority of citizens.
39 Bayne, 'The Constitution and the Franchise in Western Samoa'.
40 The commission received 351 letters about the provisional list of 2283 candidates posted on 20 January: 92 per cent of objections were about personal character and internal party problems, 5 per cent about administrative problems, and 3 per cent about past criminal records or civil lawsuits: *Jakarta Post*, 4 March 1992.
41 For South Korea, see Chan Wook Park, 'Legislators and the Constituents in South Korea', and 'Constituency Representation in Korea'.
42 KIPP (Komite Independen Pemantau Pemilu) was established as an independent body in March 1996, with former magazine editor Gunawan Mohamad as president and Mulyana W. Kusumah (former director of the Indonesian Legal Aid Institute) as secretary-general: HRW/Asia, *Election Monitoring in Indonesia*, May 1996. The government's electoral monitoring body is the Panitia Pengawas Pelaksanaan Pemilu or Panwaslak (Committee for Supervising the Implementation of the Elections). Home Affairs

Minister Yogie SM was chairman of the General Elections National Committee, Attorney-General Singgih chaired the Elections Supervisory Committee, and Governor Surjadi Sudirdja chaired the Jakarta Electoral Committee.

43 Maisrikrod, *Thailand's Two General Elections in 1992*, esp. ch. VI.
44 Representation of the People (Amendment) Act 1988, which adds Part IVA to the Representation of the People (Amendment) Act 1951.
45 'Integrity of Political Parties' (s. 129: to provide for registration of political parties with the electoral commission, for declaration of assets, income, and expenditure) and 'Integrity of Candidates' (s. 130).
46 'No Party Registered', *Post Courier*, 22 October 1999; 'Law To Control Politicians A Must – CDC Chairman', *Post Courier*, 25 October 1999.
47 *Solomons Voice*, 21 July 1995.
48 Representation of the People Act, 1950 and 1951; Presidential and Vice Presidential Elections Act 1952; Government of Union Territories Act 1963, and the Delhi Administration Act 1966.
49 Representation of People Order 1972 (PO No. 155 of 1972).
50 *Rising Nepal*, 2 December 1994.
51 *Far Eastern Economic Review*, 17 March 1994, 20.
52 *Bangkok Post*, 25 November 1994. Concerning post-election defections in 1994 that affected the government of Datuk Joseph Pairin Kitingan, see 'Sabah Victor Quits in Poll U-Turn', *Australian*, 19–20 March 1994; 'Sabah Leader Denies He Has Quit', *Australian*, 15 March 1994.
53 'Fears over Local Government Elections', *National*, 8 August 1997.

6 Head of state

Each modern constitution provides for a 'head of state', through election, appointment or descent. Traditional and neo-traditional monarchies, executive presidents and ceremonial presidents are all present in the Asia Pacific. Although the office is generally described as being either an executive one, as in Indonesia and the Philippines, or a ceremonial one, as in Japan and Papua New Guinea and other Pacific nations, the powers of yet other heads of state are far-reaching, even if rarely used. There are also states in which the nominal head of state is represented by another constitutional figure, such as a governor (or governor-general). In general terms, the most problematic issues in relation to the role and powers of the head of state have been determining methods for selection, conditions for removal, length of term, and extent of powers allocated.

Most heads of state are elected by an electoral college or by the parliament, in indirect elections. Countries having direct presidential elections include Singapore, Taiwan and Palau. The model in a particular country will set the pattern for many of the functions and powers of the office. The head of state has mostly created controversy by dismissing governments and judicial figures, and by invoking and/or revoking the use of emergency powers. In moments of constitutional crisis, the head of state has at times been positioned between the will of an elected government and the will of other sources of power, such as the military. The choices made in such moments have made the difference between the survival of democracy and recourse to non-democratic authoritarian regimes. Since some heads of state also possess residual powers (i.e. powers beyond those stated in constitutions), and given this variety of models and roles, the position of head of state is possibly one of the hardest to define in a written constitution.

Traditional monarchies

As noted in the first chapter, traditional monarchies existed in many Asia–Pacific states well before the modern period and their powers, which were often only broadly defined, often had religious as well as political legitimacy. That some traditional monarchs embody dynasties far older than the states that emerged during the periods of colonialism and national independence adds to the challenge of attempting their legal definition, for in many instances they have resisted such moves towards codification.

The 'traditional monarchies' of Thailand, Malaysia and Nepal continue to embody an association between a religious view of life and the progress of the state. The Malaysian monarch, for instance, is also supreme head of Islam in Penang, Melaka and his own state. Yet other monarchies were modified or abolished by colonial rulers or eroded and overthrown by the secular ideologies of nationalism and socialism. The once-powerful Chinese dynasty disappeared in the national revolution of 1911, and the Laotian throne was abolished as recently as 1975, following the abdication of King Savang Vatthana.

Cambodia's monarchy was overthrown in 1970 but restored in 1993.[1] Although a constitutional monarch who does not hold executive power, the king appoints three of the nine members of the Constitutional Council and chairs the Supreme Council of National Defence. The monarch is elected by a Throne Council comprising the chair and two vice-chairs of the National Assembly, the two Buddhist Patriarchs (heading each of the two Buddhist orders) and the prime minister(s). Any such election must proceed within seven days of the death of the reigning monarch. In January 1996 King Sihanouk elevated the queen from the status of 'Royal Wife' to 'Royal Supreme Wife', prompting speculation that he intended to nominate the queen his successor after his death,[2] a possibility welcomed by many but which contradicted a constitutional requirement that the monarch be descended from either King Ang Duong, King Norodom or King Sisowath – which the queen is not.

Although the Cambodian monarch's role is principally ceremonial, he retains some constitutional powers and is relied on to take other responsibilities that assist in unifying the fragmented polity. (In the lead-up to elections in 1998 there were calls for him to head an election monitoring body.)[3] He cannot declare a state of emergency or dissolve the assembly without the consent of the president of the assembly, and he needs the latter's approval before appointing the prime minister.

The powers of the Nepalese king were diminished in the 'pro-democracy' constitution of 1990. In the years prior to the democratic reforms, the government exercised 'panchayat' democracy, in which there were no parties, but also few freedoms.[4] Under the new rules of constitutionalism, Nepal's Supreme Court overruled the king's decisions on several occasions. In 1997, facing a no-confidence motion, Prime Minister Surya Bahadur Thapa had recommended to King Birendra that parliament be dissolved and general elections called. At the same time, 96 MPs submitted a petition to the king urging that parliament hold a special session. On a previous occasion, the monarch had accepted the advice of the executive to dissolve parliament but had had this decision overturned on appeal. On this occasion, he invoked Constitutional Article 88(5), which allows the king to seek an opinion from the Supreme Court 'on any complicated legal question of interpretation of this constitution or of any other law'. The Supreme Court ruled on 4 February 1998 that the parliament should meet. The no-confidence motion proceeded, but was lost.

In Thailand, the monarch is regarded by many of his subjects as a patriarchal and semi-divine figure, traditionally part of the cosmic order, and under Brahmin influence. Kingship is a symbol of *dharma* (the way), with the function of preserving sacred laws, but not legislating.[5] The ideal monarch is righteous and abides by the ten kingly virtues and pursues the four proper modes of conduct. The king is both Head of Armed Forces and Upholder of the Buddhist Religion and all other religions.

The Thai monarch is also considerably involved in assisting the population. The function of receiving of petitions, for instance, exists alongside the court system.[6] As a residual prerogative of the king, originating in practices dating to the Sukhothai period, it is not overruled by any modern constitution. As currently practised, the king processes petitions and appeals from his subjects with the advice of a Privy Council (whose members are chosen by the king for life).[7] Petitions are passed to the office of the king's personal private secretary, then to the relevant government department(s) for attention. If the explanation is acceptable, the matter may be resolved. Otherwise, it will be further investigated on the instruction of the king. Citizens are also able to direct grievances to the Petition Committee of the Office of the Juridical Council, a body within the prime minister's department.

There are several categories of petitions: (i) the asking of pardons, which are directed to the 14-member Privy Council for advice;[8] (ii) *rangsan petiti*: petitions about individual instances of claimed injustice which the king's principal private secretary decides whether or not to pursue; and (iii) petitions for assistance in time of misfortune. Only important or highly sensitive issues are handled by the Privy Council and the king, and all processes are confidential. The king seeks information from relevant government departments and passes it to the Privy Council for its recommendation. The monarch is not bound to accept the council's advice and is known to have at times ignored it. One recent example of a petition to the king was that of village headmen (*kamnan* and *puyaiban*) opposed to legislative reform that they felt reduced their status and responsibilities. The headmen also organised public rallies in an effort to gather support for their stance, but their protests were to no avail.[9]

In the Pacific, dynasties were extinguished during colonial penetration of Tahiti and Hawaii. Others continue in Tonga (where Taufa'ahau Tupou IV of Tonga has reigned since 1965, and the monarchy is possessed in perpetuity by his heirs),[10] and in Samoa, which came to independence with joint heads of state who possessed the highest *tama'aiga* (chiefly) titles and upon whose death the position will be determined by parliamentary election.

Neo-traditional monarchies

In Asia, traditional authorities were entrenched in the independence constitutions of Malaysia and Brunei, although generally with modified powers. In recommending the creation of the office of king (Yang di-Pertuan Agong), Malaysia's Constitution Commission stated that 'he will be a symbol of the unity of the country'.[11] While the king must act through and under the advice of an elected cabinet, he has held extensive prerogative powers.[12] Shah refers to a Malaysian monarch's description of the role of the king in terms extending beyond constitutional functions:

A King is a King, whether he is an absolute or constitutional monarch. The only difference between the two is that whereas one has unlimited powers, the other's powers are defined by the constitution. But it is a mistake to think that the role of a King, like a President is confined to what is laid by the Constitution. His role far exceeds those constitutional provisions.[13]

Other representatives

A number of states that gained independence from Britain have retained a 'governor-general' who acts on behalf of the British monarch, although, through convention, is not influenced by him or her. These countries include the Solomon Islands, Papua New Guinea and Tuvalu. In Kiribati, Nauru, Palau and the Marshall Islands, the head of state is also head of the executive. The President of Vanuatu and the Governor-General of Papua New Guinea are elected by their respective parliaments to hold mostly ceremonial powers. Of course, the head of state of the French Pacific territories is the President of France.

The discretionary powers allocated to the governor-general can be quite minimal. In the Solomon Islands, the governor-general, who is a Solomon Islands citizen appointed for a five-year term on the recommendation of the National Parliament, appoints a prime minister only after an election in parliament, and can only dismiss a prime minister after a successful vote of no confidence. The governor-general cannot dissolve parliament before its normal term expires unless it favours this course of action by an absolute majority vote.

For states that lacked traditional authorities, the problem is not how to influence long monarchical traditions, but how to cope with the lack of one. In the Pacific, uncertainty concerning the extent of the head of state's authority has resulted in constitutional crises in Papua New Guinea, the Solomon Islands and Vanuatu. In one instance, Papua New Guinea Governor-General Sir Seri Eri resigned after refusing to dismiss a deputy prime minister on the advice of the prime minister. Whereas Diro had been found guilty by a leadership tribunal, for which the punishment was dismissal from parliament, the governor-general appealed to the need for ethnic and national unity as justification for ignoring the requirement of the law.

In a second case, and one in which the law was less clear, the Solomon Islands High Court refused an application in 1993 by the Leader of the Opposition to overturn the governor-general's installation of Francis Billy Hilly as prime minister. The applicant had argued that the term 'absolute majority' meant 'at least one half of all the members plus one' and that, in a legislature of 47 members, that number would be 25. The court ruled, however, that 24 seats met the requirement of 'absolute majority'.

In Vanuatu, the position of head of state has proven quite eventful. In October 1996 a group of soldiers abducted President Jean-Marie Leye to discuss with him a long-standing dispute concerning payment of salaries. Although the president was returned safely to the capital from the island of Malekula, almost half of the defence force was arrested and charged with kidnapping, carrying weapons, and unlawful assembly. Prime Minister Vohor informed parliament that the soldiers had planned to establish a military government, suspend the constitution and impose martial law. The presidency of Ati George Sokomanu was brought to a more permanent end when he attempted to dissolve one government and establish another in 1998. He was arrested on the order of Prime Minister Walter Lini, convicted for sedition, and jailed. Four years later, however, Lini's fortunes had changed. In late 1992 he was battling to retain the premiership and requested President Fred Timakata to dissolve parliament to avoid a no-confidence motion. Timakata refused to grant a dissolution, stating that the issue was one of politics, not the constitution, and Lini's time as prime minister came to an end.

The 'reserve powers' of the Queen's representative have thus obtained less recognition in some jurisdictions than in others. In Pakistan, the validity of the dismissal of the elected prime minister by the governor-general in 1953 was upheld by the Supreme Court on the ground that it was a valid exercise of the royal prerogative.[14]

Ceremonial presidencies in Asia

While the President of India does not normally exercise constitutional powers on his or her own initiative, a number of powers are none the less exercisable. Executive power of the Union is vested in the president and is exercised either directly or through subordinate officers in accordance with the constitution. The president summons, prorogues, addresses, sends messages to parliament and dissolves the Lok Sabha; promulgates ordinances at any time (except when both houses are in session); makes recommendations for introducing financial and money bills and gives assent to bills; grants pardons, reprieves, respites or remissions of punishment or suspends, remits or commutes sentences in certain cases. The president is also commander-in-chief of the Armed Forces.

In the case of Singapore, a 1991 constitutional amendment introduced an elected rather than appointed head of state, and granted the president powers to veto budget spending and key appointments, and to block action by the government under the Internal Security Act and the Religious Harmony Act. These reforms to the functions of the head of state were introduced to ensure that the executive would not squander the state's accumulated financial reserves, and to preserve the integrity and meritocracy of the public services.[15] However, the president's powers were reduced by an amendment to the Act in 1996, so as to allow the government to call a referendum if the president vetoes certain constitutional changes, and to allow a two-thirds majority vote by parliament to override a presidential veto to certain civil service appointments.

Executive presidencies

In Asia, executive presidencies operate in Indonesia, the Philippines and South Korea. The powers of the Indonesian President, who is both head of state and chief executive, as established in the 1945 Constitution are executive, legislative, ceremonial and judicative. Constitutional Article 4 invests the president with executive power and art. 5 gives the power to draw up legislation 'in concurrence with the House of People's Representatives', while art. 5(2) gives the president power to establish government regulations 'to implement the legislation expediently'.

Since the president is also the 'Mandatory' of the People's Consultative Assembly, he or she must execute his or her duties in compliance with the Guidelines of State Policy.[16] During the Soeharto presidency, scholars both inside and outside Indonesia expressed concern at the concentration of power in the office of the executive president.[17] The president works with an appointed cabinet, has veto power over DPR (House of Representatives) bills, and appoints all twenty-seven governors. The president's powers are subject to almost no control by parliament, and the government cannot be overturned.

The president can declare a state of emergency, can bestow titles, awards of merit and other tokens of honour, and can ratify legislation. In times of a 'crisis which compels', the president can establish regulations in lieu of legislation. The power exists wherever the constitution refers to the need for statutes, since the president has the 'power to make statutes'. The DPR, on the other hand, merely has the 'right to make statutes'. The sole limitation of presidential authority lies in the requirement that parliament concur in the enactment of legislation, declaration of war and peace and the proclamation of treaties.

Among many formal powers, the President of Sri Lanka determines the number of ministries to which he or she appoints ministers from among members of parliament, and also appoints the judiciary, provincial governors, the attorney-general, defence forces leaders, secretaries of ministries, the commissioner of elections, the auditor-general and the ombudsman). In addition, the president can retain any portfolio, presides over cabinet, and enjoys immunity from prosecution for things either done or not done in his or her presidential capacity. The president can exercise limited powers over financial supply,[18] amend or suspend parliamentary laws, dissolve parliament (at any time except in the first year after a parliamentary election), and introduce emergency regulations. The president is hard to remove by impeachment.

The executive presidential form of government in Bangladesh led to the highly arbitrary use of power, which in turn contributed to the spread of corruption and widespread abuse of power. The importance of the legislature was diminished and there was significantly less openness and accountability of government. These conditions facilitated military take-overs and concentrated power in the office of the president, but also made the office assassination-prone. In 1991 the Twelfth Amendment to the Constitution returned the system of government to a parliamentary form. What had been an 'authoritarian' president became a head of state indirectly elected by members of parliament, with executive power once more held by a prime minister who enjoyed the confidence of the majority in parliament.

Selection

Each method for selecting a head of state has its advantages and disadvantages. A hereditary monarch is secure in his or her office and therefore quite able to remain above political forces, yet for the same reason could tend towards lack of involvement in issues of public concern. Where the head of state is elected, on the other hand, the element of competition can work to ensure that the office holder is a person of capacity who has proven abilities and commitment to the public good. This competitive element, however, could also work against the head of state's goal of unifying the polity, particularly when the office is an executive one and the president has been in political competition with other leading personalities in the government and society. In this situation, the president will have more difficulty in personifying the unity of the state and in maintaining an identity that is 'above politics'.

Eligibility

Heads of state who do not occupy the position by hereditary right must be selected in some other way, generally through an election. Many decisions have to be made, however, as to who is eligible to vote and who can stand for election. The other decision of no less significance concerns the range of powers allocated to the office of head of state. Candidates for the presidency will generally be persons of considerable experience in public life who already have a familiar public profile. The President of India must be a citizen not less than 35 years of age and qualified for election as a member of the Lok Sabha.

Under Singapore's Presidential Elections Act 1991, the elected president must: be a citizen of Singapore, aged 45 and above; not be a member of any political party on the date of nomination for election; have his or her name appear on the current register of electors; be a resident of Singapore at the time of nomination and have been a resident for a period amounting in aggregate to not less than ten years; and not be subject to any disqualification.[19] In addition, candidates must satisfy the Presidential Elections Committee (PEC) that they are 'a person of integrity, good character and reputation',[20] who has for a period of not less than three years held office in one of numerous capacities.[21] In preparation for the first elections under the new Act, at least two contenders (Joshua Jeyaretnam and Tan Soo Phuan) were judged unfit 'in regard to integrity, good character and reputation'. On 29 August 1991, 1.6 million Singaporeans (95 per cent of those eligible) first voted under the new law. Former PAP member and Deputy Prime Minister Ong Teng Cheong won with 59 per cent of the vote, defeating former accountant-general Chua Kim Yeow (41 per cent).

In Papua New Guinea, the governor-general (who at present represents the Queen of Papua New Guinea) must be a 'mature' and 'respected' citizen. In Fiji and the Marshall Islands, the head of state has generally also possessed the highest customary credentials, status or authority. Ratu Sir Penaia Ganilau became President of Fiji in 1987 following two military coups that resulted in the establishment of a republic. Ratu Sir Kamisese Mara was subsequently appointed President by the Great Council of Chiefs. The late President of the Marshall Islands, Amata Kabua, went to court while still in office to protect his title of paramount chief of Kwajalein atoll from other claimants.[22]

Direct election

A third method of selection is through direct election. States that have instituted direct presidential elections in recent times include the Philippines, Singapore (from 1991), Sri Lanka, South Korea (from 1992), Palau (1992) and Taiwan (1996). In Taiwan, Lee Teng-hui was elected president at general elections on 23 March 1996, in the first popular election for that office.

Direct election of the President of the Philippines has been problematic since the election of Manuel Roxas in 1946. At elections in 1949, the incumbent Liberal Party committed extensive electoral fraud to defeat the Nationalist Party, principally by altering electoral returns after the close of balloting. The 1961 elections, won by Diosdado Macapagal, were characterised by pre-election violence, pork-barrelling and vote-buying. In the context of Southeast Asia, the elections were nonetheless regarded as 'democratic'. Writing at the time, Wurfel commented optimistically, 'The Philippines is now the only country in Asia which has twice witnessed the transfer of power to the opposition party through constitutional processes'.[23] The failure of the president to control corruption (under President Garcia 1957–61), or to fulfil intended programs of social and economic reform (under President Macapagal 1961–65), drew attention to the problems associated with placing so much responsibility in the one office.

Some scholars suggest that a directly elected president has too much power compared to the power of other constitutional bodies, particularly parliament. A president wins 'all power', whereas, in a parliamentary system, power can be shared by a number of parties and interests. A president controls cabinet completely, whereas a prime minister appoints to cabinet parliamentary colleagues who retain their positions in parliament even if dropped from cabinet. Furthermore, presidential terms are 'rigid' compared to parliamentary terms, which may allow for a mid-term change of government if such is required. A president is shielded from the parliamentary scrutiny that monitors a prime minister and cabinet.[24]

On the other hand, an executive president does not necessarily possess legislative power, and presidential programs may be frustrated by inability to undertake legislative reform. For a number of decades, this has been the case in the Philippines. In 1961 Macapagal was only able to get half of his proposed legislation through the Congress and, thus frustrated, began to act swiftly and with little regard to due process. His decisions were overruled by the Supreme Court four times during his first year in office. Macapagal's experience may have prepared the ground for the attitudes towards the use of executive power adopted by his successor, Ferdinand Marcos.

Parliamentary election

States in which the head of state is elected by the legislature include India, Vietnam and Kiribati. In Kiribati, the president must first be elected to the 41-member Maneaba ni Maungatabu, be nominated by a parliamentarian, and then receive a majority vote from the parliament. In Papua New Guinea, the governor-general is elected by parliament for a six-year term and is eligible for re-election once only. The threshold for election to a second term rises to a two-thirds parliamentary majority.

College election

Another method for election of a head of state is through some form of electoral college. The President of India is elected by an electoral college composed of members of both the Rajya Sabha and the Lok Sabha and the state legislatures. Malaysia's monarchy is unique in that the position is chosen by nine Malay sultans who form part of a 13-member Conference of Rulers (Majlis Raja-Raja), established under art. 38 of the constitution and composed of an 'inner conference of hereditary rulers' (the Malay rulers of the nine states) plus the governors of Penang, Malacca, Sabah and Sarawak. The hereditary rulers are empowered to elect or remove the king, and to decide on matters concerning Malay and Muslim privileges. The removal of the Yang di-Pertuan Agong or the Timbalan is, of course, a serious matter and has never happened: 'He [the Yang di-Pertuan Agong] cannot be removed by the Cabinet or even by the Malaysian Parliament itself. In this respect his position is stronger than that of the President of India who can be impeached by both Houses of the Indian Parliament but not as strong as the English Monarch who cannot, it seems, be removed at all'.[25]

The Conference of Rulers meets three to four times each year to deliberate on national policy. It has the right to be consulted on the appointment of judges and other high officials, and must concur with alteration of state boundaries, legislation affecting the Muslim religion, and amendments to the constitution and regulations affecting the special position of Malays and natives of East Malaysia. 'It stands outside Parliament, yet can veto certain bills and has legislative powers of its own in relation to certain religious observances in the States of Malaya ... and it can discuss anything'.[26] King and deputy king are accountable to the Conference of Rulers while in office.[27]

The President and Vice-President of Indonesia are elected by the 1000-member People's Consultative Assembly (Majelis Permusyawaratan Rakyat, or MPR). The Indonesian Constitution (art. 6) stipulates that the president must be an indigenous Indonesian and the MPR has set the minimum age for president and vice-president at 40 years. Indonesia has had five heads of state since independence: Soekarno from 1945 until his resignation in 1966; Soeharto from 1967 until his resignation at the beginning of his fifth term, in May 1998; Bacharuddin Jusuf Habibie until elections in 1999; Abdurrahman Wahid until his dismissal in 2001; and Megawati Sukarnoputri.

The sovereignty of the state is vested in the people and exercised by the MPR. Its main functions are to determine the broad outlines of state policy; to amend the constitution; and to elect the president and vice-president. The electoral law introduced for the 1971 presidential election – the first under Soeharto's 'New Order' – gave the president the right to appoint one-third of the members of the MPR and 22 per cent of the members of parliament. In general sessions of the MPR following the last five general elections, only one candidate has been proposed for the post of president, and until 1983 both president and vice-president were elected in the one package. In 1988 there were two candidates for the position of vice-president for the first time, although one withdrew at the last minute.

In 1993 Soeharto was elected to a sixth term. He was nominated for the post by the United Development Party in April 1992 and his candidature endorsed by the Armed Forces (ABRI) on 5 October. Due to the lack of additional candidates, more attention focused on the office of vice-president, as a range of senior military and government figures indicated their interest in the position: ABRI chief, General Try Sutrisno; Minister for Research and Technology B. J. Habibie; Home Minister Rudini; and Vice-President Sudharmono.

When Soeharto was elected to a seventh presidential term, the legitimacy of the process became a focus of discussion. There was growing concern at the lack of accountability of the president to the MPR (given that a majority of that body were appointed by the president), and there was also concern at the election itself (Soeharto stood unopposed and was 'elected' by standing acclamation). A third crucial factor was a widespread perception of neglect of the rule of law, and such concomitant maladies as corruption in public offices (notably the judiciary) and abuse of human rights. Soeharto's last cabinet epitomised the cronyism of his final years: it included his eldest daughter and several political and business associates. His decision to resign followed strong signals from other branches of government. Speaker of the DPR, Harmoko, read a statement urging Soeharto to resign and calling for a special session of the MPR. In accordance with art. 8, Vice-President Habibie took over as president.[28]

Other states in which the head of state is elected by an electoral college include Hong Kong, Fiji and Vanuatu. In Hong Kong in December 1996, a 400-member selection committee established by China elected Tung Chee-hwa, the first chief executive of Hong Kong Special Administrative Region. The President of South Korea is elected by a presidential electoral college, itself elected by universal suffrage from among citizens who are not members of the National Assembly.

The selection of a head of state by an electoral college can suffer from political conflict as much as any other method of election. In Vanuatu, following the retirement of President Frederick Timakata in January 1994, an electoral college comprising all 46 MPs and the presidents of ten local governments convened in February and was boycotted by opposition politicians protesting at the insufficient notice of the election. A second election days later failed to deliver to any of the eight candidates the two-thirds required majority before a third ballot, on 2 March, elected Jean-Marie Leye.

The dismissal of a head of state can similarly be a moment of high drama. Such an event is often reported by the press as a 'constitutional crisis', although it is often more a crisis of politics and a moment in which constitutional mechanisms play the role expected of them. In Indonesia, where a president can only be dismissed by the MPR, the transfer of power from Soekarno to his successor, Soeharto, was politically sealed before the formal mechanisms required by the constitution were performed. Following a failed coup attempt on 30 September 1965, Soekarno was requested by the Provisional MPRS in its session of 20 June – 5 July 1966 to account for his role in it. Dissatisfied with his speech, the MPRS requested further elucidation, but Soekarno's response of January 1967 remained unsatisfactory and it formally terminated his presidency by decree during a special session (7–12 March). At the same time, the MPRS affirmed the powers that President Soekarno had handed to Lieutenant General Soeharto in a decree of 11 March 1966, effectively giving him presidential powers, and Soeharto was formally installed as president.[29]

Term of office

The issue as to whether the term of office of a head of state should be limited is not easy to decide. To do so combats the entrenchment of political and vested interests, but on the other hand, it limits democracy and the accountability of people who are in their last term of office. Since they will not face the electorate again, they may not feel accountable to its views or interests in their final term.

States that limit the number of terms that a president may serve consecutively include India, the Philippines, Kiribati (three four-year terms), and South Korea (a single term of seven years). In the Philippines and South Korea, these provisions were created following negative experiences. President Ferdinand Marcos held power for twenty years before being forced into exile in 1986, while South Korea had experienced twenty-seven years of military rule before constitutional amendments limited the elected president to a single six-year term.

No previous Philippines presidents had succeeded in winning a second term: Elpidio Quirino was defeated by Ramon Magsaysay, Carlos Garcia by Diosdado Macapagal, and Macapagal by Marcos. Marcos' lengthy rule might suggest to some the need to set limits, but it could also be argued that his intention to serve a third term motivated his declaration of martial law in 1972, and suggests that limiting terms are ineffective.

The first president to follow Marcos, Cory Aquino, observed the rule established in the 1987 Constitution that barred a second term. The second president, however, Fidel Ramos, fostered efforts by parties to amend the constitution to allow him to stand again. His supporters launched a people's initiative to amend the constitution so as to extend the terms of office of elected officials, including that of president. More than three-quarters of the 217-member House of Representatives, many of whom were also in their final term of office, were reported as being willing to sign the petition.[30] In December 1996 the Supreme Court was asked to stop the Commission on Elections from hearing the petition, on the basis that it lacked jurisdiction over the petition filed by the People's Initiative for Reform, Modernization and Action (Pirma). Advocates of change had attempted to gather the signatures of 12 per cent of voters nationwide (and 3 per cent of voters in each legislative district) to invoke a provision allowing for a plebiscite on the proposed constitutional amendment. Although the House Committee of the Philippine Congress agreed to reconvene Congress as a constituent assembly, and the Supreme Court dismissed an application from Opposition Senator Mirian Defensor-Santiago to halt the collection of signatures, the pro-reform initiative only ceased after Ramos decided not to proceed with his bid for a second term.[31] The movement for constitutional change met firm opposition, if not from within Congress then certainly outside it: key leaders of the 'people power' movement that had removed Marcos, including the Catholic Bishops Conference and Cory Aquino, reactivated their popular networks against the initiative.

There is an alternative view that term limits are themselves a restriction on democracy, since they restrict freedom of choice. There will also be instances, as have occurred in South Korea and in Tuvalu, where a president is constitutionally required to leave office when still widely supported by the people. In Kiribati, where the constitution allows incumbents just two terms, outgoing President Ieremia Tabai stood for election to an ordinary member's seat at general elections in 1991. In India and Indonesia, the term is five years, and in Singapore, Sri Lanka and Philippines it is six. President of the Marshall Islands, Amata Kabua, commenced a fourth term in 1992, and died in office.

Powers

Determining the length of term in office, and the number of terms, is perhaps of lesser importance than determining the powers to be exercised by a head of state. It has been noted that executive presidents exercise extensive powers because they head both the government and the state. Some traditional monarchs, such as those of Malaysia and Thailand, have legitimacy in the eyes of the people far in excess of the powers established for them in written constitutions. If the Thai monarch believes that the government is not administering in accordance with the good of the people, he has the right to be consulted, the right to encourage, and the right to warn. He is advised by a 14-member Privy Council.

The Malaysian Constitution confers on the monarch the power to appoint the prime minister, to withhold consent to dissolution of parliament, and to requisition a meeting of the Conference of Rulers when concerned solely with the privilege and honour of the Rulers Article 40(2). Further, he may issue a Proclamation of Emergency if satisfied that a emergency exists that threatens security, economic life or public order (art. 150(1)), and art. 153 gives him responsibility for safeguarding the special position of the Malays and the natives of the Borneo States (Sabah and Sarawak).

In 1996 the Singapore parliament amended the constitution, reducing the powers of the president. Constitutional amendments in 1991 had established an elected presidency, with powers to veto the cabinet appointments of senior officials, and decisions of government on the budget and expenditure of foreign reserves. The recent amendments reduce these powers. The government may now call a referendum if the president vetoes certain constitutional changes, and a two-thirds majority vote by parliament overrides any veto the president seeks to apply to certain civil service appointments.

Power to form and dismiss governments

One of the most important powers given to many heads of state is choice of political party to form government. While this power is not so important when one party or coalition obtains a clear and undisputed majority in the parliament, discretion is more important when the parties are more evenly balanced. In India, the practice of the head of state has been to distinguish between 'entitlement' and 'stability', choosing in some instances a smaller party having more chance of stability rather than the largest party automatically.

In November 1996, for the third time in seven years, the President of Pakistan used his considerable constitutional powers to dismiss a government. President Farooq Leghari dismissed Prime Minister Benazir Bhutto and dissolved the National Assembly, on grounds of corruption and undermining the judiciary. The court had clashed with the government that June, after the Chief Justice had ordered the restoration of local councils in Punjab province, which had been suspended by the government in 1993. Within a day, however, the government had passed legislation overturning the court's ruling, and the judiciary had responded with a series of public statements accusing the government of ridiculing it. A second clash concerned the allocation of power to approve judicial appointments, to which both the judiciary and the executive laid claim. Following dismissal of Bhutto's government, the Supreme Court refused to accept an application by Mrs Bhutto appealing the President's Decision, on the grounds that it contained 'scandalous' sections. General elections held in February 1997 were won by Nawaz Sharif. In 1997 the parliament removed the president's power to dissolve the National Assembly at his discretion through amending the constitution.[32] The changes also bound the head of state to make major appointments 'on the advice of', rather than in consultation with, the prime minister.[33] The political parties viewed the amendments as restoring the supremacy of parliament.

In the Solomon Islands, the governor-general moved to dismiss Prime Minister Francis Billy Hilly in October 1994 on the grounds that he no longer enjoyed the support of a majority in parliament. The Prime Minister, the Speaker, and the Commissioner of Police applied to the High Court for declarations concerning the powers of the governor-general, and it was left to the Court of Appeal to find that s. 72(1) of the constitution gives the governor-general the specific power to direct the holding of a session of parliament but not necessarily to force the prime minister's resignation. The Solomon Islands Constitution provides for the election of the prime minister by the members of parliament rather than by appointment by the governor-general, and the governor-general can only dismiss the prime minister following the latter's defeat in a motion of no confidence. Billy Hilly did resign, and the Hon. Solomon Mamaloni was elected as the new prime minister on 7 November.[34]

Power to assent to legislation

While assent to legislation is often considered a formality, the power given to the head of state to assent to legislation provides a final opportunity for suspect legislation to be checked. Not surprisingly, use of this power can be a source of friction between the head of state and the executive government.

Immunity

In Malaysia, the matter of which immunities and privileges are to be enjoyed by the head of state has been considered by the executive and the courts for some time. The constitution says that the state shall guarantee its rulers the right 'to succeed and to hold, enjoy and exercise the constitutional rights and privileges of Ruler of that State in accordance with the Constitution' and that disputes concerning 'the title to the succession as Ruler of any State' are to be resolved by means provided within the constitution. It also states that 'the sovereignty, prerogatives, powers and jurisdiction' of the rulers and of the ruling chiefs of Negeri Sembilan 'as hitherto had and enjoyed shall remain unaffected', and that 'No proceedings whatsoever shall be brought in any court against the Ruler of a State in his personal capacity'.[35]

While such provisions were no doubt meant to protect the legitimate status of the rulers, the implication of a number of subsequent court cases is that they also allow the rulers to act with impunity in civil and commercial matters, in addition to being free of scrutiny as to their choices in matters of royal succession. Rulers hid behind the clauses, for instance, to avoid the payment of commercial debts.[36]

In 1983 the government of Prime Minister Mahathir sought to amend the constitution to remove the king's right to veto legislation, except over money bills. In other cases, the king could not exert veto after the second reading and one month's delay.[37] A significant clause of the proposed changes was that the king would be obliged to act on the advice of the 'Prime Minister', rather than on that of 'Cabinet', as expressed formerly. The Conference of Rulers voted 8 to 0 against accepting the amendments, and the Yang di-Pertuan Agong refused to assent to the Constitution (Amendment).[38] A compromise was eventually devised by which the Timbalan Yang di-Pertuan Agong, as acting king (the Yang di-Pertuan Agong was, at the material time, indisposed), would assent to the Amendment Bill and the government amended the Constitution (Amendment) Bill 1984,[39] deleting the 1983 amendments.

In 1992 a majority of Malaysia's sultans signed a Proclamation of Constitutional Principles, which clarified their 'rights' in relation to: involvement in politics; appointment of the Menteri Besar (executive head) for each state and of State Executive Council Members; acting on advice; the appointment of senior government officers; involvement in business; provisions for the expenses of the royal households; religious involvements; and contact with the media.[40]

Several of these provisions do no more than restate constitutional practice: the rulers will accept the nomination of the 'person who commands the confidence of the majority of the members of the Legislative Assembly' as the Menteri Besar (Chief Minister); as constitutionally required, they will act on the advice of the State Executive Council or of the Menteri Besar in each state; in the appointment of members of the State Executive Council, they will act 'on the advice of the Menteri Besar alone'; and they will appoint senior public officers (including the state secretary, the state legal adviser and the state financial officer) on the recommendation of the appropriate Public Service Commission and on the advice of the Menteri Besar. By signing the document, the sultans agreed that they would not be 'directly or indirectly involved in party politics'; that they would only engage in commercial enterprise 'by way of trust'; that the expenses of royal households provided for in the Civil List would be controlled and administered by the Comptroller of the Royal Household; that, as heads of the religion of Islam in the respective states, they would uphold the teachings and practice of Islam; and that they would not, in accordance with constitutional practice, 'disclose to or discuss with the media any matter pertaining to the administration of the State which is likely to give rise to controversy'.

The Constitution (Amendment) Bill 1993 was introduced in the context of growing concern at the actions of some rulers that were contrary to law, including assault, failure to pay import duties on luxury cars, and abuse of logging concessions.[41] The amendment sought to allow court proceedings against rulers for alleged offences in their personal capacity but not while acting officially as king or as titular state rulers. It also sought to remove their power to pardon themselves and family members facing criminal charges, and to allow debate on royalty in parliament and state assemblies. These changes were agreed to by the Conference of Rulers on 11 February.

Laws affecting the monarchy continued to require royal assent, but the change removed the complete legal immunity they had enjoyed previously. A ruler could now face prosecution in a special court comprising the Lord President of the Supreme Court as chair, the Chief Justices of the High Courts, and 'two other persons who hold or have held office as judge of the Supreme Court or a High Court appointed by the Conference of Rulers' (s. 7a). The Special Court has the same jurisdiction, powers, practices and procedures as other courts. Its decisions are based on the majority opinion and are final and conclusive. Civil or criminal actions can only be brought against the Yang di-Pertuan Agong or the ruler of a state with the consent of the 'Attorney General personally'.

The Constitution (Amendment) Act 1994 removed the king's right to return a bill to the parliament for reconsideration within thirty days and ensured that he acted only on the advice of the government. It also ensured that the judiciary abided by a code of ethics drawn up by the government.

Conclusion

This chapter has indicated the variety that exists in the law forms, and the constitutional roles and responsibilities, given to heads of state in the Asia–Pacific region. Given this variety, one might wonder how one model could be considered superior to another. Evidently, the manner in which the office has been exercised by its incumbent has been as significant as any decisions made about the scope of the powers exercised. The ability of a head of state to communicate effectively with other offices under the constitution, and the ability to assess the mood of the population at large, have been equally vital objectives.

Notes

1 Norodom Sihanouk became monarch in 1945 but abdicated after a coup in 1970. He returned in 1991 after twenty-one years of exile. The 1993 constituent assembly vested Prince Sihanouk with powers 'inherent in his capacity and duties as head of State in order that he may save our nation', *Australian*, 15 June 1993.
2 Queen Norodom Monique Sihanouk's royal title became 'Her Majesty Preah Reach Akka-Mohesey', 'Queen Bestowed New Title', *Cambodia Times*, 7 January 1996.
3 Chheang Sopheng, 'MPs Want King To Head Independent Electoral Panel', *Cambodia Times*, 9–15 June 1996.
4 Burghart, 'The Political Culture of Panchayat Democracy'.
5 Bunnag and Aakesson, 'The Legal System of Thailand'.
6 See Aakesson et al., 'The Development of Constitutionalism in Thailand', 670–1.
7 The 1991 Constitution (s. 10) states that the king selects and appoints up to 18 persons to the Privy Council for life. The work of the Privy Council is not made public. Its members include Sanya Dharmasakti (President), General Prem Tinsulanonda, and Prof. Tanin Kraivixian.
8 Section 197. For this reason, about half of the Privy Council are retired judges. Most recently, in July 1993, the king pardoned two English women who had been jailed in Thailand for heroin trafficking. Such royal pardons, however, are not to be regarded as the outcome of judicial review, or as indications of innocence: *Nation*, 22 July 1993.

138   *The Constitution of Modernity*

9 *Bangkok Post*, 17 November 1994.
10 The Tongan monarchy, not unlike Britain's House of Windsor, maintains a nobility. In May 1997, on the passing in April of the holder of the noble title Fielakepa, Paula Longolongo'atumai Aleamotu'a, King Taufa'ahau appointed Mr Siosaia Tupou Aleamotu'a of Haveluloto to the title and estate.
11 The Reid Report (Report of the Constitutional Commission), 22 para. 58(i). The Yang di-Pertuan Agong is 'a visible symbol of unity in a remarkably diverse nation': Groves, *The Constitution of Malaysia*, 42.
12 See Hickling, 'The Prerogative in Malaysia'.
13 Shah, 'The Role of Constitutional Rulers', 17. Also published in Trindade and Lee, *The Constitution of Malaysia* as 'The Role of Constitutional Rulers in Malaysia'. Raja Azlan Shah, a member of the Perak royal family was then Lord President of the Federal Court of Malaysia. On 3 February 1984 he was installed as the Sultan of Perak. On 18 September 1989 he became the ninth Yang di-Pertuan Agong of Malaysia. See Special Commemorative Issue of the *Supreme Court Journal* 2, 1989.
14 Jennings, *Constitutional Problems in Pakistan*.
15 Tan and Thio, 'Singapore'.
16 Executive powers are treated in chs III, arts. 4–15, of the Indonesian Constitution.
17 See, for example, Muhammad Indra, *The President's Position under the 1945 Constitution*.
18 Where the president dissolves parliament before the budget has been passed, s/he may authorise the expenditure from the Consolidated Fund, monies that s/he considers necessary for the public services for a period that could amount to six months.
19 Arts. 19(2)(a), 19(2)(b), 19(2)(f), 44(2)(c), 44(2)(d). Art. 45 contains the disqualification criteria for MPs: being of unsound mind; or an undischarged bankrupt; or holding an office of profit; or failure to lodge return of election expenses; or being convicted of an offence in Singapore or Malaysia and imprisoned for not less than one year or fined not less than $2000; or have voluntarily acquired or exercised citizenship rights in a foreign country; or conviction under an election offence.
20 Article 19(2)(e). The PEC is established under art. 18 and consists of the chairman of the Public Service Commission, the chairman of the Public Accountants Board established under the Accountants Act, and a member of the Presidential Council for Minority Rights nominated by the chair of that council. Its main function is to ensure that candidates for the office of president comply with the requirements under art. 19.
21 See art. 19(2)(g). Specifically, these offices are: Minister; Chief Justice; Speaker; Attorney-General; Chairman of the Public Service Commission; Auditor-General; Permanent Secretary; chairman or chief executive officer of one of the statutory boards referred to in art. 22A read with Schedule 5 (*viz* Board of Commissioners of Currency, Singapore, Central Provident Fund Board, Housing and Development Board, Jurong Town Corporation, Monetary Authority of Singapore, and the Post Office Savings Bank of Singapore); chairman of the board of directors or chief executive officer of a company incorporated or registered under the Companies Act with a paid-up capital of at least $100 million or its equivalent in foreign currency;

or 'in any other similar or comparable position of seniority and responsibility in any other organisation or department of equivalent size or complexity in the public or private sector which, in the opinion of the Presidential Elections Committee, has given him such experience and ability in administering and managing financial affairs as to enable him to carry out effectively the functions and duties of the office of the President'.
22 *Pacific Islands Monthly*, March 1994.
23 Wurfel, 'The Philippine Elections', 25.
24 Linz, 'The Perils of Presidentialism'.
25 Trindade, 'The Constitutional Position of the Yang di-Pertuan Agong', 106.
26 Sheridan and Groves, *The Constitution of Malaysia*, 131
27 For an account of the election procedure of the Yang di-Pertuan Agong, see Trindade and Jayakumar, 'The Supreme Head of the Federation'; Trindade, 'The Constitutional Position of the Yang di-Pertuan Agong', 101, 103–5. The election should strictly follow the electoral list according to the Third Schedule of the constitution and is by secret ballot, although it is known that the list has been departed from: see Abdul Rahman, *View Points*, 72–3. For further readings on the election of the Agong, see Sinnadurai, 'The Yang di-Pertuan Agong'.
28 A number of inquiries have been undertaken into the former president's wealth. The MPR passed a decree on the eradication of corruption, collusion and nepotism (KKN) which named Soeharto as one of the targets for investigation. Attorney-General Andi Muhammad Ghalib led a government investigation, and there were calls for some form of independent commission. The parliament also initiated an inquiry into the wealth of the Soeharto family.
29 By Decree 23/1967. See Soedijana, 'People's Consultative Assembly'.
30 'Pirma Drive Brought to High Court', *Archipelago*, 20 December 1996. Earl G. Parreno, Aries Rufo and Raffy S. Jimenez, 'NPC Caves In; Sin Says Ramos Doing a Marcos', *Manila Times*, 21 August 1997.
31 *Asiaweek*, 21 June 1996.
32 The amendments deleted sub-clause (b) of clause 2 of art. 58. The power of governors to dissolve provincial assemblies was removed through deletion of sub-clause (b) of clause 2 of art. 112.
33 Art. 112(2-B). Section 58(2)(b) was the most disputed part of the Eighth Amendment, and its deletion restores the prime minister's mandatory advice in the appointment of armed services chiefs and governors.
34 Barltrop, 'Constitutional Crisis in the Solomon Islands'.
35 Articles 71(1) and 181.
36 In *Mobil Oil Malaysia Sdn. Bhd. v. Official Administrator Malaysia* (1988) 1 *Malaysian Law Journal* 518. Article 181(2) was held to absolve the estate of the deceased Sultan of Perak from liability under a commercial contract. The plaintiff had claimed the cost of diesel oil supplied to a mining company of which the late sultan was the sole proprietor, but the court decided that art. 181(2) precluded legal action against the estate.
37 Hickling, 'Malaysia'.
38 Ong, 'Malaysia in 1983'.
39 Reproduced in (1984) 1 *Commonwealth Law Journal* 7.
40 See *New Straits Times*, 6 July 1992.

41 For example, in June 1991 two members of Johore state were allegedly bashed by the Johore ruler in the presence of senior police and army officials at the opening of the Johore State Assembly. The Democratic Action Party wrote a letter of complaint to the king, who claimed in 1993 that he had not acted on the complaint as he had not received any letter: *Straits Times*, Tuesday, 2 February 1993.

7 Constitutional revision

Chiba describes the constitutional experience of Asian legal systems as the coming together of 'official law' (the legal system sanctioned by the legitimate authority of a country), 'unofficial law' (sanctioned by the consensual practice of some group within or outside a country) and 'legal postulate' (a value principle or system serving to justify and orient either unofficial or official law, which gives unique identity to the body of law).[1] When divergence between official law and customary values and practices becomes too great, some accommodation will occur, either negotiated or more revolutionary. This schemata seems plausible in a general sense and assists in understanding a tendency for the peoples of new nations to amend their constitutions, sometimes drastically, within a generation of their establishment.

There have been few exercises in constitutional reform in the Asia Pacific, and their success or otherwise is difficult to assess. In fact, a survey of reform efforts in the region suggests that exercises in complete constitutional revision appear to have failed to achieve their objectives more often than they have succeeded. A number of regional countries have swung between presidential and parliamentary forms of government, on each occasion striving to extricate themselves from the worst effects. Pakistan, Sri Lanka and South Korea have tried both systems.[2] Bangladesh and Pakistan have established parliamentary forms of government after experiencing periods of harsh military rule.

In Nepal, similarly, the parliament was established under a prime minister following the creation of a parliamentary democracy in 1991. In Thailand, regimes have changed, and new constitutions made, so constantly that their status as the supreme source of law has been seriously eroded. Constitutions are regarded in no better light than a set of rules for the playing of 'domestic political games'.[3]

Reform of a state's constitution should not be undertaken lightly, and constitutions themselves often include measures to prevent easy alteration in order to protect against change for purely strategic interests. When arguments are raised proposing constitutional reforms to meet some perceived necessity, they are invariably opposed by counter-arguments that include the warning that the constitution is not to be treated as simply another piece of legislation.

Modern constitutions and the need for expertise

Specifying who can participate in constitutional activism is a vital matter. Political science literature often presumes that 'constitutions are enacted by political elites'[4] and this may also be the case in the Asia Pacific. Yet the 'elite' nature of the origins of constitutionalism in Asia is understandable. When independence was achieved, there was little understanding of the 'modern state' among the people, hence the 'expert commissions' and 'people's representatives' who undertook the constitutional exercise on their behalf.

This also occurred in Western settings. Vanberg and Buchanan point out that whereas rational individuals, in a constitutional constituency, can be expected to have an interest in others making investments in constitutional knowledge, and such interest is likely to generate a mutually reinforced and expressed normative expectation that, as a good citizen, one should make an effort to be informed, it is still the case that the complexity of the issues results in 'rational ignorance'. This 'ignorance' can be overcome in three ways: by implementing constitutional education (and there are many instances of civic education programs), by the use of specialised experts, or simply by allowing competition between constitutional ideas and frameworks (to see what works).[5]

Reliance on constitutional experts implies a lower information cost (since constituents do not have to spend the time getting the requisite knowledge), and given the complexity of many colonial societies (ethnic and linguistic diversity, lack of 'civil society', and so on), this is the path most often taken by the metropolitan powers in the lead-up to independence. This chapter reviews three major methods of comprehensive constitutional review: that undertaken by constituent assemblies, that undertaken by parliaments and that undertaken by expert commissions.

Post-independence constitutional reform

The post-colonial experience comprises the phases of 'constituted' (independence) and 'constitutional' states. Ironically, the traditional elites of Southeast Asian societies were replaced by the new urban intelligentsia, who drew on the Western traditions that had subjugated them.

Japan, the Asian country that avoided colonisation, industrialised rapidly, and inflicted military defeat on Tsarist Russia in 1905. Following the experience of colonialism, World War II provided the historical break that allowed nationalists in such places as Dutch Indonesia and French Indochina to take command. On 12 October 1945 the nationalist Lao Issara (Free Lao) movement proclaimed the independence of Laos, but the French army quickly seized control again.

In the Pacific, modern, Westernised elites emerged more often in a context of co-operation with colonial authorities than in the adversarial circumstances which often accompanied elite formation, and the emergence of nationalism, in African and Asian colonies. Ghai suggests that independence constitutions transferred authority from traditional diffuse leadership to an educated, Westernised elite, and have consolidated power in national institutions that subordinate all traditional jurisdictions and competence.[6]

In Papua New Guinea, the first post-independence leaders spoke of renewing the constitutional order,[7] and the independence constitution has undergone partial review. In the Solomon Islands, Prime Minister Solomon Mamaloni commented in parliament: 'Twelve years after independence from British rule and the Solomon Islands constitution is lousy and very inadequate'. He said it needed to incorporate the traditions and aspirations of the country.[8] A Constitutional Review Committee had recommended in 1988 that the Solomons become a federal republic, with equal member states and an indigenous head of state as ceremonial president. It stressed, among other recommendations, making provision for due recognition of the 'traditional norms and customary practices of Solomon Islanders' in the making of laws and policies, and the inclusion of traditional leaders in decision-making at provincial and local levels.[9] No action was taken on the committee's findings.[10]

The constitutions of Tuvalu and Fiji have undergone the most significant processes of reform since independence, the former through a constitutional convention, the latter following military coups in 1987. A review of Fiji's 1990 Constitution was undertaken in 1995–97 by an expert commission. The resulting constitution of 1998 succeeded in striking a compromise between the need to recognise Fijian sovereignty and the need to accommodate other communities. While outlawing racial discrimination and guaranteeing a wide range of civil and political rights for all citizens, it reserves 23 seats in the 71-seat parliament to indigenous Fijians and 19 to Indians (there is also provision for 3 'mixed race' seats, 1 for a Rotuman, and 25 'open' seats). The constitution also guarantees freedom of speech, freedom of association, and the independence of the judiciary.

The 200-member Constitutional Convention held in Kiribati in March 1998 made only minor recommendations for change. For instance, it recommended increasing the membership of the Council of State, which runs the country's affairs in the event of an elected government or parliament being dissolved, from three (Chief Justice, Speaker of Parliament, and Chairman of the Public Service Commission) to either four or five. The government wanted the Chief Justice replaced by the Cabinet Secretary, while many delegates wanted the heads of the Roman Catholic Church and the Kiribati Protestant Church to be members. Other delegates recommended the addition of a woman member. The constitutional revisions were referred back to the people for comment before being considered by parliament.

In Tonga, a pro-democracy movement has sought constitutional reform throughout the 1990s. The fact that pro-democracy candidates won 3 of the 9 'people's seats' at general elections in February 1990 indicated the strength of popular support for reform,[11] and a 'Constitutional Convention' held in Nuku'alofa in November 1992, sponsored by the Tonga Pro-Democracy Movement, attracted some 500 international and domestic participants (cabinet ministers decided not to attend, and most were away from the capital at the time it was held).[12]

In 1996 a motion put by four of the parliament's 'People's Representatives', to amend the constitution to provide for a 30-member house fully elected by popular vote to five-year terms, was defeated.[13] If it had been approved, the king would have been required to select a prime minister and deputy prime minister from among the 30 elected members, and the members would have been able to choose their own Speaker. Under the motion, nobles seeking election in 1999 would have had to compete along with commoners for district seats, voiding their right to elect 9 representatives in the Legislative Assembly.

Debate on constitutional reform has proceeded elsewhere in the Pacific Islands, with little outcome. In Vanuatu, where a number of calls have been made for constitutional revision since the nation gained independence from Britain and France in 1980, the first substantial changes occurred in 1995, when the system of provincial government was reformed. Walter Lini, the first post-independence prime minister, spoke of revising the 1980 Constitution some time after general elections in 1991 to restrict the activities of religious groups, to increase the role of custom and the authority of chiefs, to limit access to courts of appeal, and to clarify the functions and powers of the head of state. The initiative of the subsequent Kalpokas government, which constituted parliament as a constitutional review committee, was suspended by the succeeding government of Carlot Korman, putting the whole process on hold.[14] Although President Jean-Marie Leye also suggested at a ceremony in October 1995 marking the constitution's sixteenth anniversary that a constitutional review committee be established, no such process has been implemented.

In the North Pacific, constitutional reform in countries associated with the United States is undertaken in the shadow of relations with the United States. In 1995 Palau's President Kuniwo Nakamura vetoed a bill that would have authorised a constitutional convention for that country, arguing that Palau could not risk the impact that restructuring of government might have on investment.[15] The move was ironic since the president had been instrumental in developing the bill and urging its passage.

In American Samoa, where a revised constitution took effect in 1967, official inquiries into the territory's future political status, ranging from full incorporation with the United States to full integration with Western Samoa, were conducted in 1970 and again in 1979, but resulted in no changes.[16] Governor Coleman announced in 1991 that the constitution would be reviewed to increase the level of self-government. He envisaged Commonwealth Status for American Samoa, similar to the relationship that exists between the Cook Islands and New Zealand, or between the Northern Mariana Islands and the United States, but his suggestions do not appear to have led to significant dialogue on reform.

Reform by constituent assemblies

As already noted, constituent assemblies have either failed to complete their term or failed to provide a 'constitution' in Indonesia, Bangladesh, the Philippines and Burma. Yet elsewhere, conventions have proceeded to more successful conclusions. In the Northern Marianas, the decision to hold a constitutional convention is taken by the people. The first convention was agreed by 75 per cent of the voters when asked in November 1973. The second, in 1984, proposed forty-four constitutional amendments, all of which were approved by the people. At general elections in November 1993, 75 per cent of voters approved the establishment of a third convention, and this convened in June 1995 to deliberate for a mandatory sixty days.[17]

Indonesia

Changes in Indonesia's post-independence constitutional practice have mirrored the considerable social tensions within Indonesian society. After a period of openness under the 1950 Constitution which offered liberal democracy but unstable parliamentary government, President Soekarno dissolved a constituent assembly on 5 July 1959 and reinstated the Constitution of 1945 by presidential decree. His political program sought to reintroduce such Javanese practices as *gotong-royong* (mutual co-operation) and *mufakat* (consensus). According to Abdulgani, 'guided democracy and its concomitant, guided economy, sprang from the existence of instability within Indonesia's society and governmental structure and the necessity of controlling and guiding that instability'.[18]

Soekarno's removal from power in 1965 provided General Soeharto and Indonesia with another opportunity to address constitutional issues. But, although Soeharto's New Order ended the 'revolutionary' approach to law, and the judiciary recommenced referring to legal codes in their decisions, the 1945 Constitution was not revised.

Philippines

The Philippines held a constituent assembly at the beginning of the period of martial law promulgated by Ferdinand Marcos, and held another with similar rapidity following his demise.[19] In November 1970, delegates were elected to a convention that convened in June 1971 and worked for seventy days, completing its task on 29 November 1972. However, Marcos had declared martial law on 21 September, and the commission completed its draft in the knowledge that a number of its members had been removed and taken into detention. Wary of Marcos' intentions, the Constitutional Commission recommended a parliamentary system with a strong prime minister and weak president.

Abueva describes the constitution as 'liberal, socially oriented, progressive, developmental, and nationalistic'.[20] Corte's, on the other hand, calls the Philippines' experience of constitution-making and its amendment 'spotty', and expresses concern at the lack of democratic process surrounding its ratification:

> The defect in the manner of submission was not only the absence of an election as it is usually understood. Also as salient is the fact that no one at the time, even the best informed could truly say that what was submitted was fully understood. For besides the textual provision of a document that included eclectic innovations in governmental structures it also contained a rider that all presidential issuances, would become part of the law of the land. This comprehended not only proclamations, orders, decrees, instructions and other acts already issued, the number and scope of which were not fully ascertained, but also those yet to be issued. The constitution being supreme law emanating from the sovereign people, it should go without argument that the people who promulgate it should know what they have adopted. Even granting that the ratification of that

constitution would pass muster, it cannot seriously be claimed that those who ratified it were fully informed of what that document contained or what it would include subsequently.[21]

The 1972 Constitution initiated a change from a presidential to a parliamentary form of government, but its transitory arrangements were tailored to suit the interests of President Marcos, who was able to implement it selectively. He altered the constitution so as to grant himself executive, legislative and judicial powers.[22]

Cambodia

Cambodia's new constitution was established following unprecedented efforts by the international community to re-establish peace, through United Nations action.[23] The constitution was drafted with little public scrutiny or debate, and not even the 120-member constituent assembly that convened in May 1993 previewed the final draft. Yet on 24 September 1993, the day of his enthronement as King of Cambodia, Norodom Sihanouk signed the constitution into law and formally decreed the formation of the new Cambodian government. Co-premier Hun Sen, and chairman of the constituent assembly Son Sann, had taken two alternative draft constitutions to Prince Sihanouk's palace in Pyongyang for approval. One restored constitutional democracy. The other, drafted by a joint committee of royalists and former communists, called for a parliamentary system with a head of state elected for a five-year term.

Following general elections in 1998 the political parties could not agree on coalition arrangements and refused to take their parliamentary seats. In March 1999 King Norodom Sihanouk signed amendments to the constitution to create a Senate. An upper house was established, that is, for political expediency. As with the 1993 Constitution, 'the people' were not involved, not consulted.

Burma

Although a constitutional assembly was established in Myanmar in 1993 with the ostensible purpose of rewriting that country's constitution, the circumstances surrounding it point to the overtly political, rather than constitutional, intentions of the exercise. By the late 1980s there was considerable unrest, as the socialist–military government began to unravel. Although demonstrations by students, workers and monks were suppressed, the protests had their effect, and General

Ne Win, who had been in power since 1962, resigned on 23 July 1988. The regime promised to hold a referendum to end one-party rule and institute a multi-party system. When demonstrations continued, the army established the State Law and Order Restoration Council (SLORC) under the chairmanship of Chief of Staff Senior General Saw Maung. The National Assembly (Pyithu Hluttaw), the Council of State and other governmental bodies were dissolved.

Although SLORC had promised to establish a multi-party democracy, and allowed a general election to be held on 27 May 1990, it may not have anticipated the strength of the pro-democracy vote, and, for whatever reason, did not relinquish power afterwards. The main opposition party (National League for Democracy, or NLD) won 81 per cent (392) of 485 seats, and 60 per cent of the votes. Announcing at first that declaration of the results would be postponed until the Election Commission had examined the expense accounts of all elected representatives, the regime eventually reimposed military rule. Daw Aung San Suu Kyi, daughter of Gen. Aung San (an independence hero assassinated in 1947) and general secretary of the NLD, had been banned from campaigning for the elections. She was detained on 20 July 1989 and remained under house arrest without trial until her release in 1995. In 1991 she was awarded the Nobel Prize for Peace.

In January 1993 SLORC convened a constitutional convention to lay down the basic principles of a new constitution. The 702 delegates comprised representatives from eight categories: political parties (49); those elected in the 1990 elections (107); national racial groups (215); representatives of peasants (93); representatives of workers (48); the intelligentsia and technocrats (41); state services (92); and other invited persons (57). The National Convention deliberated on six objectives provided in SLORC Order 13/92: non-disintegration of the union; non-disintegration of national solidarity; perpetuation of sovereignty; a multi-party democracy system; values such as justice, liberty and equality; and ensuring the 'national political leadership role' of the Tatmadaw (military).

The last draft clause, which sought to entrench the military's future role at the centre of government, proved the most contentious and a majority of delegates refused to accept it. It is perhaps on this point that the convention eventually broke down. Reports also began to surface suggesting that the attendance by some delegates was involuntary. Unexpectedly, Yo E La, of the Lahu National Development Party, proposed a return to the basic principles of Burma's pre-1962 federal and democratic constitution, and to provisions for local autonomy for all national minorities. This initiative forced an adjournment until June to give SLORC time to respond. Intense negotiations took place in

1993–95 within the National Convention's sub-commissions, and the regime made periodic announcements of progress made. Some of this activity will be recorded here, to indicate the manner in which the dialogue proceeded.

Towards the end of 1993, the Public Relations and Information Division of the Union of Myanmar's Ministry of Foreign Affairs produced a statement on progress towards the writing of the new constitution. In more than 100 meetings held since the establishment of the convention, the delegates had settled on the constitution's major chapter headings,[24] and in June had presented twenty-two papers (consisting of over 900 pages) focusing on the first chapter, concerning the state's 'fundamental principles'. Following a plenary session on 6–9 September, at which the panel of alternate chairmen 'presented an overall appraisal of the principles that should be laid down as basic principles of the state', the National Convention Convening Work Committee prepared a reiteration of fundamental propositions:

- The state would be constituted by the Pyidaungsu (Union) system and consist of seven regions (presently known as divisions) and seven states of equal status and authority, which would retain their present names.
- There would also be self-administered areas in regions and states for certain national races.
- The state would practise 'genuine multiparty democracy', and would be named Pyidaungsu Thamada Myanmar Naing Ngan-Daw.
- The head of state would be a president, elected by a presidential electoral system.
- There would be separation of powers between the legislative, executive and judicial branches of government, 'with reciprocal control and check and balance'. The head of the executive would be the president, and there would be 'administrative organs at Pyidaungsu, regions and states as well as those in self-administered areas'. Legislative power would be distributed among Pyidaungsu Hluttaw 'elected on basis of population' and others 'with equal number of representatives elected from regions and states'. Judicial power would be distributed among the Pyidaungsu Taya Hluttaw (Supreme Court), Region Taya Hluttaw (Regional High Court) and State Taya Hluttaw (State High Court), and law courts of different levels including in self-administered areas.
- The state would pursue a 'market economic system' and an independent, active and non-aligned foreign policy.
- The state would not nationalise economic enterprises or demonetarise currency; nor permit the deployment of foreign troops on its territory.

- Tatmadaw servicemen would participate in Pyidaungsu Hluttaw, and regional and state Hluttaws, and 'Pyidaungsu, regions, states, self-administered areas and districts' executive organs would include Tatmadaw servicemen to undertake responsibilities of defence, security, border administration, etc'.

The National Convention recessed until 18 January 1994 to give delegates time to 'carefully review and analyse what has transpired during the recent meetings', and to 'go back to the grassroots and hold consultations'. The Plenary Session on 18 January appears to have consisted of an address by Commission Chairman Lt. Gen. Myo Nyunt, and a 'clarification' by National Convention Convening Work Committee Chairman U Aung Toe. 'Group discussions' were held three days later. On 21 February four groups of delegates met to discuss draft chapters on 'The State', 'State Structure', and the 'Head of State'. Groups represented in the discussions were 'workers', state service personnel, other 'invited persons', and members of the panel of chairmen of representatives-elect delegates. The twenty-first co-ordination meeting of the National Convention Convening Work Committee was held on 28 January, although no details were made public.[25] After almost two years of discussion, just three chapters of a projected fifteen had been considered, and no votes had been taken.

Early in 1995 the delegates agreed on '104 basic principles to pave the way for the writing of a firm and enduring new State Constitution with the basic guarantees for all'. These principles included provisions for the establishment of 'self-administered areas' within regions or states for national races 'who reside in communities on the same common stretches of land in appropriate sizes of population'.[26] Deliberations continued on the chapters concerning the judiciary, the executive and the legislature. The Tatmadaw continued to insist on a constitutionally mandated role in government. The military supports its position as a politico-military force by constant reference to the need to preserve national unity in the context of a multi-ethnic nation in which many armed groups continue to threaten its existence.[27] The National Convention adjourned between 8 April and 28 November 1995, and even rapporteurs investigating on behalf of the United Nations were unable to identify the reasons for the adjournment.[28]

On 22 November Aung San Suu Kyi, who had been released from detention the previous July, criticised the undemocratic composition of the convention (just 15 per cent of its remaining 677 delegates had been elected). All 86 of the NLD delegates walked out of the 28 November meeting and two days later they were officially expelled from the convention for being absent without permission.[29]

In March 1996 the National Convention decided that the president of the state would be chosen by parliament, from among the three vice-presidents it elects, for a five-year term. The president must be at least 45 years old and have lived in Myanmar for the past twenty years. Neither the president, nor his or her parents, spouse or children, can be a subject or citizen of a foreign country.

An NLD Congress directed its Central Executive Committee to draft a state constitution, using a 1990 draft commenced by NLD MPs (which was in turn based on the 1947 Constitution, which pro-democracy parties argue was never technically nullified following military coups in 1962 and 1988). SLORC responded by passing a law in June 1996 prohibiting unauthorised discussion of the constitution, disruption of the convention, or anything that could 'belittle and create misunderstandings among the public in connection with the national convention'. Any organisation found breaching the law risked being suspended, dissolved or declared an 'unlawful association', and could have its money and property confiscated. The drafting of any alternative version of a constitution became a violation of the law and subject to a penalty of a prison sentence of up to twenty years.[30]

Little further progress towards conclusion of the exercise in constitutional revision was reported in the year, and the constraints placed on the exercise by Burma's rulers had by now created considerable scepticism internationally about the entire exercise:

> The most likely future for Burmese law and the most optimistic prognosis for it do not coincide. The following prediction favours the optimistic over the likely. Constitutional law will look after itself, in the sense the Burmese law can only hope to recover its health once some negotiated settlement (perhaps collectively guaranteed by a group of regional powers) is in place. Any such constitutional settlement will be perceived as provisional until it has lasted a couple of generations.[31]

Although its ostensible purpose was to produce a new constitution, the National Convention had not done so by the end of 1997, and after five years of drafting appeared to be simply 'another means of legitimating authoritarianism'.[32]

Thailand

In contrast to the previous instances, in which constituent assemblies failed to complete their mandate, Thailand's constitutional exercise of 1997 was considerably more successful, particularly in light of Thailand's problematic constitutional history. We will review this history briefly, before moving to a description of the most recent program of revision.

There has been a continuing struggle between political power (the politicians and the people), and state power (the bureaucrats and state enterprises) in Thailand, manifest in periodic pro-democracy movements such as those of 1972–73 and 1991.[33] The structure of the bureaucratic polity (elite control through a bureaucratic polity dominated by the military) was first described by Fred Riggs in 1966. As described by Ross Prizzia at the beginning of the 1980s, constitutionalism in Thailand has been a 'main element in the justification of political power', and a mechanism for legitimating the participation of newer groupings in the political process, in addition to the ruling bureaucratic and royal elite.[34] Pisan Suriyamongkol has suggested that recent constitutions balance three forces: 'the kingship, bureaucratic forces and extra-bureaucratic forces within some mutually accepted form of democracy'.[35]

In this tense socio-political context, some of the Thai constitutions were good, but short-lived. For example, the constitution drawn up in 1946 was scrapped by a coup d'etat one year later and replaced with a dictatorial one. In 1959, Field Marshal Sarit Thanarat established a constitution drafting council. After nine years and enormous expenditures, a new constitution was approved in 1968, only to be scrapped late in 1971 by Field Marshal Thanom Kittikachorn. After the end of the Thanom–Prapass regime, a legislative council was appointed to draft a new constitution, which was in effect from 1974 to 1976.

Following large-scale pro-democracy civil unrest in 1990 and the imposition of martial law by a self-styled National Peace-Keeping Council (NPKC) in February 1991, a new constitution (Thailand's fifteenth) was drafted and passed hurriedly in 1991. Further civil unrest followed in May 1992, as the new constitution had addressed some, but not all, of the concerns of the expanding pro-democracy movement.[36]

Successive Thai governments won favour by promising to make further reforms in the name of democracy. The Leekpai government proposed twenty-five constitutional changes, which included reducing the size of the Senate from 270 to 120 members; altering the method of selection of senators and members of cabinet; reducing the voting age from 20 to 18; introducing freedom of information; and granting financial assistance to political parties. Although the eight bills submitted by the government were drafted by a committee after one full year of work, and incorporated eight major points unanimously agreed upon by all political parties in the lower house, the first bill was defeated in its first reading (constitutional amendments must be approved by a majority of the members of both houses, that is at least 316 of 630 votes, but the government obtained only 189 votes in support when the majority in the Senate joined with the opposition).

Concern at the Thai legislature's incapacity to establish a genuinely democratic constitution provoked calls for the formation of a constituent assembly without MPs. Political activist Chalard Vorachat campaigned to make the House of Representatives the sole authority to amend or redraft the constitution and to exclude the Senate. The major issue was whether non-MPs could ensure a change to constitutional art. 211, which empowered a special drafting committee comprising three former prime ministers and ten to fifteen academics to revise the constitution. The parliament established a 35-member Democracy Development Committee early in 1994 to make recommendations on political and constitutional reforms.[37] Influenced by the non-parliamentary Committee for Democratic Development, which advocated the establishment of such accountability bodies as a constitutional court, an administrative court, an office of the auditor-general, a counter-corruption commission and an election commission, and which sought reform of constitutional art. 111,[38] the parliamentary committee, chaired by academic Prawasi Wasi, proposed vast changes to the constitution and laws:

- Introduction of a three-chamber parliamentary system, with the third chamber being a National Advisory Assembly that could freeze major decisions taken in the other two houses on affairs concerning national security, religion, and the monarchy.
- Reduction of the Senate to 150 members, with senators being appointed from party lists on the basis of the percentage of votes gained in general elections by each party.
- Subsidisation of political parties by government to prevent them from being influenced by party 'financiers'.
- Lowering of the voting age to 18 years.
- Limiting of electoral campaigns to forty-five days.
- Establishment of an independent election commission.
- Introduction of the secret ballot in parliament.
- Provision for the appointment of a non-elected prime minister.
- Empowerment of a prime minister to declare a 'state of legislative emergency', and hence the right to by-pass the lower house in order to have an 'essential' bill approved by the Senate alone.
- Restriction of censure motions by the opposition to one per year.
- Classification of constitutional amendments into three types, according to level of entrenchment (those concerning the monarchy, those concerning civil rights, and those concerning political issues).[39]

The short-lived government of Banharn Silpa-archa (May 1995 to November 1996) passed a law amending constitutional section 211, which had till then prevented non-parliamentarians from participating in constitutional revision. The new law, formulated by a 45-member committee chaired by non-MP Chai-anan Samudavanija, called for the election of a Constitution Drafting Assembly (CDA) on the basis of indirect elections and required the CDA to complete its work in 240 days.

On 15 December 1996 over 19,000 candidates stood for election to the CDA. Ten representatives were elected in each of Thailand's seventy-six provinces. On 26 December parliament elected a representative from the list of ten for each province, and a further 23 members expert in law, political science, public administration or politics, making a total of 99. Once formed, the CDA established five committees: drafting, suggestion-gathering and public hearing, public relations, research and information, and records and meeting reports. Sub-committees were established in each province comprising nine failed candidates for CDA seats and five academics and experts.

The CDA completed its task in 233 days. Thailand's sixteenth constitution was approved by a joint sitting of the Senate and House of Representatives (578 members of 651 present voting in favour), and signed into law by King Bhumibol Adulyadej in October 1997.

The new constitution sought to consolidate the democratic process and the rule of law. It established a Constitutional Court (separate from the Ministry of Law), comprising five Supreme Court judges selected by fellow judges through secret ballot. The constitution also established an independent electoral commission and replaced systems of appointment with direct elections for the 200-seat Senate, and for the position of village head '*kamnan*'. To relieve the pressure that has traditionally accompanied the desire of MPs to win places in cabinet, the constitution now requires prospective members of cabinet to nominate for the positions. If their party wins sufficient seats and they obtain a cabinet position, they must give up their parliamentary seat. To ensure against enrichment while in office, MPs are now required to declare their personal assets before and after leaving office.

As part of the agenda for constitutional reform, the new constitution stipulated that three 'organic' laws – concerning elections, political parties and the establishment of the Election Commission – be passed within 240 days. Consequently, the Thai parliament was occupied throughout 1998 creating more than twenty pieces of enabling legislation. The legislative program included a new electoral law; a law providing for the appointment of inspectors-general to a number of auditing bodies, including ombudsman and election commission; judicial reform, including the establishment of a constitutional court; and the establishment of a national counter-corruption commission and a national human rights commission. The parliament also had to revise laws now considered unconstitutional, such as the 1952 Anti-Communism Act.

Reform by parliaments

In some jurisdictions, parliaments are empowered to undertake constitutional revision and there is no need to establish an independent body, such as a constituent assembly. Parliaments in some jurisdictions even have the legal capacity to reconvene specifically as a constituent assembly. Of course, a parliament that reconvenes for this purpose has made the assumption that the election of its members to a parliamentary term is also approval by the people of their election as representatives to undertake constitutional reform. The promise of constitutional revision is often a feature of election manifestos, and in the programs of newly elected governments. In India, for instance, the Bharatiya Janata Party government of Atal Behari Vajpayee, installed following general elections in March 1998, proposed constitutional and legal reforms in its 'National Agenda'.[40]

Malaysia

In Malaysia, a significant post-independence constitutional moment occurred as a consequence of race riots in 1969. Ahmad suggests that the independence constitution was a 'bargain' made between communal leaders, and that by the late 1960s it was opposed by a younger generation of Malays.[41] The subsequent Constitution Amendment Act 1971 placed discussion of the Malay interests listed in constitutional art. 153 'beyond the reach of communal politics'. It prohibited the questioning of any matter, right, status, position, privilege, sovereignty or prerogative established or protected by the provisions of part III or arts. 152, 153 or 181, otherwise than in relation to their implementation. Following a closely contested election in 1987, the Malaysian government used racial violence as a pretext to impose martial law/emergency codes and place opposition figures in detention.

Vietnam

Socialist countries also conduct constitutional change through the legislature. In April 1992, for instance, the Vietnamese National Assembly promulgated a 'revised', which was essentially a 'new', constitution with 138 of the 148 articles subject to amendment. The Council of State, which had served as the parliament's standing committee and whose chairman acted as the ceremonial head of state, was replaced by a president and a cabinet headed by a premier. Under the revised constitution, the premier must be a member of parliament but can appoint non-elected ministers to cabinet, and the president is elected by the National Assembly. Land remains the property of the state (although farmers can now inherit), and the constitution continues to allow the Communist Party to guide state policy without giving it power to intervene in day-to-day government.

Reform by expert commissions

A third possible method for securing constitutional reform, in addition to the constituent assembly and the parliament, is the expert commission. Three Asia–Pacific countries in which constitutional reform exercises have been carried out by expert bodies are Papua New Guinea, the Philippines and Fiji.

Papua New Guinea

Parliament in Papua New Guinea has the power to alter the constitution, although the constitution also provides for a constitutional commission. Following passage of the Constitutional Commission Act in September 1993, members were appointed to the newly established commission in January 1994,[42] with instructions to propose to parliament by 30 September 1996 new organic laws and acts, to recommend review of administrative procedures and to make general recommendations about amendments. The commission was renamed the Constitutional Review Commission (CRC) and tasked to report on specific questions that the government might put to it from time to time.

In June 1995, following intensive research and presentation of findings by the commission, the parliament voted for constitutional amendments and consequently for a new Organic Law on Provincial and Local Level Governments (referred to in the chapter on devolution). On completion of this reform exercise, the government put a further seven questions to the commission.[43] These questions included:
- whether the country should retain the current system that provides for the queen and her heirs and successors as the sovereigns and heads of state of Papua New Guinea, or whether it should become a

republic or some other form of government. If the commission recommended changes in the form of government, it was to suggest a time-frame for any transition;
- whether changes needed to be made to all or any offices established under the constitution which would better co-ordinate their powers, responsibilities and accountability;
- whether there was a need to change the name of the country, and the national anthem;
- whether changes were needed to ensure that, while freedom of the press was maintained, owners, editors and journalists of all elements of the media were accountable and persons aggrieved by media abuses would have access to redress.

The CRC was also asked to recommend an outline Organic Law on the Integrity of Political Parties, in a move intended to protect elections from outside or hidden influences. Although the commission was due to report by 30 June 1996, it did not do so.

The CRC established committees to examine the issues of media accountability and the integrity of political parties. The committee addressing the issue of media freedom comprised four commissioners and five non-commissioners,[44] and was to determine:
- whether there were genuine constitutional problems arising from and in the course of the exercise of the freedom of media within Papua New Guinea;
- the range of appropriate constitutional, legal and other means available for resolving the problems;
- the appropriate resources required to implement any solutions the committee recommended;
- the realistic time-frame within which remedial actions might be taken;
- the implications any such remedial actions might have on other provisions of the constitution; and
- any such matter or matters which the committee might consider relevant under its respective terms of reference.

In addition, the committee was to refer to the proceedings of the CRC's seminar on press freedom held in January 1996, to consult relevant government authorities and other members of the public and reports of the Papua New Guinea Law Reform Commission, and to also take into consideration current law, practice and experience in other countries.

Progress with drafting an Organic Law on the Integrity of Political Parties and Candidates (as required by ss. 129 and 130) proceeded only slowly. In 1999 Bernard Mollok, chair of the Constitutional Development Commission, called on the government to undertake a total review of the Papua New Guinea Constitution rather than the 'piecemeal approaches' that had occurred in recent years.[45] As a major cause of political instability since independence has been the volatility of MP loyalty to political parties, the government was seeking to strengthen the party system and diminish the prevalence of 'party-hopping'. To achieve this, the draft organic law provided for the dismissal from parliament of an MP who defected to a political party other than the one for which he or she was elected to parliament. The draft also required a political party to have more than ten MPs to gain registration and state funding. It sought to deny registration to a party that was regionally rather than nationally based, which did not promote nationalism, or which portrayed 'sinister tactics designed to work against the National Constitution'. The law would require all registered political parties to have a registered office, a constitution, a secretariat and a national policy, and transparency of the sources of party funds.

Political parties expressed concern that the draft provisions were too harsh and penalised MPs who sought to change parties for valid reasons. They also predicted that MPs would not vote for a law that curtailed their freedom of movement within the parliament.[46]

Philippines

Through the February 1986 'people's revolution' which ousted Ferdinand Marcos, Corazon Aquino became president. In March she abolished the National Assembly (full of Marcos supporters), abrogated the 1973 Constitution, claimed all legislative powers, dismissed all Marcos appointees to the Supreme Court, and appointed a 47-member Constitutional Commission. The new constitution was drafted between June and October 1986 and ratified in a plebiscite on 2 February 1987 with 76 per cent approval. Blaustein cautioned the Filipinos against excessive copying of the US Constitution.[47] The constitution made new provisions in regard to the powers of the state but few changes in other areas. It contained a bill of rights and stipulated a bicameral legislature, with a 24-seat upper house and not more than 250 lower house members. It retained the presidential system of government but limited the office of president to a single term.[48]

Fiji

Under Fiji's 1990 Constitution, a constitutional review was required within seven years, but the method of revision was not specified. This gave the Rabuka government considerable room to move, and details of how the review would proceed emerged over a lengthy period of time. The model eventually settled on was the expert review, followed by the presentation of recommendations to the government. After elections and formation of the Rabuka government in 1992, the prime minister pledged to 'immediately initiate a process of review and change of the 1990 Constitution'. In July 1993 a cabinet sub-committee was appointed to define terms of reference prior to the establishment of a Parliamentary Select Committee on the Constitution, and a Constitutional Review Committee. In May 1994 the government established a timetable for the review and, in September, a joint parliamentary select committee (3 senators and 16 MPs) representing 'both parliamentary chambers, from political parties not in Parliament and from the Government' to discuss the membership and terms of operation of the Constitution Review Commission (CRC).

A three-member commission was chosen: former Governor-General of New Zealand Sir Paul Reeves (chair), former cabinet minister Tomasi Vakatora, and academic Brij Lal. The commission was asked to review the constitution 'bearing in mind internationally recognised principles and standards of individual and group rights', and to ensure that it 'guarantee full protection and promotion of the rights, interests, and concerns of the indigenous Fijian and Rotuman people'. It was to have regard for:
- the need for Fiji's constitution to enhance national unity;
- advancement of the interests of all of Fiji's communities;
- inclusion of full protection of the rights of Fijians, including protection of their interests and aspirations;
- protection of the interests of all other of Fiji's communities; and
- provision for the constitution to accomplish these objects within the framework of the standards provided at international law.

The CRC's review was to proceed in four phases: May–June 1994 to December 1995 (appointment of members, start of work);[49] January–June 1996 (meetings and consultations, necessary amendments, submission of second report to government, the Great Council of Chiefs and parliament); July–December 1996 (submission to parliament of final report, final report debated in parliament and approved or otherwise); and January–June 1997 (drafting of new constitution, debate on new constitution, new constitution approved by parliament).[50]

The CRC received more than 700 submissions from the major political parties and the public at large.[51] Some generated considerable controversy. The major political parties were divided on the 'paramountcy' of Fijian chiefs, the electoral system (a communal system which did not allow cross-voting), and the existence of and powers of the Senate (many of whom were appointed by the Great Council of Chiefs). The emphatic view put by the Soqosoqo ni Vakavulewa ni Taukei (SVT) was that the 1990 Constitution, which weighted the allocation of political power in favour of ethnic Fijians, should continue to form the basis of Fiji's constitutional order. The Rotumans took the opportunity to remind the Fijians that they wanted a separate political recognition. The chief of Rotuma's Royal Malmahan Clan indicated that Rotumans did not want to be mentioned in the constitution and that their island, with a population of 2800, desired some form of free association.[52]

More democratic options were offered by non-government organisations, including the Citizens Constitutional Forum (CCF), which proposed the establishment of a system of 'shared governance' which acknowledged the legitimate interests of Fijians and of Indo-Fijians but placed both within a context of 'common interests'.[53] The CCF advocated an electoral system based on multi-member constituencies of approximately equal size; a single parliamentary chamber; non-racial allocation of constitutional offices; inclusion of a bill of rights, only changeable through referenda; and the sharing of executive power 'within all public institutions and at all levels of government among political parties in proportion to their electoral representation'. An intriguing option raised during the review exercise, and at other times in Fiji's political history, concerns the creation of a 'government of national unity'. Although largely undefined, the intention was to find a constitutional structure that allowed 'all voters to participate in the formation of Government'.[54]

The CRC's final report, formally tabled in parliament in September 1996, recommended reducing the number of seats allocated on the basis of ethnicity and making 45 of 70 lower house seats elected by all communities.[55] Only 25 seats would be distributed according to ethnic criteria. It also recommended that the presidency remain reserved for an indigenous Fijian and that the Great Council of Chiefs or Senate have veto powers over legislation affecting Fijian affairs.

The final decisions of several sub-committees studying the Reeves report were tabled at a joint Parliamentary Select Committee on Constitutional Review in March, and that committee's findings were tabled in parliament on 14 May – the tenth anniversary of the 1987 military coup. The committee recommended that a new constitution include a 71-member parliament, with 46 seats reserved for voting along racial lines (23 Indian and 19 Fijian), and 25 open seats;[56] that upper house seats be reduced from 34 to 32; and that the number of these nominated by the Great Council of Chiefs be reduced from 24 to 15. As the committee had agreed in 1996 that the constitution would not be changed without the Great Council of Chiefs' approval, the onus was on it, and its chair Prime Minister Sitiveni Rabuka, to gain its acceptance of the terms of constitutional change.

In March 1997 the provincial councils of Bau, Kadavu and Cakaudrove expressed their opposition to the Reeves report, fearing that its recommendations did not sufficiently protect the rights of indigenous Fijians. The prime minister had also to assure some members of the ruling coalition (the SVT) that the proposals were adequate. At the invitation of the prime minister, Opposition Leader Jai Ram Reddy addressed the Great Council of Chiefs on 6 June, and his speech is credited with influencing the chiefs in their decision to endorse the reform proposals.

Conclusion

At the end of this survey of experience with constitutional revision, a number of comments can be made. There is immense variety in the forms of constitutional dialogue that have taken place in the Asia Pacific – from states in which discussion is banned, through to states in which constitutional dialogue is mandatory.

First, there is a distinction between genuine constitutional exercises and sham exercises less interested in constitutionalism than in seeking legitimacy for a regime. Second, the most complete constitutional dialogue will be open to all citizens. The major forms of constitutional reform exercise involve either a convention/assembly or a commission of experts. But whatever method is employed, the major challenge is distinguishing between constitutional dialogue and strategic debate. In constitutional dialogue, the parties focus on the interests of the people as a whole, prior to consideration of special interests held by sub-groups within society. In strategic debate, in contrast, those involved in the constitutional process remain advocates of special interests and take part in the dialogue to the extent that their interests are recognised and responded to. Perhaps both types of dialogue are required in designing or reforming a constitution.

Notes

1 Chiba, *Asian Indigenous Law*; also Chiba, 'Three Dichotomies of Law'.
2 South Korea's 1960 parliamentary constitution ended with a coup d'etat in 1961.

3 Mya Saw Shin, *The Constitutions of Thailand*, vi; Darling, 'Thailand in 1976', 116. Race, on the other hand, was optimistic about the impact on the polity of the 1974 Constitution: Race, 'Thailand in 1974', 165.
4 Lane, *Constitutions and Political Theory*, 188.
5 Vanberg and Buchanan, 'Constitutional Choice', 46.
6 Ghai, *Law, Politics and Government*, 49–50.
7 The first Minister for Justice Kaputin called the law 'a colonial fraud': J. Kaputin, 'The Law: A Colonial Fraud', *New Guinea*, 10:1, 1975. However, governments since independence have done little to substantially change the law.
8 The Solomon Islanders are not happy that their constitution is merely a schedule in the British parliament, and wish to 'repatriate' it: *Post Courier*, 8 August 1991, 9.
9 *Commonwealth Law Bulletin*, 15:1, January 1989.
10 Writing in 1977, Campbell had viewed the prospects for decentralised government favourably: Campbell, 'Devolution in the Solomon Islands'.
11 *Pacific Islands Monthly*, March 1990, 16.
12 *Matangi Tonga*, September–November 1992; Powles, *The Tongan Constitution*.
13 The 8 November motion, tabled by 'Akilisi Pohiva, Viliami Fukofuka, Tie-in Fuko and 'Uliti Uata, was lost 9–5, with 3 abstentions.
14 The constitutional review commission was headed by Joseph Calo and included all 46 MPs plus other representatives.
15 *Pacific Magazine*, May–June 1995.
16 Laughlin, 'The Application of the Constitution'.
17 *Pacific Magazine*, 12, January–February 1994. Of the 27 delegates, 19 were from Saipan and the northern islands, 4 from Rota, and 4 from Tinian and Aguigan.
18 Abdulgani, 'Indonesia's National Council', 103.
19 The failure of such exercises to bring any fundamental reforms to Filipino society prompted Ruel Padua's thesis, Understanding Revolution.
20 Abueva, 'Ideology and Practice in the "New Society"', 37.
21 Corte's, 'Constitutionalism in the Philippines', 343.
22 *ICJ Review* 33, December 1984, 21–5.
23 The Cambodian Peace Agreement signed on 23 October 1991 comprised four documents: (1) Agreements on a Comprehensive Political Settlement of the Cambodia Conflict; (2) Agreement Concerning the Sovereignty, Independence, Territorial Integrity and Inviolability, Neutrality and National Unity of Cambodia; (3) Declaration on Rehabilitation and Reconstruction of Cambodia; and (4) the Final Act of the Paris Conference on Cambodia.
24 (a) Fundamental Principles of the State, (b) Structure, (c) Head of State, (d) Legislature, (e) Executive, (f) Judiciary, (g) The Tatmadaw, (h) Citizens and Their Fundamental Rights and Responsibilities, (i) Elections, (j) Political Parties, (k) Emergency Provisions, (l) Constitutional Amendments, (m) State Flag, State Emblem, National Anthem and Capital, (n) Transitory Provisions, and (o) General Provisions.
25 *Embassy of the Union of Myanmar News Bulletin*, 18 October 1993, 31 January, 16, and 31 March 1994.

26 See Maung Kyi Lin, 'Sixth Major Task Accomplished by National Convention: Self-Administered Divisions and Self-Administered Zones', *Embassy of the Union of Myanmar Newsletter* 11/95, 25 May 1995; 'National Convention Plenary Session Commences', *Newsletter* 9/95, 10 May 1995.
27 See, for example, a statement by Khin Nyunt, chairman of the Work Committee for Development of Border Areas and National Races and first secretary of SLORC: 'Secretary-1 Recalls Lessons from History, Warns To Beware of Dangers, Safeguard Unity and Stability', *Embassy of the Union of Myanmar Newsletter* 17/95, 30 August 1995. In 1997 the National Convention agreed to allocate 110 of 440 parliamentary seats to the Armed Forces, with the remaining 330 to be elected. Fifty-six of 224 seats in the upper house (House of Nationalities) would be military appointees.
28 UN Commission on Human Rights, 52nd session, Item 10 of the provisional agenda, 'Question of the Violation of Human Rights and Fundamental Freedoms in Any Part of the World, with Particular Reference to Colonial and Other Dependent Countries and Territories: Report on the situation of human rights in Myanmar, prepared by Mr Yozo Yokota, Special Rapporteur of the Commission on Human Rights, in accordance with Commission resolution 1995/72'.
29 See 'National Convention Convening Commission's Press Release in Connection with the Action of National League for Democracy Delegates at the National Convention', *Embassy of the Union of Myanmar Newsletter*, Sp. H/95, 30 November 1995.
30 'EU Rejects Burma Coming to Berlin EU–ASEAN Meeting', *Deutsche Presse-Agentur*, 14 March 1999. The EU's rejection of Burma is to protest the lack of democracy and the violations of human rights carried out by its military leaders.
31 Huxley, 'The Last Fifty Years of Burmese Law', 19.
32 Alamgir, 'Against the Current', 346. Some National Convention documentation is available in English: Address by the Chairman of the National Convention Convening Work Committee U Aung Toe regarding the Formulation of Basic Principles for Framing A New State Constitution. Yangon, Printing and Publishing Enterprise, 1993; Address by the Chairman of the National Convention Convening Commission Major General Myo Nyunt on opening day of the National Constitutional Convention. Yangon, Printing and Publishing Enterprise, 1993.
33 See, for example, Laothamatas, 'Business and Politics in Thailand'; Somvichian, 'The Oyster and the Shell'; Jumbala, 'Towards a Theory of Group Formation'; Heinze, 'Ten Days in October'; Zimmerman, 'Student "Revolution"'; Dhiravegin, *Demi-Democracy*, esp. 91–224; Keyes, *Thailand*, esp. chs 4 and 5.
34 Prizzia, *Thailand in Transition*, 87.
35 Suriyamongkol, *Institutionalization of Democratic Political Processes*, 92. See also McKinnon, 'Can the Military be Sidelined?' (this view is shared by William Kintner, a former US ambassador to Thailand, who nevertheless argued the potential of Thailand's 'democratic roots': Kintner and Zimmerman, 'Thailand's Search for Constitutional Government'); Riggs, *Thailand*; Prizzia, *Thailand in Transition*, 87.
36 Maisrikrod, *Thailand's Two General Elections in 1992*.

37 The committee wanted to preclude the political community from involvement in constitutional revision and wanted the new constitution to be approved by referendum.
38 *Bangkok Post*, 6 April 1995. Constitutional art. 111 needed to be changed if non-MPs were to be involved in the drafting of a new constitution. This committee further proposed that such a drafting body be appointed by the king and that its proposals be put to the people for approval.
39 *Bangkok Post*, 12 August 1995; *Nation*, 12 August 1995.
40 In the section on 'Governance', the report proposed appointment of a commission to review the Constitution of India; a move towards 'more financial and administrative powers and functions to the States', following the recommendations of the Sarkaria Commission; special attention to states 'where the percentage of population below the poverty line has increased during the last five decades'; consideration of treating all nineteen languages included in schedule 8 of the constitution as official languages; implementing electoral reforms recommended by the Goswami Committee; and establishing a National Judicial Commission to recommend judicial appointments in High Courts and the Supreme Court and to draw up a code of ethics for the judiciary.
41 Zakaria, 'Malaysia', 355.
42 The chair was Ben Micah and the deputy chair, Bernard Narokobi. Additional appointees were 14 MPs, 9 nominees of non-government organisations (Melanesian Council of Churches, National Council of Women, Papua New Guinea Trade Union Congress, and Papua New Guinea Urban Authority Association), the Premiers Council, and the prime minister. Following elections in 1998, the commission was renamed the Constitutional Development Commission, with Vincent Auli as chair. Its brief under the Skate government was to draft laws on the integrity of the political parties, to continue provincial government reforms, and to examine the constitutional provisions on votes of confidence.
43 *National Gazette*, 26 October 1995.
44 Commissioners Prof. John Waiko, MP, Philemon Embel, MP, Leo Hannett and John Paska; and non-commissioners Sir Paulius Matane, Neville Togarewa, John Taylor, Charles Turi and John Napu.
45 'Mollok Wants a Total Review', *Post Courier*, 20 October 1999. The CRC had been renamed in 1998.
46 'Diro Sees Loophole Already', *Post Courier*, 20 October 1999.
47 Blaustein, 'On a Constitution for the Philippines'.
48 Burke, 'Philippine Constitution'.
49 Comprising: (a) planning and implementation of a program to inform the public of all aspects of the constitutional review; (b) discussions and hearing of submissions from the public, government, political parties, other organisations and legal advisers; (c) compilation of the first report; and (d) submission of this report to government, the Great Council of Chiefs and parliament.
50 *Review*, November 1994; *Pacific Magazine*, November–December 1994.
51 Reeves et al., *The Fiji Islands*.
52 'Rotuma Council Wants Greater Representation', *Fiji Times*, 20 September 1995.

53 Citizens Constitutional Forum, *One Nation, Diverse Peoples*; Citizens Constitutional Forum, *Protecting Fijian Interests*; Citizens Constitutional Forum, *Electoral Systems and Power Sharing*; Chapman, *Recommendations Concerning the Constitution of Fiji*.
54 'Include Unity Concept in Constitution, Says Party', *Fiji Times*, 20 July 1995.
55 Reeves et al., *The Fiji Islands*; Lal, 'Towards a United Future'; Lal and Lamour, *Electoral Systems in Divided Societies*.
56 Fiji Labour Party leader Mahendra Chaudhry dissented on the seat allocation issue, saying Fiji's history showed that a voting system on racial or communal lines would perpetuate the racial divide. The only way to break that cycle would be to reduce the number of seats allocated for specific races. He said that a multiracial cabinet would have a better chance of success if it were based on a non-racial voting system.

Part III

Democracy and the Rule of Law

8 Courts and the judiciary

This chapter considers the powers and functions of courts, and the ways in which courts are established and staffed to conduct these functions. The judicial system of a country generally consists of a hierarchy of courts, including a Supreme or High Court, a court of appeal, and other courts established by the constitution or by parliament. Those states that have retained customary laws and authorities may also have lands and titles courts. Judicial review refers to the power of a court or other body to review the lawfulness of a law or an action by one or other branch of government. Such review is necessary since all constitutional systems require clarity as to what acts are constitutional, and which institutions are authorised to give a final determination on the constitutionality of a law or government action. While most constitutional systems include institutions and procedures to conduct judicial review, others do not. Judicial restraint on executive agencies of government is seen as essential to constitutional government. Courts, however, are generally empowered to consider matters of procedural justice, as opposed to substantive justice, which is the responsibility of the legislature and the government.

Courts solve disputes by finding the relevant law, either from existing statutes or from 'common law'. In this way, courts can assist citizens who are in conflict with each other, or with a business, or with a branch of the government (and for this reason courts are regarded as the 'guardian of the people').[1] Most importantly, courts can also assist branches of government when they are in conflict. They also fulfil other functions in the state: mediating between political rivals, and sometimes working to preserve the unity of the polity. It is useful to consider the intentions of the executive and the judiciary as much as the practice. Buxbaum has suggested that:

> the role of the formal judiciary in pre-modern society is often different from its role in modern industrial states. Furthermore social institutions such as guilds, lineages, clans and even the family often have important legal responsibilities in pre-literate and peasant societies. Thus one cannot merely examine the court system and the formal legal institutions and hope to understand the Asian and

African judiciary. Therefore the study of these matters requires the endeavours not only of legal scholars, but also of anthropologists, political scientists, sociologists and perhaps psychologists.[2]

Judicial 'activism' and 'quietism'

At times these objectives are met by remaining conservative and cautious and at other times by making progressive and even 'active' decisions. Judicial activism refers to the degree to which courts actively 'make law'. One line of reasoning restricts the role of courts to that of adjudicating on matters in a 'strictly legal' way, making sure not to make orders that trespass on the duties of the legislature or the executive. A more activist model of judicial responsibility suggests, on the other hand, that courts are empowered to not only interpret the law but also direct other branches of government in the conduct of their duties.

Judicial activism in such countries as India has prompted questions about appropriate limits and how they might be expressed. There the judiciary has found and upheld the doctrine of a 'fundamental framework' within the Indian Constitution, which it prevents the executive from altering. Article 50, part of the non-justiciable 'Directive Principles of State Policy', states: 'The State shall take steps to separate the judiciary from the Executive in the public services of the State'. In 1973 the Supreme Court decided that parliament has no power to amend the basic structure of the constitution. This was held to be an inherent limitation on the power of amendment in spite of the manner and form having been adhered to by parliament.[3]

In Taiwan, the Council of Grand Justices, the organ of the Judicial Yuan,[4] responsible for interpreting the constitution, has become increasingly assertive in recent years, accepting more review applications from individuals and in some cases finding government measures unconstitutional.[5]

In contrast to judicial activism are courts characterised by 'quietism'. Such courts may have valid power which they do not exercise for any number of reasons. In Indonesia, the chief justice allowed in 1959 that President Soekarno's actions followed an unwritten legal principle, which allowed deviation from existing procedures in cases of extreme emergency threatening the very existence of the state.[6]

In South Korea, the 1962 Constitution adopted a presidential form of government and a judicial branch having the power to review the constitutionality of legislation and legality of administrative actions, but the Supreme Court remained 'cautiously silent' in exercising its judicial review power until 1971.[7] During more than forty years there were only four cases in which a law was found to be null and void for its unconstitutionality. Two of these were the Judicature Act and the State Indemnity Act, which deprived members of the Armed Forces of the right to claim damages against the state.[8] The justices who held those Acts unconstitutional were forced to leave the Supreme Court and no other Acts or statutes have been declared unconstitutional. As a result, constitutional clauses concerning judicial review have remained no more than nominal. Use of judicial power at this time prompted retaliation against the judiciary by the executive, which in turn fuelled growing public opposition to the government.

The impact of colonial and post-colonial experience

As with other aspects of Asia–Pacific constitutions, it is necessary to bear in mind the colonial experience. In Indonesia, the judicial system continues to bear the legacy of Dutch colonial rule, but has also experienced a period of revolution under President Soekarno and a period of authoritarianism under President Soeharto. During the Dutch period, there were separate courts for Europeans and for Indonesians. Chinese appeared in European courts as they were subject to the European civil code. This dualistic system ceased with Law 1 of 1951, which brought uniformity to the courts and abolished customary courts. The constitution does not indicate the relation between the judiciary and other branches of government, nor is the relationship between the court and the People's Consultative Assembly (MPR) clear. As the judiciary is defined by statute, and statutes are made by the president and the House of Representatives (DPR), then the judiciary is dependent on these two powers. Since independence, the most important laws relating to the judiciary are the Basic Law on Judicial Powers (Law 19, 1964), and the Basic Act 14/1970 on the Judiciary. The 1964 Law empowered the Supreme Court to undertake cassation hearings from not only the general courts but also the religious, military and administrative courts.

The authoritarian aspects of the 1945 Constitution were challenged by more liberal elements within the Indonesian leadership, and in the liberal period from 1950 parties and unions were allowed maximum freedom to organise, the press was free, and the courts functioned with relatively little interference from the executive. Soekarno's decree of 5 July 1959, which introduced Guided Democracy, recommenced a revolution that had consequences for the development of law. Regulation 2/1945 was recalled.

In 1962 Minister for Justice Dr Sahardjo argued that Dutch-era civil and commercial codes be regarded as 'commentaries', rather than as codes of law. The Supreme Court's 'Circular No. 3' of 1963 directed that existing laws (and eight codes in particular) were invalid because they had been enacted by the Dutch to further their own interests in Indonesia. The circular provided no reasoning but 'assumed' the listed articles were no longer in force. Such 'circular letters' purporting to interpret legislation were probably not binding on the lower courts, but the lower courts observed them.[9]

Soekarno had been saying at about this time that jurists were unfit to make a revolution, and perhaps spurred by his comments, and encouraged by Sahardjo, many judges adopted this approach and stopped referring to the codes in their judicial decisions. Guatama argues that only four of the eight codes mentioned were contrary to the constitution, or related to the constitution at all, but that the others did not raise constitutional questions.[10]

With the installation of the Soeharto government, this 'revolutionary' approach to law was curtailed, and judges once more used the Dutch codes in their decisions in the search for legal certainty. In 1968 the restructuring of the Supreme Court was completed to meet the conditions set out in the 1945 Constitution, that is, to be free from government intervention in the exercise of justice. At least in theory, the 1970 Law emphasised the principle of independence and prohibited interference. Since the removal of Soeharto from power, the courts have been less politically controlled but have not yet had sufficient time to define sound judicial practice.[11]

Judicial practice in Thailand has been shaped in part by the experience of no fewer than seventeen military coups in the twentieth century. No Thai constitution has been effective for more than a handful of years, and successive courts have faced the challenge of determining which constitution, which laws and which decrees form part of the enduring law of Thailand. Other courts that have operated under periods of emergency rule or authoritarian government include those of the Philippines, South Korea, Taiwan and Bangladesh. In the Philippines, the courts lost all sense of independence during the Marcos administration. A 1983 report from the International Commission of Jurists concerning the Philippines judiciary questioned the 'astonishing argument' put forward by the Philippines Supreme Court for the continued detention of prisoners under Presidential Order 2045.[12] In assessing the path of judicial development in a specific country, therefore, one has to recognise the challenges that have confronted those institutions most affected by constitutional reform or renewal.

The common law and customary law

Post-independence, states took up to greater or lesser degrees the challenge of creating their own 'common law' from their own, rather than from English, customs. Consequently, constitutions direct the parliament and judiciary, whether expressly or implicitly, on the role of custom as a source of law. The common-law tradition is in fact a recognition of customary law. However, 'custom' in the British context refers to custom found and recognised by the courts. In many parts of the Asia Pacific, 'custom' refers to very specific codes of behaviour and values which predate the operation of the courts and which often run parallel with statute law as an authoritative source of legal norms. This becomes problematic for courts that are attempting to unify the law or to build up a common legal framework in the face of pluralism.

Reporting on the small Pacific territory of Tokelau, Angelo has pointed to the anomalies that arise from applying British common law as the underlying law for Tokelauans, who speak a different language and live in a quite different cultural context.[13] In American Samoa, a villager was killed in 1993 on the orders of the Matai council. The enforcement of traditional law and order by the Matai relieves the state of much police work at local level, but in this instance it provoked discussion about whether customary law had gone beyond the boundaries set for it by the constitution.[14] To admit custom as a source of law thus allows the potential for conflicting value norms. However, to deny custom is to deny the norms that actually govern communities at local level. Customary law is most easily incorporated into plural legal systems where traditional leaders remain to enforce it, and also in areas where law and morality have rapidly disintegrated in the absence of Western-type legal codes.

The independence constitution of Papua New Guinea anticipated the adoption of customary law wherever possible, but difficulties in its definition and in proving its widespread applicability have led to the retention of much common law. Despite the constitutional expectation that the judiciary would contribute to the development of an underlying law, the court only made its first submission towards this in its 1987 annual report.[15] Weisbrot, Bayne and others have pointed to a continuing failure to address constitutional aspirations outlined in the National Goals and Directive Principles, and the continued interpretation of law in conformity with the non-traditional system of common law.[16]

Former Deputy Chief Justice Sir Mari Kapi noted that 'very few customary concepts were integrated in the system'.[17] The courts have been accused of preferring to adopt common law as it exists in England and in Australia, rather than 'find' customary law, because the former path is the easier. Kapi, writing in defence of the judiciary, has suggested that it is the task of the lawyers representing parties to a dispute to use arguments based in custom, so that the judges have the opportunity of determining 'customary law'. An alternative view is that in the 1980s the judiciary in fact commenced the task of developing the underlying law but were hampered by the low frequency of litigation in the country.[18]

Consideration of customary law can have an impact on legal procedures as much as on outcomes. Again, in the context of Papua New Guinea, Chalmers and Paliwala have observed that form of law and legal processes are not necessarily rigid and that as a result rules of law are often stated in the form of argument. The forms of dispute settlement give much greater emphasis to what the parties wish – in particular, the need to come to amicable settlement of disputes between people and groups – rather than to the 'winner takes all' form found elsewhere. Since principles are more important than processes, rules exist but can be transgressed in order to meet an overriding principle, particularly the goal of having a harmonious society. However, because of the traditional lack of some paramount leadership, and because parties to a dispute were generally in charge of their own efforts at resolution, they resorted to their own forms of sanction (such as revenge, shaming, pay-back or compensation), if a dispute could not be resolved peacefully. This fluid approach to law also means that it is not easy to separate law from politics, or religion, or the interests of the extended family.[19]

In Indonesia, 'adat law' is that part of custom that has consequences in law.[20] Although scholars differ in opinion on the extent to which received Islamic law forms part of 'adat', the term refers to all the (uncodified) customary law of the non-European population of Indonesia, as opposed to the codified law introduced by the Dutch and continued by the Indonesian government. It flourishes in small semi-autonomous communities throughout the archipelago, can vary from region to region, and is not necessarily the same as Islamic law. Most Indonesians are subject to Islamic law, rather than adat, and as both systems concern 'the totality of life' rather than merely legal relationships, the two can come into conflict. There is also the difficulty of reconciling acceptance of custom as a source of law with constitutional art. 27, which refers to the equality of all citizens before the law.

The establishment and dis-establishment of courts

Whereas courts are often viewed as permanent and stable institutions within the constitutional order, a surprising degree of court creation and transformation continues to take place in the Asia–Pacific states. In

Box 8.1 *Sino-British agreement on Hong Kong's Court of Final Appeal*

10 June 1995

THIS is the full text signed between the senior British and Chinese representatives of the JLG [Joint Liaison Group]:

AFTER full consultations, the two sides of the Sino-British Joint Liaison Group have reached the following agreement on the question of the Court of Final Appeal in Hong Kong:

The British side agrees to amend the Court of Final Appeal Bill on the basis of the eight suggestions published by the Political Affairs Sub-group of the Preliminary Working Committee of the Preparatory Committee of the Hong Kong Special Administrative Region on May 16, 1995.

The Chinese side agrees to the British side amending the Court of Final Appeal Bill to make it clear that Section 83P of the Criminal Procedure Ordinance applies in a case where an appeal has been heard and determined by the Court of Final Appeal, and that there is therefore no need for further legislative or other provisions in relation to the power to inquire into the constitutionality of laws or to provide for post-verdict remedial mechanisms.

The British side agrees to amend the Court of Final Appeal Bill to include the formulation of 'acts of state' in Article 19 of the Basic Law and to provide that the Court of Final Appeal Ordinance shall not come into operation before 30 June, 1997.

The Chinese side agrees that, after the Chinese and British sides reach this agreement, the legislative procedures for the Court of Final Appeal Bill, on which the two sides have reached a consensus through consultation, will be taken forward immediately to enable them to be completed as soon as possible before the end of July 1995. The Chinese side will adopt a positive attitude in this regard.

The Chinese and British sides agree that the team designate of the Hong Kong Special Administrative Region shall, with the British side (including relevant Hong Kong Government departments) participating in the process and providing its assistance, be responsible for the preparation for the establishment of the Court of Final Appeal on 1 July, 1997 in accordance with the Basic Law and consistent with the provisions of the Court of Final Appeal Ordinance.

1995 the Hong Kong Legislative Assembly approved legislation concerning Hong Kong's Court of Final Appeal to operate in the Hong Kong Special Administrative Region after 1 July 1997 (see Box 8.1). The court comprises four local judges and one overseas judge. Its jurisdiction excludes acts of state. Although critics have expressed concern that the Act's failure to specify the meaning of 'acts of state' will allow China's National People's Congress to gradually broaden what it deems to fall under this term, the Hong Kong government insists that the issue is addressed in art. 19 of the Basic Law, that is, that the courts in Hong Kong will determine what constitutes an 'act of state'.

In Malaysia, a special court was established in 1993 through Act A848 (now provided for in art. 182 of the Federal Constitution) to hear cases involving offences and civil cases by or against the rulers.[21]

Judicial reform has also occurred in the socialist states. Proposals for law reform made at the Vietnam Lawyers Association's 8th congress, held in Hanoi in May 1993, included establishing special courts to deal with commercial disputes between bureaucrats and citizens, establishing district courts (which would be a new judicial level, between the people's court and the central Supreme Court), reforming the juvenile court system, enlarging the notary public function, and establishing 'legal consultancies'.[22]

Changes in appeal courts were also made in Pacific jurisdictions. From 1965 until 1981 the Cook Islands Constitution recognised a right of appeal from the High Court of the Cook Islands to the Court of Appeal of New Zealand. Constitutional Amendment No. 9 (Act 1980–81) ended recourse to the New Zealand courts and established a Cook Islands Court of Appeal, while retaining a right to appeal to 'Her Majesty the Queen in Council, with the leave of the Court of Appeal, or, if such leave is refused, with the leave of Her Majesty the Queen in Council'.

A Tongan Court of Appeals was established in 1990, to have jurisdiction in all appeal cases except those dealing with traditional titles and estates, which continue to be heard by the Privy Council Court of Appeal. The Appeals Court is the highest court in the land. The king, as the Supreme Judge, oversees the Appeals Court with his cabinet and a selected judge. Cases are brought to this court on appeal from judgements of the Supreme Court.[23]

The Privy Council

A number of countries formerly under British rule retained appeal to the Privy Council: Cook Islands, New Zealand, Fiji, Malaysia and

Singapore. Before 1985, for example, the Federal Court of Malaysia was the highest court in that country but its decisions were further appealable to the Privy Council in London. However, in 1978 Privy Council appeals in criminal and constitutional matters were abolished, as were all other appeals, such as civil appeals except those filed before that date, in 1985. In place of the Privy Council, a Federal Court of Appeal was established in 1994 through amendment to the Federal Constitution by Act A885, and in 1995 trial by jury and judicial preliminary inquiries were both abolished.

Singapore's Judicial Committee (Repeal) Act of 1994 abolished all appeals to the Privy Council and installed the Court of Appeal in Singapore as the final court of law in the land. The small state of Brunei allowed appeals to the Privy Council from independence in 1984 until a declaration of a state of emergency[24] provided that 'no appeals in any criminal cause nor matter shall lie from the Courts to the Judicial Committee of the Privy Council'.

In the small Pacific archipelagos, constitutions provide for the establishment of courts with jurisdiction on specific islands. The Constitution of Vanuatu allows parliament to make law for village or island courts, and seven such courts have been established.[25] Each consists of three lay justices, one of whom must be a chief. The body of decisions of the island courts provides 'guidance' for new cases, but not precedent. Settlements may be based on custom, as far as the Supreme Court. Lawyers have no right to appear, and there are no technical rules (e.g. for evidence).

Constitutional courts

Apart from new appeals courts, which redistribute authority to resolve disputes that have already gone to trial, the establishment of constitutional courts and tribunals was one of the more significant developments in the region in the late twentieth century. In Indonesia, the process for determining the constitutionality of law was not made clear in the 1945 Constitution. The chapter which deals with the judiciary reads, in its entirety: 'Judicial powers are carried out by the Supreme Court and other courts as may be established by statute. The organisation and authority of those courts as well as the conditions for appointing and dismissing judges shall be determined by statute.'[26]

While the Basic Law on Judicial Powers empowered the Supreme Court to undertake cassation hearings, no court was empowered to determine the constitutionality or otherwise of statutes. Subekti, Chief Justice of the Supreme Court of Indonesia from 1967, wrote in 1973 that the question of granting powers to the Supreme Court to annul unconstitutional laws was being 'heatedly debated':

> Some hold the opinion that these powers should be granted to the Supreme Court while others maintain that such powers should be granted to a Court of the Constitution and not to the Supreme Court. It is generally agreed that since such powers are not granted by the Constitution, they would have to be granted by the People's Consultative Congress; it would not be possible to do this by means of an Act of Parliament. There are also moves to transfer the administrative, organizational affairs of the general courts of justice from the hands of the Minister of Justice to the hands of the Supreme Court.[27]

The powers of the Supreme Court were recast in Statute 14/1985. It could give legal advice to other state institutions (art. 37), could advise the president on questions of granting grace (art. 35), and was to remain free of all influences (art. 2). While the court could not deal with the facts of a case, only with procedure, it could determine whether administrative regulations and decisions conflicted with higher legislation. It could not review laws of parliament but could, in theory, review cabinet decisions, and in the early 1990s it began to hear challenges to such decisions as decrees banning media.[28]

In South Korea, a Constitutional Court established in 1988 in accordance with provisions of the 1987 Constitution brought considerable change to political practices.[29] During the presidency of Rhee (1948–60), a Constitutional Committee comprising the vice-president, five justices and five National Assembly members had exercised judicial review of legislative power upon the request of a court.[30] While the new court can review the constitutionality of Acts passed by the National Assembly, conduct impeachment trials upon the indictment of the National Assembly, settle jurisdictional disputes between branches of government, and hear 'constitutional grievances', the pre-existing Supreme Court has ensured that it cannot review the decisions of other courts. Nonetheless, its decisions nullifying statutes challenged for their unconstitutional character have brought a normative effect to the constitution.

In the 1990s there was considerable discussion in Thailand about which court or institution should have the right to determine the constitutionality of Acts. The allocation of powers of constitutional review to the quasi-judicial Constitutional Tribunal, rather than to the Supreme Court or some other constitutional court, ensured that the judiciary made virtually no judgment on the constitutionality of military and executive action and legislation by successive regimes.[31] Comment has been made about the plethora of outdated laws that remain on the statute books as a legacy of successive decree-making regimes.[32]

Until reforms in 1997, Thailand's Constitutional Tribunal included both judicial and non-judicial figures, and had both political and legal functions. It comprised the Supreme Public Prosecutor and three legal experts each appointed by the House and Senate, the Attorney-General, the Speaker of the Senate as a proxy of the bureaucracy, the Speaker of the House of Representatives, and the President of the Supreme Court.[33] The tribunal examined the constitutionality of bills before the parliament, at the request of not less than one-fifth of the members of both houses, or the prime minister, and could also interpret provisions of the constitution at the request of the prime minister or the presidents of the parliament, the Senate or the House of Representatives.[34]

Given the composition of the Constitutional Tribunal and the manner in which legal references were made to it, its findings were often regarded as based more on political than on legal considerations, and a desire for reform grew through the early 1990s. A particular catalyst for reform was a tribunal ruling upholding the constitutionality of an executive decree issued by the Suchinda Kraprayoon government (National Peace-Keeping Council Order No. 26), granting a blanket amnesty to those involved in suppression of pro-democracy demonstrators in May 1990. The Supreme Court found the NPKC's order to be unconstitutional under the 1991 interim Constitution and so disagreed with the tribunal's ruling, and Justice Minister Suvit Khunkitti proposed to an extraordinary house committee on constitutional amendments that the courts be empowered to decide the constitutionality of any law applied in their rulings.

The Cambodian Constitution of 1993 established a Constitutional Council to examine the constitutionality of both government and court decisions. Although the composition of the council – three members appointed by the Supreme Council of Magistry, three by the king and three by the National Assembly – was set out in the Supreme Council of Magistracy Law of 1994, only the king's representatives had been appointed by late 1995, and the legislation required to establish the council had not been passed. This prompted Chakrei Nhiek Tioulong, a royal representative to the Constitutional Council, to claim that all laws thus far passed by the National Assembly were unconstitutional.[35]

Religious courts

Religious courts have been established in countries that are Islamic or have large Islamic populations. These include Pakistan, Malaysia, the Philippines and Indonesia. In 1988 the Malaysian parliament amended the constitution so as to deprive civil courts of jurisdiction in respect of

Box 8.2 *Provision for religious and tribal courts in the Philippines*

Republic Act No. 6734, 1 August 1989, Organic Act for the Autonomous Region in Muslim Mindanao:

Sec. 5. The Shari'ah Appellate Court shall have the following powers:
(1) Exercise original jurisdiction over petitions for certiorari, prohibition, mandamus, habeas corpus, and other auxiliary writs and processes in aid of its appellate jurisdiction; and
(2) Exercise exclusive appellate jurisdiction over all cases tried in the Shari'ah District Courts as established by law.

Sec. 6. The decisions of the Shari'ah Appellate Court shall be final and executory: Provided, however, That nothing herein contained shall affect the original and appellate jurisdiction of the Supreme Court as provided in the Constitution.

Sec. 7. The Presiding and Associate Justices of the Shari'ah Appellate Court shall serve until they reach the age of seventy (70) years, unless sooner removed for cause in the same manner as Justices of the Court of Appeals or become incapacitated to discharge the duties of their office.

Sec. 8. The Presiding Justice and Associate Justices of the Shari'ah Appellate Court shall receive the same compensation and enjoy the same privileges as the Presiding Justice and Associate Justices of the Court of Appeals, respectively.

Sec. 9. (1) The Supreme Court shall, upon recommendation of the Presiding Justice of the Shari'ah Appellate Court, appoint the court administrator and clerk of court of said Appellate Court. Such other personnel as may be necessary for the Shari'ah Appellate Court shall be appointed by the Presiding Justice of said court.
(2) The pertinent provisions of existing law regarding the qualifications, appointment, compensation, functions, duties and other matters relative to the personnel of the Court of Appeals shall apply to those of the Shari'ah Appellate Court.

Sec. 10. The Members of the Shari'ah Appellate Court and of other Shari'ah Appellate courts established by law shall not be designated to any agency performing quasi-judicial or administrative functions.

Sec. 11. The official seat of the Shari'ah Appellate Court shall, unless the Supreme Court decides otherwise, be in the seat of the Autonomous Government.

Sec. 12. Proceedings in the Shari'ah Appellate Court and in the Shari'ah lower courts as are established in the Autonomous Region shall be governed by such special rules as the Supreme Court may promulgate.

Shari'ah Courts

Sec. 13. The Shari'ah District Courts and the Shari'ah Circuit Courts created under existing laws shall continue to function as provided therein. The judges of the Shari'ah courts shall have the same qualifications as the judges of the Regional Trial Courts, the Metropolitan Trial Courts or the Municipal Trial Courts as the case may be in. In addition, they must be learned in Islamic law and jurisprudence.

Tribal Courts

Sec. 14. There is hereby created a system of tribal courts, which may include a Tribal Appellate Court, for the indigenous cultural communities in the Autonomous Region. These courts shall determine, settle and decide controversies and enforce decisions involving personal, family and property rights in accordance with the tribal codes of these communities. The Regional Assembly shall define their composition and jurisdiction in accordance with this Act.

matters within the jurisdiction of Syariah courts. The Malay Rulers hold the title of head of the religion of Islam in their respective states. However, as Malaysia has a federal system and Islamic law and personal and family law of Muslims are governed by state legislation, federal law did not clarify all issues (part of clause (2) of art. 76 expressly prohibits legislation in respect of Islamic law).

Islamic law is also a significant factor in Indonesia. If Muslims had succeeded in having the seven-word 'Jakarta charter' inserted into the constitution at the time of independence, the phrase 'Belief in God both for the people in general and for every Indonesian personally in accordance with his own religion and with respect for the religion of others' would have continued on to say 'with the obligation for adherents of Islam to practise Islamic Law', and this would have ensured that Muslims were subject to the laws of Islam.

Although Singapore's legal system is predominantly a common-law one, there is a small degree of legal pluralism. Muslim law, which governs the Muslim community in religious, matrimonial and related matters, is administered by a separate system of courts and judicial officers.

182   *Democracy and the Rule of Law*

In the Philippines, the organic law of the autonomous region of Muslim Mindanao provides for not only religious courts but also 'tribal' courts (see Box 8.2). Article IX(2) establishes a Shari'ah Appellate, whose judges are to hold qualifications in Philippines law and 'shall also be learned in Islamic law and jurisprudence'.[36]

Administrative courts

The establishment of courts to review administrative action by government agencies may be an indicator of the spread of constitutional thinking in the Asia Pacific. In Indonesia, an Administrative Court was established in 1991, at what might be considered the beginning of the decline of executive supremacy in that country. After the popular news weekly *Tempo* was banned in June 1994, the Administrative Court found, on appeal in May 1995, that Information Minister Harmoko had acted unlawfully in revoking the licence. Although this decision was upheld by the State Appellate Court on 22 November 1995, it was subsequently overturned by the Supreme Court (Mahkamah Agung), which ruled in June 1996 that the minister had the right to revoke publication licences and that *Tempo* had ignored six warnings from the minister.[37] Despite the overturning of such decisions, the questioning of the legality of the decrees of the president and the members of his cabinet contributed to a mood change in Indonesian society.

The establishment of an Administrative Court in Thailand contained a similarly symbolic element. In 1992 the Chuan government presented to parliament a policy statement that promised to upgrade the Juridical Council's Law and Petition Analysis division into an Administrative Court within four years. Consequently, the Juridical Council drafted the Establishment of Administrative Court and Administrative Procedure Bill. The judiciary, on the other hand, argued that any new body named a 'court' could only be established under the jurisdiction of the Ministry of Justice, and drafted its own bill accordingly. In both bills, Administrative Court judges were to be recruited from among public prosecutors, senior civil servants, and academics, but the bills differed on the issue of judicial independence. The Juridical Council proposed the establishment of a body similar to the Judicial Commission for the supervision of the Administrative Court of first instance, an appeals court and a supreme administrative court, and that these new courts come under its administrative supervision. The judiciary, on the other hand, advocated supervision of any new courts by the Ministry of Justice. The two bodies also disagreed on whether the Administrative

Court should adopt the adversarial or the inquisitorial approach, and over the method of appointment of the Supreme Administrative Court Chief Justice.[38] There was also a view outside of the judiciary that judges had little knowledge of public law (which considers the structure, powers and operations of government, and the rights and duties of a citizen in relation to government).

The judiciary

Effective constitutionalism requires, in addition to the creation of relevant court structures and the passage of relevant laws, the creation of a judiciary that is competent, autonomous and stable. To achieve this, the constitutional order must address the key issues of judicial appointment, promotion, dismissal and independence.

The civil- and common-law traditions find judges differently. In the civil-law tradition, the judiciary is a career path open to lawyers soon after graduation. Promotion to higher courts is gained through years spent in the lesser courts. In Thailand, for instance, judge trainees who have a law degree and a minimum of two years experience can take oral and written exams at about age 25 to gain entry to judicial service. Competitive exams, held annually, eliminate 'possible unsuitable candidates' and help to establish 'an order in seniority on the appointments'.[39]

In the common-law tradition, in contrast, appointments are made to the judicial bench from among the lawyers who have distinguished themselves before it as members of 'the bar'. Judges are generally appointed by the executive, or by some form of judicial commission. The nine judges of the Constitutional Court of South Korea are formally appointed by the president, although three are recommended by the Chief Justice of the Supreme Court and three by the National Assembly. Despite such diverging career paths, however, both the civil- and common-law systems have been challenged to find methods for judicial appointment that raise the exercise above political interests.

The Indian Constitution provides that judicial appointments be made by the president, on the advice of the government, following consultation with the chief justice.[40] The judiciary is independent of the executive and is the guardian and interpreter of the constitution. From 1950 to 1973 the senior-most judge of the Supreme Court was appointed Chief Justice of India on a vacancy arising. When Chief Justice Sikri retired in April 1973, Indira Gandhi appointed Justice A. N. Ray (the fourth in seniority) as Chief Justice of India over Justices Shelat, Hedge and Grover, who promptly resigned. During 1975–77 Prime Minister Gandhi transferred sixteen 'inconvenient' judges to 'irrelevant posts', and later amended the rules in order to make some judicial appointments posts for political patronage.[41] In October 1993 a Nine-Judge Bench ruled that responsibility for the selection of judges for the High Court and the Supreme Court rests with the chief justice, not with the government. Justice J. S. Verma delivered the leading judgment on behalf of himself and four other judges constituting a clear majority. Two other judges (Pandian J and Kuldip Singh J) agreed with the principal point (with small disagreements) but delivered concurrent judgments giving separate reasons. It was held among others by clear majority that:

(a) in the appointment of Judges to the Supreme Court of India and High Courts of various States the opinion of the Chief Justice of India after consulting with two senior most Judges of the Supreme Court will have primacy and will be binding on government except in a couple of exceptional cases;
(b) The Government can not make any appointment to the Supreme Court or the High Court unless it is in conformity with the opinion of the Chief Justice of India;
(c) The recommendation of the Chief Justice of India is to be arrived at by a detailed process of consultation including the views of the Government, two senior-most Judges of the Supreme Court and any other Judge of the Supreme Court whose opinion would be regarded as significant, and
(d) the decision of the Supreme Court in S.P. Gupta v Union of India (1982) 2 SCR 365 (a bench of seven Judges) stands overruled.[42]

The High Court of Bangladesh relied on the Indian court's 1993 decision in *SCAORA* to reject judicial appointments made by the Zia government in February 1994. Chief Justice Shahabuddin Ahmed asserted that the judiciary lacked independence from the government and that members of the Bar were not satisfied that the appointments were made through 'effective consultation' between the government and the chief justice. Prime Minister Khaleda Zia responded by stating at the opening of the Bangladesh National Parliament's winter session that the government had total confidence in judicial independence.[43]

In Malaysia, senior judicial appointments are made by the king on the advice of the prime minister after consulting the Conference of Rulers. In Indonesia, responsibility for judicial appointments rests with the president, who is supplied with a list of candidates by the parliament. The 1970 Basic Act on the Judiciary emphasised judicial independence but gave responsibility for the administration of the courts, the budget, and matters of transfers, promotions and postings, to the Ministry of Justice.[44]

Other jurisdictions make appointments through some form of judicial commission. Thailand's Judicial Services Commission (JSC) was established by the Judicial Service Act of 1957. According to both the constitution and the provisions of the Judicial Service Act, BE 2521 (1978), the king makes all appointments, promotions, transfers and removals of judges upon the recommendation of the JSC. Section 192 of the 1991 Constitution states:

His Majesty the King shall appoint and relieve the judge and adjudicator from their position. Before taking over the responsibility for the first time the judge and adjudicator shall give an oath to His Majesty the King with the wording which the Judicial Council under the law has prescribed concerning the judicial government official.[45]

Section 193 states:

The appointment and relieve [sic] of the judge in the Court of law shall have first to be approved by the Judicial Council under the law concerning judicial government official. The promotion, raise in salary and penalising the judge in the Court of Law shall have to be approved by the Judicial Council under the law concerning judicial government official.

The commission's twelve members are elected for renewable terms of two years. Four members are ex officio: the Chief Justice of the Supreme Court, the Chief Justice of the Court of Appeal, the Deputy Chief Justice of the Supreme Court, and the Under Secretary of the Ministry of Justice. Another four are elected from among senior members of the judiciary (i.e. members of the Supreme Court or equivalent service ranks) by all judges in Thailand (approximately 1300), while a further four members are elected from the ranks of retired judges (who are not practising lawyers or legislators, or holding political posts). The election of four representatives is modelled on a French system (which has since been discontinued in France).[46]

The justice minister has the right to forward to the JSC recommendations concerning promotions and appointments, which the JSC takes as non-binding advice. The decisions of the JSC are subsequently forwarded through the justice minister to the prime minister, who forwards them to the king for consent. Should the justice minister not approve of the recommendations, he has the right to return them to the JSC within thirty days, for reconsideration.

A similar body exercises responsibilities for judicial appointment in Cambodia. The nine-member Supreme Council of Magistry, established in 1994, has the role of ensuring the independence of the judiciary. It makes recommendations on the appointment, promotion, disciplining and dismissal of judges. It comprises King Sihanouk or his nominated representative as chair, an appointee of the justice minister, and seven judges and prosecutors. The draft law proposed that the justice minister be a member of the Supreme Council, but this was modified in the parliament following protests that such inclusion was unconstitutional and, besides, would threaten the separation of powers. Justice Minister Chem Snguon agreed with this, and a compromise position provides for the inclusion of the minister's nominee. The constitution explicitly bars National Assembly members and government ministers from holding other public functions, and states that 'legislative, executive and judicial powers shall be separate'.

A less used practice is election of judicial officers. In Laos, for example, the President of the People's Supreme Courts and the Republic Prosecutor-General are elected by the National Assembly on the recommendation of the People's Assembly Standing Committee (the Vice-President of the People's Supreme Court and the judges of the people's courts at all levels are appointed by the National Assembly Standing Committee). In Vietnam, judges are elected but have limited autonomy, since the Supreme Court is accountable to the National Assembly and the state. Processes of election are also used within multi-member bodies, such as judicial services commissions, which are charged with putting forward the names of judicial figures for appointment, promotion or dismissal.

In a number of countries, the duty of governments to consult other offices before appointing senior judges is becoming more widespread. Whatever the process used, the power to appoint the judiciary is becoming a responsibility rather than a privilege given to the executive.

Regional appeals courts

In courts that lack judicial capacity, including most Pacific Island courts, higher judicial offices, including appeals courts, were occupied in the first post-independence decades by expatriate judges[47] (although legally-trained judges are appointed to the higher courts, some lower courts and the specialist lands courts admit 'assessors' having knowledge of local custom and procedure). This brought both advantages and disadvantages. Among the former was an ability to adjudicate on sensitive matters without fear or favour, but the disadvantages were also several: expatriate judges were not necessarily well placed to adjudicate on matters involving custom, and there was always the possibility that judicial independence was compromised when judges were employed on fixed-term contracts.[48] In Vanuatu, tensions emerged in 1995 between the government of Maxime Carlot Korman and Robert Kent, an Australian citizen on a three-year contract as a judge of the Supreme Court of Vanuatu, who resigned in 1995 after one and a half years, expressing concern at the lack of independence shown by Chief Justice Charles Vaudin d'Imèecourt, a British citizen.[49] In the 1990s four chief justices of the Marshall Islands were forced to resign or were impeached.

An example of visiting expatriate judges determining the outcome of significant issues of constitutional and customary law is found in the August 1995 sitting of the Western Samoan Court of Appeal. In the case of *Italia Taamale and Taamale Toelau v. Attorney General* (unreported), the court (New Zealand judges Sir Robin Cook, Sir Gordon Bisson and Sir Maurice Casey) held that banishment from a village was a reasonable restriction on the rights of freedom of movement and residence imposed by existing law, in the interest of public order.[50] A second significant case concerned the constitutionality of the Electoral Amendment Act of 1990. The Act extended the franchise to all Western Samoan citizens, which MP Le Tagaloa Pita argued contravened the constitution's granting of suffrage to those holding Matai (chiefly) titles. He applied to Sir Maurice Casey, sitting as a judge of the Supreme Court of Western Samoa, to find the Act unconstitutional. Pita lost this application and was reported as fearing that the Court of Appeal would not sit prior to the April 1996 general election.[51]

In the case of the Vanuatu Court of Appeal, foreign judges were invited to sit by the chief registrar and the chief justice.[52] When in September 1991 an appeal bench of the Supreme Court of Vanuatu heard an application by the government for an injunction to stop a no-confidence motion in the leadership of then Prime Minister Walter Lini, the court comprised Australian Federal Court Judge Trevor Morling, Solomon Islands Chief Justice Gordon Ward and Tongan Chief Justice Geoffrey Martin.

By the 1990s indigenous judicial figures were also sitting on appeals courts beyond their own jurisdiction. In 1992 Papua New Guinean judge (now Chief) Justice Arnold Amet served on Fiji's Supreme Court, following an agreement reached between Papua New Guinea and Fiji. The then Chief Justice, Sir Biri Kidu, was already serving on this court of appeal. Papua New Guinea has a similar arrangement to assist the Solomon Islands, Vanuatu and Kiribati. The Samoan Court of Appeal comprises judges from Niue, Tonga and New Zealand.[53] Initiatives such as the establishment of the Pacific Judicial Council, PILOM (Pacific Islands Law Officers Meeting), and so on, have strengthened regional co-ordination of legal policy and practice.[54]

Judicial independence

In assessing the position of courts in constitutional systems, one encounters an intriguing duality of intention: whereas constitutional doctrine holds that courts are 'impartial' and 'independent' in their duties before the law, each and every activity of the court is at the same time either one that supports or one that erodes the legitimacy of the constitutional order. Yet such duality need not be viewed sceptically: a judicial system that buttresses a just constitutional order will generally have only beneficial implications for the social order. Of more concern are judicial acts that appear to buttress self-interested holders of public power.

The notion of judicial independence is strong in countries coming from the British or common-law tradition, and many regard judicial independence as a more important objective than other aspects of the separation of powers. However, the constitutional doctrine of autonomy is an idea which is not always put into practice. Indeed, in some legal systems the relationship between courts and other branches of government is one of co-operation rather than separation. This may be the case more with courts that have adopted the civil-law tradition. In Thailand, the phrase 'judicial independence' generally refers to judicial impartiality and an absence of influence in judicial decision-making by other factors.[55]

In Indonesia, court officials speak of the idea of family '*keluaga*' to describe a 'division of labour' among government branches, rather than a separation of powers. According to the 1970 law on the judiciary, 'the judicial authority is a state authority which is freely exercising judicature in order to uphold law and justice according to Pansasila, for the sake of implementing the state law of Indonesia'. The MPR, and not the courts, has the authority to strike down legislation, and the court is not necessarily regarded as the defender of a citizen's individual rights. Consequently, Lev describes Indonesian courts as an intra-elite institution which looks to its own interests as much as to those of others in society.[56] The 1970 law emphasised the principle of independence and prohibited interference.

Oda notes the connections between personnel in the ruling party and in the judiciary in the socialist states, suggesting law's utilisation as an instrument of political power.[57] Some regional constitutional philosophies reject the concept of separation of powers. Scholars in the People's Republic of China, for instance, are discussing how review of executive action and legislation can be built into China's system of 'constitutional supervision'.[58] Elsewhere, judicial independence is under pressure from the influence of other branches of government, and indeed from social pressures.

Attacks on judicial independence have taken many forms, from the most subtle, to violent. In 1989 the Centre for the Independence of Judges and Lawyers (1988–89) reported to the UN sub-commission on the Prevention of Discrimination and the Protection of Minorities on 145 harassed or persecuted judges and lawyers in thirty-one countries. The Philippines topped the list (6 judges killed, and 17 attacked or threatened with violence), higher scores than Colombia and Peru.[59]

More generally, however, the capacity and willingness of courts to act independently have been vitiated through procedures for dismissal, suppression of promotion, and forms of relegation. Among the more well-known incidents of dismissal is that of Malaysian Supreme Court President, Salleh bin Abas, in 1988. In the midst of a highly sensitive case involving Malaysia's ruling party (dissident members of UMNO had claimed that some UMNO candidates in the April 1987 elections were not legally registered, and that UMNO should not have won the election; the Supreme Court ruled UMNO an unlawful society, and the organisation was appealing), Abas had complained to the head of state about government attacks on the independence of the judiciary. Two months later he was suspended from the bench by order of Prime Minister Mahathir, who alleged he had made misrepresentations to the king. This suspension coincided with an appeal to the Supreme Court against the court's earlier ruling on the legal status of UMNO, over which Salleh was to have presided. In the course of subsequent legal attempts by Salleh to secure his reinstatement, five additional judges were suspended for supporting his submissions, and in August 1988 he was replaced by Abdul Hamid Omar, formerly Chief Justice of the High Court of Peninsular Malaysia.

In the small Pacific Island states, the courts have been required to rule frequently since independence in cases of dispute between contending political parties. In doing so they have risked offending the political branches of government, yet at the same time have contributed to an evolving set of case law establishing proper exercise of executive and legislative power.

After Papua New Guinea Prime Minister Pais Wingti attempted to prolong his tenure as chief executive in September 1993 by resigning his position and being re-elected the following day, the opposition parties appealed to the Supreme Court to find his action illegal. The court's concurrence, finding on 25 August 1994 that Wingti's resignation was lawful but that his re-election the same day was not, implied the need for a new election for the position and allowed Sir Julius Chan to seek and win the office.

In Vanuatu, perhaps more than elsewhere in the Pacific, the courts have been relied on extensively to adjudicate what have been essentially political disputes.[60] In September 1991 an appeal bench heard an application by the government for an injunction to stop a no-confidence motion in the leadership of then Prime Minister Walter Lini. When this was withdrawn, it heard an application (which it denied) to find that MP Donald Kalpokas had been elected to the position of president of the Vanua'aku Party in breach of party rules. Then, in February 1996 MPs Walter Lini and Serge Vohor challenged the election of Maxime Carlot as prime minister on five grounds, including that the standing orders had been violated, but the Vanuatu Supreme Court dismissed all five claims one week later, ruling that Carlot had been duly elected. Chief Justice d'Iméecourt said that Vohor's resignation had been read out in parliament and endorsed, and later gazetted. The plaintiffs' lawyer Roger de Robillard stated their intention to appeal against the decision but was reminded by the chief justice that the Court of Appeal, which must consist of three foreign judges, could not convene before October. De Robillard left Vanuatu on 2 March and on 12 March he and a Mauritian judge, who was about to be sworn in as a judge of the Vanuatu Supreme Court, were declared to be 'undesirable aliens' by Vanuatu's Council of Ministers.

The Supreme Court continued to be drawn into disputes between parliamentary factions. Following the chief justice's rejection in March 1996 of an application by former Prime Minister Vohor that he be reinstated to office, the court ordered Vohor and other members of his former government to return all government property in their possession and to pay the costs of the case. The Korman government faced a no-confidence motion in September in which the opposition parties were sure to hold the numbers, and after the government cancelled a parliamentary session, opposition MPs once more petitioned the Supreme Court, this time to order parliament's resumption.[61] Although the court ruled that parliament should sit on the morning of 30 September, Parliamentary Speaker Edward Natapei defied the order and cancelled the session, arguing that as the petition calling for the no-confidence vote had been signed by two suspended MPs, the court's ruling was incorrect. Opposition leader Willie Jimmy threatened to prosecute the Speaker for contempt of court and called on the country's police and paramilitary Mobile Force to obey the Supreme Court rather than the government.

The position of Vanuatu's expatriate chief justice was now being affected by political events. After he had issued arrest warrants for the leaders of a revolt (which had seen the president temporarily abducted and flown to the island of Malekula for 'discussions', as noted above), he was sacked by the new acting Prime Minister Barak Sope, accused of 'gross misconduct' and attempting to undermine an agreement ending the revolt by the Armed Forces. After the Judicial Services Commission found the chief justice guilty of serious misconduct, President Jean-Marie Leye terminated his appointment as a judge in the Supreme Court and he was ordered to leave the country. Clerk of the Court Vincent Lunabeck was appointed acting chief justice. D'Iméecourt appealed his dismissal, and although Supreme Court Judge Kalkot Mataskelekele ordered the government not to attempt deporting him until completion of the hearing in late October, the ex-chief justice made his departure.

These instances exemplify the sensitive role played by the higher courts in small states, and the vulnerability that judicial figures face. Similar challenges have faced the courts in Nepal, Bangladesh, Pakistan, and elsewhere in the region. In the Philippines, court rulings played a crucial role in mediating the struggle between supporters and opponents of President Ramos, as he sought ways around the constitutional prescription of a single term for the incumbent president.

In light of the struggle to establish judicial independence in numerous countries, the United Nations endorsed the Basic Principles on the Independence of the Judiciary in 1985:

1. The independence of the judiciary shall be guaranteed by the State and enshrined in the Constitution or the laws of the country. It is the duty of all governmental and other institutions to respect and observe the independence of the judiciary.
2. The judiciary shall decide matters before it impartially, on the basis of facts and in accordance with the law, without any restrictions, improper influences, inducements, pressures, threats or interferences direct or indirect, from any quarter or for any reason.
3. The judiciary shall have jurisdiction over all issues of a judicial nature and shall have exclusive authority to decide whether an issue submitted for its decision is within its competence as defined by law.
4. There shall not be any inappropriate or unwarranted interference with the judicial process, nor shall judicial decisions by the courts be subject to revision. This principle is without prejudice to judicial review or to mitigation or commutation by competent authorities of sentences imposed by the judiciary, in accordance with the law . . .
10. Persons selected for judicial office shall be individuals of integrity and ability with appropriate training or qualifications in law. Any method of judicial selection shall safeguard against judicial appointments for improper motives. In the selection of judges, there shall be no discrimination against a person on the grounds of race, colour, sex, religion, political or other opinion, national or social origin, property, birth or status, except that a requirement that a candidate for judicial office must be a national of the country concerned shall not be considered discriminatory . . .
13. Promotion of judges, where-ever such a system exists, should be based on objective factors, in particular ability, integrity and experience.

In 1995 chief justices from twenty jurisdictions across the Asia Pacific, from both common-law and civil-law traditions, and from both liberal-democratic and socialist political cultures, endorsed a similar document on judicial independence known as the 'Beijing Statement'.[62] The post-independence judicial experience of many states in the region pointed to the essential role that courts play – whatever weaknesses their systems inevitably still displayed - in upholding the rule of law, and in improving the chances of justice being dispensed to the people.

Notes

1 'The Judiciary – the Guardian of the People', Lawasia '93, Sri Lanka, 12–16 September, S.11 The Judiciary, Bar Association of Sri Lanka, 1993: Shri Indrajeet Roy, 27–9; Justice Saleem Akhtar, 1–4.
2 Buxbaum, *Traditional and Modern Legal Institutions*, 1.
3 *Keshavananda Bharati v. State of Kerala* (1973 [Supp.] SCR1), popularly known as the Fundamental Rights case was decided 7 for and 6 against.
4 The 1947 Constitution divides government into five branches or Yuan (Executive, Legislative, Judicial, Examination and Control).
5 Liu, 'Judicial Review and Emerging Constitutionalism'; and Fa, 'Constitutional Developments in Taiwan'.
6 Thoolen, *Indonesia and the Rule of Law*, 54.
7 70 DA 1010, 22 June 1971 decision. Daebopwon pankyoljip (Supreme Court Case Report), vol. 19, no. 2, 110–24. In the decision which had indeed embarrassed the executive government, two separate statutory provisions, the State Redress Act (art. 2, s. 1 proviso) and the Court Organisation Act (art. 59, s.1 proviso), were held unconstitutional. According to the Court Organisation Act provision, the presence of more than two-thirds of all the justices and the concurrence of more than two-thirds of all the justices present were required for the Supreme Court to declare a statute unconstitutional instead of a simple majority, a governmental scheme to make such a ruling harder.
8 Supreme Court Decision 71 DA 1010, 22 June 1971; 72 DA 986, 25 July 1972.
9 In another instance, the Supreme Court declared unconstitutional two non-code provisions (R.V. arts. 834 and 836) and indicated that arts. 108, 110 and 284 of the code – three articles referred to in the 1963 circular – were also unconstitutional.
10 Guatama and Hornick, *An Introduction to Indonesian Law*, 7.
11 Some of the calls for judicial renewal have come from within. Purwanto Gandasubroto, for instance, who replaced Lt. Gen. Ali Said as Supreme Court chairman in July 1992, called in a parliamentary hearing for bold reforms to bolster the independence of the judiciary: *Inside Indonesia*, December 1992, 12.

12 *ICJ Review*, 30, July 1983, 15–17. A three-member ICJ mission to the Philippines in 1984 found evidence of continuing and increased militarism, arbitrary arrests and torture, and other legal limitations and restrictions on human rights: *ICJ Review*, 33, December 1984, 21–5.
13 Angelo, 'The Common Law in New Zealand and Tokelau'.
14 *Pacific Islands Monthly*, November 1993.
15 *Commonwealth Law Bulletin*, 15:1, January 1989, 334.
16 Gawi, 'The Status of the Common Law', 16–17; Weisbrot, 'Papua New Guinea's Indigenous Jurisprudence', 1–45; Bayne, 'Judicial Method', 121–66.
17 Kapi, 'The Underlying Law in Papua New Guinea'. On the problems of interpreting customary law, see Stewart, 'Stone Age and Twentieth Century Law', 48–71.
18 See 'Judiciary and the Development of the Underlying Law', *Commonwealth Law Bulletin*, 15:1, January 1989, 334–7.
19 Chalmers and Paliwala, *An Introduction to the Law in Papua New Guinea*, 17.
20 Thoolen, *Indonesia and the Rule of Law*, 33. On Dutch efforts to codify adat law, see Bisschop, 'Adat Law in Indonesia'.
21 The origins of this court are discussed in Gillen, 'The Malayan Rulers' Loss of Immunity'.
22 *Indochina Chronology*, April–June 1993, 7.
23 Chief Justice Geoffrey Martin was President of the Tongan Court of Appeals in 1995. Other judges appointed to the court were Sir Clinton Roper, of the Privy Council Court, Justice Trevor Morling of the Federal Court of Australia, and Justice Frederick Cooke, Chief Justice of Vanuatu. In September 1995 Mr Nigel Kenneth Hampton OBE, QC, of Christchurch, NZ, replaced Mr Justice Gordon Ward as Chief Justice of the Supreme Court of Tonga.
24 For example, Emergency (Supreme Courts Act Amendment) Order 1995.
25 Efate, Tanna, Malekula, Ambrym, Sheppard, Banks and Torres, and Santo. The chief clerk has a role in uniting the island courts, works with the chief registrar and the chief justice to unify solutions. Although there are never sufficient funds to bring the administrators and justices of island courts to the capital for meetings or training, lay justices get a sitting allowance and receive training in situ. In the instance of Ambrym Island court, established in October 1988, the Islands Court Act 10 of 1983 delimits the courts' criminal jurisdiction to: (a) offences under the penal code; (b) offences against the Joint Regulations; and (c) offences against Ambrym regional laws. In its civil jurisdiction, the court is limited to: disputes concerning ownership of land irrespective of value of the land; claims in tort and contract to Vatu 50,000; civil claims under Ambrym regional laws to Vatu 50,000; and applications for maintenance made under Joint Maintenance of Children Regulation 13 of 1966.
26 Translation from Undang-undang Dasar Republik Indonesia, C.V. Amin, Surabaya, 1978.
27 Subekti, *Law in Indonesia*, 34.
28 *Far Eastern Economic Review*, 26 November 1992, 21.
29 Constitutional arts. 111–13.

30 The committee made six constitutional rulings. In two, it held statutory provisions in question unconstitutional (1952 honsim 1, 9 Sept. 1952 decision; 1952 honsim 2, 9 Sept. 1952 decision). Two rulings out of the remaining four are equally significant in that, although the committee avoided holding statutory provisions in question outright unconstitutional, it thwarted the executive government's real intention by resorting to a narrow interpretation so as to have them accord with what the constitution said (1953 honsim 2, 8 Oct. 1953 decision; 1954 honsim 1, 26 Mar. 1954 decision). The Constitutional Committee Decisions are reported in Taebopwon haengjong panraejip (Administrative Law Case Reports of the Supreme Court), vol. 1 (1952–57), ed. by Omunkak; Chusok hankuk panraejip (Annotated Case Reports of Korea), ed. by Law Research Institute, Seoul National University.

31 Following the 1991 coup, New Aspiration Party leader Chavalit attempted to sue coup leader Suchinda, but the court ruled that there were no grounds, as the coup was effective. The court thus indicated that it will not review the legality of change in government if the transfer of power is effective. But my informant Jaran emphasised that this case was limited, and does not imply that the court will act similarly in future but will be ready to consider each case. If, for example, coup leaders are toppled before making a decree granting amnesty, the courts may have the opportunity to find against them on certain applications. For a comparative note on the efficacy of political as opposed to judicial machinery for the enforcement of the constitution, see Cappelletti, 'The Expanding Role of Judicial Review in Modern Societies'.

32 *Nation*, 22 September 1992. It has been suggested that at least 50 of some 500 decrees issued by past military juntas are outdated, or in conflict with existing laws: 'Scrap Obsolete Decrees, Says Justice Official', *Nation*, 14 February 1993. This is not the first reference to the problem: in 1986 the Juridical Council was reviewing 'outdated revolutionary decrees': *Bangkok Post*, 15 February 1985. In 1989 Bovornwak Uwanno recommended the establishment of a commission to review outdated legislation: *Bangkok Post*, 22 April 1989. On this occasion the Prime Minister's Office Minister, Meechai Ruchupan, suggested this work be carried out by the Judicial Commission. Current limitations of the legal system as applied to environmental protection are outlined in Charoenpanij, 'The Thai Legal System'.

33 Chapter 10 (ss. 200–210) of the 1991 Constitution.

34 Sections 205[1], 205[2], 207. The tribunal, as established by ch. 10, s. 202 of the 1974 Constitution, was empowered (s. 213) to decide in cases of disputes on the jurisdiction of the Court of Justice and any other court, and disputes between other courts.

35 Matthew Grainger, 'King's Advisor Bemoans Lack of Constitution Council', *Phnom Penh Post*, 6–8 October 1995. First Prime Minister Prince Norodom Ranariddh called for reform: 'Reform the Judiciary', *Cambodia Times*, 22–28 October 1995.

36 Section 4(1) of Republic Act No. 6734, 1 August 1989, Organic Act for the Autonomous Region in Muslim Mindanao.

37 *Far Eastern Economic Review*, 7 December 1995, 26, 30; 'Up Tempo', *Far Eastern Economic Review*, 18 May 1995; Romano, 'The Open Wound'.

38 Thana Poopat, 'Disorder in the Courts', *Nation*, 13 November 1994; Vitit Muntarbhorn, 'Birth Pains of an Administrative Court', *Nation*, 16 November 1994.
39 Bunnag and Aakesson, 'The Legal System of Thailand', 340.19.
40 Art. 124(2): 'Every Judge of the Supreme Court shall be appointed by the President by warrant under his hand and Seal after consultation with such of the Judges of the Supreme Court and of the High Courts in the States as the President may deem necessary for the purpose and shall hold office until he attains the age of sixty-five years'.
41 *Economist*, 16 October 1993. Some High Court judges were transferred and others were not confirmed as permanent after having been appointed additional judges. This circular and transfers were challenged in public interest litigations and ultimately the matter was pronounced upon by a Seven-Judge Bench in the case (*S.P. Gupta v. Union of India* (1982) 2 SCR 365), a decision which stood until overturned in 1993.
42 *SCAORA (Supreme Court Advocates on Record Association) v. Union of India*, Lawasia Comparative Constitutional Law Newsletter, 1:7, December 1993.
43 *Kathmandu Post*, 6 February 1994.
44 Lev, 'Judicial Authority and the Struggle for an Indonesian Rechtsstaat'. The articles relevant to judicial appointments are: The conditions to be appointed and dismissed as a judge and the procedures of appointment and dismissal are regulated by statute (art. 30); Judges are appointed and dismissed by the head of state (art. 31); Matters concerning rank, salary and extra allowance of judges are regulated by special regulation (art. 32).
45 The 1974 Constitution stated: 'The King appoints and removes judges. Before taking office for the first time, a judge is required to make a solemn declaration before the King with the words to be prescribed by the Judicial Commission' (s. 208); 'The appointment and the removal from office of a judge of a Court of Justice must be approved by the Judicial Commission under the law on judicial service before they are tendered to the King' (s. 209); 'The promotion, increase of salaries and punishment of judges of the Courts of Justice must be approved by the Judicial Commission under the law on judicial services'.
46 Previous constitutions configured the JSC only slightly differently. Under the 1974 Constitution (s. 210), it comprised: the Chief Justice of the Supreme Court as chairman, three judicial officials as commissioners ex officio as provided by the law on judicial service, and eight qualified commissioners to be selected by judicial officials, four of whom to be selected from judicial officials and the other four from retired judges receiving gratuities or pensions who do not hold any political position and are not senators, members of the House of Representatives, or advocates. The positions of judicial officials who have the right to be selected as qualified judicial commissioners and the selection of qualified judicial commissioners shall be in accordance with the law on judicial service. The 1978 Constitution, having referred to the functions of the Judicial Services Commission in ss. 75 and 76, was silent as to its composition.
47 In Fiji, for example, foreign judges were commissioned to serve on the bench of the Supreme Court's November 1995 session: 'Supreme Court Session Dates Set', *Fiji Times*, 16 September 1995. In Kiribati, British

lawyers appointed to judicial posts included Richard Lussick as chief justice, Brian Suttill as chief registrar, and Amanda Ford as magistrate trainer: 'New Judiciary Named by Kiribati Government', *Pacific Magazine*, July–August 1995, 12.
48 For example, Peter T. Hoffman, a professor at University of Nebraska's Clinical Law Program, was appointed an associate justice, thus filling Palau's Supreme Court: *Pacific Magazine*, November–December 1993, 58.
49 'Vanuatu Threatens Australian Lawyer with Legal Action', *Fiji Times*, 23 June 1996. Kent implied that, in making his decisions, the chief justice was mindful of the fact that he was receiving a salary of US$300,000 per year: *Solomon Star* 23 June 1995.
50 Country Report: Western Samoa, PILOM, Port Vila, 1995.
51 'MP Pursues Special Court of Appeal Hearing', *Solomon Star*, 27 October 1995.
52 In accordance with the constitution and s. 35(1) of the Courts Regulation No. 30 of 1980. For instance, in 1988 President Ati George Sokomanu appointed then Chief Justice of the Solomon Islands, Gordon Ward, and Justice Louis Cazandres, as acting judges of the Supreme Court of Vanuatu for a period of one month.
53 For example, on 19 December 1990 the editor of the *Samoa Times*, Leota Uelese Petaia, had his conviction for contempt of court overturned. Petaia had printed an editorial on 26 January 1990 critical of a case in which then Acting Chief Justice and Attorney-General Tiavaasue Falefatu Sapolu presided over a murder trial for which the judge's sister, who was a partner in the private law firm Sapolu and Co. of which the judge was principal, was acting as defence counsel. At a fifteen-minute hearing on 1 February 1990, the judge had found the editor to be in contempt of court. A three-member court of appeal (comprising Niue's Chief Justice John Dillion, Tonga's Chief Justice Geoffrey Martin and New Zealand District Court Judge Finton Latham) held that the articles did not bring the judicial process into disrepute, nor were they likely to diminish public confidence in the judicial system.
54 In 1992 eight western Pacific judges formed the Pacific Judicial Council to facilitate co-ordination between Micronesian judicial systems. The forum elected Guam Superior Court Presiding Judge Alberto C. Lamorana III as president. Others elected were Palau Chief Justice Mamoru Makamura, Commonwealth of the Northern Mariana Islands Judge Jose dela Cruz, and Pohnpei Judge Edwel Santos. Other judges in the organisation came from the Marshall Islands, Yap, Chuuk and Kosrae: *Pacific Magazine*, March–April 1992, 52.
55 In November 1991 Maj. Gen. Attasit Sittisunthorn, chair of the Juridical Council, suggested he was ultimately influential.
56 Lev, 'Judicial Authority'; Lev, 'The Politics of Judicial Development'; Lev, 'Judicial Institutions and Legal Culture in Indonesia'.
57 Oda, 'The Procuracy and the Regular Courts as Enforcers'.
58 Cai, 'Constitutional Supervision and Interpretation'; Ren Jainxin, 'The All-Round Growth of People Courts'.
59 Brody, *The Harassment and Persecution of Judges and Lawyers*.

60 On 4 August 1991 the Supreme Court dismissed an appeal by Lini to have a congress of the Vanua'aku Party scheduled to be held in Mele ruled illegal. In August 1992 the chief justice ruled unconstitutional a proposed business law, giving the finance minister power to grant or revoke business licences without fear of a court challenge. He was yet to consider whether he or the president had the power to remove the offending clause, or whether it had to be referred back to parliament.
61 'Outside the court, jubilant opposition supporters honked their car horns as opposition leader Willie Jimmy predicted his group would now be able to topple the government': BBC Summary of World Broadcasts, Thursday 5 September 1996.
62 The Beijing Statement indicated a consolidation of support for standards concerning judicial independence, appointment, tenure, jurisdiction, relationship with executive, and states of emergency. It is reproduced as 'Independence of the Judiciary' in *Australian Bar Review* 15 (1996–97).

9   The suspension of constitutional power

In recent decades, a significant number of states in the Asia–Pacific region have imposed 'extraordinary security laws in times of crisis'.[1] In some instances, emergency powers[2] have been used to meet a crisis, then revoked when the crisis is over. In other instances, however, the crisis is over-extended or frequent use of emergency powers has provoked concern. By definition, reliance on 'emergency powers' implies suspension of normal constitutional processes, including legal protections of individual rights. The latter, in turn, often involves extended powers of arrest and interrogation to deal with terrorism and other forms of politically motivated behaviour and restrictions on freedom of movement, thought, belief, and other civil and political rights. *Habeas corpus*, judicial review of government action, and the normal operation of the legislature are usually suspended. The regular courts may be restricted in operation or suspended as well, in favour of the use of military or other special courts for the prosecution of what would otherwise be regarded as civil and criminal cases.

Such extensive divergence from the normal rule of law points up the paradoxical nature of emergency rule. Emergency powers theoretically are conferred for the sole purpose of protecting and preserving the constitution in times of crisis. The rights and freedoms which constitutionalism is considered to protect are suppressed under conditions of emergency. The paradox can be resolved by restricting emergency rule to the powers necessary to preserve the existence and well-being of the state, however that is identified.[3] It follows that emergency rule need not be co-terminous with regime change, or prolonged martial rule:[4] emergency powers properly used preserve rather than shatter the democratic and constitutional framework. Since emergency powers derive from the constitution, it can be argued that they are not unlimited: they are used to suspend or otherwise override other constitutional provisions, but are not intended permanently to nullify them.

Recent experience in a wide number of states suggests, however, that return to normality is not easy and has prompted studies of how states of emergency are declared, monitored and ended. Thus, the International Law Association examined the characteristics of states of emergency, the relationship between emergency powers and the protection of the individual, and the scope of non-derogable rights and freedoms. This led, in 1984, to its 'Paris Minimum Standards of Rights Norms in a State of Emergency'.[5] The International Commission of Jurists (ICJ) has also monitored the impact of states of emergency on human rights, reporting its conclusions at length in 1983.[6] The reasons for the concern of these bodies are obvious. Whereas the effective use of emergency powers seeks to preserve the state and to restore its effective functioning, their illegitimate exercise strikes at the heart of constitutionalism and democracy and is destructive of all facets of a state's social, political and economic life.

In a 1994 study, Fitzpatrick identified two *de jure* forms of emergency, and no less than four *de facto* forms of legal arrangements implied by the terms 'emergency powers' and 'state of emergency'.[7] Where genuine emergencies exist, *de jure* emergency rule may be invoked through a formal declaration (a 'good' *de jure* emergency). Alternatively, a *de facto* state of emergency may be established through the use of law without any such formal declaration. Where, on the other hand, no real state of emergency exists, authorities may for some reason formally declare a state of emergency (a so-called 'bad' *de jure* emergency). Alternatively, in these circumstances emergency rule may be established *de facto* where emergency powers are exercised without a formal declaration in 'ambiguous or potential' emergency conditions, emergency powers are institutionalised after an emergency has ceased to exist, or permanent laws place extreme restrictions on human rights and democratic constitutional processes in the absence of any particular emergency at all, which Fitzpatrick describes as 'ordinary repression'. Fitzpatrick's study suggests that states now possess a sophisticated array of legal devices that can potentially cloak human rights abuses in the guises of constitutionalism and the rule of law.[8]

Despite Philips' view that, ultimately, emergency powers are 'elastic concepts' which make attempts to define them 'futile',[9] definitions of emergency powers cannot be avoided, if only because the operation of important constitutional provisions depends on an emergency being claimed or framed. Emergency powers may be defined in constitutions, case law, or statutes. Their varied evolution in countries throughout the region is the result of differing approaches to constitutional amendment, judicial activism, and the effectiveness of legislatures. In some states, constitutionalism has been taken less seriously, and the protection of individual rights has been evidently less important than the unity and solidarity of the system as a whole.

In practice, there is considerable variation in the extent to which constitutions define an 'emergency'. Broadly speaking, there are four sources of emergency conditions: natural disasters (earthquake, flood, famine, fire),[10] economic circumstances, civil unrest, and external aggression represented, usually, by war. Chowdhury categorises these under three headings: serious political crises, *force majeure*, and particular economic circumstances.[11] By contrast, Soluta refers to 'securing public safety, the defence of the nation, the maintenance of public order and efficient prosecution of any war in which the government may be engaged, [and] maintaining supplies and services essential to public welfare'.[12]

In the Asia–Pacific region, numerous independence constitutions were drafted in circumstances of national assertion against colonial rule. In some countries, such as Indonesia, there was little time for constitutional elaboration prior to the declaration of independence. Elsewhere, these constitutions were drafted in the face of communist insurgency, communalism, separatism, and conflict with neighbours. India, for instance, faced separatist movements in Kashmir, Hyderabad and Junagarh, and conflict with neighbouring Pakistan. These circumstances inevitably influenced the nature and scope of emergency rule for which the constitutions provided.[13]

South Asia

The Indian Constitution distinguishes between emergencies caused by war, external aggression or internal disturbance (National Emergency, art. 352); the failure of constitutional machinery in a state or states (State Emergency, art. 356); and financial crises (Financial Emergency, art. 360). It also distinguishes between all-India and part-India declarations of emergency (art. 352.1). Following the restoration of normalcy after an emergency period in 1977, the parliament amended the constitution so that a state of emergency could only be proclaimed for reasons of 'war, external aggression or armed rebellion',[14] and so that the protections of life and liberty in article 21 could not be suspended during a state of emergency.[15] In 1988, however, in the face of deteriorating political conditions in the Punjab, the fifty-ninth amendment authorised proclamation of an emergency 'if the integrity of the country is threatened by internal disturbance in any part of the territory of India', and once more allowed suspension of art. 21.

The concept of emergency in the 1962 Constitution of Pakistan was similarly extensive. Article 232(1) refers to 'grave emergency . . . in which the security of Pakistan, or any part thereof, is threatened by war or external aggression, or by internal disturbance beyond the power of a Provincial Government to control'. Article 235(1) refers to 'a situation . . . whereby the economic life, financial stability or credit of Pakistan, or any part thereof, is threatened'. In the event, Pakistan has experienced considerable economic and political instability which has not only tested such provisions but also resulted in the overthrow of several constitutions and regimes.

Since coming into existence in 1972, the state of Bangladesh may be said to have developed and even refined a 'martial law culture'. The country had experienced political instability during the period it formed the province of East Pakistan.[16] The new constitution of 1972 and later amendments defined states of emergency and provided familiar constitutional safeguards. In particular, under art. 141a(1) an emergency could be declared to exist when 'the security or economic life of Bangladesh, or any part thereof, is threatened by war or external aggression or internal disturbance'. The proclamation had to be put to parliament, and expired after 120 days unless approved by a resolution of parliament. The Constitution (Second Amendment) Act 1973 added safeguards concerning arrest and detention and the establishment of procedures for the proclamation of an emergency to part IXA of the new constitution. When the proclamation of emergency was in operation, provision was made for the suspension of fundamental rights.

Although states of emergency existed in 1974–79,[17] 1981,[18] and 1982–90, a number of legal processes continued. Amendments were made to the constitution;[19] parliament continued to meet, albeit with limited powers; rules and regulations took the form of presidential decrees, rather than laws emerging from a legislature; and elections were held. During this period, the constitution was suspended and the Supreme Court deprived of all jurisdiction over the protection of fundamental rights made under the authority of martial law (although the courts continued to function, subject to the provisions of proclamations, orders and other instruments).

Sri Lanka's constitutional chapter XVIII, concerning 'Public Security', refers to the power to make 'emergency regulations' (art. 155(2)) but does not define 'emergency'.

Southeast Asia

The struggle to define a viable legal order in Burma began with independence in 1948 and remains unfinished. When Premier U Nu resigned in September 1958 and General Ne Win formed an interim non-political cabinet, a 'constitutional coup d'etat' took place. Elections were held in 1960 but a political crisis continued. In 1961 Ne Win dissolved the parliament and established a Revolutionary Council. Ne Win himself was invested with full legislative, judicial and executive power. The Supreme Court and high courts were abolished in March 1962, and in 1966–67 the parliamentary system was disbanded in favour of Workers Councils. With the approval of a new constitution by referendum in 1973, the Burmese Socialist Programme Party became the 'only political party leading the state'. Constitutional arts. 76–78 provide for emergency rule 'if an emergency affecting the defence and security of the State should arise'.[20] The 1974 Constitution operated until the Tatmadaw (Armed Forces) responded to civil unrest in 1988 by establishing the 21-member State Law and Order Restoration Council (SLORC). Although multi-party democracy general elections were held in 1990, SLORC refused to accept the results and retained power.

Malayan independence was achieved in 1957 in the face of opposition from communist insurgents, providing the principal cause of the state of emergency from 1948 to 1960. Consequently, part XI of the Malayan Constitution (1957) provided 'Special powers against subversion, organised violence, and acts and crimes prejudicial to the public and emergency powers'. Specific procedures for legislation against subversion, proclamations of emergency, and restrictions on preventive detention have been issued subsequently on several occasions, not necessarily related to the original source of danger.[21] Article 149(1) specified six grounds on which 'Special Acts of Parliament' can be lawful despite inconsistency with other constitutional provisions. Article 150(1) refers to 'a grave emergency . . . whereby the security, or the economic life, or public order in the Federation or any part thereof is threatened'.

Article 12 of Indonesia's 1945 Constitution states: 'The President declares the state of emergency. The conditions governing, and the consequences of the state of emergency shall be prescribed by statute.'[22] Article 22 grants the president the right to issue government regulations in lieu of statutes during periods of emergency, which must 'obtain the consent of the Dewan Perwakilan Rakyat [parliament] in its next session'. If such consent is not obtained, the government regulation shall be revoked. This provision gives the president, nonetheless, authority with the force of law for up to a year before parliamentary ratification is obtained. Following a seven-year period of liberal but unstable democracy during 1950–57, President Soekarno used these powers to suspend the 1950 Constitution and established instead 'Guided Democracy'.[23]

Coups, counter-coups, and periods of martial law have been an integral part of Thailand's constitutional history.[24] Article 172 of the 1990 Constitution allows the king to issue an Emergency Decree 'for the purpose of maintaining national or public safety or national economic security or averting of public calamity'. On 23 February 1991, the National Peace-Keeping Council (NPKC) took over the administration of the country with the objective of strengthening democratic processes through a revised constitution.[25] The take-over was peaceful and widely endorsed by the people and the media. The NPKC promulgated a provisional constitution and selected Anand Panyarachun to head a civilian interim government until general elections were held in 1992.

The Philippines' independence constitution in 1935, drafted under North American influence, provided for the suspension of *habeas corpus* and the declaration of martial law 'in case of invasion, insurrection, or rebellion or imminent danger thereof'. As is well known, that country was governed under martial law by President Ferdinand Marcos during 1972–84. Presidential Proclamation No. 1081 of 21 September 1972 committed 50 per cent of the Armed Forces to 'suppress rebellion and insurrection': 'the rebellion and armed action undertaken by these lawless elements of the communist and other armed aggrupations organized to overthrow the Republic of the Philippines by armed violence and force have assumed the magnitude of an actual state of war against our people and Republic of Philippines'.[26] In the post-Marcos era, the 1987 Constitution refers to 'lawless violence, invasion or rebellion' and gives the president, as commander in chief, powers for the suppression of lawless violence, for suspension of the writ of *habeas corpus*, and for declaration of martial law (art. VII, 18).

East Asia

From its foundation in 1949 to the promulgation of its first constitution in 1954, the People's Republic of China was under martial law. Articles 67 and 89 of the 1982 Constitution referred to martial law without defining the circumstances in which it might be invoked. In contrast, the Constitution (1948) of Taiwan, a state that emerged in the shadow of communist victory on the mainland, and greatly affected the path of constitutional development on the island,[27] included an appendix regarding 'Temporary provisions effective during the period of Communist rebellion' which referred to 'emergency measures to avert an imminent danger to the security of the State or of the people or to cope with any serious financial or economic crisis'.[28]

Article 76 of the Constitution of South Korea refers to conditions under which the president may make 'urgent measures for the maintenance of national security or public peace and order, and there is no time to await the convocation of the National Assembly'.²⁹ Article 77(1) allows the president to proclaim martial law 'when it is required to cope with a military necessity or to maintain the public safety and order by mobilization of the military forces in time of war, armed conflict or similar emergency', while art. 77(2) distinguishes between extraordinary and precautionary types of martial law ('Under extraordinary martial law, special measures may be taken with respect to the necessity for warrants, freedom of speech, the press, assembly and association, or the powers of the Executive and the Judiciary as prescribed by law').³⁰ Ironically, martial law was not declared during the Korean war (1950–53), but since then has been 'regularly enforced to facilitate passage of laws of a kind which would normally pose problems, if placed before the National Assembly or the public under ordinary circumstances'.³¹

Pacific Islands

Our final grouping of countries comes from the Pacific Islands. Part X of the Papua New Guinea Constitution provides for 'Emergency Powers'. An emergency can be a military or natural disaster, or 'action taken, or immediately threatened, by any person that is of such a nature and on so extensive a scale, as to be likely to endanger the public safety or to deprive the community of any substantial portion of the community of supplies or services essential to life'. An emergency is either national or provincial and is declared by the National Executive Council (NEC) (art. 228). It is revoked either by the NEC or the parliament (art. 229). Emergency regulations – laws made on advice of the NEC – must be forwarded immediately to the Speaker and to an emergency committee. They expire in twenty-eight days unless extended by parliament (art. 231). Emergency laws can alter all existing laws except constitutional laws (art. 233).³²

An Organic Law on Provincial Government (1976) allows for the suspension of provincial governments during states of emergency, which are sometimes prompted by 'tribal fighting', particularly in the Highlands provinces.³³ They can also be suspended for other reasons, including corruption and gross mismanagement. In 1989 a state of emergency was declared in North Solomons Province, where the self-styled Bougainville Revolutionary Army had succeeded in closing down the Panguna copper mine.

The execution of the first military coup in the Pacific Islands by Col. Rabuka in Fiji in 1987 provides an interesting illustration in the (non) use of emergency provisions, as little effort seems to have been made by the governor-general to protect the constitution by declaring a state of emergency.³⁴ Following an initial period of military rule, an interim civilian government was appointed in December 1987. Instruments issued under this regime included decrees to restore basic human rights and fundamental freedoms, and to create a High Court, a Fiji Court of Appeal, and a final appellate court known as the Supreme Court of Fiji. A new constitution, in 1990, provides that the military answer to the commander of the military forces, rather than to the government, and that it be responsible 'to ensure at all times the security, defence and the well being of Fiji and its peoples'.³⁵ Drawing on the Malaysian Constitution, art. 162(1) specifies five grounds on which 'Special Acts of Parliament' can be lawful despite inconsistency with the provisions of ch. II.³⁶ Section 163 now provides for the use of emergency powers in the event of a threat to Fiji's security or economic life.

The Solomon Islands Constitution provides (s. 16) for two types of emergency, depending on whether the country is at war or facing some other 'public emergency'. In Tuvalu, an emergency includes war or any circumstances deemed by the head of state to be an emergency. In Vanuatu, an emergency may be war, a natural calamity, or a threat to public order. In Western Samoa, an emergency exists if the security or economic life of either the whole or part of the country is threatened, 'whether by war, external aggression, internal disturbance, or natural catastrophe'. The constitutions of the Marshall Islands, Mariana Islands, Federated States of Micronesia, and Palau carry similarly phrased provisions.³⁷ The Tongan Constitution does not define what constitutes an emergency but allows the sovereign in council to make regulations 'for securing the public safety, the defence of the Kingdom, the maintenance of public order and for the maintaining of supplies and services essential to the life of the community'. In 2000, states of emergency were enacted in the Solomon Islands, in relation to an anti-Malaitan uprising on Guadalcanal, and in Fiji, following a 'civil coup' agitating for the interests of indigenous Fijians that removed the Chaudhury government and President Ratu Sir Kamisese Mara.

Characteristics and use of emergency powers

Declaring a state of emergency

Important questions have arisen concerning who holds the power to invoke emergency powers, and the processes by which this decision is made. Most regional constitutions confer the power on the head of state. Effectively, this means that the power rests with executive government, whether the head of state is also head of the government or is a non-executive, titular head, acting on advice. The principal focus of interest therefore concerns the requirement for checks and balances through the involvement of cabinet more widely, the legislature, or the courts. By way of illustration, in Bangladesh, it depended initially on the satisfaction of the president: after extensive use of emergency powers, however, a new sentence required the 'prior counter signature' of the prime minister as well (art. 141a(1)).

The Constitution of India refers to the satisfaction of the president as well and requires a decision of the Union cabinet in writing (art. 352). In recent years 'President's Rule' has been declared in Sikkim (1984), the Union Territory of Pondicherry (1983), Punjab (1987), Tamil Nadu (1988), Nagaland (1988), and Karnataka (1971, 1977 and 1989). In Pakistan, also, the decision rests with the president (art. 232). In South Korea, the president is to 'promptly notify the National Assembly and obtain its approval' (art. 76). In Malaysia, the decision is formally taken by the Yang Di-Pertuan Agong (the king), in accordance with art. 150, and is expressly non-justiciable (art. 142, 8a). In the Philippines, the president can declare a state of emergency for a period of up to sixty days. However, such a declaration must be presented within forty-eight hours to Congress for approval, and it cannot suspend the constitution or supplant the functioning of the civil courts and legislative assemblies. In the People's Republic of China, the Standing Committee of the National People's Congress decides on the 'enforcement of martial law throughout the country or in particular provinces, autonomous regions or municipalities directly under the central government' (art. 67(20)), while the State Council decides on the 'enforcement of martial law in parts of provinces, autonomous regions and municipalities directly under the central government' (art. 89(16)).

Pacific Island constitutions exhibit a range of provisions concerning the declaration of emergencies. Under Fiji's 1990 Constitution, emergencies were proclaimed by the president 'if satisfied' (art. 163), and the parliament was to be summoned. States of emergency are also declared by the president in Vanuatu, on the advice of the Council of Ministers, and in the Marshall Islands (if not already declared by the cabinet). In Tonga, an emergency is declared by the prime minister on the advice of the police minister, or 'a Governor to whom authority is delegated'; in Tuvalu, by the head of state acting on the advice of the prime minister; and in Western Samoa, by the head of state, following consultation with cabinet.

A number of regional constitutions state that an emergency may be 'imminent' rather than 'real': Malaysia (art. 150(2)), Bangladesh (art. 141a), and India (art. 352). The degree to which the state is under threat from 'imminent' danger is hard to assess: in the Philippines, Marcos declared a state of emergency while 'Congress was in session, the Supreme Court and inferior courts were open, the Constitutional Convention was in session, and none of the provincial governments was under Communist control'.[38]

Duration of an emergency

A survey of constitutional provisions specifying the duration of emergencies shows great similarity across jurisdictions. In Fiji, an initial state of emergency lasts for six months unless approved by parliament (art. 163). In this event, it may be renewed an indefinite number of times, for periods of up to six months each (art. 163). In Malaysia, an emergency can be declared for an initial period of six months. Requests for its extension 'shall be laid before both Houses' (art. 140). In Bangladesh, emergency orders are to be laid before parliament 'as soon as may be'; states of emergency last initially for 120 days and can be extended with the approval of parliament (art. 141a). Emergency proclamations also must be laid before parliament, as must presidential orders that suspend fundamental rights.

In India, emergencies last for one month unless approved by a resolution of both houses of parliament, which authorises them for up to six months (art. 352). Article 356 allows for the extension of a declaration of a state of emergency for a period beyond the expiration of one year from the date of issuance if the Election Commission certifies that it is necessary 'on account of difficulty in holding general elections'. The same article allows the president to assume the powers of government or to give them to the legislature of the state, or to suspend the constitution, but not to take the powers of the court. If the president is to take legislative powers, he or she is to do so only with the approval of the parliament (art. 357).

In Pakistan, emergencies last initially for two months, unless approved by the National Assembly. They are to be placed before a joint sitting of parliament within thirty days of their proclamation; proclamations may last four months if parliament is currently dissolved (art. 323). Extensions can be obtained through parliamentary approval. In South Korea, an emergency ceases immediately if it is not approved by the National Assembly (art. 76).

In the Pacific Island states, emergencies may be declared for initial periods from three days in Tuvalu (or fourteen days if parliament is not sitting) to six months in Fiji. In the Marshall Islands, the initial period is ten days if the Nitijela is in session, and thirty-one days if it is not; in Samoa, the first declaration may last up to thirty days.

Most constitutions, this suggests, specify the period for which a state of emergency exists following its initial proclamation. They also generally specify the review procedures to be followed in order to legitimate a continued use of the power. In application, however, there have been notable instances in the region in which emergency conditions have been retained for considerable periods of time. Martial law in Taiwan lasted from 20 May 1949 to 15 July 1987.[39] The Philippines remained under martial law between 1972 and 1981. Reference has already been made to the extended periods of martial law in Pakistan and Bangladesh. A state of emergency declared in Malaysia in 1964, at the time of 'confrontation' with Indonesia, has not been expressly revoked. A state of emergency imposed in Burma on 3 August 1988 likewise remains in force.

Review of emergency powers

Whereas many of the provisions noted above suggest that a number of constitutions in the region provide for review of the use of emergency powers, the reality is that, on more occasions than not, those invoking such powers act so as to minimise the availability of such review mechanisms. In consequence, there are few controls on the declaration of emergency powers and virtually no protection for constitutional and human rights once declared. Furthermore, where those in authority have abused their power under emergency conditions, the process of restoring full democracy has proven to be lengthy.

Article 150 of the Malaysian Constitution was invoked five times between 1963 and 1977.[40] Despite this frequency, a degree of uncertainty exists as to whether a state of emergency is proclaimed by the head of state on his or her own judgement, or only on the advice of the prime minister.[41] Furthermore, the pretexts for the use of emergency powers sometimes includes intra-elite conflict (that is, conflict among political leaders, as distinguished from conflict between mass followers of political parties). In 1966, for instance, a state of emergency was declared in Sarawak by the federal government after the High Court upheld a petition by the state's chief minister who believed he had been wrongfully dismissed by the governor. To the Filipino jurist Fernando, this constituted the use of emergency powers to meet a constitutional impasse. To another commentator, it exemplified an executive giving in to the 'irresistible' temptation of using emergency powers to 'validate unconstitutional action'.[42]

A similar source of instability has provoked the use of emergency powers in Pakistan, where a constitution adopted in March 1956 remained in force only until late 1958.[43] 'Far from containing the main points of conflict or retailing a system of checks and balances,' argues Ayasha, 'the constitutional framework was a veritable time bomb with the fuse box in the custody of the president. The powers of the president far exceeded those normally bestowed upon a ceremonial head of state in a parliamentary system.'[44] According to Bhargava, the 'Ayoub' constitution that followed 'provided no checks and few balances'.[45] Since 'economic instability and internal disturbances attracting the exercise of emergency powers under Art. 191' were everyday occurrences, the president could at any time intervene in provincial affairs, disrupt the political process and take charge of the entire administration, with the exception of the high courts.[46] This helps to explain why emergency powers were relied on six times between 1947 and 1977.[47]

Revocation of states of emergency

Constitutionally, the revocation of states of emergency is generally a simple procedure: they either expire or are revoked by the head of state. In Malaysia, a state of emergency may be repealed, or will cease to have effect 'if annulled by resolution of both Houses' (art. 149(2)). In Bangladesh, they are terminated by a subsequent proclamation (art. 141A (2a)) or '30 days after parliament meets without having approved the proclamation' (art. 141A (2c)). If the South Korean National Assembly requests the president to remove a state of emergency, the president must comply (art. 77(5)).

While some declarations of states of emergency end with the cessation of the threat, a greater number continue longer than the time during which a threat can be perceived. The continued use of emergency powers in such circumstances provides a multiple dilemma. First, it becomes difficult to determine which laws are in force, since the condition of a state of emergency generally suppresses the operation of a number of other laws, mostly concerning fundamental and democratic rights. Second, the continued imposition of emergency conditions impacts on the constitutional life of the nation.

In addition to difficulties that may arise in determining the legality of orders made during periods of emergency, confusion of laws can result when emergency powers are repealed if 'unconstitutional' laws and orders made during the emergency remain in force. A case in point arose in Malaysia in 1976 in *Teh Cheng Poh v. Public Prosecutor,* in which the appellant Teh Cheng Poh had been charged with possessing a revolver and ammunition in a security area. A central issue concerned the king's purported action in 1975 under the Emergency (Essential Powers) Ordinance 1969 to make the 1975 Regulations which provided for special procedures in trials for security offences.[48] The 'special procedures' applying to security areas included the absence of a jury. Poh was found guilty and sentenced to death. An appeal to the Federal Court was dismissed and an appeal to the Privy Council also failed.

A related concern when periods of martial law are terminated concerns the status of the principal actors in martial law regimes. Those who wield emergency powers are frequently reluctant to come under the law, lest their actions during the period of emergency or martial law result in their prosecution. This leads to the adoption of immunity or amnesty clauses during transition back to constitutional authority. The Fourth Schedule of the Constitution of Bangladesh, for instance, prevents legal action being taken against martial law administration.

Some current issues

The role of the courts

By convention, the decision that conditions exist which necessitate the invoking of emergency powers has been non-justiciable. Judicial review may continue under emergency conditions, however, in matters relating to due process, *ultra vires*, and other civil and criminal matters. What has also occurred, however, and what has caused concern, has been the suspension of judicial processes during periods of emergency beyond what is required and to the detriment of the people, who are denied access to justice. Another cause for concern has been the fragility of courts which have, in some instances, privileged 'constitutional authoritarianism' over due process and the rule of law – supposedly in the name of preserving authority and the state.[49]

The use of emergency powers generally implies a reduction in court powers.[50] Fundamental human rights usually cannot be enforced through the courts, nor can the constitutionality of emergency laws be tested. The very existence of a 'state of emergency' cannot be tested, as this is likely to be held to be a 'political judgement' on which the executive, rather than the courts, can pass judgement. A challenge to the suspension of the writ of *habeas corpus* in the Philippines in 1951, for example, failed when the Supreme Court ruled that only the president had the authority to determine whether an emergency existed.[51] There have been a number of challenges to emergency powers in Malaysia, none of which seem to have been successful. In earlier times the Privy Council declined to find that the government in any way acted in bad faith or *ultra vires*.[52]

There are thus several factors that have contributed to the ineffectiveness of courts in monitoring or moderating emergency power. Consistent with Kelsen's theory of effective power, courts have generally supported the *de facto* regime, rather than rule any regime change 'unconstitutional'. Even where no regime change has occurred, courts have traditionally refused to rule on the appropriateness of invocation of emergency powers, as this is viewed as a political rather than a legal judgement.[53] The 'roll-call of emergency cases', at least in the British Commonwealth, according to Edward Philips, displays a 'sad conformity of judicial passivity and a reluctance to uphold the very constitution they have been sworn to protect. Neither has the Privy Council, in the increasingly rare situations where it is still the final court of appeal, supplied the tenacity lacking in Commonwealth jurisdictions.'[54]

Where courts have not been suspended or otherwise removed by emergency regimes, they remain empowered to determine cases on the basis of the law as it has been argued before them. Where emergency powers are expressed in the constitution, and where the wording allows for wide interpretation of such words as 'emergency', courts have little room to move. Only in cases where gaps exist in the laws, or where executive action is beyond power, can courts control the use of emergency provisions.

Reference to developments in Pakistan offers an example of judicial resistance to encroachment on constitutionalism through the application of emergency powers. Iyer suggests that the courts in Pakistan have resisted the imposition of military government on the state under the guise of legality and the term 'martial law'.[55] Bhargava, similarly, has suggested that in Pakistan 'the judiciary was perhaps the lone upholder of the tradition of independence'.[56] The court's role in defining the scope of emergency powers commenced in 1954. On 24 October 1954 Governor-General Ghulam Mohammad dismissed the constituent assembly. The government he put in place was essentially a 'constitutional dictatorship', a 'cabinet of talents', with Bogra as prime minister. East Bengali President Maulvi Tamizuddin Kahn challenged the governor-general's action in the Sind High Court. This was also a test of judicial independence.

On 9 February 1955 the Sind High Court upheld Tamizuddin's appeal, ruling that the governor-general had 'no power of any kind to dissolve the constituent assembly', nor appoint a cabinet without reference to the people's representatives. The government appealed, knowing that Chief Justice Mohammad Munir favoured the centre. On 21 March the High Court's ruling was overturned by the Federal Court, which ruled that the court had no jurisdiction to issue a writ in Tamizuddin's favour:

> The federal court did not . . . consider whether the governor-general had rightly dissolved the constituent assembly; it merely overruled the court's decision on the grounds that section 223a under which it had heard the appeal did not have the Governor-General's assent and was, therefore, not part of the law.
> . . . After the federal court's verdict, Pakistan was not only without a parliament but as many as forty-six acts had lost their legal sanction . . . within a week of the federal court's decision, the governor-general had issued the emergency powers ordinance IX, declared a 'state of grave emergency' throughout Pakistan, and placed a blanket prohibition on all proceedings against the central government in connection with the dismissal of the first constituent assembly. The ordinance empowered him to frame a constitution, to convert west Pakistan into a single unit of administration, to validate thirty-five of the forty-six laws passed by the constituent assembly but for which his assent had not been sought, to pass the central budget and, finally, to rename the eastern wing 'east Pakistan'.

However, the governor-general's actions lost him support and led to calls for more democracy. On 13 April 1955 the Federal Court ruled that in the absence of a constituent assembly, the governor-general could not validate laws retrospectively. It followed that the section of the emergency ordinance giving him such powers was *ultra vires*.[57]

Elsewhere in the region there have been instances where courts have positively supported emergency measures. When Soekarno, citing growing rebellion in outer regions, dissolved Indonesia's constituent assembly using martial law powers,[58] his chief justice suggested that Soekarno's actions followed an unwritten legal principle, which allowed deviation from existing procedures 'in cases of extreme emergency threatening the very existence of the state'.[59]

It has been argued that part of the reason that Marcos was able to declare martial law in the Philippines with relative ease was that the courts had shown a readiness to admit the existence of the necessary conditions.[60] Having accepted the existence of genuine emergency conditions, the Supreme Court was subsequently emasculated by the provisions of the 1973 Constitution.[61] Commentators on constitutionalism in the Philippines recognised the necessity for the doctrine of martial law but asked questions about the conditions under which necessity required their use.[62] The courts continued to function under martial law but could not be called on by those held in administrative detention. General Order No. 3 allowed the judiciary to 'try and decide in accordance with existing laws all criminal and civil cases', except 'those involving the validity, legality or constitutionality of any decree, order or acts issued, promulgated or performed' by the president or by his representatives and 'those involving the validity, legality or constitutionality of any rules, orders or acts issued, promulgated or performed by public servants pursuant to decrees, orders, rules and regulations issued and promulgated' by the president.[63]

At first the Supreme Court 'asserted jurisdiction to entertain challenges to government actions alleged to be in violation of the constitution and unduly restrictive of the people's sacred rights'.[64] The courts entertained numerous writs of *habeas corpus* and required the military 'to explain the detention of some people' shortly after promulgation of General Order No. 3. The president submitted initially to the court's jurisdiction, but later suspended the writ of *habeas corpus* from 1971 to 1972.[65] His 'New Society' was established under the 1973 Constitution, during which the courts were emasculated and no longer presented a threat to executive power.

In January 1973 Marcos submitted the constitution approved by the Constitutional Convention to the public in a plebiscite. He called this 'Filipino style grass-roots democracy':

Referendum voting was by *viva voce* or acclamation in citizen assembly meetings, not by secret voting supervised by the Commission on Elections. The 1973 constitution was proclaimed ratified by the president on the basis of a report that 95 percent of the voters had favoured it. Marcos also declared that the interim National Assembly would not be convened and that martial law would continue for an unstated period.[66]

This action was contested in *Planas v. Comelec* by petitioners who claimed that the power to submit a new constitution lay with Congress, and that 'there was no proper submission of the proposed Constitution to the people for lack of time and the absence of freedom of speech, press and assembly'.[67] The court, however, upheld the new constitution, giving the president the crucial 'cloak of legality'.[68]

During the period of martial law in the Philippines, reports of human rights violations surged. A 1983 report from the International Commission of Jurists questioned the 'astonishing argument' put forward by the Philippines Supreme Court for the continued detention of prisoners under Presidential Order 2045.[69] A three-member ICJ mission to the Philippines in 1984 found evidence of continuing and increased militarism, arbitrary arrests and torture, and other legal limitations and restrictions on human rights.[70]

A further example comes from India. A state of emergency proclaimed by Indian Prime Minister Indira Gandhi for reasons of 'internal disturbances' in 1975 lasted until 1977. When suspension of art. 21 of the constitution, protecting *habeas corpus*, was challenged in the Supreme Court of India,[71] the court upheld its validity: 'article 21 shall remain suspended during the entire period of the state of emergency and no writ petition could be filed to challenge the legality of any detention orders or other orders'.[72] Through this decision, some argued, the 'rule of law became a casualty'.[73] Das argued that the courts did not have the power to question the validity of emergency power proclamations.[74]

De facto emergency rule

In some cases, *de facto* emergency rule exists or has existed where, in the absence of specifically named legal conditions, or in the absence of constitutional language and practice, the directives of the government have the same consequences for the people, the state and the operation of law, as *de jure* emergency rule in constitutional states. Such states have articulated powers similar to emergency powers, without giving them this name: the indication of the presence of such similar powers, and their use, is in the impact on the functioning of state organs, and on individuals and society.

Anti-subversion laws, or internal security laws, as opposed to emergency powers, may be used at any time and generally grant the executive extraordinary powers, while not suspending the constitutional rights of all members of society. Such has been the case in Singapore and Taiwan.[75] Since the lifting of martial law in Taiwan in 1987, civilians can no longer be tried in military courts, but under the National Security Law judgements or sentences passed by military courts during martial law cannot be appealed or challenged in civilian courts, and other laws enacted during martial law remain in force.

In Malaysia, an Internal Security Act allows arrest and detention without trial for up to two years, while an Emergency (Essential Powers) Ordinance allows *in camera* trials, anonymous witnesses, and presumption of guilt rather than innocence. A Constitution (Amendment) Act 1971 restricts discussion of ethnically sensitive topics in the media. In October 1987 Prime Minister Dr Mahathir interned 106 people under the Internal Security Act, stating that the move was necessary to pre-empt a recurrence of the 1969 'race riots'. At approximately the same time, a group of elder statesmen, judges and academics called for the bringing of hereditary rulers within the power of the law, for changes in procedures for holding general elections, and for restrictions on the prime minister's power to declare a state of emergency. The following year the prime minister removed from office the Lord President of the Supreme Court and two of five Supreme Court judges.

When Marcos lifted martial law in the Philippines in 1981, he wielded the equivalent of martial law powers through Presidential Order No. 2045, which renewed martial law 'in all but name'.[76] In examining this 'Constitutional Authoritarianism', Payoyo suggests that the strong executive style was dependent on a 'whole philosophy of government' which negates the philosophy of constitutionalism.[77]

Future directions

The role of international covenants and international law

The experience of Asia–Pacific states with emergency powers prompts questions about how such powers can be regulated so as to ensure they are not misused. Other regions – Africa, Europe and America – have formalised a charter of rights, although compliance is variable in practice. The states in the Asia–Pacific region have not taken this step, and by not establishing some form of regional human rights declaration, treaty or obligations are denying their peoples the protections for basic freedoms which are gradually emerging elsewhere.[78]

In one view, states in the Asia–Pacific region have been reluctant to expose themselves to obligations internationally from which they cannot withdraw without condemnation. To cite one example, by effectively restoring the emergency powers of the executive held in India before 1977, the Indian Constitution violates India's obligations under the International Covenant on Civil and Political Rights, art. 4 of which says that:

In time of public emergency which threatens the life of the nation and the existence of which is officially proclaimed, the States Parties to the present Covenant may take measures derogating from their obligations under the present Covenant to the extent strictly required by the exigencies of the situation, provided that such measures are not inconsistent with their other obligations under international law and do not involve discrimination solely on the ground of race, colour, sex, language, religion or social origin.[79]

The question as to whether derogation of responsibilities under international agreements is also involved in a derogation of domestically derived constitutional rights is contested. The International Law Association would limit the conflict through non-derogable standards, such that: 'No state party shall, even in time of an emergency threatening the life of the nation, derogate inter-alia from the Covenant's guarantees of the right to life, and freedom from torture, or other cruel, inhuman or degrading treatment or punishment'.[80]

In fact, the use of emergency powers does not require abrogation of the constitution, dissolution of parliament, dismissal of the courts, in addition to the suspension of fundamental rights and freedoms – although on occasion all of these steps have been taken. A growing body of opinion accepts that 'a minimum floor of fair trial' exists under international instruments in regard to emergency situations.[81]

Emergency powers and constitutionalism: some proposals

There is a clear need for fundamental reassessment of the construction, monitoring and use of emergency powers by states in the Asia–Pacific region. Constitutional provisions intended for use on those rare occasions on which the life of the state is imperilled have too frequently become the legal cloak for arbitrary use of power and for the suppression of fundamental rights. If constitutional use of emergency powers occurs where the executive 'can demonstrate in the legislature and in the courts that these powers are both absolutely necessary and that existing powers are inadequate',[82] states' constitutions should include comprehensive and secure mechanisms providing for consultation in the decision-making processes that lead to the initial declaration of a state of emergency.

From this review of emergency powers as they have operated in the Asia–Pacific region, it is evident that a number of steps can be taken towards minimising their misuse. Some of these have been noted above. In summary, constitutional provisions defining the scope of emergency powers are most appropriate where they include:
- a clear definition of what is intended by the term 'emergency';
- a declaration of an emergency that follows deliberation between the highest state organs and to the smallest extent necessary through the conclusion of any single person, including the head of state;
- clear parameters to the initial period for which emergency conditions may apply; and the period of renewals;
- limits to emergency powers so that other organs of government, such as parliament and the courts, may not be suspended, or may only be suspended in accordance with stringent and specified regulations;
- limits to emergency powers, such that limits to the fundamental rights of individuals are minimised;

- clear guidelines for monitoring the use of emergency powers, and authority to lift their use as soon as possible; and
- provisions ensuring that powers lapse totally and automatically after a specific period, rather than provisions that require their express revocation.

Whereas traditional thinking concerning the doctrine of emergency powers suggests that the executive should be left free to determine the steps to be taken to protect the constitution and to secure the life and security of the state and its people, experience suggests that – the declaration of a state of emergency notwithstanding – executive action should continue to be accountable to some degree, whether to the people's representatives or to the highest courts. To construct emergency power as 'access to unlimited power' is to invite the attention of those who covet such power. Rarely has an authority in command of such power returned it freely to the people, by whom it was originally entrusted.

In addition to the retention of some domestic capacity to monitor and review the use of emergency powers, it is also desirable for international monitoring capacity to be strengthened. In some way, mechanisms must be developed which assist those in authority to distinguish between crises which threaten the life of the state, and crises of a more political nature, which simply threaten the life of a particular government. Inability to make this distinction has provided opportunity to imperilled governments and regimes to sustain unpopular rule through recourse to emergency provisions.

Although emergency powers are articulated in domestic constitutions, the security and stability of states is of more than purely domestic concern, for instability in one nation affects the stability of its neighbours and its region. The question of emergencies, therefore, is not of singularly national concern and interest. At some point, the relationship between emergency power and national sovereignty will require investigation. As national sovereignty diminishes, the expectation that nations will solve state-threatening crises without international support is similarly decreasing. Put another way, some elements of the emergency may have an international origin, whether political, economic or environmental in nature, and thus require a corresponding international solution. To bracket emergencies in purely national terms is becoming anachronistic. Support for international norms establishing the extent of derogations from major international treaties and covenants is thus to be encouraged.

Notes

1. Fitzpatrick, *Human Rights in Crisis*, 6.
2. Defined by Philips as 'those extraordinary powers permitted to government to deal with threats to the nation that cannot adequately be met with ordinary powers': Philips, 'Drastic Solutions', 59.
3. Cf. the Philippines: 'The word "emergency" as used in Sec. 26. Art. VI of the Constitution means a temporary emergency, or it cannot be said to be an emergency', *Araneta v. Dinglasan*, 84, Phil 376.
4. Strictly speaking, emergency rule implies the acquisition of extraordinary powers by a civilian government, whereas martial law implies the suspension of civilian government for a period of rule by military rather than civilian leaders. Either may be authorised by the constitutional and legal framework, as the examples of Indonesia, Thailand, Pakistan and Burma show.
5. See Chowdhury, *The Rule of Law in a State of Emergency*.
6. International Commission of Jurists, *States of Emergency*. This 480-page report examined states of emergency in twenty countries, including India, Malaysia and Thailand, and generated forty-four recommendations for national and international measures that can be taken to ensure better respect for human rights during emergencies.
7. Fitzpatrick, *Human Rights in Crisis*.
8. Cf. Pakistan in the 1950s where Ayasha suggests that 'the civil bureaucracy and the army high command' maintained a 'facade of constitutionalism for what in effect was a bureaucratic coup d'etat underwritten by the military high command': Ayasha, *The State of Martial Rule*, 197. Similarly, Peiris refers to the 'veneer of constitutional normality' in the Philippines under Marcos: Peiris, 'Judicial Activism and Civil Disorder', 156.
9. Philips, 'Drastic Solutions'.
10. An instance of emergency powers being declared in the region due to natural disaster occurred in Papua New Guinea in September 1994, in relation to East New Britain Province, following the eruption of Mt Tavurvur.
11. Chowdhury, *The Rule of Law*.
12. Soluta, 'On the Alternative Approach', 485.
13. Das points out that the traumatic times during which the constitution was written are reflected in the emergency power provisions of Part XVIII, and especially arts. 360, 356: Das, 'Emergency Provisions'.
14. The amendment substituted for 'internal disturbance' under the previous art. 352(1).
15. (1988) 40 *ICJ Review*, 4. Article 21 states that 'no person shall be deprived of his life or personal liberty, except according to procedure established by law'.
16. See Ayasha, *The State of Martial Rule*, 275.
17. A state of emergency was proclaimed by President Muhammadullah on 28 December 1974. Proclaimed to meet the state's immediate needs, the emergency continued as a legal condition until 1979.
18. A state of emergency was proclaimed at the end of May 1981, when President Zia was assassinated. Acting President Justice Abdus Sattar

invoked clause 1 of const. art. 141a to proclaim the emergency. Events of this period are summarised in 'Human Rights in the World: Bangladesh', (1983) 30 *ICJ Review*, 4–6.
19 The Constitution (Fourth Amendment) Act 1975 adopted a presidential form of government in Bangladesh. At other times, however, the constitution was amended by decree rather than legislation. For example, the Proclamation (Amendment) Order 1977 amended the preamble and articles of the constitution relating to fundamental principles of state policy, foreign policy, and acquisition, nationalisation and requisition of property by the state, and citizenship.
20 Art. 76 of the 1974 Constitution states: 'The Council of State may declare a state of emergency and promulgate martial law in specified areas or in the entire State, if an emergency affecting the defense and security of the State should arise. It may order mobilization in certain areas or in the entire State. Such measures shall be submitted for approval to the nearest session of the Pyithu Hluttaw [People's Assembly].'
21 See Jayakumar, 'Emergency Powers in Malaysia: Development of the Law 1957–1977'.
22 Indonesia called on its emergency powers several times soon after independence. With the formation of the Republic of the United States of Indonesia (RUSI) in December 1949 came calls for the abolition of some Dutch-created states, and calls by other legislative councils (East Java, Madua, Central Java, and East Kalimantan) for incorporation in the republic. On 8 March 1950 the cabinet enacted an emergency law sanctioning the voluntary union of one state or territory with another. By 4 April 1950 only four separate entities continued to exist outside RUSI. A revolt in the state of East Indonesia was quickly suppressed, and a newly installed leadership there sought incorporation in RUSI.
23 Soekarno, in a speech entitled 'Saving the Republic of the Proclamation' (1957), excerpted in Feith and Castles, *Indonesian Political Thinking*, 84.
24 See Nuechterlein, 'Thailand', 121; Hickling, 'The Thai Constitution of 1974'.
25 Led by General Sundhorn Kongsompong, then Supreme Commander of the Royal Thai Armed Forces,
26 Cited in Escobido, 'Judicial Review and National Emergency', 474.
27 See Chiu, 'Constitutional Development'.
28 This phrase has been reinstated in toto in provisions for emergency powers added to the constitution (art. 7) in 1991.
29 Art. 76(1) refers to 'internal turmoil, external menace, natural calamity or a grave financial or economic crisis', and art. 76(2) refers to 'major hostilities affecting national security'.
30 Art. 77(3).
31 Yoon, *Law and Political Authority in South Korea*, 73.
32 The Constitution of Papua New Guinea seems to provide for the use of additional powers in at least two other circumstances. Art. 204 allows the governor-general, on the advice of the NEC, to 'call out' the military 'to provide assistance to the civilian authorities'. This power was exercised in March 1991, in conjunction with the Curfew Act 1987, in response to growing concern at the level of crime in Port Moresby. Second, in a society where

'tribal fighting' still occurs, provincial executives can declare parts of a province 'fighting zones'.
33 For example, states of emergency were declared in the provinces of Eastern Highlands, Western Highlands, Southern Highlands, Simbu and Enga in 1980. See Gordon and Meggitt, *Law and Order in the New Guinea Highlands*.
34 Ghai and Cottrell, *Heads of State in the Pacific*, esp. ch. 5.
35 See Ghai, 'A Coup by Another Name?'.
36 These grounds are activities which are held: to cause, or to cause a substantial number of citizens to fear, organised violence against persons or property; to excite disaffection against the president or the government; to promote feelings of ill-will and hostility between different races or other classes of the population likely to cause violence; to procure the alteration, otherwise than by lawful means, of anything by law established; or which is prejudicial to the security of Fiji.
37 President Jacob Nena declared a state of emergency throughout the Federated States of Micronesia in February 1998 because of severe drought, attributed to the El Niño effect. Water shortages were contributing to disease, and there was increasing risk of fires, requiring rapid expenditure of disaster relief funds.
38 Del Carmen, 'Constitutionality and Juridical Politics', 87. See Republic of the Philippines, Constitutional Commission of 1986, *The Constitution of the Republic of the Philippines*, National Book Store, 1986; Bernas, *Dismantling the Dictatorship*.
39 Chiu, 'Constitutional Development', 28; 'Human Rights in the World: Taiwan', (1988) 40 *ICJ Review*, 10–11. Although Taiwan professed a democratic system, a multi-party system was only legalised in March 1989. Parliamentary elections were held in November 1946, and not again until December 1991.
40 At the time of 'confrontation' with Indonesia in 1964; the Emergency (Essential Powers) Act 1964; the 1966 proclamation of emergency for Sarawak; the 1969 state of emergency following post-election race riots which ended in 1971; and the 1977 state of emergency covering Kelantan.
41 Jayakumar, 'Emergency Powers in Malaysia: Can the Yang Di-Pertuan Agong Act in His Personal Discretion and Capacity'.
42 Fernando, *Governmental Powers and Human Rights*, 39; Philips, 'Drastic Solutions', 60.
43 Choudhury, 'Failure of Parliamentary Democracy in Pakistan'.
44 Ayasha, *The State of Martial Rule*, 215.
45 Bhargava, *Pakistan in Crisis*, 81.
46 Ayasha, *The State of Martial Rule*, 218–19.
47 Philips, 'Drastic Solutions', 59.
48 Lee, 'Emergency Powers in Malaysia'.
49 Payayo, 'The Rule of Law and the Decree-Making Power', 173.
50 A related issue concerns the expansion of the jurisdiction of military courts during periods of emergency: see Sming Tailangka, 'The Military Judicial System of Thailand', 157.
51 *Montenegro v. Casaneda* (92 Phil. 882 (1952)), cited in Fernando, *Governmental Powers*, 24.

52 Fernando, *Governmental Powers*, 41–3. See also Iyer, 'Constitutional Law in Pakistan'.
53 Iyer, 'Constitutional Law in Pakistan'.
54 Philips, 'Drastic Solutions', 68–9.
55 Iyer, 'Constitutional Law in Pakistan'.
56 Bhargava, *Pakistan in Crisis*, 71.
57 Ayasha, *The State of Martial Rule*, 203–4, 205.
58 Presidential Decree No. 2 of July 1959.
59 Thoolen, *Indonesia and the Rule of Law*, 54. On this period generally, see Nasution, *The Aspiration for Constitutional Government*.
60 These had been acknowledged, for instance, in *Lansang v. Garcia* 42 SCRA 448 (1971), where the Supreme Court declared: 'We entertain, therefore, no doubts about the existence of a sizeable group of men who have publicly risen in arms to overthrow the government and have thus been and are still engaged in rebellion against the Government of the Philippines'.
61 Art. X required that the judiciary submit a report annually to the legislature, specified that judges continue in office until retirement or 'until otherwise provided by law or decreed by the incumbent President', and pre-empted the court's power to rule on the constitutionality of presidential actions taken prior to the constitution's promulgation: see Del Carmen, 'The Philippine Judicial System'.
62 Escobido, 'Judicial Review and National Emergency', 475; Soluta, 'On the Alternative Approach'.
63 Cited in Escobido, 'Judicial Review', 478.
64 Escobido, 'Judicial Review', 479.
65 Fernando, *Governmental Powers*, 21.
66 Abueva, 'Ideology and Practice in the "New Society"', 38.
67 Escobido, 'Judicial Review', 480.
68 Tiglao, 'The Consolidation of the Dictatorship', 29.
69 *ICJ Review*, 30, 1983, 15–17.
70 *ICJ Review*, 33, December 1984, 21–5.
71 *ADM Jabalpar v. Shirkant Shukla*.
72 *ICJ Review*, 40, 1988, 4.
73 Venugopal, 'Emergency Powers and the Federal Structure', 88.
74 Das, 'Emergency Provisions', citing *Emperor v. Benocrilal*, 72, 57: AIR (1945).
75 *ICJ Review*, 40, 1988, 8–11.
76 *ICJ Review*, 30, 1983, 15–18.
77 Payoyo, 'The Rule of Law', 153.
78 This process of regional standards setting is slow, but ultimately valuable: see Hartman, 'Derogation from Human Rights Treaties'.
79 *ICJ Review*, 40, 1988, 4.
80 *ICJ Review*, 40, 1988, 5.
81 Stavros, 'The Right to a Fair Trial in Emergency Situations', 364.
82 Philips, 'Drastic Solutions', 60.

10 Devolution

All governments devolve some decision-making powers from higher to lower levels of authority. The challenge is determining the extent of the devolution and the methods for co-ordinating devolved delivery of government. A unitary state in which all power is held and exercised at the 'centre' may have a high degree of co-ordination, but risks having too little regard for decision-making at lower levels. Conversely, a system that allows two much devolution of authority and program implementation faces two major risks: unnecessary duplication of activities (e.g. where states make similar laws about similar subjects), and lack of co-ordination, leading to deterioration of the system as a whole. States need not have a formal federal structure in order to achieve decentralisation. A unitary state can decide to devolve responsibilities to regional and local branches of government. On the other hand, the executive can also decide to remove responsibilities from lower levels, and it is this level of uncertainty that formal federal systems seek to avoid. In an ideal federal system, one state will not be legally subordinate to another, and the system as a whole is not centralised.

Although Frenkel suggests that federalism is an organisational principle rather than a legal term that can be given a legal form, such as a federation or confederation,[1] it is generally set out in a formal arrangement, particularly a constitutional arrangement. Federalism can be set out in structures of parliament (for law-making) and courts (for dispute resolution), and federal constitutions will define the powers that remain at 'the centre' and those that devolve to 'the states', as well as defining the remedies to be used when this allocation of powers is unclear or insufficient (the distribution of amending powers). Federal systems often also define powers which may be exercised at both federal and state levels.[2]

If, as is suggested in the theoretical literature, federalism is a good principle to use in plural societies, we might well ask why it is not used more widely in the Asia Pacific, a region that is undoubtedly composed of pluralism. In the Pacific Islands, federalism has been adopted in the Federated States of Micronesia, and discussed by other states. Other states have implemented programs of devolution, including Papua New

Guinea, the Solomon Islands and the Philippines. There are, too, unique arrangements, such as the Special Administrative Region status accorded to Hong Kong and Macau, and the 'Compacts' of free association linking Pacific Island states with the United States of America.

With modern constitutions came many laws aimed at standardising and homogenising societies, including in practices of language and education. Thus the challenge for multi-ethnic societies has been to restructure political and constitutional institutions to better cope with the demands and expectations of their plural societies. Theoretically, federalism allows for compromise, for identity, and for membership in a larger community. Genuine decentralisation, whether through federalism or a system of provincial government, will assist in preventing the centralisation of power. It is obvious, then, that effective decentralisation will only occur where governments have no intent to centralise. Devolution may be administrative or political, or both.

Federalism in Asia

In Asia, federalism characterises the constitutional systems in India and Malaysia, but few other states.[3] In the past, federal systems operated in Indonesia (1949–50) and Burma (1948–62). Singapore was part of Malaysia's federal system during 1963–65. The Special Administrative Regions established for Hong Kong and Macau are in a sense forms of federalism, certainly of devolved power. During 1962–69 Pakistan, which had a nominally federal structure, experienced a highly centralised presidential form of government, and this imposed serious strains on federal–state relations and fuelled the demand for regional autonomy in the eastern wing.

The Republic of Indonesian States was a federation (1949–50) sponsored by the Dutch, which many Indonesians viewed as an effort to 'divide and rule' the states. Thus, its dissolution after nine months in favour of a unitary system was seen as a victory for nationalism over colonialism, and implanted forever the idea that devolution was similar to favouring the break-up of the republic. This was unfortunate because a nation of such size and diversity subsequently endured an extended period of increasingly centralised control.

In the mid-1990s the principles of federalism continued to be discussed in Bangladesh and Burma. The Nepalese parliament also considered a decentralisation bill.[4]

Burma's 1947 Constitution provided for a federal system of government with separate executive, legislative and judicial branches. On 12 February

1947, Gen. Aung San and leaders of Shan, Kachin and Chin groups had signed an agreement that guaranteed 'full autonomy' in internal administration for the frontier areas, and right of secession (although this could not be exercised until ten years after the constitution came into force). In March 1948 the Communist Party of Burma commenced an armed insurgency against the then government, which various minority ethnic groups joined. In 1962 the federal system was dismantled by General Ne Win's coup d'etat and any subsequent efforts to return to a federal system have been actively opposed.

In 1993, for instance, the government was attempting to rename the Shan, Karen, Mon, Astrakhan, Kayah, Chin and Kachin States the 'Kambawza Division', at a time when ethnic minorities seeking a federal structure were resisting the government's efforts to maintain a centralised executive. A Shan lawyer, Shwe Ohn, was sentenced to a year's imprisonment for writing and distributing the guidelines for a federal constitution.[5] Burma's ethnic minority groups met in January 1997 to discuss the autonomy promised them under the agreement signed fifty years previously. Although some groups have made peace with the current authorities, they remain disillusioned with the results of the outcome and maintain contact with the remaining militant organisations.

Malaysia

In 1963 the states that had formed the Federation of Malaya in 1957 joined with the states of Sabah, Sarawak and Singapore to form the independent state of Malaysia. The federal principle was for a strong central government that could hold together states of considerable ethnic diversity which desired considerable regional autonomy. The federation was one between thirteen equal states (nine Malay and four others). Legislative powers were divided into federal, state, and concurrent lists. The federal constitution aimed to preserve the levels of autonomy expected by the pre-existing states.[6]

The legislative authority in Malaysia consists of the Yang di-Pertuan Agong (monarch and head of state), and two Majlis: Dewan Negara (Senate) and Dewan Rakyat (House of Representatives). The Yang di-Pertuan appoints the Senate. The federal government has power to legislate for external affairs, defence, internal security, civil and criminal law, administration of justice, finance, trade, commerce and industry, education, labour, and social security.

Each of the thirteen states has an executive council or cabinet headed by a chief minister (Menteri Besar). The cabinet is collectively responsible to the state legislature. The legislatures are directly elected, although there are still some appointed seats in Sabah, and they mostly meet for brief periods four or five times a year. The states can make laws on matters not reserved for federal parliament or not included in the joint list; that is, they can legislate for Muslim law, land, agriculture and forestry, and local government.

Subjects on the concurrent list, concerning which both the federal and state governments have power to legislate, are social welfare, town and country planning, and public health.[7] The federal government is the main taxing authority and controls the borrowing powers of states, so that, apart from land revenue, states enjoy no significant sources of income.

The special position of Sabah and Sarawak

While the federal constitution has proven resilient, federal–state relations in Malaysia have been turbulent and have reflected tensions existing in the wider Malaysian society. Despite the federal system, the structures of government have come under the strong political control of the dominant United Malays National Organisation (UMNO). The loss of two states, Sabah and Kelantan, to opponents of UMNO in elections in the early 1990s prompted threats of funding retaliation by the central government.[8] Disputes have also occurred between Kuala Lumpur and UMNO-controlled states over the centre's move into previously state-regulated areas. In 1993, in an action which can be interpreted as either enhancement of the accountability of leaders or enhancement of the power of the executive, the Yang di-Pertuan Agong and other members of the Conference of Rulers (Majlis Raja-Raja) lost their privileged positions of immunity from prosecution.[9]

There has been discussion about reviewing the terms under which Sabah agreed to become part of the federation in 1963. Sabah and Sarawak were granted special provisions and safeguards in matters of land law, local government, finances, official language and official religion. In recent years, issues of concern in Sarawak–Kuala Lumpur (federal) relations have included immigration, sharing of oil revenue, development-fund allocations, and tourism. Roads, identity cards and rural amenities come under the federal government, and the government of Sarawak has sought to distance itself from problems in these areas. In 1996 the federal government argued that the '20-point agreement for Sabah' required change because amendments to Sabah's constitution since independence had limited the state's authority over a number of fields. Specifically, the federal government argued for limiting the powers of the chief minister.

Indonesia

Indonesia's 1945 Constitution provides:

The division of the area of Indonesia into large and small regional territories, and their structures of governmental administrations, shall be prescribed by statute, with regard for and in observance of the principle of deliberation in the governmental system of the State, and the traditional rights of a special character in the regional territories.[10]

There are twenty-seven provinces, each administered by a governor.[11] Although provincial legislatures hold elections for governors at provincial level, the minister for home affairs selects the winner from among the top candidates, who is then appointed governor by the president. Provincial governors have a similar power over the appointment of officials elected at district level. There is a three-tier system of elected provincial, regency and village assemblies at local and regional levels.[12]

As Indonesia is a 'unitary state', the autonomy of provinces and minorities is quite limited. A report of the International Commission of Jurists recommended 'that the government of Indonesia accept within the present constitutional boundaries a broader margin of free expression on the question of regional autonomy'.[13]

The status of Aceh within the republic remains problematic. The separation of East Timor from Indonesia in 1999 has fuelled separatist aspirations elsewhere in the republic. On 8 November approximately two million people, half the population of the province, attended a rally organised by the Center for Aceh Referendum (SIRA) at which a 'Declaration for Referendum in Aceh' was read by the head of the Acehnese legislature, M. Yus.

Hong Kong

The entirety of Hong Kong was returned to China as a Special Administrative Region on 1 July 1997, as a result of a process established by the Joint Declaration of 1984 between Britain and China. It was formalised on Britain's part in the Hong Kong Act 1985 and in the Chinese parliament's 1990 Basic Law of Hong Kong. The Declaration, and the Basic Law which now acts as a regional constitution for Hong Kong, are intended to preserve the 'previous capitalist system and way of life'.[14] A Basic Law has also been drafted for Macau, which returned to Chinese sovereignty in December 1999. Chinese authorities hope these arrangements will provide a model for the reintegration of Taiwan.[15]

Sri Lanka

In Sri Lanka, devolution was at the heart of proposals for constitutional reform proposed by the government in 1995 in an effort to end the ongoing ethnic conflict. But debate on draft proposals continued through the remainder of the decade. Some governmental powers had been devolved in 1987 under the Gandhi–Jayawardene Accord. But the devolution of powers through the Provincial Councils Act 42 of 1987 was not successful,[16] and de Silva described the idea of federalism being applied to Sri Lanka as 'facile'.[17]

The devolution proposals advanced by the president on 3 August 1995 sought to divest the central government of a range of powers and to establish a clearer division of powers between the centre and the regions. Specific proposals were:

a) that the Republic of Sri Lanka shall be united and sovereign. It shall be a Union of Regions; b) that the territory of the Republic will consist of regions, the names of which are set out in the first schedule, and its territorial waters;
c) that the legislative power of the People will be exercised by Parliament, Regional Councils and the People at a Referendum to the extent hereinafter provided; and d) that the executive power of the People will be exercised by the President of the Republic acting on the advice of the Prime Minister and the Cabinet of Ministers, and the Governors acting on the advice of the respective Chief Ministers and Regional Boards of Ministers to the extent hereinafter provided.

Article 2, which provides for the unitary character of the state, would be amended and the constitution would instead declare the Republic of Sri Lanka to be a united nation. The state would be redefined as a Union of Regions. Article 76, which accords the status of supreme legislative competence in every sphere to the Parliament of Sri Lanka, would be deleted. Legislative power would be devolved.[18]

The 1995 proposals balanced a demand by Tamil separatists for a Tamil homeland in the north of the island, and the concerns of the Sinhala majority. The Kumaratunga government required the cooperation of the opposition United National Party (UNP) to pass any constitutional reforms.

Regional experts appeared to approve of President Kumaratunga's plan.[19] Following the report of the Moonesinghe Select Committee, the ruling Sri Lanka Freedom Party and the UNP agreed on the 'establishment of two separate units of administration for the Northern and Eastern provinces', and to a scheme of devolution patterned on the Indian Constitution. Constitutional change, however, requires two-thirds majority support in parliament and the people's approval at a referendum. An enlarged Parliamentary Select Committee on Constitutional Change chaired by Justice and Constitutional Affairs Minister and Deputy Finance Minister Prof. G. L. Peiris, and including representatives of all the parliamentary parties, met in March 1996 to finalise its proposals.[20] Despite considerable optimism surrounding the talks, no significant change to Sri Lanka's political crisis occurred by century's end.

Thailand

Thailand is another unitary state in Asia which has implemented a program of devolution. Each of the country's seventy-six provinces (except Bangkok) is governed by a provincial governor, who is appointed by the Interior Ministry and who represents the central government. Provinces are divided into districts, and districts are divided into *tambon* (a group of villages). The heads of the *tambon* and villages, as established in the Pokrong Thontee Act of BE 2457, are popularly elected but are nonetheless accountable to the Interior Ministry and the district offices.[21] Appointed local officials (*kamnan*) and village heads had been part of the traditional process of government since the abolition of absolute monarchy in 1932.

Passage of the 1994 Tambon Council and Tambon Administration Act, in the face of considerable opposition from the *kamnan*, marked the first significant alterations to local-level government since the 1914 Local Administration Act and Coup Announcement No. 326 of 1972 which authorised the formation of sub-district councils nationwide. The councils (Ongkarn Borihan Suan Tambon) comprised both elected and appointed members (the *tambon* and village headmen were elected members of regional government).[22] The 1994 law recognised approximately 6000 *tambon* councils. Those with annual revenues of less than Baht 150,000 retained their status but were transformed from totally government-dependent bodies to full legal entities in their own right, capable of making legal transactions.[23]

The new law empowered *tambon* councils to build and maintain local transit; maintain public places; administer waste disposal; prevent communicable diseases; organise civil defence; promote education, religion and the Thai culture; promote the welfare of women, children, the elderly, and the disabled; protect the environment and manage natural resources; and implement government policy. The councils could find alternative means to generate electricity; construct public meeting places, sports and recreational facilities and public parks; organise farmers and create agricultural co-operatives; promote household manufacturing; promote occupations and create jobs; maintain government property, and generate income from property in the *tambon* administrative organisation.[24]

The 1914 and 1972 laws had recognised the *kamnan* as the ex-officio chair of the *tambon* council and allowed a government-paid teacher to act as secretary. Village headmen and *kamnan* were elected for five-year terms but, once elected, were appointed to *tambon* councils automatically.[25] The 1994 law retained the *kamnan* as council chair but added the position of deputy chair. The law allows for a four-year transitional period, but the amendments were also opposed by officials of the Interior Ministry, who argued that the introduction of elections at local level would lead to calls for the election of provincial governors, whom it presently appoints.

The decentralisation of political and bureaucratic power aimed to reduce the possibilities for high-level corruption by limiting the power of senior officials.[26] Ironically, the opposition to these reforms was led by then Minister for the Interior Chavalit Yongchaiyudh, head of the New Aspiration Party, who, despite the party's membership in the five-member coalition government of the time, argued that changes would disturb the government's traditional methods and reduce the status and privileges of traditional leaders.[27]

Philippines

The Philippines shares some of the features of centralised bureaucratisation present in the Thai system, yet has an even greater need for devolutionary trends. The desire for autonomy has long been expressed by the Cordillera region of Luzon and in the Mindanao region in the south, and some steps have been taken to this end. The Marcos administration made plans in 1979 to establish autonomy zones. Although the Aquino government created the Cordillera Administrative Region in 1987, with a 250-member Cordillera Regional Assembly, the terms of autonomy proved unacceptable to the people subject to it. The Organic Act for the Creation of an Autonomous Cordillera Region was rejected at a 1990 plebiscite in all provinces but Ifugao. The Supreme Court subsequently ruled that Ifugao could not constitute an autonomous region on its own.[28]

Similar difficulties have accompanied efforts to establish an autonomous zone centred on Mindanao. The 1976 Tripoli Agreement granted autonomy to certain provinces[29] and promised Muslims a package of rights to administer their own Shariah courts, schools, colleges and universities, and financial and economic system. The agreement also established a regional legislative assembly and executive council, and a special regional security force. It gave rights to representation and participation in the central government, and guaranteed a reasonable percentage of revenues from mines and minerals.[30] Although these powers were articulated in the Organic Act for the Autonomous Region in Muslim Mindanao, the issue was far from settled, since the eleven provinces affected by the Act disagreed among themselves on its application. Some provisions were immediately appealed to the Supreme Court, and when provinces were asked in a November 1989 plebiscite to approve the Act, only four agreed. By the end of the century the autonomous province was not functioning as anticipated.

Federalism in the Pacific

From the first, the archipelagic basis of Pacific Island societies produced significant cultural diversity. One legacy of colonial rule was the ordering of this diversity under new political authorities, and in accordance with a range of introduced systems of law. The post-colonial states of the Pacific thus seek their identity in the tensions that exist between traditional and introduced systems of law and politics, which are sometimes open to synthesis but just as often resistant to it.

Because such states as Papua New Guinea, the Solomon Islands and Vanuatu in the South Pacific and the Federated States in the North Pacific contain a diversity of cultures and 'Pacific nations', federal arrangements between several states and the central government have been vital to successful state functioning. Nevertheless, such federalism continues to change shape and problems in relations between the state and diverse ethnic aspirations remain. Some 'decentralisation' of government in the Pacific Islands was achieved *de facto* when the colonial powers departed, leaving newly established national governments to build government services on many scattered islands.

Rodman suggests, for example, that Vanuatu is best viewed as 'a weak state with a local people who have responded to the challenges of the colonial and postcolonial era by actively seeking control over their own destiny'.[31] Following passage of the Decentralization and Local Government Regulations Act 1 of 1994, the country's provincial councils were replaced by six local government regions.[32] Although there was some resistance to these amalgamations, the bill was introduced to parliament and passed with little discussion.

Devolution in the Pacific

Forms of devolved power are used more widely in the Pacific than are explicitly federal arrangements. In some cases, devolution clarifies the relationship between a Pacific Island state and a metropolitan power, while elsewhere the devolution focuses on internal governmental arrangements.

French Polynesia

Internal autonomy was granted to the Territory of French Polynesia in 1984. In 1990 the French High Commissioner took control of the territorial budget.[33] The move, however, cast doubt on the degree of autonomy delegated by France to the territorial government. The Act specifies that if the territorial budget is not balanced and, after due notification by the Territorial Audit Chamber, no action is taken by the government to rectify the situation, the high commissioner is empowered to seize control and implement the necessary budgetary measures. A mixture of economic and political considerations influenced the timing of the high commissioner's intervention: reduction of the territory's public finances consequent to the moratorium on nuclear testing announced in April; France's failure to comply with promises on financial transfers; the possibility of financial mismanagement by past and present territorial governments; and political animosity between the territorial government of Gaston Flosse and the French socialist government.

New Caledonia

Although French Overseas Territories were granted the right of representation in the French national assembly in 1948, and Kanaks gained the right to vote in French parliamentary elections in 1951,[34] New Caledonia only became an overseas territory in 1956. The *loi Cadre*

(Framework Law) of 1956 increased local powers through new 'councils of Government' in overseas territories. In 1964 the role of the executive council was reduced to an advisory one and the powers of the elected Assembly were further reduced in 1976 and 1979, virtually placing New Caledonia once more under full French administration.

The Matignon Accord of 1988 established progress indicators in institutional development, training and education, economic development, employment, regional relations, and cultural policy which were to be monitored closely for a decade, in preparation for a referendum. The Noumea Accord, concluded in Paris on 5 May 1998, sets out an agreement between the French government and New Caledonian parties that anticipates a constitutional law for New Caledonia to be enacted by the French parliament, followed by a twenty-year period of 'shared sovereignty' at the end of which New Caledonia will attain 'an international status of full responsibility'. A referendum concerning the final transfer of sovereign powers will be held at a date to be determined by the Territory's Congress.

Papua New Guinea

Papua New Guinea's system of government is unitary, but it has also been described as 'quasi-federal' in the manner of Tanzania.[35] Prior to independence, the Constitutional Planning Committee had advocated political decentralisation along the lines of a federal system, but had had its arguments countered by others and recommended a federal rather than unitary system of government. However, the argument that decentralisation would increase the speed in decision-making and involve the people in processes of development and government was met by fears that local-level political participation might further divide an already fragmented society or even endanger national unity.

Following the collapse of negotiations between Bougainvillean leaders and the central government over future financial policy, the House of Assembly withdrew the provisions regarding federalism from the draft constitution. The House of Assembly approved the constitution in August 1975 and independence was attained in September 1975. Meanwhile, Bougainville declared independence as North Solomons on 1 September. The disputing parties resumed negotiations in January 1976, and one year after independence the first amendment to the constitution introduced a 'decentralised' form of government to appease Bougainville province.[36]

The provisions concerning the number of legislative seats, fiscal arrangements concerning grants and taxation, devolution and delegation of administrative and legislative powers were to be enacted in a later organic law (s. 187b). Some powers were to come from the Organic Law on Provincial Governments, while others were delegated by the national government. The nineteen provincial governments had elected legislatures empowered to pass legislation and to make policy decisions at provincial level.

The Organic Law on Provincial Governments of 1983 identified provincial and concurrent subjects; established certain provincial taxes; stipulated refunds of national government taxes collected from within the province; and established a derivation grant of 1.25 per cent of all export revenue deriving from the province. The law also established conditional and unconditional national government grants. Each provincial assembly elected a premier, who chaired a provincial executive council. Provincial governments had many powers similar to those of state governments in a federal system, but their legislation could be overridden by the national government.

However, few provincial governments had effective capacity to govern, and as the years passed concern grew at their inability to provide services. Not all nineteen provinces were able to establish full financial responsibility. Serious difficulties in the establishment and operation of the system included fiscal, managerial and legal difficulties, and ranged from incompetence to lack of political will and blatant and pervasive corruption. Reports by the auditor-general to parliament in May 1991 indicated that most provincial governments were performing poorly in crucial areas: 'inadequate controls over payment, recording and acquitting of advances, procedural deficiencies relating to payment of accounts, lack of accountability of grants given and inadequate internal controls'. Books of accounts and records were incomplete, notably in Sandaun, Gulf, Central and Fly River provinces.[37]

By 1981 there was a serious breakdown of the provincial government system. Political power had not gone to village people but to regional elites. Elections for provincial assemblies had 'set clan against ancient opponent clans leading to war'. Provincial politicians felt insecure and engaged in wasteful prestige politics and even corruption. They lacked the sophistication to direct public servants with policy. Because of the structure of state power, politicians saw their task as pulling resources to the small group, and not as the people's representative whose task was to consider the common good of the whole electorate or nation.[38]

Inefficiencies were compounded by corruption. Between 1983 and 1991 at least nine provincial governments were suspended, and a parliamentary select committee was appointed to assess: 'the powers and functions of Provincial Governments and their exercise and performance of them; their financial powers; and the effectiveness of the operation of the Provincial Government system'. Subject to the findings of this committee, and to their implementation, the stability of national–provincial government relations should be improved.[39]

The Hesingut report[40] concluded that the provincial government system was absorbing funds unnecessarily and that provincial government elections were not an accurate assessment of popular leadership. It recommended abolition of provincial assembly elections and the reconstitution of provincial assemblies with presidents of local government councils and national MPs from the province. The head of the provincial government would be elected from among the council presidents. Only the governor would receive a salary, and all other members of the assembly would be paid Kina 200 per daily sitting.[41] The intention of the reform was to reduce the cost and improve the effectiveness of provincial government by reducing the number of provincial legislators. Politically, it can be seen as the triumph of national politicians over their provincial counterparts for limited political space in what is, after all, a small polity.

Micah Report on Provincial Government

Following the tabling of the Hesingut report, the Micah Bipartisan Committee on the future of provincial governments was established to decide on its implementation. In the tradition of parliamentary committee inquiries, the committee toured the country to gauge public opinion. In February 1993 the auditor-general described for the committee serious failures in co-ordination and supervision by the Department of Provincial Affairs, Personnel Management, Finance and Planning, and the National Computer Centre. The auditor-general noted that provincial governments remained dependent on the national government for 55 per cent of their annual revenues, and that administration consumed 28 per cent of their annual expenditure. The general thrust of evidence put to the committee was that the provincial government system required streamlining to reduce administrative costs.[42]

The Micah Committee's report, tabled in parliament in August 1993, recommended replacement of provincial governments with small political units ('provincial authorities') comprising all local government representatives, non-government representatives and all national parliament members. Local-level government would be re-established and given constitutionally protected financial and administrative support. The auditor-general would be empowered to audit government bodies at provincial and local level without notice, and a commission for provincial and local legal services would manage, provide and train manpower needs of provincial authorities and local-level governments.

In addition to recommending major changes to the system, the report recommended the establishment of a nine-member constitutional committee to implement and monitor its recommendations. National parliament acted on this, passing the Constitutional Commission Act (1993).

Following adoption of the Micah report by the national parliament, provincial government leaders rejected its main proposals and forced the executive to desist from implementing immediate and drastic change. Leaders of the New Guinea Islands region threatened secession and prepared to hold a referendum in their provinces to determine the people's preferred system of provincial government.[43] Despite such opposition, however, the Organic Law on Provincial Governments and Local-level Governments repealed and replaced the Organic Law on Provincial Governments on 18 July 1995. The changes in the Organic Law required changes in associated legislation.[44]

Bougainville

Whatever improvements were secured by revision of the provincial government system, the issue of the state of Papua New Guinea's relations with North Solomons Province (Bougainville) remained a separate and continuing challenge. We have noted the origins of the problem in the colonial period (see Chapter 1). At independence, the question of Bougainville's position remained unresolved. The neglectful practices of the Australian administration, which allowed missionary organisations to assume all responsibility for social advancement and which contributed little itself towards economic development on the island; the forceful manner in which the administration negotiated the establishment of the copper mine at Panguna; the different notions of land ownership and land use held by the colonial government and the traditional occupants of the mine-site; the lack of dialogue between the administration, the representatives of self-government and Bougainvillean leaders as to the arrangements under which the island was incorporated into the nation-state – these and other reasons fuelled Bougainvillean nationalism and the attempt in 1975 to secede from the newly independent state.[45]

Following the introduction of a devolved system of government through constitutional amendment in 1976, North Solomons Provincial Government was established on 1 September, with its premier directly elected by the people and a provincial assembly granted considerable executive and legislative powers. Although these changes enticed the island to relinquish its quest for independence, little else occurred to ameliorate the other sources of conflict mentioned above. To the contrary, the grievances intensified as the negative effects of the mine – notably environmental degradation, failure to renegotiate royalty payments, and continued occupation of scarce land-holdings – began to outweigh such positive effects as career and education opportunities, enhanced social services, and greater transport and communication facilities.

The operation since 1972 of one of the world's biggest copper mines among the Nasioi people at Panguna aggravated the long-standing desire for independence. A former mine worker began a campaign of sabotage in November 1988 and efforts by the Papua New Guinea Defence Force to solve the problem militarily only exacerbated the problem. In June 1989 the central government declared a state of emergency and the conflicting parties alternated between negotiations and battle throughout the 1990s. The Bougainville Revolutionary Army (BRA) proclaimed independence on 17 May 1990,[46] but also signed the Honiara Declaration in January 1991, agreeing to defer talks on Bougainville's constitutional status and to embark on 'a joint programme of peace, reconciliation and rehabilitation, within the current constitutional framework'.

A constitutional crisis was triggered in 1997 after the state entered a confidential contract with Sandline International to impose a military solution on the secessionist issue. Army Chief General Singirok refused orders to work with the mercenaries hired by the government of Sir Julius Chan. He was sacked, then demanded the resignation of the prime minister, the deputy prime minister and the defence minister. Although the prime minister won a parliamentary vote of confidence, he stepped aside for the duration of an inquiry and his government was defeated at general elections held over two weeks commencing 14 June. Sir Julius lost his seat and Port Moresby Governor Bill Skate was elected prime minister, as head of a coalition government, in July.

A permanent cease-fire was established on Bougainville in April 1998, following accords facilitated in 1997 by New Zealand, the state of Papua New Guinea and Bougainvillean separatists. The issue of the future constitutional status of Bougainville, however, was yet to be addressed.

When the Papua New Guinea parliament failed to pass a law creating a provincial government for Bougainville in December 1998, the three main parties to the peace process – the Bougainville Interim Government, the BRA and the resistance force – decided to proceed the same month with the formation of a reconciliation government. They commenced by establishing the Bougainville People's Congress and convening a constituent assembly. Two hundred representatives adopted the constitution after four days of discussion.[47]

Solomon Islands

In April 1997 the Solomon Islands High Court invalidated the Provincial Government Act, passed by parliament in August 1996. The Act, which had replaced provincial premiers with elected provincial councils in an effort to decrease cost and to improve the efficiency of government services, had been strongly opposed by the larger provinces. During debate on the bill, the Malaita and Guadalcanal provinces had threatened secession if it were passed. It was challenged by Guadalcanal's provincial government. There are nine provincial governments in the Solomon Islands. The three provincial governments in which the Act was in operation were placed under caretaker premiers.

Notes

1 Frenkel, *Federal Theory*.
2 The Constitution of Malaysia, for instance, includes a 'Concurrent List' in its Ninth Schedule: see Part VI Relations between the Federation and the States, Chapter 1 – Distribution of legislative powers.
3 Each Indian state has a legislature comprising a governor and at least one house, and in some cases, two (Bihar, Jammu and Kashmir, Karnataka, Maharashtra and Uttar Pradesh). Schedules to the Indian Constitution allocate different powers to state governors in accordance with the particular circumstances of some state. Thus, in Arunachal Pradesh, the governor has special responsibility for law and order issues (art. 371 H); the Sixth Schedule gives governors discretionary power over the sharing of royalties with district councils of tribal areas in Assam, Meghalaya, Tripura and Mizoram; the Governor of Sikkim has special responsibility for peace and social and economic advancement of different sections of the population; and so on.
4 Abdul Quader, 'On a Framework for Governance', *News from Bangladesh* (daily internet edition), 23 July 1997; Nussara Sawatsawang, 'Minorities Determined To Pursue Autonomy', *Bangkok Post*, 12 February 1997; 'NC Seeks Local Bill from Govt', *Kathmandu Post*, 3 August 1997. The Decentralisation Bill offering autonomy to local bodies failed to get through parliament when the Nepali Congress-led coalition government fell.
5 *Far Eastern Economic Review*, 15 July, 29 July 1993.
6 Ibrahim, 'Malaysia as a Federation'.
7 Shafruddin, 'The Constitution and the Federal Idea'.
8 The detention of Sabah Foundation executive director Datuk Jeffrey Kitingan under the Internal Security laws on 13 May 1991 occurred in the context of a deterioration of state–federal relations dating to Parti Bersatu Sabah's rise to power in Sabah in 1985: *Far Eastern Economic Review*, 23 May 1991.

9 Faruqi, 'The Sceptre, the Sword and the Constitution'.
10 Chapter VI 'Local Government' (art. 18). This article is elaborated in the Basic Law on Autonomous Regions (No. 1/1957, LN No. 6/1957).
11 Twenty-four provinces (*propinsi-propinsi*, singular = *propinsi*), 2 special regions* (*daerah-daerah istimewa*, singular = *daerah istimewa*), and 1 special capital city district** (*daerah khusus ibukota*): Aceh*, Bali, Bengkulu, Irian Jaya, Jakarta Raya**, Jambi, Jawa Barat, Jawa Tengah, Jawa Timur, Kalimantan Barat, Kalimantan Selatan, Kalimantan Tengah, Kalimantan Timur, Lampung, Maluku, Nusa Tenggara Barat, Nusa Tenggara Timur, Riau, Sulawesi Selatan, Sulawesi Tengah, Sulawesi Tenggara, Sulawesi Utara, Sumatera Barat, Sumatera Selatan, Sumatera Utara, Timor Timur, Yogyakarta*.
12 The provinces are divided into 246 districts, each under a district head, and 55 municipalities, each headed by a mayor. The districts are further divided into sub-districts, each headed by a *camat*.
13 Cited in Thoolen, *Indonesia and the Rule of Law* , 29.
14 Art. 5: 'The socialist system and policies shall not be practised in the Hong Kong Special Administrative Region, and the previous capitalist system and way of life shall remain unchanged for 50 years'.
15 People have migrated from the mainland to Taiwan since the sixteenth century. When the Communist Party took power on the mainland in 1949, the nationalist Kuomintang consolidated their authority on Taiwan and established a system of government. The status of Taiwan has been disputed ever since, by the mainland which regards Taiwan as part of China, by the Taiwan independence movement, and by a declining nationalist movement that has anticipated for five decades reclaiming control over mainland China.
16 Edrisinha, *Provincial Councils and Local Government*.
17 de Silva, *An Appraisal of the Federal Alternative for Sri Lanka*.
18 'Government's Proposals for the Devolution of Power to Regions', *Sunday Observer*, 28 January 1996.
19 See, for example, Jayadeva Uyangoda, 'A Bold Step in Sri Lanka', *Hindu*, 17 August 1995.
20 Amal Jayasinghe, 'President, Ranil Agreed on Need To Expedite Constitutional Reforms, *Sunday Observer*, 27 February 1996.
21 Likhit Dhiravegin, 'Bureaucracy vs Democracy', *Thailand Times*, 16 November 1994.
22 The *tambon* and village headmen could retain their posts on the Ongkarn Borihan Suan Tambon by resigning and standing in elections.
23 Prakobpong Panapool, 'Inauspicious Bill Finally Sees the Light of Day', *Nation*, 13 November 1994.
24 Prakarn Sanubol and Amornrat Monkholchart, 'Rural Folk Poised for a Fresh Start', *Nation*, 20 November 1994.
25 *Bangkok Post*, 20 November 1994.
26 Likhit Dhiravegin, 'Bureaucracy vs Democracy', *Thailand Times*, 16 November 1994.
27 *Nation*, 24 November 1994.
28 *Pacific News Bulletin*, February 1994.
29 Basilan, Sulu, Tawi-Tawi, Maguindanao, Sultan Kudarat, Zamboanga del Sur, Z. del Norte, North Cotabato, Davao del sur, South Cotabato, and Palawan.

Devolution   239

30 Basman et al., *Autonomy for Muslim Mindanao*.
31 Rodman, 'The Law of the State and the State of the Law in Vanuatu', 56.
32 TAFEA – Tanna, Anatom, Futuna, Erromango and Aniwa; SHEFA – Efate, Shephards Islands and Epi; MALAMPA – Malekula, Ambrym and Paama; PENAMA – Pentecost, Ambae and Maewo; SANMA – Santo and Malo; and TORBA – Torres and Banks Is.
33 Under art. 77 of the Statutory Law of 6 September 1984 (modified by the law of 12 July 1990).
34 A 1952 decree established a single electorate with five districts (*arrondissements*). The Territory's *caldoche* (French settlers) had campaigned for separate electorates. In 1964 a system of proportional representation was introduced, to end the electoral dominance of the pro-Kanak political party, Caledonian Union.
35 General Constitutional Commission, Final Report 1983, 105.
36 Constitutional Amendment No. 1 of 1976 (s. 187a).
37 *Post Courier*, 10 May 1991.
38 Standish, 'Power to the People?'.
39 The provincial system of government has been subject to considerable analysis: Axline, 'Financial Foundations'; Axline, *Decentralisation and Development Policy*; Ghai and Regan, 'The Constitutional Arrangements'; Ghai and Regan, *The Law, Politics and Administration*; May and Regan, *Political Decentralization*; Regan, 'Papua New Guinea (c) National–Provincial Relations'.
40 The parliamentary select committee was chaired by Finschhafen MP Henu Hesingut.
41 With four proposed sittings, each of fourteen days, the committee calculated a saving of Kina 8.8 million over what is currently spent on provincial governments. The media of the time included considerable coverage of alleged over-spending at provincial level: for example, that in the first six months of 1991 Eastern Highlands Provincial Government spent Kina 500,000 on internal travel (accusation by Lufa MP Jerry Kavori, *Post Courier*, 12 September 1991); that MPs in Morobe province were calling meetings even when there was insufficient work to justify the sitting, so that they could claim sitting allowances, accommodation, airfares and other incidental allowances (*Post Courier*, 12 September 1991); that the Provincial Affairs Department, which administers the Law on Provincial Governments, lacked the legal authority to question provincial governments about their investment of public funds (a claim put by Dept. Sect. Kepas Watangia to the Parliamentary Accounts Committee, *Post Courier*, 18 October 1991). In May 1991 serious allegations were made about over-expenditures on transport, public utilities, travel and accommodation by members of the Southern Highlands Provincial Government; in June, reports of non-payment of Kina 500,000 for road and building contracts were evidence that that government was facing financial difficulties (*Times of Papua New Guinea*, 6 June 1991).
42 *Times of Papua New Guinea*, 18 February 1993.
43 *Times of Papua New Guinea*, 19 August and 2, 9, 16 September 1993. Opposition from the Islands region and their threats to secede altered the extent of the government's reform program: *Pacific Magazine*, January–February 1995.

44 The Organic Law on National and Local-level Government Elections (No. 3 of 1997), which commenced on 9 April 1997, repealed and replaced the Organic Law on National Elections and the Electoral Regulations 1977 and also amended the Organic Law on Provincial Governments and Local-level Governments. The principal purpose of these amendments was to allow for two separate elections to be conducted in 1997.
45 The strength of the Australian government's resolve to proceed with the copper mine is described in the official history of Australia's administration of Papua New Guinea: Downs, *The Australian Trusteeship*.
46 With Francis Ona as head of state, Sam Kauona as minister for defence, and former North Solomons Premier Joseph Kabui as minister for justice. Other members of the North Solomons Provincial Government have similarly revealed their alignment with the BRA. Former academic Lembias Magasu became foreign minister, and former provincial planner Bernard Simiha joined a ten-member committee to design a permanent political structure for an independent Bougainville. The secessionists propose having an elected president presiding over a two-house assembly, and replacing civil courts with village elders.
47 Phillip Kepson, 'Bougainville Adopts Reconciliation Government Charter', *National*, 28 December 1998.

Conclusion: Postmodernity and constitutionalism

This study has suggested that contemporary states in the Asia Pacific have been shaped by history, colonial experience and the struggle for independence, and that they gained independence in forms determined by and acceptable to the metropolitan powers. The first written constitutions of the region were in fact responses to the threat of colonialism and to a desire for 'modernity'.

The 'modern' constitutions of these states have regarded law as a tool for regulating the use of public power, prescribing the rights and duties of their citizens, establishing order and conformity, and managing progress. While they contemplate constitutional amendments, they also generally proclaim the nation-state to be the most highly evolved embodiment of the people's sovereignty. Paradoxically, while most independence constitutions claim to be 'autochthonous',[1] they were invariably influenced by the constitutions and the legal systems of their colonial masters.[2]

A majority of states in the Asia Pacific can thus be regarded as 'post-colonial' in that their constitutional values and practices were either copied from colonial authorities or established in reaction to them. They favour, as a consequence, access to the state by elites, whether as representatives or as beneficiaries. 'The language of the law' is not that of 'the people'.

At the same time, these modern formal systems of law and political authority often intertwined with pre-existing rules of custom. Western systems based on majoritarian rule have traditionally been premised on homogeneous societies; studies of plural societies show that the permanent relegation of ethnic groups to the status of electoral minorities leads in time to dissatisfaction with the system. This also raises the question as to whether ethnic communities actually have different, even competing, needs.

The link between law and justice is often expressed as concern for procedural fairness, while that between law and prosperity is described in terms of equity. Societal cohesion is framed by laws delimiting the rights of individuals in relation to the interests of the community, and those of the state.³ Intense debates on the upholding of human rights link the circumstances of particular jurisdictions to the notion of global values;⁴ and the notion of global values raises philosophical questions concerning the role of law as an agent of modernity. Ultimately, a study of constitutional systems is interested in the extent to which they serve the interests, and meet the needs, of the majority of the people who live under them.

There has been debate in recent years as to whether the theory and practice of constitutionalism is global, or culturally specific. The emergence of human rights norms, principally through gradual adherence to the principles established in the United Nations Universal Declaration of Human Rights of 1945, and in two subsequent instruments of international law created in 1966, the International Covenant on Civil and Political Rights and the International Covenant on Economic, Social and Cultural Rights, has led to dialogue between those wishing to see such human rights norms established globally, and those who argue that such rights can only be established in accordance with culturally specific traditions and contemporary conditions. Whereas a strong and vibrant democracy, premised on some notion of 'civil society', is an essential component of the constitutional process,⁵ some Asian countries have proposed an alternative constitutional philosophy premised on the protection of the interests of the community by the state on duties owed to the state by its citizens.⁶ The result is renewed debate on 'Asian' versus 'Western' concepts of individual and community rights.⁷

If rights are viewed as being embedded in 'sets of relationships', they are 'universal' to the extent that the discourse that constructed them embraced everyone who was to be affected by them. There may be universal values, but this does not mean that there need be universal methods for their application. Justice, for instance, is an abstract norm, which may find expression through various means. This study has treated the elements of democratic or constitutional governance as interrelated but flexible points of reference in considering the structure and operation of Asia–Pacific constitutional systems. The application of general or global rules must be supplemented and qualified by reference to the continued operation of customary law, and to modification in the face of differences in approach to problems of governance. Inevitably, there will be differences in practice between societies having profoundly different cultures and histories.

The twentieth-century constitutions thus struggled with a number of recurring questions: Do rigid definitions of ethnic legitimacy, and the discriminatory laws associated with them (such as those defining citizenship), hinder the establishment of a fully democratic state? Is it possible to both retain traditional values and structures and adopt the aspirations of modern constitutionalism and democracy? In chiefly societies, how can the right to free expression be reconciled with respect for the authority of chiefs? In democratic societies, how can the need for freedom of assembly and thought be balanced by the preservation of order? Should chiefly offices retain privileges or become 'accountable to the people'? Democratic systems need not disenfranchise traditional authority, nor need they establish such authority at national level. If chiefly power were exercised at local or regional level, its powers could be de-limited accordingly. A distinction might well be made between *state* political institutions, whose members are *elected*, and *appointed* or hereditary leaders, who, not having been elected by the people, have *consultative status* only.

Asia–Pacific states have addressed the problem of representation in heterogeneous societies by adopting non-majoritarian principles of representation, appointing representatives, for instance, on the basis of function or ethnicity, to represent groups rather than individuals, for the purpose of bringing to the parliament a variety of capacities and expertise not necessarily obtained for it through open electoral contests. While the use of appointment to legislatures does increase the potential for the executive to manipulate the 'representative system', it also ensures systematic as opposed to populist coverage of interest groups.

A corollary of this post-colonial heritage is challenge from the periphery. Which Asian state is not perplexed by struggles for autonomy or independence by peoples at the margins who claim to have never been consulted on their constitutional choices? Continued conflict between India and Pakistan over Kashmir drains the governance resources of both countries. Similarly, while the Dutch fixed the borders of the Netherlands East Indies in relation to British Malaya, and the French defined the borders of Indochina, Vietnam, Laos and Cambodia, questions remain about the sovereignty of border areas and about other areas that had always resisted colonial rule. Independence constitutions have not resolved problems in Indonesia's troubled province of Aceh, nor those of Mindanao in the southern Philippines, or Bougainville on the borders of Papua New Guinea and the Solomon Islands.

Conflicts also remain concerning the methods by which acts of 'self-determination' were conducted. In resolving the status of Dutch New Guinea at the beginning of the 1960s, for instance, the Indonesian government refused UN proposals for universal suffrage, claiming that West Papuans were too ill-educated to vote. The territory was incorporated into Indonesia after a UN-sponsored 'act of free choice', involving just 1026 selected people. On 15 August 1962 the United Nations officiated at the signing of an agreement to transfer the territory to Indonesia on 1 May 1963.[8] While the status of West New Guinea (Irian Jaya) has been 'settled' in international law, some sections of the population of the Indonesian province still do not recognise the legitimacy of the transfer and resist Indonesian sovereignty. Surely such disputes strengthen the idea of intervention by a global authority, as occurred in the eventual solution of the problem of East Timor, annexed by Indonesia in 1976 and finally able to exercise self-determination with UN assistance in 1999–2001.

Under the 'constitution as power', the constitution is merely a legal tool with which to keep power, rather than a tool to protect the rights of the people. Having political power does not bring command of state power. Lack of legitimacy for constitutional authority therefore begins with a lack of grounding of constitutions in the will of 'the people'.

The use of military force by the Chinese at Tiananmen Square in 1989, by the State Law and Order Restoration Council in Rangoon in 1988, by the Indonesian security forces throughout the 1990s, and by the Cambodian government in 1998, have all eroded constitutional values within these countries and in the region as a whole. Clearly, the idea of 'constitutionalism' is yet to triumph in a number of political cultures in the region, where competing ideologies of power continue to exert influence (particularly money politics and patronage). Issues of effective governance (including accountability and adherence to the rule of law), and equity (especially provision of services to outer regions), also remain important. Furthermore, it appears that 'constitutional review' is seldom able to rise above the strategic action of political interests, whereas ideally the constitution should, following Habermas, be the result of communicative action.

Apart from questions relating to the establishment of the modern constitutions, this study has focused on the practices of democracy and representation that they have encouraged. Attention to this question emerges from the challenges that the Asia–Pacific states continue to face in establishing stable and just systems of governance. Because effective democracies require representatives of the highest quality in public life, whether in the parliaments, the courts or the bureaucracy, the quality of candidates drawn to public life under current conditions of electoral democracy must be of concern. Political parties are increasingly drawing media personalities, athletes and entertainers into electoral contests, and current methods of finding representatives do not tend to attract to high public office candidates with such qualities as sagacity and impartiality, and the ability to put the public interest before their own.

Partisan political processes are inherently destabilising. Western societies are generally able to meet this source of instability through the presence of compensatory stabilising factors (historically, a homogeneous electorate, and a cultural acceptance of the rules limiting permissible actions within political life). The absence of this 'culture of political restraint' in Asia–Pacific societies results in a willingness by actors to transgress the stabilising rules, and to push political games into destabilising patterns. Given the experience with political parties over the second half of the twentieth century, it may now be timely to examine the role of parties and investigate whether they contribute to the conduct of government or detract from it.

A number of elements of contemporary constitutional processes have added to conflict, rather than alleviated it. Among small Pacific Island communities, for instance, the processes of candidature, electioneering and, in general, running for political office can cause disunity at village level (a 'modern' leader defeating a 'traditional' leader, or person of lower rank defeating someone senior). There are instances, on the other hand, where the existence of electoral frameworks, whatever their continuing inadequacies, has provided an ordered means for conflict resolution. In New Caledonia, a struggle between several parties — the FLNKS seeking Kanak sovereignty, the RPCR seeking to remain within French sovereignty – had led to violent confrontation prior to 1984, when the Kanaks elected to re-enter the constitutional path.

The quality of representation has a bearing on all other aspects of constitutional practice, notably the performance of the legislature and the executive. But, since it is by representation through elections that the people exercise their power, the quality of civil society becomes particularly important. There must surely be a link between an expanding class of citizens who are not only educated but who have the capacity to voice opinions in the public sphere, and the operation of the constitutional order. Telephony, fibre optics and satellite technology are becoming the weapons of choice of the discontented. Ironically, however, the technology that enables the democratisation of knowledge and decision-makng also enables levels of surveillance and control equal to those achieved by the most coercive of colonial or post-colonial masters.

A third theme threaded through this study has been a concern with the future of the constitutional framework derived from Westminster. During modern times the rule of law and constitutionalism have come to signify the principles of government that purposively aim to attain and fulfil human rights through the mechanism of separation of powers in government. However, the institutionalisation of an 'opposition' to the government, as occurs in the Westminster constitutional system, is a foreign concept to communities whose highest aspiration had been social cohesion and harmony: the application of such a model in such countries adds an element of instability to an already unstable environment. With an absence of political ideology, and party loyalty, the constitutional device known as the 'vote of no confidence' became the legal loophole used by political actors to seek power (office of the prime minister) once they had failed at general elections. It may be noted here that parliamentary practice, as borrowed by Asia–Pacific countries from their metropolitan patrons, ignores most of the conditions required for success in conflict resolution: active listening to all views, speaking with respect to all parties, investing sufficient time in dialogue, and probing the consequences of a range of possible outcomes.

Although the desire to establish governments that are both accountable and inclusive is addressed to a certain extent by current systems of representation, other aspects of the democratic process, notably the organisation of political discourse through the party system, compound the problem. Democracies desire communicative action, but through formalisation of the party system they are more beholden to strategic action. This formalisation of the party system, so required by the modern constitutions but so at variance with the need for genuine consultation on constitutional issues and public policy matters alike, has been adopted as an undesirable necessity throughout the Pacific and in some Asian states. Parties are based more on matters of patronage and personality than on ideology or nationalism.[9]

The 'postmodern' constitution?

The constituting of modernity through acts of independence assists in understanding the persistence of fundamental conflicts in states previously more often premised on pluralism than order. Modernity privileges conformity and uniformity, and these purposes are identical to the aspirations of modern law. The modern law is one that renders all actors 'equal' before it; unique responses, or exceptions, are not normally allowed. Legal procedures are routinised.

But societies have always been 'de-centred'; modernity hoped to make us believe that an ordering was possible. Actors possess worldviews, and these address notions of past, present and future values. Physical conditions, including geography and the economy, also have their impact on worldviews. Values are linked to religion, philosophy and culture, and not just to material conditions. Whereas pre-modern variety resulted from the small scale of communities and the limits of the communicative action, postmodern variety is consciously so. Postmodernism refers to a paradigm shift that involves new understandings of relations between law and power.

The postmodern idea is that there is no need to submit to the presupposition of an 'exhaustion of possibilities' of modernity (as proclaimed by, for instance, Fukayama). The 'realism' of positive law has not proven effective, and through observation of society we can frame normative proposals. What is required, rather, is recognition of 'complexity',[10] a valuing of 'difference' rather than conformity, a renewed appreciation of the normativity of law, and an expectation of 'constitutional learning'.[11] The complexity recognised by postmodernity, and the positive response to sceptical concerns offered by such theorists as Habermas, are useful in the analysis of constitutional thought and practice.[12] Habermas is conscious of the postmodern paradigm that frames his analysis. What is required is a paradigm shift, not simply a tinkering with the system. This involves critical rethinking of relations between law and power.

There is a dimension to democracy beyond the nation-state – in what can be termed the 'international constitution' – that remains unexplored. If constitutional law is to concern itself with human dignity, and with freedom and welfare, it must now address global issues. Global constitutionalism, the new constitutionalism, can complement traditional constitutionalism which focuses on protecting individual freedoms. National constitutions need to take into account international instruments, especially concerning human rights and minority rights. In this way fundamental and universal rights can be co-ordinated with nationally or ethnically unique political and legal structures and values.

There is increasing appreciation of diversity, and respect for diversity, but the same dynamic process is raising questions about the boundaries between national and supra-national jurisdictions. Could it be that an era of international co-operation is looming in which the advantages of internationalism will outweigh the disadvantages and that the national interest will be best served through regional and global co-operation? One implication of such a development would be an increase in the importance of collective ('supra-national') decision-making. International agreements, accords and treaties are already entered into throughout the region, but to view their increasing number and range from a more global perspective raises questions about the ways in which states can and do enter into international agreements.

Clearly, the nation-states are increasingly caught between national self-interest and the realities of an emerging globalism. The basic model for national constitutionalism emerged before the spread of international and supra-national organisations in the second half of the twentieth century, and the co-ordination of regional policy-making was a major challenge for the Asia–Pacific states. Traditional constitutional law is only now opening itself to consideration of global law and diplomacy. Isolationist models of national economies have generally been discarded in favour of co-operative arrangements at both regional and global levels.[13] Concepts of the homogeneous nation-state are being replaced by recognition of the value of diversity and difference.[14] These developments are having a significant impact on thinking about constitutions, and on the proper operation of government.[15] As the democratic element of constitutional practice becomes more deliberative and less conflictual, and as the spread of global values leads to critical revision of current notions of state sovereignty, constitutional dialogue in the Asia Pacific may well become resurgent sooner than anyone expects. The result may be a revision of constitutional practices more far-reaching than current experts in modernist law are able to foresee.

Notes

1 Blaustein, 'On a Constitution for the Philippines'.
2 Benedito, 'Law and Nationhood'.
3 See Prior, 'Constitutional Fairness or Fraud on the Constitution?'
4 This was especially the case in Hong Kong: see Chan and Edwards, *Hong Kong's Bill of Rights: Two Years before 1997*, and *Hong Kong's Bill of Rights: The Final Year*; Jones, 'A Leg to Stand On?' A similar concern was also expressed in relation to the role of customary law in contemporary legal orders: for the Pacific Islands, see Banks, 'Devolution of Justice in Papua New Guinea'; Lawson, 'Cultural Relativism and Democracy'.
5 Walzer, *Toward a Global Civil Society*. For a discussion of constitutional process and modernity, see Rosenfeld, 'Modern Constitutionalism as Interplay between Identity and Diversity'.
6 See, for example, Mahbubani, 'The Pacific Way'.
7 Liebich et al., *Citizenship East & West*; Hill and Fee, *The Politics of Nation Building and Citizenship in Singapore*.
8 Dr Thomas Wapai Wainggai was detained after proclaiming the state of 'West Melanesia' on 14 December 1988.
9 See, for example, Paia, 'Nationalism and the Solomon Islands'.
10 Zolo, *Democracy and Complexity*.
11 See Vanberg and Buchanan, 'Constitutional Choice, Rational Ignorance and the Limits of Reason'.
12 Is Habermas' theory (and categories, e.g. 'law' and 'life-world') useful in appraising non-Western experience? If yes, it may be universally useful; if no, it is yet another culturally-bound Western theoretical construct.
13 Commission on Global Governance, *Issues in Global Governance*. New organisations in the Asia Pacific include ASEAN (Association of South East Asian Nations), South Pacific Forum, and APEC (Asia–Pacific Economic Co-operation). In the 1990s Kiribati, Niue, Nauru, Tuvalu and the Cook Islands, the five smallest island nations in the Pacific, established a group called the Small Island States to consider joint action in such areas as fishing rights, controlling access to shipping lanes that pass through their exclusive economic zones, and global warming.
14 Basta, 'Constitutions and Peace within States'; Fleiner, 'Basic Concepts for Autonomy Decentralisation and Minority-Protection'; Divan, 'Constitutional Protection of Special Groups'; Sanghi, 'Human Rights Protection';

Mohsin, 'Rights of the Minority Communities'; Endo, 'Minority Community and Japanese Culture'; Chiba, 'Legal Pluralism in Mind'.
15 In the Pacific Islands, for instance, a number of projects have emerged devoted to the study of governance: Macdonald, *Governance and Political Process in Kiribati*; Paeniu, 'South Pacific'; Gonzales, 'Governance, Socio-Economic Development and the East Asian Miracle'; Taafaki and Oh, *Governance in the Pacific*.

Appendix: Chronology of constitutional events in the Asia Pacific

Bangladesh

1953 Constituent assembly dissolved. Elected prime minister dismissed by governor-general.
1956 Constituent convention adopts constitution with parliamentary form of government, president as head of state, and prime minister as head of government.
1958 1956 Constitution abrogated and martial law proclaimed.
1962 Constitution promulgated. Presidential form of government introduced.
1969 Constitution abrogated by military intervention.
1970 Election held for constituent assembly. **3 March:** constituent assembly halted by military head of state. **16 December:** Pakistani military forces defeated.
1971 Independence gained following civil war with West Pakistan. **10 April:** first meeting of Constituent Assembly of Bangladesh.
1972 **4 November:** constitution adopted. Parliamentary system introduced.
1975 **24 January:** presidential system introduced. **15 August:** president assassinated. Constitution suspended, and a former minister assumes office of president until removed by military intervention.
1978 **April:** presidential election. Opposition parties seek reversion to parliamentary form of government.
1981 **29 May:** president assassinated. **October:** incumbent vice-president elected president.
1982 **24 March:** president removed by military coup.
1986 'Election' to office of president widely considered rigged.
1991 Twelfth Amendment restores parliamentary form of government.
1994 **March:** three main opposition parties boycott parliament and eventually resign en masse in bid to have general elections held under neutral caretaker government.

1995 **25 November:** prime minister asks president to dissolve parliament.
1996 **12 February:** elections held under government of Prime Minister Khaleda Zia, widely regarded as rigged. **12 June:** general elections; 2574 candidates contest 300 parliamentary seats, and voter turnout highest ever but no single party obtains a clear majority.
1998 General elections.

Burma

1896–1948 British rule (province of India until 1937).

1947 12 February: Panglong agreement signed by the Shan Saohpalong, Kachin Duwas, Chin chiefs, and Bama leaders led by Bogyoke Aung San; regarded as foundation for forming a national state. **April:** elections for constituent assembly. **July:** assassination of Aung San. **2 September:** constitution. Assembly resolves for independent Republic of Burma.

1948 Constitution. Independence gained from Britain; first independent Prime Minister U Nu. Karen ethnic minority commence fighting for independence from Burma.

1958 Army take–over.

1960 General elections. Last civilian government elected.

1962 2 March: military coup by General Ne Win. Constitution suspended. Burma becomes one-party state controlled by military-dominated Burma Socialist Programme Party (BSPP). U Nu goes into exile.

1971 Ne Win government appoints constituent assembly.

1974 New constitution (commitment to socialist economy and life) and unicameral people's congress. Constitutionally elected single-party.

1980 Ne Win proclaims general amnesty; U Nu returns from exile.

1988 March–August: mass demonstrations demanding end to one-party rule; resignation of BSPP government; free elections for multi-party democracy. Several thousand demonstrators killed by army and police. **23 July:** Ne Win resigns, replaced by Sein Lwin. **18 September:** SLORC issues Political Parities Registration Law, legalising political opposition for first time since 1962. Aung San Suu Kyi forms National League for Democracy (NLD).

1989 June: NLD and other opposition parties begin demonstrations against SLORC. **July:** Aung San Suu Kyi placed under house arrest. **December:** U Nu placed under house arrest.

1990 27 May: general elections; NLD wins 392 out of 485 seats. SLORC refuses to step down. Aung San Suu Kyi remains under house arrest.

1992 January–February: SLORC begins military offensive to 'annihilate all insurgent movements'; Muslim members of Rohingya ethnic minority flee into Bangladesh; Karen rebels seek refuge in Thailand; rebel members of Naga ethnic minority take refuge in India. **April:** SLORC announces clemency program and begins release of prisoners; U Nu freed from house arrest; Aung San Suu Kyi receives first visit from family members since arrest. **July:** Aung San Suu Kyi receives second family visit; US Secretary of State Baker calls on ASEAN to send collective message to Burmese military to 'Release all political prisoners immediately and begin a genuine dialogue aimed at rapidly transferring power to a democratically elected government'; ASEAN members prefer policy of 'constructive engagement' with SLORC. **September:** SLORC lifts martial law, remains in power.

1993 January: constitutional convention starts meetings.

1994 20 September: Aung San Suu Kyi meets with SLORC members, who will only discuss conditions of her leaving Burma; she refuses to discuss leaving; SLORC refuses to discuss elections; she remains under house arrest.

1995 26 January: main Karen guerrilla base at Manerplaw taken by SLORC; Karens retreat into Thailand. **February:** major Karen base at Kawmoora taken by SLORC; Karens announce intention to continue guerrilla war inside Burma. **8 April:** national convention adjourns; Chief Justice U Aung Toe states that agreement reached on laying down principles for designation of self-administered divisions and zones. **10 July:** military ends 6-year house arrest of Aung San Suu Kyi. **3 August:** Foreign Minister Ohn Gyaw attends ASEAN meeting as guest, but told that more progress towards normalising political life necessary before can become full member. **27 October:** regime frees another 30 political prisoners; 2277 now freed but still at least 1000 in prisons. **28 November:** national convention reconvenes. **29 November:** deadline for NLD participation in convention, but NLD withdraws.

1996 28 May: NLD plans to draft a constitution separately from government panel. **7 June:** SLORC adopts new law declaring unauthorised constitution drafting an offence punishable by up to 20 years in prison. **23 July:** Myanmar admitted by ASEAN to a security forum for first time.

Cambodia

1863–1941 French colonial rule relatively stable due to French patronage of king.
1941 Prince Norodom Sihanouk installed as king by French colonial authority.
1947 First constitution.
1948 First general elections held.
1953 Second constitution. Cambodia gains independence.
1958 General elections.
1962 **10 June:** general elections.
1970 Prince Norodom Sihanouk (head of state) deposed. Gen. Lon Nol remains prime minister, declares Cambodia a republic.
1975 **April:** Khmer Rouge seize power; regime headed by Pol Pot.
1976 New constitution abolishes private property and bans organised religion.
1978 Khmer Rouge government removed by Vietnamese forces.
1979 Third constitution.
1981 Constitution. National Assembly comprises deputies elected to 5-year terms. A 7-member council of state elected from National Assembly members. A council of ministers acts as government. Local people's revolutionary committees established in provinces, municipalities, district communes and wards. Judiciary comprises people's courts and military tribunals.
1991 **1 May:** cease-fire. **23 October:** peace agreements signed in Paris by the 4 Khmer factions, 19 countries and UN Secretary-General; UN Security Council authorises establishment of peace-keeping mission to oversee implementation of agreements.
1993 UN-sponsored general elections for 120-seat National Assembly; seats won by Funcinpec (58), CPP (51), Buddhist Liberal Democratic Party (10), and Molinaka (1). **September:** new constitution promulgated establishing constitutional monarchy, with Sihanouk as head of state and Prince Norodom Ranariddh and Hun Sen as first and second prime ministers, respectively.
1994 Nine-member Supreme Council of Magistry established.
1998 **26 July:** general elections.

China

1911 China proclaimed a republic under Sun Yat Sen.
1949 Communist revolution succeeds. China placed under martial law.
1954 **20 September:** first formal constitution adopted; defines People's Congresses system as basic political system. Congresses

elected at all levels, and people's governments and courts founded.
1966–76 Cultural Revolution Group of Central Committee takes power. NPC inactive 1965–75. Revolution committees set up at local levels to administer state powers and these arrangements confirmed in 1975 and 1978 constitutions.
1975 Constitution completely revised.
1977 22 July: Deng Xiaoping elevated to vice-premier.
1978 Constitution completely revised. 32nd plenum of 11th National Congress of CPC re-establishes system of People's Congresses.
1982 New constitution.
1988 Constitutional reforms.
1989 3–4 June: People's Liberation Army troops enter Beijing and fire on student-led pro-democracy demonstrators.
1993 Constitutional reforms.
1997 China signs international covenant on economic, social and cultural rights.

Cook Islands

1964 Cook Islands Constitution Act.
1965 4 August: Cook Islands Constitution enters into force.
1966 Electoral Act.
1980–81 Constitution Amendment (No. 9) Act transfers legislative capacity to Cook Islands Assembly.
1981–82 Constitution Amendment (No. 10) Act provides that there 'shall be a representative of Her Majesty the Queen in the Cook Islands, to be known as the Queen's Representative'.
1989 General elections.
1994 General elections and referendum on term of subsequent parliaments, flag and national anthem.
1999 General elections; Dr Joe Williams becomes prime minister. **18 November:** Dr Terepai Moate replaces Williams as prime minister.

Federated States of Micronesia

1965 Convening of First Congress of Micronesia.
1979 11 May: beginning of constitutional government.
1982 Constitutional convention, Pohnpei. **October:** Compact of Free Association with US.

1986 **14 January:** compact approved by US Congress. **3 November:** compact brought into full force.
1989 New constitution for Truk; name changed to Chuuk.
1990 **April:** state elections. **16 July:** constitutional convention commences.
1991 **5 March:** elections to Congress. **11 May:** Bailey Olter (Pohnpei) wins third presidential election. **17 September:** admission to UN membership.
1993 **March:** elections to Congress.

Fiji

1970 Constitutional conference in London determines 22 Fijian seats, 22 Indian, and 8 Europeans and others. **10 October:** independence.
1983 Sir Penaia Ganilau appointed governor-general.
1985 Formation of Fijian Labour Party (FLP).
1987 **14 May:** general elections. Ratu Sir Kamisese Mara replaced as prime minister by Dr Timoci Bavadra. Bavadra deposed in military coup of Colonel Rabuka. **26 August:** second military coup. **September:** decree overthrows 1970 Constitution. **October:** independent republic proclaimed.
1990 **25 July:** Constitution of Sovereign Democratic Republic of Fiji proclaimed (2nd).
1991 Electoral decree.
1992 **May:** general elections; Rabuka wins government. 170 candidates contested 65 seats; Fijian Political Party (SVT) wins 30 and FLP, 13.
1993 **30 November:** parliament fails to pass 1994 budget. Rabuka government falls. **16 December:** President Ratu Sir Penaia Ganilau dies in Washington, DC.
1994 **12 January:** Ratu Mara becomes governor-general. **18–25 February:** general elections. Rabuka becomes prime minister. Seats won by SVT (31), Fijian Association (5), General Voters Party (4). SVT establishes coalition with General Voters Party and two independents to command 37 of 70 seats.
1996 **10 September:** Constitution Review Commission report tabled in parliament.
1998 **27 July:** new constitution (3rd) comes into effect.
1999 General elections; Mahendra Chaudhury becomes prime minister.

French Polynesia

1986 General elections; 73% voter turnout.
1991 March: general elections for Territorial Assembly's 41 seats.
1992 13 March: French general elections; 2 representatives elected from French Polynesia.
1996 General elections.
1999 General elections.

Guam

1976 US Congress grants Guam right to frame its own constitution, but terms restricted such that the people rejected it at referendum.
1982 People vote in favour of commonwealth status.
1987 Plebiscite held to approve negotiating draft for commonwealth status to be sent to US Congress.

Hawaii

1852 Constitution.
1864 Constitution.
1893 17 January: Queen Lili'uokalani, Hawaii's last monarch, overthrown.
1894 Republic of Hawaii declared.
1898 Hawaii formally annexed as US territory.
1945 Hawaii placed under art. 73 of UN Charter, under administering authority of US.
1959 Hawaiians vote to become a US state.
1978 A state constitutional convention creates Office of Hawaiian Affairs to administer to needs of Native Hawaiians and to get share of proceeds from use of 1.7 million acres of public land that once belonged to Kingdom of Hawaii.

Hong Kong

1842 Treaty of Nanking. Hong Kong becomes British Crown Colony.
1971 (UK) Immigration Act denies Hong Kong citizens right of abode in Britain.
1981 British Nationality Act changes status of Hong Kong citizens

from Citizens of United Kingdom and Colonies to British Dependent Territory Citizens. Latter status to expire 1 July 1997.
1984 Sino-British Declaration on Future of Hong Kong.
1989 30 June: British House of Commons Foreign Affairs Committee rejects right of abode in UK for 3.25 million Hong Kong British subjects. **21 December:** 225,000 citizens eligible for British passport with right of abode under new British Nationality Scheme.
1990 4 April: National People's Congress approves Basic Law of Hong Kong.
1991 5 June: bill of rights passes into law.
1992 July: Chris Patten becomes governor.
1995 Britain and China reach agreement on question of Court of Final Appeal in Hong Kong.
1996 11 December: Tung Chee-hwa voted first chief executive by 400-member selection committee.
1997 1 July: Hong Kong reverts to Chinese sovereignty.

India

1947 Constituent assembly in India outlaws untouchability. **15 August:** independence. Pandit Jawaharlal Nehru, first prime minister.
1949 26 November: federal constitution adopted by constituent assembly.
1950 26 January: constitution promulgated. India becomes republic.
1951 Representation of the People Act.
1951–52 First general elections on basis of adult suffrage; simultaneous elections for Lok Sabha and all state legislative assemblies.
1957 Second general elections.
1962 Third general elections.
1967 Fourth general elections.
1971 President's Rule imposed in Karnataka.
1975 June: PM Indira Gandhi declares Internal Emergency (1975–77). Fifth general elections.
1977 March: sixth general elections. Gandhi defeated by Janata Party. President's Rule imposed in Karnataka.
1980 Seventh general elections. Indira Gandhi regains power.
1983 21 June: Union Territory of Pondicherry placed under President's Rule.
1984 25 May: Sikkim placed under President's Rule.
1984 Eighth general elections.
1985 Anti-defection constitutional amendments.

1986 Mizoram granted statehood.
1987 Constitution (Fifty-seventh Amendment) Act. **20 February:** Arunanchal Pradesh granted statehood. **11 May:** President's Rule imposed in Punjab. **30 May:** Goa granted statehood.
1988 **30 January:** President's Rule imposed in Tamil Nadu. **7 August:** President's Rule imposed in Nagaland. **7 September:** Mizoram assembly dissolved by presidential proclamation.
1988 Representation of the People (Amendment) Act. Constitution (Sixty-first Amendment) Act amends art. 326, lowering voting age from 21 to 18.
1989 **30 January:** Tamil Nadu put under President's Rule. **21 April:** President's Rule imposed in Karnataka.
1991 **12 March:** ninth Lok Sabha dissolved. Elections held (20 May – 15 June).
1992 **13 July:** Dr Shanker Dayal Sharma elected ninth president.
1996 General elections. **28 May:** government of Atal Behari Vajpayee falls after 13 days. H. D. Deve Gowda becomes prime minister, heading a 13-party United Front coalition government.
1998 **March:** general elections won by Bharatiya Janata Party. Prime minister is Atal Behari Vajpayee.
1999 General elections.

Indonesia

1500–1900 Portuguese, British and Dutch traders establish various levels of control over 'East Indies' at various times.
1941–45 Occupied by Japanese.
1945 **March:** Investigating Committee for Preparation of Independence established; total members 62, incl. Soekarno, Hatta and other nationalists, and also Japanese, some ignorant of Bahasa Indonesia. **May–July:** basic agreement reached concerning constitutional and economic questions. **1 June:** Soekarno delivers Pancasila speech before committee. **15 August:** Japanese surrender. **17 August:** independent republic proclaimed by Soekarno and Hatta. War begins with Dutch.
1949 **27 December:** Republic of United States of Indonesia receives complete and unconditional sovereignty, with exception of western part of New Guinea. Constitution of 1945 abrogated by federal constitution. New Guinea issue remains unresolved until 1962.
1950 **17 August:** new provisional constitution comes into force. Federal government system, established at independence,

abolished and Indonesia becomes unitary state. Beginning of seven years of liberalism.
1955 **5 July:** 1945 Constitution reinstated and constituent assembly dissolved. Soekarno continues to play key role in government. **29 September:** first general elections. **15 December:** election of 520-member constituent assembly.
1957 Law No. 1 of 1957 concerning regional autonomy.
1961 **14 December:** plebiscite held in Dutch New Guinea. UN recognises integration of Irian Jaya.
1962 **15 August:** UN officiates at signing of agreement to transfer territory to Indonesia on 1 May 1963.
1963 Anti-Subversion Law of 1963 characterises wide range of activities as 'subversion'.
1965 **30 September:** attempted coup results in downfall of Soekarno.
1966 Indonesian Communist Party outlawed and Soekarno forced to resign. Basic Principles of the Press (Act 11 of 1966) (amended in 1967 and 1982) requires all newspapers, journals and other publications to obtain licence and to comply with vaguely defined list of duties and 'national responsibilities', including adherence to state policy of Pancasila.
1967 Lt. Gen. Soeharto officially recognised as president.
1968 **27 March:** Soeharto elected chief of state and head of government by MPRS.
1969 **19 November:** UN General Assembly resolves to take note of report of Secretary General on fulfilment of his tasks under Indonesian–Dutch Agreement of 15 August 1962.
1970 Basic Act on the Judiciary (replaces Statute 19 of 1964).
1971 DPR elections.
1972 **1 October:** MPR formally inaugurated.
1976 Indonesia annexes former Portuguese colony of East Timor.
1984 Conditions and procedures prescribed for granting of media licences. Prominent victims of press censorship include *Sinar Harapan* and *Prioritas* newspapers.
1985 Law on Social Organisations imposes stringent restrictions on establishment and functioning of NGOs; all obliged to adopt Pancasila and to register with Department of Home Affairs.
1986 Transmigration policy introduced. **October:** *Sinar Harapan* newspaper licence revoked.
1987 **June:** *Prioritas* newspaper licence revoked.
1988 Soeharto elected for fifth term. Travel restrictions to East Timor eased.
1990 **September:** government orders closure of *Monitor*, following publication of public opinion poll in which prophet Muhammad

came eleventh in popularity, after Soeharto and a leading rock music performer. Editor arrested and sentenced to 5 years' imprisonment for blasphemy.
1991 Massacres in East Timor.
1992 DPR elections; Golkar remains major group, winning 68% of vote (73% in 1987), Democratic Party (PDI) 15% and Development Party (PPP) 17%.
1993 **March:** Soeharto begins sixth term. Gen. (ret.) Try Sutrisno elected vice-president.
1994 **June:** government revokes publishing licences of *Tempo*, *Editor* and *DeTik*, on grounds that they violated journalistic code of ethics and endangered national security.
1997 **29 May:** general elections; Golkar wins 73.4% of vote, PPP 23.6% and PDI 2.8%. 75 seats reserved to military.
1998 **10 March:** Soeharto begins seventh term. **May:** Soeharto resigns; Habibie becomes president.
1999 **28 January:** passage of laws required for first post-Soeharto general election. **5 May:** governments of Indonesia and Portugal, and UN Secretary-General Kofi A. Annan, reach agreement on conducting of East Timor ballot. UN deploys personnel in East Timor. **June:** general elections; Abdurrahman Wahid elected president and Megawati Sukarnoputri vice-president. **30 August:** UN supervises referendum in East Timor which results in huge vote for independence. Large-scale violence fomented by military-aligned militia.
2001 Abdurrahman Wahid resigns as president and is replaced by Megawati Sukarnoputri.

Kiribati

1978 General elections.
1979 **12 July:** independence; constitution promulgated.
1982 General elections.
1983 No-confidence motion leads to national elections.
1987 General elections.
1991 **May:** general elections. President Ieremia Tabai replaced by Teateo Teannaki.
1998 **2–6 March:** first post-independence constitutional convention. General elections.
1999 Presidential election.

Laos

1893 Becomes French protectorate under Franco-Siamese treaty.
1907 Acquires present borders.
1941–45 Japanese occupation.
1945 Independence declared. Lao Issara government established.
1946 France reasserts dominance.
1947 11 May: constitution promulgated by King Sisavong Vong. Laos became constitutional monarchy under Luang Prabang Dynasty.
1949 Recognised as independent sovereign state within French Union.
1953–73 war between Pathet Lao (supported by North Vietnamese) and Lao government (backed by US bombing and Thai mercenaries).
1954 Full sovereign status gained.
1956 Constitution amended to extend suffrage to women.
1958 General elections; Lao Patriotic Front (LPF or Pathet Lao) gains 13 seats.
1960 10 September: constitution suspended by Boun Oum.
1961 January: constitution reapplied, and remains until communist take-over.
1973 Protocol ends war.
1974 April: new (provisional) government established with royalist, neutralist and LPF participation. LPF increases its power and eventually gains effective control. Tough economic and political policies lead to mass emigration.
1975 29 November: King Savang Vatthana abdicates and monarchy abolished. **2 December:** 264-member People's Congress proclaim People's Democratic Republic of Laos. Prince Souphanouvong becomes head of state and Kaysone Phomvihane prime minister.
1986 Prince Souphanouvong retires. Phoumi Vongvichit becomes acting president.
1989 Communist take-over. First assembly elections; Kaysone Phomvihane elected president. Gen. Khamtay Siphandone becomes premier.
1991 14 August: constitution promulgated, affirming monopoly on power of Lao People's Revolutionary Party and formalising goal of market-oriented economy. Kaysone Phomvihane elected president. Khamtay Siphandone appointed prime minister.
1992 Death of Phomvihane, replaced by Nounak Phoumsavan. **December:** elections.

Macau

1951 Becomes overseas province of Portugal.
1976 **17 February:** Organic Law of Macau; basic law drafted primarily by Beijing and awaiting final approval.
1991 **10 March:** general elections for 23-seat Legislative Assembly.
1999 Reversion to Chinese sovereignty.

Malaysia

1819 Raffles arrives in Singapore; Crown Colony (1867–1941) had Executive Council and Legislative Council comprising official and unofficial members.
1874–1930 British signed treaties of protection with Malay rulers.
1888 Sarawak and North Borneo (Sabah) become British protectorates.
1896 Federated Malay States (Selangor, Pahang, Negeri Sembilan and Perak). British establish system of indirect rule using sultans. FMS had Federal Council and Resident General; ruler of each state presided over a state council able to legislate for that state.
1906 North Borneo brought under Crown rule.
1942–45 Japanese occupation.
1946 Union of Malaya 9 states of Malay peninsula and British settlements Penang and Malacca. British make sultans sign to union under duress, and protests result. North Borneo becomes Crown Colony. **March:** congress of 39 Malay organisations declare British document illegally obtained. **May:** United Malays National Organisation (UMNO) established, with Dato Onn as president, to 'struggle for the restoration of Malay Sovereignty'.
1948 Malayan Union established but opposition to it, so federation formed by all Malay states and Straits Settlements but not Singapore.
1951 **1 December:** first elections in federation, for Municipal Council of George Town, Penang.
1955 **27 July:** first general elections; 51 of 52 seats won by UMNO/MCA/MIC Alliance.
1957 **31 August:** Federation of Malaya formed through agreement between UK and rulers of Malay states. Emphasis placed on 'peace, order, and good government'. Sarawak becomes Crown Colony but amid protests of Malays, who prefer Brooks Rajah rule.
1959 General elections.

1962 **1 September:** Singaporeans support proposal at referendum to join federation.
1963 **9 July:** Sabah (formerly North Borneo), Sarawak and Singapore join Malaya in Federation of Malaysia. **16 September:** Malaysian federation formed.
1964 Federal elections.
1965 **9 August:** Singapore separates from Malaysia.
1969 General elections; Alliance coalition loses its two-thirds majority in parliament. **13 May:** communal riot in Kuala Lumpur. Government invokes emergency powers, creates National Operations Council. Parliament suspended.
1970 Tun Abdul Razak succeeds Tunku Abdul Rahman as prime minister.
1971 Ruling coalition forms National Front parliamentary rule. Government establishes New Economic Policy. **March:** constitutional amendments, incl. art. 159 to require consent of Conference of Rulers for any law that seeks to change arts. 38 (Conference of Rulers), 70 (Precedence of Rulers) and 71 (Right of a Ruler to Hold and Exercise Constitutional Rights and Privileges of Ruler of the State).
1976 Tun Hussein Onn becomes prime minister following death of Tun Razak.
1981 Datuk Seri Dr Mahathir Mohamad becomes prime minister.
1983 Constitutional crisis results in removal of king's right to veto legislation.
1988 Suspension of President of Supreme Court Salleh bin Abas.
1990 **21 October:** general elections; National Front 52%, other 48%; of 180 seats, National Front 127 (incl. UMNO 71, MCA 18), DAP 20, PAS 7, independents 4, other 22.
1995 **24–25 April:** general elections; 14-party ruling coalition returned to power, with Mahathir returned as prime minister. Number of seats in lower house expanded to 192; opposition seats reduced from 52 to 30.

Marshall Islands

1934 Japan withdraws from League of Nations but retains possession of Marshall Islands.
1943–44 Allied invasion and occupation begins.
1945 End of World War II grants effective control to US.
1947 Marshall Islands becomes one of six entities in Trust Territory of Pacific Islands (TTPI) established by UN, with US as Trustee.

1951 US responsibility for TTPI moves from Department of Navy to Department of Interior.
1965 Congress of Micronesia formed, with representatives from all TTPI islands. Created by US administration in preparation for greater self-governance by Micronesians.
1978 Marshall Islands Constitutional Convention adopts first constitution.
1979 Government of Marshall Islands officially established, and country becomes self-governing. Amata Kabua elected president (1979–96).
1982 Official name changed to Republic of the Marshall Islands (RMI).
1983 Voters in RMI approve Compact of Free Association with US.
1986 US Congress approves Compact, which grants sovereignty and provides for aid and defence in exchange for continued US military use of missile testing range at Kwajalein atoll. **21 October:** Compact of Free Association comes into force.
1990 UN Security Council terminates trusteeship status.
1991 RMI joins UN.
1992 **6 January:** general elections and presidential election. Amata Kabua re-elected for fourth term.
1997 Imata Kabua elected to succeed Amata Kabua (died 1996).
1998 **September:** no-confidence motion against government of Imata Kabua.
1999 **15 November:** general elections.
2000 **January:** Kessai H. Note elected president.
2001 Current Compact of Free Association expires.

Nauru

1919–67 Former German colony administered by Australia under Mandate System of League of Nations and International Trusteeship System of United Nations.
1968 Gains independence.
1989 **December:** Bernard Dowiyogo replaces Sir Hammer De-Robert as president.
1999 **April:** Rene Harris elected president after successful no-confidence vote against Dowiyogo. Nauru joins UN.

Nepal

1951 **18 February:** King Tribhuvan announces establishment of democracy.

1961 **January:** King Mahendra imposes ban on political parties.
1962 **December:** new constitution provides for partyless panchayat system.
1972 King Birendra Bir Bikram Shah Dev ascends throne.
1990 Democratic revolt curtails powers of monarch. **9 November:** new constitution.
1991 **12 May:** general elections.
1994 **15 November:** general elections; Nepal Communist Party (United Marxist-Leninist) UML) gains power under PM Man Mohan Adhikari.
1995 **13 June:** king dissolves parliament on advice of Prime Minister Adhikari, who says government unable to rule effectively because of opposition blocking tactics. **28 August:** Supreme Court rules dissolution unconstitutional and reinstates house. **10 September:** Adhikari defeated in no-confidence motion in parliament. Bahadur Deuba becomes prime minister and wins vote of confidence by 107 to 86.
1997 **March:** Lokendra Bahadur Chand becomes prime minister.
1999 **3 May:** general elections.
2001 King Birendra assassinated by his son.

New Caledonia

1946 Becomes a French Overseas Territory.
1987 **September:** 61% vote to stay French (57% of pop. is European, Polynesian and Asian stock).
1988 Matignon Accord grants substantial autonomy, promising referendum on self-determination in 10 years.
1998 **5 May:** Noumea Accord signed, postpones referendum on independence.

Niue

1966 Elections; Robert Rex becomes chief minister, serving until his death in December 1992.
1974 Niue attains self-government in free association with New Zealand.
1985 **April:** constitutional review committee recommends maintaining status of self-government in free association with New Zealand.
1992 Death of Sir Robert Rex. Young Vivian elected Premier.
1993 **March:** general elections.

1999 March: Sani Lakatani elected prime minister.

North Korea

1993 November: regional elections.
1994 8 July: death of President Kim Il Sung.
1998 September: constitutional amendments adopted during 10th Supreme People's Assembly. Kim Jong Il, general secretary of Workers Party of Korea, is re-elected as chair of National Defense Commission.
1999 7 March: regional elections; voter turnout recorded at 99.9%.

Northern Mariana Islands

1973 6 November: general elections and vote on establishing a constitutional convention (75% approval).
1975 15 February: covenant with US concluded by US and Marianas Political State Commission.
1976 24 March: covenant approved by US Congress.
1984 Second constitutional convention proposes 44 constitutional amendments (all approved).
1986 3 November: Covenant Agreement and Constitution of Commonwealth of Northern Mariana Islands become effective.
1989 November: election for governor won by Lorenzo I. DeLeon Guerrero.
1991 November: Senate elections.

Pakistan

1947 Pakistan created by partition from India.
1958 Gen. Ayub Khan stages military coup; martial law until 1962.
1969 Gen. Yahya Khan reimposes martial law.
1971 East Pakistan breaks away to form Bangladesh; army discredited. Zulfikar Ali Bhutto becomes president and then prime minister.
1973 Parliamentary form of government established.
1977 Military intervention. Gen. Zia-ul-Haq ousts Bhutto. Office of president given enhanced powers but still within parliamentary form.
1985 Martial law lifted after 16 years.
1986 Benazir Bhutto returns from exile.

1988 Gen. Zia killed in aircrash. Benazir Bhutto elected prime minister.
1993 Government suspends local councils in Punjab Province. **April:** President Ghulam Ishaq Khan dismisses PM Nawaz Sharif and parliament (but both president and PM resign). **May:** Supreme Court orders reinstatement of Sharif.
1996 **5 November:** PM Benazir Bhutto sacked by President Farooq Leghari on grounds of corruption and undermining judiciary. Caretaker government formed by Malik Merak Khalid.
1997 **February:** general elections; Nawaz Sharif becomes prime minister. 13th Constitutional Amendment reduces presidential powers.
1998 **9 October:** National Assembly passes 15th Constitutional Amendment Bill, making Islamic teachings supreme law of Pakistan but promising protection of personal laws, religious freedom, traditions and customs of non-Muslims.
1999 **13 October:** coup by Gen. Pervaiz Musharraf ousts Nawaz Sharif. State of emergency declared and parliament suspended.

Palau

1985 President Remeliik assassinated.
1988 President Lazarus Salii commits suicide. Ngiratkel Etpison wins presidential election.
1992 Passage of presidential Primary Law (with 26% of vote, a mere 31 votes more than opponent Roman Tmetuchel). **16 July:** constitution changed. **September:** Kuniwo Nakamura wins presidential election. **4 November:** vote in favour (61.8%) of amending constitution, paving way for approval of Compact of Free Association with US.
1993 7-member advisory review committee appointed by President Nakamura to work on compact. **9 November:** vote on compact.
1994 **1 October:** independence.

Papua New Guinea

1949 Papua New Guinea Act passed by Parliament of Australia to provide for governance of Papua New Guinea.
1964 First House of Assembly elections.
1968 Second House of Assembly elections.

1972 Third House of Assembly elections. Constitution Planning Committee established.
1974 Self-government.
1975 **1 September:** Bougainville declares independence as North Solomons. **16 September:** Papua New Guinea gains independence.
1976 Constitutional Amendment No. 1 establishes provincial system of government.
1977 General elections.
1980 Julius Chan becomes prime minister.
1982 General elections.
1987 General elections.
1988 **April:** Bougainvillean Francis Ona demands secession and Kina 14 billion as compensation for damage to Jaba River. **November:** sabotage of power plants, airstrips, then assassinations, riot police, state of emergency.
1990 **May:** declaration of Republic of Bougainville.
1991 **23 January:** Honiara Declaration provides for restoration of essential services. **April:** government troops land on Bougainville.
1992 General elections; Paias Wingti becomes prime minister.
1993 **23 September:** Wingti resigns and is re-elected next day.
1994 Court rules Wingti gained premiership unconstitutionally and orders fresh ballot. **30 August:** Sir Julius Chan elected prime minister.
1995 **18 July:** Organic Law on Provincial Governments and Local Level Governments repealed and replaced by Organic Law on Provincial Governments.
1997 **July:** general elections. Bill Skate becomes prime minister. Burnham Declaration commits government and Bougainvillean secessionists to working towards ending conflict.
1998 **December:** national parliament fails to pass constitutional amendments granting recognition to Bougainville Reconciliation Government (BRG). Skate prorogues parliament to forestall no-confidence motion.
1999 **January:** Bougainville Constituent Assembly adopts BRG Basic Agreement and BRG Constitution; National Executive Council subsequently endorses agreement but does not consider constitution. **May:** Bougainvilleans elect 69 members to BRG; Joseph Kabui elected president. **7 July:** Skate government falls. Sir Mekere Morauta becomes prime minister. **15 December:** Hutjena Record recognises Bougainville's right to maximum possible autonomy and promises that National Executive Council will consider holding independence referendum.

Philippines

1785 Royal Company of Philippines established for direct Philippines–Spanish trade.
1781 Tobacco monopoly established.
1800 Governors appointed.
1834 Manila declared a 'free port'.
1896 Revolution. **December:** Rizal killed.
1898 **12 June:** Filipino revolutionaries declare independence from Spain.
1899 **29 January:** Malalos constitution proclaimed. First Philippines Commission (Schurman Commission) recommends territorial government with two legislatures; replacement of military government by civilian; conservation of natural resources; organisation of autonomous municipal and provincial governments; establishment of schools; and appointment of 'men of good ability and character' to important government offices.
1900 **March:** Second Philippines Commission (Taft Commission) instructed to legislate and act as executive government (from September to August 1902, commission enacted 499 laws). **December:** Martial law declared.
1901 Appointment of William Howard Taft (judge, later US president) as first administrator. Municipal elections.
1902 Provincial elections and congressional legislation for lower house. Political parties: Nacionalista Party, Osmena, Quezon. Pronounced binational loyalties; public call for independence but private guarantees of loyalty.
1907 Lower house legislature; Sergio Osmena elected Speaker.
1935 Constitution of (Third) Philippine Commonwealth.
1946 General elections; Liberals defeat Nacionalistas; Manuel Roxas (d. 1947) elected first president. **July:** independence. Constitution of (Third) Republic of the Philippines.
1949 Presidential election; Elpidio Quirino re-elected.
1953 Presidential election; Ramon Magsaysay becomes president.
1957 Presidential election; Carlos P. Garcia becomes president.
1961 General elections; violence, vote-buying. Diosdado Macapagal elected 5th president.
1965 Presidential election; Ferdinand Marcos becomes president.
1971 Constitutional Convention Act authorises amendments and governs conduct of election of delegates to constitutional convention. **June:** convention begins work (finishes 29 November 1972).
1972 **21 September:** Marcos imposes martial law.
1973 Constitution of (Fourth) Republic of the Philippines.

1976 Tripoli Agreement between government and Moro National Liberation Front to establish autonomous province in south. Constitution amended.
1977 December: Marcos seeks approval to continue as president and prime minister; referendum passed (99%).
1981 Constitution amended. Presidential election; Marcos re-elected.
1984 Batasang Pambansa elections. Marcos repeals martial law.
1986 7 February: presidential election; massive anti-government demonstrations and revolt within army; Marcos flees into exile; Corazon Aquino assumes presidency. **March:** National Assembly abolished (full of Marcos supporters); 1973 Constitution abrogated; all legislative powers claimed; Marcos appointees to Supreme Court dismissed; Moro National Liberation Front and Philippines government sign peace pact. **June–October:** new constitution drafted.
1987 2 February: Constitution of (Fifth) Republic of the Philippines ratified in plebiscite (76% approval).
1988 Organic Act for Autonomous Region in Muslim Mindanao.
1989 19 November: plebiscite in provinces concerning inclusion in Autonomous Province of Mindanao; four agree (Lanao del Sur, Maguindanao, Sulu, and Tawi-Tawi).
1992 General elections; Fidel Ramos becomes president.
1998 May: general elections; List Proportional Representation Scheme used for first time; Joseph Estrada becomes president.

Samoa

1961 Referendum grants only chiefs right to vote.
1962 Independence. Mataafa Fiame Faumuina becomes first prime minister.
1976 Tupuola Efi becomes prime minister.
1990 29 October: referendum agrees to extend suffrage to all adults aged 21 and older. 52.4% (53,000) of all eligible voters (75,000) registered to vote, of whom 49.4% voted in favour of, and 44.4% against, reform.
1991 General elections, first under universal suffrage.

Singapore

1826 Second Charter of Justice granted to East India Company.

Singapore received law of England as it stood on 27 November 1826.
1945 British forces return.
1946 **March:** end of British Military Administration; Straits Settlements dissolved. **1 April:** Singapore becomes Crown Colony (Penang and Malacca become part of Malayan Union).
1947 **July:** separate Executive and Legislature established.
1948 Formation of Federation of Malaya.
1948 **20 March:** first general elections. **June:** uprising by Communist Party of Malaya leads to declaration of state of emergency.
1953 British appoint commission under Sir George Rendel to review constitutional position and make recommendations for change. Rendel proposals accepted by government and serve as basis of new constitution giving a greater measure of self-government.
1955 General elections; Labour Front wins 10 seats, People's Action Party (PAP) 3. **6 April:** David Marshall becomes first chief minister.
1958 UK promulgates new constitution for Singapore, providing for self-government with a fully-elected assembly and control over most matters except defence and external security.
1959 Singapore granted self-governing status. Office of Governor becomes that of Yang di-Pertuan Negara (head of state). **May:** first general elections for 51-member Legislative Assembly; PAP wins 43 seats. **3 June:** new constitution comes into force. Sir William Good becomes first Yang di-Pertuan Negara. **5 June:** Government sworn in, with Lee Kuan Yew as first prime minister.
1963 Singapore joins Federation of Malaysia. 13 PAP MPs defect to Barisian Socialis Party.
1965 **9 August:** Singapore leaves federation.
1966 Wee Chong Jin Constitutional Commission.
1968 General elections; PAP wins all seats.
1972 General elections; PAP wins all seats.
1976 General elections; PAP wins all seats.
1980 General elections; PAP wins 78% of valid vote and all seats.
1984 General elections; PAP wins all but two seats.
1990 **28 November:** Goh Chok Tong becomes prime minister. Six nominated members added to parliament.
1991 **August:** general elections; PAP wins 77 of 81 seats, 41 uncontested, and 61% of valid vote. Parliamentary Elections Act amended to provide that a group representation constituency shall elect a group of three or four members of parliament as may be designated by the president for that constituency.
1992 **4 December:** PM Goh succeeds Senior Minister Lee Kuan Yew

as secretary-general of PAP. **19 December:** Marine Parade by-election; PAP wins 72.9% (48,965) of total 67,126 valid votes. SDP, NSP and SJP obtain 24.5% (16,447), 1.4% (950) and 1.1% (764) of votes.

1993 **March:** Dr Chee Soon Juan loses job in National University of Singapore. **June:** Opposition MP Chiam See Tong resigns as secretary-general of SDP and Chee Soon Juan becomes acting secretary-general. **29 June:** BT publishes article citing official estimate of economic growth in second quarter of 1992 and is charged under Official Secrets Act. **August:** *Economist* gazetted by government for refusing to print reply by High Commissioner to London to published article by J. B. Jeyaretnam on prosecution of 5 men under Official Secrets Act. Chiam See Tong summoned to face CEC of SDP on charges of indiscipline and is expelled. **29 August:** presidential election; Ong Teng Cheong becomes first directly elected president, with 58.7% of valid votes, while Chua Kim Yeow obtains 41.3%; both meet requirements laid down by Presidential Election Committee but NMP Chia does not. **December:** Chiam See Tong reinstated by High Court. Lee Hsian Loong appointed sole deputy prime minister.

1995 **17 March:** High Court scrutinises powers of elected president. **20 April:** Tribunal rules that president has no veto power over constitutional bills, and government can amend powers without his assent. **10 November:** Chiam files complaints about Ling's insults in parliament (over motion to censure SDP and chief Chee Soon Juan for endorsing fugitive Francis Seow's unfounded attacks on judiciary).

1996 **28 October:** constitutional amendment increases number of multi-member group representational constituencies and number of representatives eligible for election from each constituency from 4 to 6, prior to establishment of community development councils.

Solomon Islands

1893 British Protectorate.
1976 Self-government.
1978 Independence.
1988 Constitutional Review Committee recommends that Solomons become a Federal Republic, with equal member states and indigenous head of state as ceremonial president.
1993 **26 May:** national elections; number of constituencies raised from

38 to 47. **18 June:** Francis Billy Hilly replaces Solomon Mamaloni as prime minister.
1994 **13 October:** governor-general dismisses prime minister and orders Speaker to convene parliament on 31 October. **7 November:** Mamaloni elected as new prime minister.
1997 **May:** Deputy Speaker Benedict Kinika gives notice of parliamentary motion of no confidence in prime minister Mamaloni. **August:** general elections; Bartholomew Ulufa'alu becomes prime minister.
1999 **June:** government invokes state of emergency; former Fiji Prime Minister Sitiveni Rabuka negotiates peace accord with Isantabu Freedom Fighters.

South Korea

1948 Democratic People's Republic of Korea established.
1950–53 Korea divided into North and South.
1960 New constitution establishes parliamentary form of government.
1961 Coup d'etat; military junta established.
1962 New constitution.
1972 New constitution.
1980 New constitution.
1987 New constitution. Presidential election; Roh Tae Woo beats Kim Dae Jung and Kim Young Sam. Constitutional Court established.
1992 **18 December:** presidential election won by Kim Young Sam (first elections since 1963 in which government candidate not a military figure).
1996 **April:** general elections. New Korea Party, headed by President Kim, wins 139 of 299 assembly seats.
1997 Presidential elections.

Sri Lanka

1948 Independence from Great Britain. Constitution.
1956 General elections won by J. R. Jayawardene.
1957 Bandaranaike Chelvanayakam Pact.
1965 Dudley Senanayake Chelvanayakam Agreement.
1970–72 Constituent assembly.
1972 **22 May:** first republican constitution, based on parliamentary sovereignty.
1977 general elections won by Jayawardene.

1978 January: select committee for revision of constitution appointed. New constitution. Prime Minister Jayawardene introduces presidential system.
1983 Jayawardene wins second term as president.
1987 Indo-Lanka Accord. New constitution. 13th Amendment to Constitution.
1990 Interim report of Mangala Moonesinghe Select Committee. Peace talks between Liberation Tigers of Tamil Eelam and government.
1994 November: general elections; Chandrika Kumaratunga becomes president, subsequently re-establishes Westminster form of government.
1997 October: new draft constitution presented in parliament. Federalist principles called on as potential solution to ongoing separatist conflict, but constitutional solution not found by 2001.

Taiwan

1895–1945 Japanese occupation.
1946 November: first National Assembly elected.
1947 25 December: constitution.
1949 Nationalists arrive from mainland, fleeing communist victory in China.
1986 December: supplementary election for legislature.
1989 March: multi-party system legalised.
1990 March: President Lee Teng-hui wins new 6-year term.
1991 1 May: Lee Teng-Hui announces end of communist rebellion and restoration of suspended provisions of 1947 Constitution. **December:** second National Assembly elections (of 403 seats, KMT 318, DPP 75, other 10).
1992 December: general elections for Legislative Yuan (KMT 60%, DPP 31%, independents 9%; seats (304 total, 161 elected) KMT 96, DPP 50, independents 15).
1993 23 February: Dr Lien Chan appointed premier (serves until 1996 presidential election).
1995 2 December: members of Third Legislature elected.
1996 23 March: Lee Teng-hui wins first direct presidential election. The 334 members of Third National Assembly elected to serve a 4-year term (until 19 May 2000).
1997 July: constitutional changes expand presidential powers and diminish provincial government. **December:** presidential election.

Thailand

1932 **24 June:** secret People's Party coup against King Prajadhipok (Rama VII) who returns to Bangkok following day. Interim constitution of Siam; 70-member National Assembly. **10 December:** king promulgates constitution of Kingdom of Siam. Phaya Monapahorn Nitithada appointed first prime minister.

1933 **November:** first national elections for 78 elective seats in assembly.

1935 **2 March:** king abdicates. Assembly proclaims his nephew, Prince Ananda Mahidol (b. 1925), Rama VIII and appoints Council of Regency.

1946 **February:** general elections, Khuang Aphaiwong becomes prime minister but resigns after a few weeks. **April:** Pridi Panomyong becomes prime minister. **10 May:** Constitution of Kingdom of Thailand enacted. **9 June:** king found shot dead; brother Bhumibol Adulyadej proclaimed King of Siam under royal title King Rama IX. **August:** Thawal Dhamrongnawaswasti becomes prime minister.

1947 **8 November:** coup d'etat by Col. Sarit Thanarat. **9 November:** new provisional constitution proclaimed. Khuang Aphaiwong becomes prime minister.

1948 **29 January:** general elections; Democratic Party wins majority; Khuang re-elected prime minister. **6 April:** Khuang forced to resign. Phibul Songkhran becomes prime minister.

1949 **23 March:** permanent constitution proclaimed. Name changed to Thailand.

1951 **29 November:** Gen. Sarit Thanarat and Gen. Pao Sriyanonda dissolve assembly in 'radio coup'. 1932 Constitution reinstated. Phibul Songkhran prime minister.

1952 Government appoints 'upper' half of unicameral assembly members. **February:** general elections for 'lower' half of assembly.

1957 **February:** general elections; massive cheating attributed to introduction of multiple party system. **16 September:** military coup by Sarit Thanarat.

1958 **January:** general elections; Thanom Kittikachorn becomes prime minister. **20 October:** coup d'etat by Sarit Thanarat.

1959 **28 January:** Revolutionary Party of Sarit Thanarat (formerly Military Party) proclaims new constitution and forms National Assembly with Thanarat as prime minister (d. in office 8 Dec. 1963).

1968 **20 June:** new constitution promulgated, creating a bicameral parliament.

1969 **10 February:** general elections; Thanom Kittikachorn becomes prime minister.
1971 **17 November:** Thanom Kittikachorn stages coup d'etat, abrogates constitution, dissolves parliament and proclaims martial law. 5-member National Executive Council formed.
1972 **December:** junta places judiciary under direct government control; students protest. New legislative Interim Assembly established. Interim constitution (9. Temporary Charter for Administration of Kingdom).
1973 **14 October:** 400 die in student–military confrontation. Junta leaders leave country. Sanya Dhammasakdi appointed prime minister.
1974 **7 March:** National Assembly begins deliberating draft of new constitution. **15 August:** draft approved. **7 October:** tenth constitution takes effect.
1975 **5 January:** general elections contested by 22 parties; Seni Pramoj elected prime minister by 3-party coalition but resigns three weeks later. **17 March:** Kukrit Pramoj becomes prime minister.
1976 **12 January:** Pramoj dissolves parliament. **4 April:** general elections; of 19 parties, Democratic Party wins 114 of 279 seats; Seni Pramoj elected prime minister. **6 October:** student riots. National Administrative Reform Council replaces Pramoj government with Gen. Thanin Kraivixien. Parliament dissolved and political parties banned. New constitution.
1977 **20 October:** coup against Thanin. Kriangsak becomes prime minister.
1978 **December:** constitution with temporary clauses that favour military; 2-chamber parliament.
1979 **22 April:** general elections. Kriangsak becomes prime minister.
1980 **12 March:** Gen. Prem Tinsulanonda becomes prime minister.
1983 **16 March:** parliament rejects constitutional provision preserving key role of military. **18 March:** royal decree dissolves National Assembly. **18 April:** general elections; Prem becomes prime minister.
1986 **27 July:** general elections; Prem becomes prime minister.
1988 **29 April:** parliament dissolved. **24 July:** general elections. **4 August:** Chart Thai Party leader Chatichai Choonhavan becomes 17th prime minister.
1991 **23 February:** military coup. National Peace-Keeping Council invokes martial law. Charter for Administration of Kingdom 1991. Anand Panyarachun becomes prime minister. **7 December:** Constitution for Administration of Kingdom.
1992 **March:** general elections. **10 June:** constitution amended;

number of senators fixed at 270 (two-thirds of 360 House of Representatives). **September:** general elections; Chuan Leekpai becomes prime minister.
1995 **2 July:** general elections; Banharn Silpa-archa forms 7-member coalition government.
1996 Banharn dissolves parliament. **17 November:** general elections; Chavalit Yongchaiudh, leader of NAP, forms 6-party coalition government.
1997 Constituent Drafting Assembly drafts new constitution. **27 September:** parliament approves Thailand's 16th constitution.

Tonga

1875 **4 November:** Tongan Constitution.
1967 **1 January:** constitution revised.
1990 **14–15 February:** Legislative Assembly elections; of 29 total seats, 9 elected (6 pro-reform, 3 traditionalist); 'Akilisi Pohiva, Laki Niu and Viliami Fukofuka elected on platform of greater government accountability.
1992 **November:** Pro-Democracy Convention on Constitution and Democracy.
1993 **February:** general elections; 6 of 9 'commoner' seats won by pro-reform candidates, including 'Akilisi Pohiva, Laki Niu and Viliami Fukofoka.
1994 First political party (People's Party) formed out of pro-democracy movement.
1996 General elections; 4 of 9 elected seats won by pro-democracy candidates. **8 November:** motion (tabled by 'Akilisi Pohiva, Viliami Fukofoka, Tie-in Fuko and 'Uliti Uata) to amend constitution to provide for 30-member popularly elected parliament defeated by 9–5 vote with 3 abstentions. King Taufa'ahau Tupou IV prorogues parliament.
1999 General elections.
2000 King appoints Prince Ulukalala Lavaka Ata 4th prime minister.

Tuvalu

1974 referendum leads to separate constitutions for Gilbert and Ellice Islands.
1976 **1 January:** administrative separation implemented.
1978 **1 October:** full independence. Constitutional monarchy with

Queen as head of state, represented by Tuvaluan governor-general.
- **1989 28 September:** parliamentary elections for 12 seats.
- **1993 September:** general election votes for post of prime minister split 6–6 between outgoing PM Bikenibeu Paeniu and Tomasi Puapua on each of three successive ballots. **10 December:** Kamuta Laatasi elected prime minister, defeating Paeniu 7–5.
- **1998 26 March:** general elections; Paeniu re-elected prime minister.

Vanuatu

- **1886–88** Joint Naval Commission established, charged with protecting lives and property of British and French subjects.
- **1906** Anglo-French Condominium agreed to, in light of German attempts to enter islands.
- **1914** Protocol Respecting the New Hebrides validated.
- **1922** Protocol forms basis of government until 1970s.
- **1957** Advisory council established.
- **1980 30 July:** independence from France and UK. Independence constitution.
- **1988 16 May:** riots in Port Vila. **December:** President Ati George Sokomanu attempts to dissolve parliament, is charged with sedition by PM Walter Lini and jailed.
- **1991 September:** Donald Kalpokas replaces Lini as Vanua'aku Party leader and prime minister. **2 December:** general elections. **16 December:** coalition formed by Union of Moderate Parties and National United Party; Maxime Carlot Korman becomes prime minister but party associations fluid; of 46 total seats, UMP 19, NUP 10, VP 10, MPP 4, TUP 1, Nagriamel 1, Friend 1.
- **1994 2 March:** J. M. Leye elected president. Decentralisation Act.
- **1995** Ombudsman Act. **November:** 4th general elections. **21 December:** Serge Vohor replaces Korman as prime minister.
- **1996 8 February:** Vohor resigns after 48 days to avoid facing no-confidence motion. **September:** Korman loses no-confidence vote; Vohor becomes prime minister.
- **1997 20 May:** new coalition formed; Vohor becomes prime minister. **November:** Vohor resigns.
- **1997** Ambae chiefs write constitution for their island.
- **1998 6 March:** general elections; seats in 52-seat parliament won by VP (18), UMP (12), NUP (11), MPP (incorporating Fren

Melanesian Party) 6, John Frum (2), independents (2), and Vanuatu Republican Party (1).
1999 Presidential election.

Vietnam

1862 Treaty of Saigon cedes three southern provinces.
1874 Treaty of Saigon recognises French sovereignty over all of Cochin China.
1884 Treaty of Hue confirms French protectorate over Annam-Tonkin.
1897 French governor-general Paul Doumer reorganises and centralises colony.
1940 Japanese land in Indochina.
1945 Japanese coup; return of French.
1946 Start of first war of independence. **March:** first general elections, First plenary session of National Assembly passes first constitution and approves then coalition government.
1949 Chinese Communist Party victory in China.
1954 Defeat of French at Dien Bien Phu; Geneva Accords.
1956 Proposed elections not held.
1960 Constitution.
1980 Constitution.
1991 **18 April:** promulgation of revised constitution. **19 July:** election of 395 members (in 158 constituencies) to National Assembly; former defence minister Le Duc Anh becomes president and Vo Van Kiet reappointed premier.
1996 8th National Congress of Communist Party of Vietnam.
1997 **20 July:** general elections for 450-seat National Assembly.

Bibliography

Archipelago, Asiaweek, Australian, Bangkok Post, Bulletin (Australia), *Cambodia Times, Courier-Mail, Daily Post* (Fiji), *Deutsche Presse-Agentur, Dominion* (New Zealand), *Embassy of the Union of Myanmar News Bulletin* (Australia), *Evening Post* (New Zealand), *Far Eastern Economic Review, Fiji Times, Financial Review, Hindu* (India), *Hindustan Times, Indochina Chronology, Inside Indonesia, Kathmandu Post, Lawasia Comparative Constitutional Law Newsletter, Manila Bulletin, Manila Times, Matangi Tonga, Nation, National* (Papua New Guinea), *New Straits Times, New Zealand Herald, Pacific Islands Monthly, Pacific Magazine, Pacific News Bulletin, Phnom Penh Post, Post Courier* (Papua New Guinea), *Radio Australia, Review, Rising Nepal, Samoa News, Solomon Star* (Solomon Islands), *Solomons Voice, Sunday Observer* ((Sri Lanka), *Thailand Times, Times of Papua New Guinea*

Aakesson, Preben A. F., Marut Bunnag and Rujira Bunnag 1992, 'The Development of Constitutionalism in Thailand: Some Historical Considerations', in L. Beer (ed.), *Constitutional Systems in Late Twentieth Century Asia*, University of Washington Press.

Abad, A. M. E. G. U. 1988, 'Initiative and Referendum: An Experimentation of People Empowerment', *Philippine Law Journal* 63, 375–402.

Abas, T. M. S. 1987, 'Legal Perspective of the Third World', *New Zealand Law Journal*, August, 250–4.

Abas, Tun Salleh 1990, *May Day for Justice*, Magnus Books, Kuala Lumpur.

Abdul Rahman, Tunku 1978, *View Points*, Pelandok Press, R.L.

Abdulgani, R. 1958, 'Indonesia's National Council: The First Year', *Far Eastern Survey* 27(7), 97–104.

Abdullah, S. 1983, 'Citizens' Rights and Enforcement of Conservation Laws: A Plea for a Comparative and Multi-Faceted Approach', *Journal of Malaysian and Comparative Law* 9–10, 33–43.

Abueva, Jose V. 1994, 'Filipino Constitutional Democracy: Its Development, Performance, and Viability', 2nd International Conference of Committee on Viable Constitutionalism, State University of New York at Albany.

Abueva, Jose Veloso 1979, 'Ideology and Practice in the "New Society"', in David A. Rosenberg (ed.), *Marcos and Martial Law in the Philippines*, Cornell University Press, Ithaca and London, 32–83.

Adas, Michael 1981, 'From Avoidance to Confrontation: Peasant Protest in Precolonial and Colonial Southeast Asia', *Comparative Studies in Society and History* 23, 217–47.

Adhikari, Bipin 1995, 'House Dissolution Case: Its Relevance for Future', *Spotlight*, 1 September.
Adhikari, Bipin 1995, 'Nepal', in Saunders and Hassall, *Asia–Pacific Constitutional Yearbook 1993*, 103–40.
Adhikari, Bipin 1996, 'Nepal', in Saunders and Hassall, *Asia–Pacific Constitutional Yearbook 1994*.
Adhikari, Bipin 1997, 'Nepal', in Saunders and Hassall, *Asia–Pacific Constitutional Yearbook 1995*.
Adhikari, Bipin 1998, 'Nepal', in Saunders and Hassall, *Asia–Pacific Constitutional Yearbook 1996*, 219–44.
Adhikari, Bipin 1999, 'Nepal', in Saunders and Hassall, *Asia–Pacific Constitutional Yearbook 1997*.
Agpalo, R. E. 1992, 'Modernization, Development, and Civilization: Reflections on the Prospects of Political Systems in the First, Second and Third Worlds', in K. E. Bauzon (ed.), *Development and Democratization in the Third World: Myths, Hopes and Realities*, Crane, Russak, New York.
Ahmed, Nizam 1998, 'Reforming the Parliament in Bangladesh: Structural Constraints and Political Dilemmas', *Commonwealth and Comparative Politics* 36(1), March, 68–91.
Alamgir, Jalal 1997, 'Against the Current: The Survival of Authoritarianism in Burma', *Pacific Affairs* 70(3), 333–50.
Alexis Heraclides 1991, *The Self-Determination of Minorities in International Politics*, Frank Cass, UK.
Ambrose, David 1996, 'A Coup That Failed? Recent Political Events in Vanuatu', *Journal of Pacific History* 31(3), 53–66.
Anand Panyarachun 1997, 'Constitutionalism and Democracy in Asia', *Nation*, 3 September.
Anderson, B. 1983, *Imagined Communities: Reflections on the Origin and Spread of Nationalism*, Verso, London.
Angelo, A. H. 1988, 'The Common Law in New Zealand and Tokelau', *Melanesian Law Journal* 16.
Anglim, John 1988, 'Palau's Strategic Position Places Palauan Democracy at Risk', Working Paper No. 40, Peace Research Centre, Australian National University, Canberra, May.
Arato, Andrew and Jean Cohen 1988, 'Civil Society and Social Theory', *Thesis Eleven* 21, 199–219.
Arinanto, Satya 1997, 'Indonesia', in Saunders and Hassall, *Asia–Pacific Constitutional Yearbook 1995*.
Arinanto, Satya 1998, 'Indonesia', in Saunders and Hassall, *Asia–Pacific Constitutional Yearbook 1996*, 199–210.
Axline, W. A. 1986, 'Financial Foundations of Provincial Policy Making in Papua New Guinea', Research Monograph No. 45, Centre for Research on Federal Financial Relations, Australian National University, Canberra.
Axline, W. A. 1986, *Decentralisation and Development Policy: Provincial Government and the Planning Process in Papua New Guinea*, Papua New Guinea Institute of Applied Social and Economic Research, Port Moresby.
Ayasha, Jalal 1990, *The State of Martial Rule: The Origins of Pakistan's Political Economy of Defence*, Cambridge University Press.

Banks, Cyndi 1996, 'Devolution of Justice in Papua New Guinea: Village Courts and Probation Service', *International Journal of Comparative and Applied Criminal Law* 20(2), 257–76.

Barltrop, Roger 1995, 'Constitutional Crisis in the Solomon Islands', *Round Table* (335), 343–51.

Basman, T. M., M. S. Lalanto et al. 1989, *Autonomy for Muslim Mindanao*, B-Lal Publishers, Manila.

Bass, Jerome R. 1970, 'The PKI and the Attempted Coup', *Journal of Southeast Asian Studies* 1(1), March, 96–105.

Basta, L. R. 1995, 'Constitutions and Peace within States: Minorities, Human Rights and Welfare State', 4th World Congress of International Association of Constitutional Law, Tokyo.

Baum, Jullian 1997, 'Perilous Politics', *Far Eastern Economic Review*, 1 May, 18.

Baxi, Upendra 1979, 'People's Law, Development, Justice', *Verfassung und Recht in Obersee* 12, 97–114.

Bayne, Peter J. 1980, 'Judicial Method and the Interpretation of Papua New Guinea's Constitution', *Federal Law Review* 11, 121–66.

Bayne, Peter J. 1985, 'The Constitution and the Franchise in Western Samoa', *Queensland Institute of Technology Law Journal* 1, 201–23.

Beer, L. (ed.) 1992, *Constitutional Systems in Late Twentieth Century Asia*, University of Washington Press.

Beer, Lawrence Ward (ed.) 1978, *Constitutionalism: Asian Views of the American Influence*, University of California Press, Berkeley.

Benedito, Roberto M. 1984, 'Law and Nationhood: Transcending the Cracks in the Parchment Curtain', *Philippine Law Journal* LIX, December, 393–415.

Bernas, Joaquin G. 1990, *Dismantling the Dictatorship*, Centre for Social Policy and Public Affairs, Ateneo de Manila University, Manila.

Bhargava, G. S. 1969, *Pakistan in Crisis*, Vikas Publications, Delhi.

Bisschop, W. R. 1934, 'Adat Law in Indonesia', *Journal of Comparative Legislation and International Law* (3rd Series) 16, 304–7.

Blaustein, Albert H. 1984, 'On a Constitution for the Philippines: Axioms and Certainties', *Philippine Law Journal* LIX, June, 99–110.

Bone, Robert C. 1955, 'Organization of the Indonesian Elections', *American Political Science Review* 49, 1067–84.

Bonoan, Rual J. 1977, 'Rizal on Divine Providence and Nationhood', *Philippine Studies* 25, 145–62.

Bott, Elizabeth 1981, 'Power and Rank in the Kingdom of Tonga', *Journal of the Polynesian Society* 90(1), March, 7–81.

Branch, James A. 1980, 'The Constitution of the Northern Mariana Islands: Does a Different Cultural Setting Justify Different Constitutional Standards?', *Journal of International Law and Policy* 9(35), 35–67.

Brody, Reed (ed.) 1988–89, *The Harassment and Persecution of Judges and Lawyers (Jan 88 – June 89)*, Centre for the Independence of Judges and Lawyers, Geneva.

Brown, Carolyn Henning 1978, 'Ethnic Politics in Fiji: Fijian–Indian Relations', *Journal of Ethnic Studies* 5(4), 1–17.

Brown, David 1986, 'Judicial Independence: An Examination', *Australian Quarterly*, Summer, 348–50.

Brown, David 1989, 'The State of Ethnicity and the Ethnicity of the State: Ethnic Politics in Southeast Asia', *Ethnic and Racial Studies* 12(1), January, 47–61.
Brown, R. J. (ed.) 1969, *Fashion of Law in New Guinea*, Butterworths, Sydney, Melbourne, Brisbane.
Bui, Kim Chi 1996, 'The Role of Law in Vietnam', in Saunders and Hassall, *Asia–Pacific Constitutional Yearbook 1994*.
Bunbongkarn, Suchit 1995, 'Thailand', in Saunders and Hassall, *Asia–Pacific Constitutional Yearbook 1993*, 272–85.
Bunnag, Marut and Preben A. F. Aakesson 1987, 'The Legal System of Thailand', in K. R. Redden (ed.), *Modern Legal Systems Cyclopedia*, William S. Hein & Co., USA, suppl. 1, vol. 9, part 1, 340.1–340.58.
Burdick, Alan 1986, 'The Constitution of the Federated States of Micronesia', *University of Hawaii Law Review* 8, 419–81.
Burdick, Alan B. 1988, 'The Constitution of the Federated States of Micronesia', in Yash Ghai (ed.), *Law, Politics and Government in the Pacific Island States*, Institute of Pacific Studies, Suva.
Burghart, Richard 1994, 'The Political Culture of Panchayat Democracy', in Michael Hutt (ed.), *Nepal in the Nineties: Versions of the Past, Visions of the Future*, Oxford University Press, Delhi.
Burke, Teresa 1987, 'Philippine Constitution', *Harvard International Law Journal* 28, 568–74.
Burton, John W. 1993, 'Conflict Resolution as a Political Philosophy', in D. J. D. Sandole and H. van der Merwe (eds), *Conflict Resolution, Integration and Practice*, Manchester University Press.
Buxbaum, David C. (ed.) 1967, *Traditional and Modern Legal Institutions in Asia and Africa*, E.J. Brill, Leiden.
Cai, D. J. 1995, 'Constitutional Supervision and Interpretation in the People's Republic of China', *Journal of Chinese Law* 9(2), 219–45.
Cai, Din Jiang 1999, 'China', in Saunders and Hassall, *Asia–Pacific Constitutional Yearbook 1997*.
Campbell, M. J. 1977, 'Devolution in the Solomon Islands: A Study of Major Reforms', *Journal of Administration Overseas* 16(4), October, 228–39.
Cappelletti, Mauro 1988, 'The Expanding Role of Judicial Review in Modern Societies', in Shimon Shetreet (ed.), *Role of Courts in Society*, Martinus Nijhoff, Dordrecht, 79–96.
Carens, Joseph H. 1992, 'Democracy and Respect for Difference: The Case of Fiji', *University of Michigan Journal of Law Reform* 25, Spring/Summer, 547–631.
Chalmers, D. R. C. and A. H. Paliwala 1984, *An Introduction to the Law in Papua New Guinea*, Law Book Co., Sydney.
Chan, Johannes and George Edwards (eds) 1996, *Hong Kong's Bill of Rights: Two Years before 1997*, Hong Kong University Law Faculty, Hong Kong.
Chan, Johannes and George Edwards (eds) 1996, *Hong Kong's Bill of Rights: The Final Year*, Hong Kong University Law Faculty, Hong Kong.
Chan Wook Park 1988, 'Legislators and the Constituents in South Korea', *Asian Survey* 28(10), October, 1049–65.
Chan Wook Park 1988, 'Constituency Representation in Korea: Sources and Consequences', *Legislative Studies Quarterly* 13(2), May, 225–42.

Chan Wook Park 1997, 'The National Assembly in the Consolidation Process of Korean Democracy', *Asian Journal of Political Science* 5(2), December, 96–113.
Chandler, David 1992, *Brother Number One: A Political Biography of Pol Pot*, Allen & Unwin, Sydney.
Chapman, D. 1995, *Recommendations Concerning the Constitution of Fiji*, Democracy Design Forum, Suva.
Charoenpanij, Sriracha 1989, 'The Thai Legal System: The Law as an Agent of Environmental Protection', in Siam Society, *Culture and Environment in Thailand*, The Siam Society, Bangkok, 463–74.
Chen, Albert H. Y. 1988, 'Civil Liberties in China: Some Preliminary Observations', in R. Wacks (ed.), *Civil Liberties in Hong Kong*, Oxford University Press, Hong Kong.
Chiba, M. 1995, 'Legal Pluralism in Mind: A Non-Western View', in Hanne Petersen and Henrik Zahle (eds), *Legal Polycentricity: Consequences of Pluralism in Law*, Dartmouth Publishing, Brookfield.
Chiba, Masaji (ed.) 1986, *Asian Indigenous Law: In Interaction with Received Law*, KPI, London and New York.
Chiba, Masaji 1992, 'Three Dichotomies of Law in Pluralism', in Peter Sack and Jonathan Alek (eds), *Law and Anthropology*, Dartmouth, Aldershot.
Chiu, Hungdah 1993, 'Constitutional Development in the Republic of China in Taiwan', in Steve Tsang (ed.), *In the Shadow of China: Political Developments in Taiwan since 1949*, University of Hawaii Press, Honolulu.
Choudhury, G. W. 1958–59, 'Failure of Parliamentary Democracy in Pakistan', *Parliamentary Affairs* 12, 60–70.
Choudhury, G. W. 1974, '"New" Pakistan's Constitution, 1973', *Middle East Journal* 28, 10–18.
Chowdhury, Subrata R. 1989, *The Rule of Law in a State of Emergency: The Paris Minimum Standards of Human Rights Norms in a State of Emergency*, Pinter Publishers, London.
Citizens Constitutional Forum (ed.) 1995, *Protecting Fijian Interests and Building a Democratic Fiji: A Consultation on Fiji's Constitution Review*, Citizens Constitutional Forum (Fiji) and Conciliation Resources (London), Suva.
Citizens Constitutional Forum 1995, *Electoral Systems and Power Sharing: Report of a Consultation on Fiji's Constitution*, Citizens Constitutional Forum and Conciliation Resources, Suva.
Citizens Constitutional Forum 1995, *One Nation, Diverse Peoples: Building a Just and Democratic Fiji. A Submission by the Citizens Constitutional Forum (CCF) to the Constitution Review Commission*, Citizens Constitutional Forum and Conciliation Resources, Suva.
Clark, Alan 1987, 'Conflict Formal and Informal: Elections in New Caledonia, 1984–1986', *Pacific Studies* 10(3), July, 91–106.
Commission on Global Governance 1995, *Issues in Global Governance*, papers written for the Commission on Global Governance, Kluwer Law International in association with the Commission on Global Governance, London and Boston.
Cooray-Peiris, L. J. M. 1979, 'Fundamental Rights, Judicial Review and the Constitutional Court of Sri Lanka', *Lawasia N.S.* 1, 24–73.

Corfield, Justin 1995, *Khmers Stand Up! A History of the Cambodian Government 1970–1975*, Monash Asia Institute, Monash University, Melbourne.
Corrin, Jennifer C. 1995, 'Solomon Islands', in Saunders and Hassall, *Asia–Pacific Constitutional Yearbook 1993*, 243–71.
Corrin, Jennifer 1996, 'Solomon Islands', in Saunders and Hassall, *Asia–Pacific Constitutional Yearbook 1994*.
Corrin Care, Jennifer 1997, 'Solomon Islands', in Saunders and Hassall, *Asia–Pacific Constitutional Yearbook 1995*.
Corrin Care, Jennifer 1998, 'Solomon Islands', in Saunders and Hassall, *Asia–Pacific Constitutional Yearbook 1996*, 337–58.
Corrin Care, Jennifer 1999, 'Solomon Islands', in Saunders and Hassall, *Asia–Pacific Constitutional Yearbook 1997*.
Corte's, Irene R. 1984, 'Constitutionalism in the Philippines: A View from Academia', *Philippine Law Journal* 59, 338–48.
Crawford, James 1988, 'Outside the Colonial Context', in W. J. Allan Macartney (ed.), *Self-Determination in the Commonwealth*, Aberdeen University Press, 1–22.
Crawford, James 1989, 'Islands as Sovereign Nations', *International and Comparative Law Quarterly* 38, April, 277–98.
Creyke, R. J. and J. Disney et al. (eds) 1996, *Aspects of Administrative Review in Australia and Indonesia*, Australian National University, Canberra.
Crocombe, Ron (ed.) 1987, *Land Tenure in the Pacific*, University of the South Pacific, Suva.
Cullen, Richard and H. L. Fu 1998, 'China', in Saunders and Hassall, *Asia–Pacific Constitutional Yearbook 1996*, 111–31.
Darling, Frank 1977, 'Thailand in 1976: Another Defeat for Constitutional Democracy', *Asian Survey* 17, 116–32.
Das, B. C. 1977, 'Emergency Provisions in the Indian Constitution', *Indian Journal of Political Science* 38, 247–52.
Davidson, J. W. 1967, *Samoa Mo Samoa: The Emergence of the Independent State of Western Samoa*, Oxford University Press, Melbourne.
de Silva, H. L. 1991, *An Appraisal of the Federal Alternative for Sri Lanka*, de Silva, Deliwala.
Deklin, Tony 1989, 'In Search of a Home-Grown Constitution', in S. Latukefu (ed.), *Papua New Guinea: A Century of Colonial Impact, 1884–1984*, National Research Institute and University of Papua New Guinea in association with the PNG Centennial Committee.
Del Carmen, Rolando V. 1974, 'The Philippine Judicial System under the New Constitution and Martial Law', *Texas International Law Journal* 9, 152.
Del Carmen, Rolando V. 1979, 'Constitutionality and Juridical Politics', in David A. Rosenberg (ed.), *Marcos and Martial Law in the Philippines*, Cornell University Press, Ithaca.
Dhavan, Rajeev 1996, 'India', in Saunders and Hassall, *Asia–Pacific Constitutional Yearbook 1994*.
Dhavan, Rajeev 1997, 'India', in Saunders and Hassall, *Asia–Pacific Constitutional Yearbook 1995*.
Dhavan, Rajeev 1998, 'India', in Saunders and Hassall, *Asia–Pacific Constitutional Yearbook 1996*, 175–98.
Dhavan, Rajeev 1999, 'India', in Saunders and Hassall, *Asia–Pacific Constitutional Yearbook 1997*.

Diamond, L., L. Linz and S. Lipset (eds) 1989, *Democracy in Developing Countries: vol. III, Asia*, Adamantine Press, London.

Diamond, Larry (ed.) 1988, *Democracy in Developing Countries: Africa*, Lynne Rienner, Boulder.

Diamond, Larry 1990, 'Three Paradoxes of Democracy', *Journal of Democracy* 1(3), Summer.

Diamond, Larry, Juan J. Linz and Seymour Martin Lipset 1988, 'Preface', in Diamond, *Democracy in Developing Countries: Africa*, xvi.

Divan, A. 1995, 'Constitutional Protection of Special Groups: The Indian Perspective', 14th Lawasia Biennial Conference, Beijing.

Douglass, William A. 1988, 'A Critique of Recent Trends in the Analysis of Ethnonationalism', *Ethnic and Racial Studies* 11(2), April.

Downs, Ian 1980, *The Australian Trusteeship: Papua New Guinea 1945–75*, Australian Government Publishing Service, Canberra.

Edrisinha, R. (ed.) 1992, *Provincial Councils and Local Government: Their Role in Strengthening Liberal Democracy*, Council for Liberal Democracy, Dehiwela.

Edrisinha, Rohan 1999, 'Sri Lanka', in Saunders and Hassall, *Asia–Pacific Constitutional Yearbook 1997*.

Edwards, A. R. 1991, 'Communication and Steering', in 't Veld et al., *Autopoiesis and Configuration Theory: New Approaches to Societal Steering*, Kluwer, Dordrecht.

Endo, H. 1995, 'Minority Community and Japanese Culture', 4th World Congress of International Association of Constitutional Law, Tokyo.

Escobido, Jose L. 1975, 'Judicial Review and National Emergency', *Philippine Law Journal* 50.

Fa, J. 1991, 'Constitutional Developments in Taiwan: The Role of the Council of Grand Justices', *International and Comparative Law Quarterly* 40.

Falk, Richard 1992, *Explorations at the Edge of Time: The Prospects for World Order*, Temple University Press, Philadelphia.

Faruqi, Shad Saleem 1993, 'The Sceptre, the Sword and the Constitution at a Crossroad (A Commentary on the Constitution Amendment Bill 1993)', *Current Law Journal*, March, xiv–lix.

Feith, Herbert 1962, *The Decline of Constitutional Democracy in Indonesia*, Cornell University Press, Ithaca, New York.

Feith, Herbert and Lance Castles (eds) 1970, *Indonesian Political Thinking, 1945–1965*, Cornell University Press, New York.

Fernando, Enrique M. 1978. *Governmental Powers and Human Rights in Times of Emergency: A Brief Survey of the Malaysian and Philippine Constitutions*, Malayan Law Journal, Singapore.

Fieldhouse, D. K. 1981, *Colonialism, 1870–1945: An Introduction*, Weidenfeld & Nicolson, London.

Firth, Stewart 1989, 'Sovereignty and Independence in the Contemporary Pacific', *Contemporary Pacific*, 1(1–2), 75–96.

Fitzpatrick, Joan 1994, *Human Rights in Crisis: The International System for Protecting Rights during States of Emergency*, University of Pennsylvania Press.

Fleiner, T. 1995, 'Basic Concepts for Autonomy Decentralisation and Minority-Protection in a Post-Modern World', 4th World Congress of International Association of Constitutional Law, Tokyo.

Frame, Alex 1987, 'The External Affairs and Defence of the Cook Islands: The "Riddiford Clause" Considered', *Victoria University of Wellington Law Review* 17, 141–51.
Frenkel, Max 1986, *Federal Theory*, Centre for Research on Federal Financial Relations, Australian National University, Canberra.
Gawi, John 1985, 'The Status of the Common Law under the Constitution', in D. Colquhoun-Kerr and J. Kaburise, *Essays on the Constitution of Papua New Guinea*, University of Papua New Guinea Press, Port Moresby.
Ghai, Y. P. and A. J. Regan 1991, 'The Constitutional Arrangements for Decentralisation in Papua New Guinea: An Overview', *Melanesian Law Journal*, Special Issue, 11–37.
Ghai, Y. and A. J. Regan 1992, *The Law, Politics and Administration of Decentralisation in Papua New Guinea*, National Research Institute, Boroko.
Ghai, Yash (ed.) 1988, *Law, Politics and Government in the Pacific Island States*, Institute of Pacific Studies and University of the South Pacific, Suva.
Ghai, Yash 1988, 'Constitution Making and Decolonisation', in Ghai, *Law, Politics and Government in the Pacific Island States*.
Ghai, Yash 1990, 'A Coup by Another Name? The Politics of Legality', *Contemporary Pacific* 2, 11–35.
Ghai, Yash 1990, 'Constitutional Foundations of Public Administration', in Yash Ghai (ed.), *Public Administration and Management in Small States: Pacific Experiences*, Commonwealth Secretariat and University of the South Pacific, Fiji.
Ghai, Yash and Jill Cottrell 1990, *Heads of State in the Pacific: A Legal and Constitutional Analysis*, Institute of Pacific Studies, Suva.
Giddens, Anthony 1991, *Modernity and Self-Identity: Self and Society in the Late Modern Age*, Stanford University Press.
Gillen, M. 1995, 'The Malayan Rulers' Loss of Immunity', *University of British Columbia Law Review* 29(1), 163–97.
Gonzales, J. L. 1996, 'Governance, Socio-Economic Development and the East Asian Miracle: Some Lessons for the Philippines', *Asian Journal of Political Science* 4(1).
Gordon, R. and M. Meggitt 1985, *Law and Order in the New Guinea Highlands: Encounter with Enga*, University of Vermont, Hanover and London.
Goto, Mitsuo 1998, 'Japan', in Saunders and Hassall, *Asia–Pacific Constitutional Yearbook 1996*, 211–18.
Gottlieb, Gidon 1994, 'Nations without States', *Foreign Affairs*, May/June, 100–12.
Gouttes, B. 1995, *Custom and the Napoleonic Code*, Pacific Islands' Law Officers Meeting, Port Vila.
Groves, H. E. 1964, *The Constitution of Malaysia*, Malaysia Publications Ltd, Singapore.
Guatama, Sudargo and Robert N. Hornick 1983, *An Introduction to Indonesian Law: Unity in Diversity*, Penerbitalumni, Bandung.
Habermas, Jurgen 1996, *Between Facts and Norms: Contributions to a Discourse Theory of Law and Democracy*, Polity Press, Cambridge.
Hajisalah, Alayas 1999, 'Thailand', in Saunders and Hassall, *Asia–Pacific Constitutional Yearbook 1997*.
Han, Sang-Hie 1996, 'The Way to Constitutional Democracy – Judicial Review in the Republic of Korea', in Saunders and Hassall, *Asia–Pacific Constitutional Yearbook 1994*.

Harijanti, Susi 1999, 'Indonesia', in Saunders and Hassall, *Asia–Pacific Constitutional Yearbook 1997*.
Hartman, Joan F. 1981, 'Derogation from Human Rights Treaties in Public Emergencies', *Harvard International Law Journal* 22, 1–52.
Hartono 1982, *In Search of New Legal Principles*, Binacipta, Bandung.
Hasnan, Habib 1992, 'The Role of the Armed Forces in Indonesia's Future Political Development', in Harold Crouch and Hal Hill (eds), *Indonesia Assessment 1992: Political Perspectives on the 1990s*, Political and Social Change Monograph 17, Research School of Pacific Studies, Australian National University, Canberra.
Hassall, Graham 1990, Religion and Nation-State Formation in Post-War Melanesia: 1945 to Independence, PhD thesis, Australian National University.
Hassall, Graham 1991, 'Ethnicity and the State: Constitutional Provisions in Some Pacific Island States', *Ethnic Groups*, vol. 9, 83–105.
Hassall, Graham 1991, 'Nationalism and Ethnic Conflict in the Pacific Islands', *Current World Leaders* 34, April, 283–96.
Hassall, Graham 1991, 'Church and State in Vanuatu 1945–1980: A "Pacific" Contest for Power', *South Pacific Journal of Mission Studies* 2(2), December, 2–12, 26–8.
Hassall, Graham 1994, 'Problems of Representation in the Asia–Pacific Region', *Legislative Studies* 9(1), Spring, 7–16.
Hassall, Graham and Sean Cooney 1993, 'Democracy and Constitutional Change in Asia', *Asian Studies Review* 17(1), July, 2–9.
Hassall, Graham and Cheryl Saunders (eds) 1994, *The Powers and Functions of Executive Government: Studies from the Asia Pacific Region*, Centre for Comparative Constitutional Studies, Melbourne.
Hassall, Graham and Truong Truong (eds) 1994, *Infrastructural Development and Legal Change in Vietnam*, Centre for Comparative Constitutional Studies, Melbourne.
Heinze, Ruth-Inge 1974, 'Ten Days in October – Students vs. the Military: An Account of the Student Uprising in Thailand', *Asian Survey* 14(6), June.
Henderson, Dan Fenno 1967, 'Promulgation of Tokugawa Statutes', in Buxbaum, *Traditional and Modern Legal Institutions in Asia and Africa*.
Henkin, L. (ed.) 1981, *The International Bill of Rights: The Covenant on Civil and Political Rights*, Columbia University Press, New York.
Henningham, Stephen 1988–89, 'A Dialogue of the Deaf: Attitudes and Issues in New Caledonian Politics', *Pacific Affairs* 61(4), Winter, 633–52.
Henningham, Stephen 1993, 'The Uneasy Peace: New Caledonia's Matignon Accords at Mid-Term', *Pacific Affairs*, Winter, 519–38.
Hickling, R. H. 1975, 'The Prerogative in Malaysia', *Malayan Law Review* 17.
Hickling, R. H. 1976, 'The Thai Constitution of 1974', *Hong Kong Law Journal* 6, 100–07.
Hickling, R. H. 1984, 'Malaysia: Constitution (Amendment) Act 1983 and Constitution (Amendment) Act 1984', *Journal of Malaysian and Comparative Law* 11.
Hill, M. and L. K. Fee 1995, *The Politics of Nation Building and Citizenship in Singapore*, Routledge, London and New York.

Hills, Howard Loomis 1984, 'Compact of Free Association for Micronesia: Constitutional and International Law Issues', *International Lawyer*, Summer, 583–608.
Hirayasu, Naomi 1987, 'The Process of Self-Determination and Micronesia's Future Political Status under International Law', *University of Hawaii Law Review*, Fall, 487–532.
Hooker, M. B. 1978, *A Concise Legal History of Southeast Asia*, Oxford University Press.
Hooker, M. B. 1986, *The Laws of South-East Asia, Vol. I: The Pre-Modern Texts*, Butterworths, Singapore.
Hooker, M. B. 1988, *The Laws of South-East Asia, Vol. II: European Laws in South-East Asia*, Butterworths, Singapore.
Howe, K. R., R. C. Kiste and Brij V. Lal (eds) 1994, *Tides of History: The Pacific Islands in the Twentieth Century*, University of Hawaii Press, Honolulu.
Hsia, Tao-Tai and Constance A. Johnson 1989, 'The Chinese Communist Party Constitution of 1982: Deng Xiaoping's Program for Modernization', in R. H. Folsom and J. H. Minan (eds), *Law in the People's Republic of China: Commentary, Readings and Materials*, M. Nijhoff Publishers, Dordrecht and Boston.
Hung, Veran Mei-ying 1997, 'Hong Kong', in Saunders and Hassall, *Asia–Pacific Constitutional Yearbook 1995*.
Hung, Veran Mei-ying 1998, 'Cambodia', in Saunders and Hassall, *Asia–Pacific Constitutional Yearbook 1996*, 69–110.
Hung, Veran Mei-ying 1998, 'Hong Kong', in Saunders and Hassall, *Asia–Pacific Constitutional Yearbook 1996*, 132–74.
Huxley, Andrew [1996–97], 'The Last Fifty Years of Burmese Law: E Maung and Maung Maung', *Lawasia Journal*, 9–20.
Hwang, Jau-Yuan and Jiunn-rong Yeh 1997, 'Taiwan', in Saunders and Hassall, *Asia–Pacific Constitutional Yearbook 1995*.
Ibrahim, Ahmad 1974, 'Malaysia as a Federation', *Journal of Malaysian and Comparative Law* 1(1), May, 1–27.
Ibrahim, Ahmad 1975, 'The Administration of Muslim Law in Sabah', *Journal of Malaysian and Comparative Law* 2(2), December.
Ibrahim, Ahmad 1985, 'Towards an Islamic Law for Muslims in Malaysia', *Journal of Malaysian and Comparative Law* 12, 37–52.
Indra, M. R. 1989, *The President's Position under the 1945 Constitution*, CV Haji Masagung, Jakarta.
Indra, M. R. 1990, *The 1945 Constitution: A Human Creation*, The Author, Jakarta.
International Commission of Jurists 1983, *States of Emergency: Their Impact on Human Rights*, ICJ, Geneva.
Islam, M. Amir-ul 1997, 'Bangladesh', in Saunders and Hassall, *Asia–Pacific Constitutional Yearbook 1995*.
Iyer, T. K. K. 1973, 'Constitutional Law in Pakistan: Kelsen in the Courts', *American Journal of Comparative Law* 21, 759–71.
Jackson, K. (ed.) 1992, *Cambodia 1975–1978: Rendezvous with Death*, Princeton University Press.
Jackson, Syd 1990, 'Indigenous Rights: Protecting Rights for All', *Pacific News Bulletin*, August, 8–10.

Jayakumar, S. 1976, 'Emergency Powers in Malaysia: Can the Yang Di-Pertuan Agong Act in His Personal Discretion and Capacity', *Malaya Law Review* 18, 149–56.
Jayakumar, S. 1978, 'Emergency Powers in Malaysia: Development of the Law 1957–1977', *Malayan Law Journal*, ix–xxv.
Jayasinghe, Amal 1996, 'President, Ranil agreed on need to expedite constitutional reforms', *Sunday Observer*, 27 February.
Jennings, Peter 1990, 'Political and Constitutional Change', in Peter Polomka (ed.), *The Security of Oceania in the 1990s, vol. 2: Managing Change*, Canberra Papers on Strategy and Defence No. 68, Strategic and Defence Studies Centre, Australian National University, Canberra.
Jennings, W. Ivor 1975, *Constitutional Problems in Pakistan*, Cambridge University Press.
Jeong, Y. 1997, 'The Rise of State Corporatism in Vietnam', *Contemporary Southeast Asia* 19(2), 152–71.
Jones, David 1989, 'A Leg to Stand On? Post-1997 Hong Kong Courts as a Constraint on PRC Abridgment of Individual Rights and Local Autonomy', in R. H. Folsom and J. A. Minan (eds), *Law in the People's Republic of China*, M. Nijhoff Publishers, Dordrecht and Boston.
Jumbala, Prudhisan 1974, 'Towards a Theory of Group Formation in Thai Society and Pressure Groups in Thailand after the October 1973 Uprising', *Asian Survey* 14(6), 530–45.
Kahin, George McTurnan 1961, Nationalism and Revolution in Indonesia, Cornell University Press, Ithaca (published under auspices of International Secretariat of Institute of Pacific Relations).
Kapi, M. 1990, 'The Underlying Law in Papua New Guinea', in *9th Commonwealth Law Conference*, Commerce Clearing House (New Zealand), Auckland, 129–34.
Kasemsup, Preedee 1986, 'Reception of Law in Thailand, A Buddhist Society', in Chiba, *Asian Indigenous Law in Interaction with Received Law*, 171–215.
Kedourie, Elie (ed.) 1970, *Nationalism in Asia and Africa*, Weidenfeld & Nicolson, London.
Kele-Kele, Kalkot Matas 1977, 'The Emergence of Political Parties', in Chris Plant (ed.), *New Hebrides: The Road to Independence*, Institute of Pacific Studies and University of the South Pacific, Suva.
Keyes, Charles 1989, *Thailand: Buddhist Kingdom as Modern Nation-State*, Editions Duang Kamol, Bangkok.
Khng, Russell Heng Hiang 1992, 'The 1992 Revised Constitution of Vietnam: Background and Scope of Changes', *Contemporary Southeast Asia* 14(3), December, 221–30.
Kim, Chin 1981, 'Recent Developments in the Constitutions of Asian Marxist-Socialist States', *Case Western Reserve Journal of International Law* 12, 483–500.
Kintner, William R. and Robert F. Zimmerman 1976, 'Thailand's Search for Constitutional Government', *Freedom at Issue* 38, November–December, 16–22.
Kutlesic, Vladon 1995, 'The New Constitution in the Former Socialist Countries of Eastern Europe', Belgrade 1995 4th World Congress of International Association of Constitutional Law, Tokyo.

Lal, Brij 1997, 'Towards a United Future: Report of the Fiji Constitution Review Commission', *Journal of Pacific History* 32(1), 71–84.
Lal, Brij V. 1988, *Power and Prejudice: The Making of the Fiji Crisis*, New Zealand Institute of International Affairs, Auckland.
Lal, Brij and Peter Lamour (eds) 1997, *Electoral Systems in Divided Societies: The Fiji Constitution Review*, National Centre for Development Studies and International Institute for Democracy and Electoral Assistance, Canberra.
Lamour, Peter 1985, 'Niue', in Peter Lamour and Ropate Qalo (eds), *Decentralisation in the South Pacific*, University of the South Pacific, Suva.
Lane, Jan-Erik 1996, *Constitutions and Political Theory*, Manchester University Press, Manchester and New York.
Laothamatas, Anek 1988, 'Business and Politics in Thailand: New Patterns of Influence', *Asian Survey* 28(4), April.
Lasaqa, Isireli 1984, *The Fijian People before and after Independence*, Australian National University Press, Canberra.
Latukefu, S. 1974, *Church and State in Tonga*, Australian National University Press, Canberra.
Laughlin, Stanley K. 1980–81, 'The Application of the Constitution in United States Territories: American Samoa, A Case Study', *University of Hawaii Law Review* 2(2).
Lawson, S. 1995, *Tradition versus Democracy in the Kingdom of Tonga*, Regime Change and Regime Maintenance in Asia and the Pacific Discussion Paper No. 13, Research School of Pacific Studies, Australian National University, Canberra.
Lawson, Stephanie 1991, *The Failure of Democratic Politics in Fiji*, Clarendon Press, Oxford.
Lawson, Stephanie 1996, 'Cultural Relativism and Democracy: Political Myths about "Asia" and the "West"', in R. Robison (ed.), *Pathways to Asia: The Politics of Engagement*, Allen & Unwin, Sydney.
Lee, H. P. 1986, 'Emergency Powers in Malaysia', in Trindade and Lee, *The Constitution of Malaysia*.
Leibowitz, A. H. 1989, *Defining Status: A Comprehensive Analysis of United States Territorial Relations*, Martinus Nijhoff Publishers, London.
Lev, D. 1965, 'The Lady and the Banyan Tree: Civil-Law Change in Indonesia', *American Journal of Comparative Law* 14, 282–307.
Lev, D. 1986, 'Adnan Buyung Nasution: Indonesian Civil Rights Lawyer under Attack', *HRI Reporter* 11(2), 4–5.
Lev, D. S. 1962, 'The Supreme Court and Adat Inheritance Law in Indonesia', *American Journal of Comparative Law* 11, 205–24.
Lev, D. S. 1964–65, 'The Politics of Judicial Development in Indonesia', *Comparative Studies in Society and History* 7, 173–202.
Lev, D. S. 1972, 'Judicial Institutions and Legal Culture in Indonesia', in C. Holt (ed.), *Culture and Politics in Indonesia*, Cornell University Press, Ithaca.
Lev, D. S. 1972, *Islamic Courts in Indonesia*, University of California Press, Berkeley and London.
Lev, D. S. 1973, 'Judicial Unification in Post-Colonial Indonesia', *Indonesia* 16, 1–37.

Lev, D. S. 1973, 'Bushlawyers in Indonesia: Stratification, Representation and Brokerage', Law and Society Program Working Paper No. 1, Berkeley.
Lev, D. S. 1978, 'Origins of the Indonesian Advocacy', *Hukum dan Keadilan* 3 & 4 (September–Oktober & Nopember–Desember), 34–40, 14–28.
Lev, D. S. 1985, 'Colonial Law and the Genesis of the Indonesian State', *Indonesia* 40, 57–74.
Lev, D. S. 1987, *Legal Aid in Indonesia*, Monash Centre for Southeast Asian Studies, Melbourne.
Lev, Daniel S. 1978, 'Judicial Authority and the Struggle for an Indonesian Rechtsstaat', *Law and Society Review* 13(1).
Li, Yahong 1999, 'Hong Kong', in Saunders and Hassall, *Asia–Pacific Constitutional Yearbook 1997*.
Liebich, A. and D. Warner et al. (eds) 1995, *Citizenship East & West*, Kegan Paul International, London and New York.
Lijphart, A. (ed.) 1992, *Parliamentary versus Presidential Government*, Oxford University Press.
Lijphart, A. 1994, *Electoral Systems and Party Systems 1945–1990: A Study of Twenty-Seven Democracies*, Oxford University Press.
Lijphart, Arend and Bernard Grofman (eds) 1984, *Choosing an Electoral System: Issues and Alternatives*, Praeger, New York.
Likhit Dhiravegin 1992, *Demi-Democracy: The Evolution of the Thai Political System*, Times Academic Press, Singapore.
Lini, Walter 1980, *Beyond Pandemonium: From the New Hebrides to Vanuatu*, Asia Pacific Books, Wellington.
Linz, Juan 1990, 'The Perils of Presidentialism', *Journal of Democracy*, Winter, 51–69.
Liu, S. L. 1991, 'Judicial Review and Emerging Constitutionalism: The Uneasy Case for the Republic of China on Taiwan', *American Journal of Comparative Law* 39, 509.
Loughlin, Martin 1992, *Public Law and Political Theory*, Clarendon Press, Oxford.
Lovelock, A. 1995, *Review of the Operations and Administration of the National Parliament of the Solomon Islands*, Honiara.
Macdonald, B. 1996, *Governance and Political Process in Kiribati*, National Centre for Development Studies, Canberra.
Macdonald, Barrie 1982, *Cinderellas of the Empire: Towards a History of Kiribati and Tuvalu*, Australian National University Press, Canberra.
Macdonald, Barrie 1986, 'Decolonization and Beyond: The Framework for Post-Colonial Relationships in Oceania', *Journal of Pacific History* XXI, 3–4.
Macnaught, Timothy J. 1982, *The Fijian Colonial Experience: A Study of the Neo-Traditional Order under British Colonial Rule prior to World War II*, Pacific Research Monograph No. 7, Australian National University, Canberra.
Mahbubani, K. 1993, 'The Dangers of Decadence: What the Rest Can Teach the West', *Foreign Affairs* 74(4), 10–14.
Mahbubani, K. 1995, 'The Pacific Way', *Foreign Affairs* 74(1), 100–10.
Maisrikrod, Surin 1992, *Thailand's Two General Elections in 1992: Democracy Sustained*, Research Notes and Discussion Paper No. 75, Institute of Southeast Asian Studies, Singapore.

Mansfield, H. 1993, *Taming the Prince: The Ambivalence of Modern Executive Power*, Free Press, New York.
Mara, Kamisese, Ratu Sir 1997, *The Pacific Way: A Memoir/Ratu Sir Kamisese Mara*, University of Hawai'i Press, Honolulu.
Mataitoga, Isikeli 1992, 'The Failure of Westminster Model Government in the South Pacific: A Critique of the Fijian Experience', *Melanesian Law Journal* 20, 61–76.
Maung Kyi Lin 1995, 'National Convention Plenary Session Commences', *Embassy of the Union of Myanmar Newsletter* 9, 10 May.
Maung Kyi Lin 1995, 'Sixth Major Task Accomplished by National Convention: Self-Administered Divisions and Self-Administered Zones', *Embassy of the Union of Myanmar Newsletter* 11, 25 May.
May, R. J. and A. J. Regan (eds) 1995, *Political Decentralization in a New State: The Experience of Provincial Government in Papua New Guinea*, Crawford House Publishing, Bathurst.
McKinnon, John 1992, 'Can the Military be Sidelined?', *Pacific Viewpoint* 33(2), 128–34.
McLachlan, Campbell 1987, 'The Fiji Constitutional Crisis of May 1987: A Legal Assessment', *New Zealand Law Journal*, June, 175–81.
Mellor, Norman 1984, 'Traditional Leaders and Modern Pacific Island Governance', *Asian Survey* 24(7), 759–72.
Mezey, Michael L. 1979, *Comparative Legislatures*, Duke University Press, Durham, NC.
Milne, R. S. 1988, 'Bicommunal Systems: Guyana, Malaysia, Fiji', *Publius* 18, Spring, 101–13.
Mohsin, A. F. M. 1995, 'Rights of the Minority Communities under Bangladesh Constitution', 4th World Congress of International Association of Constitutional Law, Tokyo.
Molisa, Grace, Nikenike Vurobaravu and Howard Van Trease 1982, 'Vanuatu: Overcoming Pandemonium', in Ron Crocombe and Ahmed Ali (eds), *Politics in Melanesia*, Institute of Pacific Studies and University of the South Pacific, Suva.
Moore, Mike 1982, *A Pacific Parliament: A Pacific Idea: An Economic and Political Community for the South Pacific*, Asia Pacific Books, Wellington, and University of the South Pacific, Suva.
Mya Saw Shin 1981, *The Constitutions of Thailand*, Law Library, Library of Congress, Washington DC.
Narokobi, Bernard 1986, 'In Search of Melanesian Jurisprudence', in Sack and Minchin, *Legal Pluralism*.
Narokobi, Bernard 1989, 'Law and Custom in Melanesia', *Pacific Perspective* 14(1), 17–26.
Narokobi, Bernard 1989, 'Lo Biling Yume Yet', in R. Crocombe, J. May and P. Roche (eds), *Law and Custom in Melanesia*, Melanesian Institute for Pastoral and Socioeconomic Service, University of the South Pacific, Goroka.
Nasution, Adnan Buyung 1992, *The Aspiration for Constitutional Government in Indonesia: A Socio-Legal Study of the Indonesian Konstituante 1956–1959*, Pustaka Sinar Harapan, Jakarta.

Nederman, Cary J. 1990, 'Conciliarism and Constitutionalism: Jean Gerson and Medieval Political Thought', *History of European Ideas* 12(2), 189–209.
Nelkin, David and Michael Levi 1996, 'The Corruption of Politics and the Politics of Corruption', *Journal of Law and Society* 23(1), 1–17.
Nicholson, Pip 1998, 'Vietnam', in Saunders and Hassall, *Asia–Pacific Constitutional Yearbook 1996*.
Nicholson, Pip 1999, 'Vietnam', in Saunders and Hassall, *Asia–Pacific Constitutional Yearbook 1997*.
Nicholson, Pip and Phan Nguyen Toan 1997, 'Vietnam', in Saunders and Hassall, *Asia–Pacific Constitutional Yearbook 1995*, 335–43.
Nielsson, Gunnar P. 1985, 'States and "Nation-Groups": A Global Taxonomy', in Edward A. Tiryakian and Ronald Rogowski (eds), *New Nationalisms of the Developed West: Toward Explanation*, Allen & Unwin, Boston.
Nizam, Ahmed 1998, 'Reforming the Parliament in Bangladesh: Structural Constraints and Political Dilemmas', *Commonwealth and Comparative Politics* 36(1), March, 68–91.
Norton, Robert 1990, *Race and Politics in Fiji*, University of Queensland Press, Brisbane.
Nuechterlein, Donald E. 1966, 'Thailand: Year of Danger and of Hope', *Asian Survey* 6(2), 119–24.
Oda, Hiroshi 1987, 'The Procuracy and the Regular Courts as Enforcers of the Constitutional Rule of Law: The Experience of East Asian States', *Tulane Law Review* 61, 1339–63.
O'Kane, Rosemary H. T. 1993, 'Cambodia in the Zero Years: Rudimentary Totalitarianism', *Third World Quarterly* 14(4), 735–48.
Oliveira, Jorge Costa, Paulo Cardinal and Paulo Pereira Vidal 1995, 'Macau', in Saunders and Hassall, *Asia–Pacific Constitutional Yearbook 1993*, 71–102.
Ombudsman 1985, *Thirteenth Annual Report of the Ombudsman (March 1984 – February 1985)*, Parliamentary Paper 35, Fiji.
Ong, Michael 1984, 'Malaysia in 1983', *Southeast Asian Affairs 1984*, Institute of Southeast Asian Studies, Singapore, 202–3.
Padua, Ruel 1994, 'Understanding Revolution: Struggles for Domination and Freedom in the Philippines', *Bulletin of the Australian Society of Legal Philosophy* 19, issue 62–63.
Paeniu, B. 1995, 'South Pacific: Traditional Governance and Sustainable Development in the Pacific', Economic Division Working Paper No. 6, Research School of Pacific and Asian Studies, Australian National University, Canberra.
Paia, Warren A. 1974, 'Nationalism and the Solomon Islands', *Yagl-Ambu* 1(2), June, 97–116.
Paterson, D. E. 1995, *South Pacific Customary Law and Common Law: Their Interrelationship*, Pacific Islands' Law Officers Meeting, Port Vila.
Paterson, Don 1997, 'Vanuatu', in Saunders and Hassall, *Asia–Pacific Constitutional Yearbook 1995*.
Paterson, Don 1998, 'Vanuatu', in Saunders and Hassall, *Asia–Pacific Constitutional Yearbook 1996*, 359–72.
Paterson, Don 1999, 'Vanuatu', in Saunders and Hassall, *Asia–Pacific Constitutional Yearbook 1997*.
Patten, Chris (Governor of Hong Kong) 1992, 'Our Next Five Years: The Agenda for Hong Kong', 7 October.

Paxton, John 1974, *World Legislatures*, Macmillan, UK.
Payoyo, Peter B. 1984, 'The Rule of Law and the Decree-Making Power of the President: Some Reflections on the Crisis of Constitutional Authoritarianism in the Philippines', *Philippine Law Journal* 59, 152–80.
Peiris, G. L. 1991, 'Judicial Activism and Civil Disorder: The Philippine Experience in Retrospect', *University of Queensland Law Journal* 16, 151–74.
Peterson, Glenn 1989, 'Pohnpei Ethnicity and Micronesian Nation-Building', in Michael C. Howard (ed.), *Ethnicity and Nation-Building in the Pacific*, United Nations University, Tokyo.
Philips, Edward 1990, 'Drastic Solutions: A Comparative Study of Emergency Powers in the Commonwealth', *Denning Law Journal* 59, 57–75.
Podolefsky, Aaron 1984, 'Contemporary Warfare in the New Guinea Highlands', *Ethnology* 23(2).
Powles, C. G. 1990, 'Traditional Authority in the Contemporary Pacific: Conflict and Compromise in Legal and Political Systems', in *9th Commonwealth Law Conference*, Commerce Clearing House, Auckland.
Powles, G. 1995, *Transformations of Customary Law: Legal Pluralism in Pacific Island States*, Pacific Islands' Law Officers Meeting, Port Vila.
Powles, Guy 1988, 'The Relationship between the Executive and the Public Service in Pacific Constitutions', in Ghai, *Law Politics and Government*, 135–46.
Powles, Guy 1992, 'The Tongan Constitution: Some Realities', Convention on the Tongan Constitution and Democracy, Nuku'alofa, November.
Powles, Guy 1995, 'Tonga', in Saunders and Hassall, *Asia–Pacific Constitutional Yearbook 1993*, 286–305.
Powles, Guy 1995, 'Western Samoa', in Saunders and Hassall, *Asia–Pacific Constitutional Yearbook 1993*.
Premdas, Ralph R. 1987, 'Melanesian Socialism: Vanuatu's Quest for Self-Definition and Problems of Implementation', *Pacific Studies* 11(1), November, 107–29.
Prior, E. J. 1996, 'Constitutional Fairness or Fraud on the Constitution? Compensatory Discrimination in India', *Case Western Reserve Journal of International Law* 28, 63–99.
Prizzia, Ross 1985, *Thailand in Transition: The Role of Oppositional Forces*, Asian Studies at Hawaii No. 32, University of Hawaii Press, Honolulu.
Qetaki, Alipate 1996, 'Fiji', in Saunders and Hassall, *Asia–Pacific Constitutional Yearbook 1994*.
Qetaki, Alipate 1997, 'Fiji', in Saunders and Hassall, *Asia–Pacific Constitutional Yearbook 1995*.
Quader, Abdul 1998, 'Bangladesh', in Saunders and Hassall, *Asia–Pacific Constitutional Yearbook 1996*, 55–68.
Race, Jeffrey 1975, 'Thailand in 1974: A New Constitution' *Asian Survey* 15, February.
Rasul, Jainal T. 1984, 'Muslim Personal Law and Its Incorporation into the Philippine Legal System: A Constitutional Perspective', *Philippine Law Journal*, December.
Reeve, David 1985, *Golkar of Indonesia: An Alternative to the Party System*, Oxford University Press, Singapore.

Reeves, Paul, Tomasi Tayalu Vakatora and Brij Vilash Lal 1996, *The Fiji Islands: Towards a United Future. Report of the Fiji Constitution Review Commission*, Parliamentary Paper No. 34, Parliament of Fiji.
Regan, Anthony J. 1996, 'Papua New Guinea', in Saunders and Hassall, *Asia–Pacific Constitutional Yearbook 1994*.
Regan, Anthony J. 1998, 'Papua New Guinea', in Saunders and Hassall, *Asia–Pacific Constitutional Yearbook 1996*, 267–316.
Regan, Anthony J. 1999, 'Papua New Guinea', in Saunders and Hassall, *Asia–Pacific Constitutional Yearbook 1997*.
Regan, Tony 1985, 'Papua New Guinea (c) National–Provincial Relations', in Peter Lamour and Ropate Qalo (eds), *Decentralisation in the South Pacific*, University of the South Pacific, Suva.
Regan, Tony 1997, 'Papua New Guinea', in Saunders and Hassall, *Asia–Pacific Constitutional Yearbook 1995*.
Ren Jainxin 1995, 'The All-Round Growth of People Courts in China's Era of Reform and Opening Up', *China Law* 2, 15 June, 49–57.
Riggs, Fred W. 1966, *Thailand: The Modernization of a Bureaucratic Polity*, East-West Center Press, Honolulu.
Robie, David 1989, *Blood on Their Banner: Nationalist Struggles in the South Pacific*, Pluto Press, Sydney.
Rodman, M. and Mathew Cooper (eds) 1979, *The Pacification of Melanesia*, University of Michigan Press.
Rodman, William L. 1985, '"A Law unto Themselves": Legal Innovation in Ambae, Vanuatu', *American Ethnologist* 12, 602–24.
Rodman, William L. 1993, 'The Law of the State and the State of the Law in Vanuatu', in V. S. Lockwood, T. G. Harding and B. J. Wallace (eds), *Contemporary Pacific Societies: Studies in Development and Change*, Prentice Hall, Englewood Cliffs, New Jersey.
Romano, Angela 1996, 'The Open Wound: Keterbukaan and Press Freedom in Indonesia', *Australian Journal of International Affairs* 50(2), 157–69.
Rosenau, James N. and Ernst-Otto Czempiel 1992, *Governance without Government: Order and Change in World Politics*, Cambridge University Press, Cambridge.
Rosenfeld, M. 1993, 'Modern Constitutionalism as Interplay between Identity and Diversity: An Introduction', *Cardozo Law Review* 14, 497–531.
Rosenfeld, Michel 1994, *Constitutionalism, Identity, Difference, and Legitimacy: Theoretical Perspectives*, Duke University Press, Durham.
Sack, P. 1982, 'Constitutionalism and "Homegrown" Constitutions', in P. Sack (ed.), *Pacific Constitutions*, Research School of Pacific Studies, Australian National University, Canberra.
Sack, Peter and Elizabeth Minchin (eds) 1986, *Legal Pluralism: Proceedings of the Canberra Law Workshop VII*, Research School of Social Sciences, Australian National University, Canberra.
Sahlins, Marshall 1966, 'Poor Man, Rich Man, Big Man, Chief: Political Types in Melanesia and Polynesia', in I. Hogbin and L. R. Hiatt (eds), *Readings in Australian and Pacific Anthropology*, Melbourne University Press, Melbourne.
Samudavanija, Chai-Anan 1987, 'Political History', in Somsakdi Xuto (ed.), *Government and Politics of Thailand*, Oxford University Press, Singapore.

Samuels, Harriet 1995, 'Hong Kong', in Saunders and Hassall, *Asia–Pacific Constitutional Yearbook 1993*, 22–54.
Samuels, Harriet 1996, 'Constitutional Developments in Hong Kong', in Saunders and Hassall, *Asia–Pacific Constitutional Yearbook 1994*.
Sanday, Jim 1989, 'The Military in Fiji: Historical Development and Future Role', Working Paper No. 201, Strategic and Defence Studies Centre, Australian National University, Canberra, December
Sanghi, G. L. 1995, 'Human Rights Protection with Regional Stability and Economic Development and Legal Protection of the Rights of the Minority', 14th Lawasia Biennial Conference, Beijing.
Santos, Sol 2001, *The Moro Islamic Challenge: Constitutional Rethinking for the Mindanao Peace Process*, University of the Philippines Press, Quezon City.
Sartori, Giovanni 1987, *The Theory of Democracy Revisited: Part One: The Contemporary Debate*, Chatham House Publishers, USA.
Saunders, Cheryl and Graham Hassall (eds) 1995–99, *Asia–Pacific Constitutional Yearbook*, vols 1–5, 1993–1997, Centre for Comparative Constitutional Studies, Melbourne.
Schuster, Donald R. 1992, 'The Last Trusteeship – Island of Opportunists: A Personal View of the Republic of Belau', *Journal of Pacific History* 27(1), June, 73–82.
Sciulli, D. 1992, *The Theory of Societal Constitutionalism: Foundations of a Non-Marxist Critical Theory*, Cambridge University Press.
Senate Select Committee on Protection of Fijian Fishing Grounds 1994, *Report*, Parliamentary Paper 10, Fiji.
Shafruddin, Hashim 1984, 'The Constitution and the Federal Idea in Peninsular Malaysia', *Journal of Malaysian and Comparative Law* 11.
Shah, Raja Tun Azlan 1982, 'The Role of Constitutional Rulers: A Malaysian Perspective for the Laity', *Journal of Malaysian and Comparative Law* 9(1), 1–18.
Shaw, William 1987, 'The Neo-Confucian Revolution of Values in Early Yi Korea: Its Implications for Korean Legal Thought', in Brian E. McKnight (ed.), *Law and the State in Traditional East Asia: Six Studies on the Sources of East Asian Law*, University of Hawaii Press.
Sheridan, L. A. and H. E. Groves 1987, *The Constitution of Malaysia*, 4th edn, MLJ Publications, Kuala Lumpur.
Shim Jae Hoon 1996, 'Swift, Tough Justice', *Far Eastern Economic Review*, 15 August, 16–17.
Shrestha, Kusum 1994, 'In Re Snap Poll for the House of Representatives', *Spotlight*, 23 September.
Shuster, D. R. 1994, 'Custom versus a New Elite: Palau's 16 State Constitutions', *Journal of Pacific History* 29(2), 188–202.
Simorangkir, J. C. T. 1980, *Around and About the Indonesian Constitution of 1945*, Djambatan, Jakarta.
Sinnadurai, Dato Dr Visu 1989, 'The Yang di-Pertuan Agong: The Appointment Process under the Federal Constitution', *Supreme Court Journal* 2, 65–9.
Sklar, Richard L. 1987, 'Developmental Democracy', *Comparative Studies in Society and History* 29, 686–714.
Sming Tailangka 1974, 'The Military Judicial System of Thailand', *Military Law Review* 64, 151–9.

Smith, Anthony 1979, *Nationalism in the Twentieth Century*, Australian National University Press, Canberra.
Soedijana 1972, 'People's Consultative Assembly (Majelis Permusyawaratan Rakyat)', *Indonesian Quarterly* 1, 31–60.
Soluta, Jose A. 1975, 'On the Alternative Approach to the Judicial Review of Emergency Power Cases', *Philippine Law Journal* 50, 484–510.
Somvichian, Kamol 1978, "The Oyster and the Shell': Thai Bureaucrats in Politics', *Asian Survey* 18, 829–37.
Sopheng, Chheang 1996, 'MPs Want King To Head Independent Electoral Panel', *Cambodia Times*, 9–15 June.
Standish, B. 1979, *Provincial Government in Papua New Guinea: Early Lessons from Chimbu*, Institute of Applied Social and Economic Research, Boroko.
Standish, B. 1983, 'Power to the People? Decentralization in Papua New Guinea', *Public Administration and Development* 3, 223–38.
Standish, B. 1990, 'Bougainville: Undermining the State in Papua New Guinea', *Pacific Research* 3(1), 8–11.
Stavros, Stephanos 1992, 'The Right to a Fair Trial in Emergency Situations', *International and Comparative Law Quarterly* 41.
Stepan, Alfred 1990, 'On the Tasks of a Democratic Opposition', *Journal of Democracy* 1(2), Spring, 41–9.
Stewart, William John 1983, 'Stone Age and Twentieth Century Law in the Independent State of Papua New Guinea', *Boston College Third World Law Journal* 4(1), 48–71.
Stokes, S. C. 1998, 'Pathologies of Deliberation', in Jon Elster, *Deliberative Democracy*, Cambridge University Press.
Subekti 1973, *Law in Indonesia*, P.T. Gunung Agung, Jakarta.
Sucharitkul, Sompong 1997, 'Thailand', in Saunders and Hassall, *Asia–Pacific Constitutional Yearbook 1995*.
Sureda, A. Rigo 1973, *The Evolution of the Right of Self-Determination: A Study of United Nations Practice*, A.W. Sijthoff, Leiden.
Suriyamongkol, Pisan 1988, *Institutionalization of Democratic Political Processes in Thailand: A Three-Pronged Democratic Polity*, Arunee Indrasuksri, Bangkok.
Sutherland, William 1992, *Beyond the Politics of Race: An Alternative History of Fiji to 1992*, Political and Social Change Monograph 15, Australian National University, Canberra.
Taafaki, T. and J. Oh 1995, *Governance in the Pacific: Politics and Policy Success in Tuvalu*, National Centre for Development Studies, Australian National University, Canberra.
Takabwebwe, Michael N. 1997, in Saunders and Hassall, *Asia–Pacific Constitutional Yearbook 1995*.
Tamanaha, Brian 1988, 'The Role of Custom and Traditional Leaders under the Yap Constitution', *University of Hawaii Law Review*, Summer, 81–104.
Tan, Kevin L. Y. 1999, 'Singapore', in Saunders and Hassall, *Asia–Pacific Constitutional Yearbook 1997*.
Tan, Kevin L. Y. and Li-Ann Thio 1995, 'Singapore', in Saunders and Hassall, *Asia–Pacific Constitutional Yearbook 1993*, 191–242.
Tan, Kevin L. Y. and Thio Li-ann 1998, 'Singapore', in Saunders and Hassall, *Asia–Pacific Constitutional Yearbook 1996*, 317–36.

Tan, Kevin, Yeo Tiong Min and Lee Kiat Seng 1991, *Constitutional Law in Malaysia and Singapore*, Malayan Law Journal, Singapore and Kuala Lumpur.

Tate, D. J. M. 1971/1979, *The Making of Modern South-East Asia*, Oxford University Press, Kuala Lumpur (vol. 1: 1971), vol. 2: 1979).

Taumoepeau, 'Aisea and 'Alisi Taumoepeau 1999, 'Tonga', in Saunders and Hassall, *Asia–Pacific Constitutional Yearbook 1997*.

Thayer, Carlyle 1991, 'Renovation and Vietnamese Society: The Changing Role of Government and Administration', in Dean K. Forbes et al. (eds), *Doi Moi: Vietnam's Renovation Policy and Performance*, Political and Social Change Monograph 14, Research School of Pacific Studies, Australian National University, Canberra.

Thio, Li-ann 1997, 'Singapore', in Saunders and Hassall, *Asia–Pacific Constitutional Yearbook 1995*.

Thio, Li-ann and Kevin Y. L. Tan 1996, 'Singapore', in Saunders and Hassall, *Asia–Pacific Constitutional Yearbook 1994*.

Thompson, Kenneth W. (ed.) 1988, *The U.S. Constitution and the Constitutions of Asia*, vol. IV, Miller Center Bicentennial Series on Constitutionalism, University Press of America.

Thoolen, Hans (ed.) 1987, *Indonesia and the Rule of Law: Twenty Years of 'New Order' Government*, Francis Pinter, London.

Thornberry, Patrick 1989, 'Self-Determination, Minorities, Human Rights: A Review of International Instruments', *International and Comparative Law Quarterly* 38, October, 867–89.

Tiglao, Robert 1988, 'The Consolidation of the Dictatorship' in Aurora Javate-Dedios et al. (eds), *Dictatorship and Revolution*, Conspectus, Manila.

Trindade, F. A. 1978, 'The Constitutional Position of the Yang di-Pertuan Agong', in Tun Mohamed Suffian, H. P. Lee and F. A. Trindade (eds), *The Constitution of Malaysia: Its Developments, 1957–1977*, Oxford University Press, Kuala Lumpur and New York.

Trindade, F. A. and S. Jayakumar 1964, 'The Supreme Head of the Federation', *MLR* 6(280), 282–4.

Trindade, F. A. and H. P. Lee (eds) 1986, *The Constitution of Malaysia: Further Perspectives and Development: Essays in Honour of Tun Mohamed Suffian*, Oxford University Press, Singapore and New York.

Troutman, Charles III 1997, 'Guam', in Saunders and Hassall, *Asia–Pacific Constitutional Yearbook 1995*.

Twitchett, Kenneth J. 1969, 'The Colonial Powers and the United Nations', *Journal of Contemporary History* 4(1), 167–85.

Van Trease, Howard 1987, *The Politics of Land in Vanuatu: From Colony to Independence*, Institute of Pacific Studies, Suva.

Vanberg, Victor J. and James M. Buchanan 1996, 'Constitutional Choice, Rational Ignorance and the Limits of Reason', in Karol Edward Soltan and Stephen L. Elkin (eds), *The Constitution of Good Societies*, Pennsylvania State University Press.

Venugopal, K. K. 1977, 'Emergency Powers and the Federal Structure', *Indian Advocate* 17.

Walzer, M. 1995, *Toward a Global Civil Society*, Berghahn Books, Providence.

Wang, De-Xiang and Wang Zhen-Min 1994, 'Development of the Concept of Government and the People's Congresses System in PRC', in Hassall and Saunders, *The Powers and Functions of Executive Government*, 94–6.
Ward, Alan 1992, 'The Crisis of Our Times: Ethnic Resurgence and the Liberal Ideal', *Journal of Pacific History* 27(1), June.
Weeramantry, Christopher 1992, *Nauru*, Melbourne University Press.
Weightman, Barry and Hilda Lini (eds) 1980, *Vanuatu*, Institute of Pacific Studies, Suva.
Weisbrot, D. 1982, 'The Impact of the Papua New Guinea Constitution on the Recognition and Application of Customary Law', in P. Sack (ed.), *Pacific Constitutions*, Research School of Pacific Studies, Australian National University, Canberra.
Weisbrot, David 1988, 'Papua New Guinea's Indigenous Jurisprudence and the Legacy of Colonialism', *University of Hawaii Law Review* 10, 1–45.
Wenk, Klaus 1968, *The Restoration of Thailand under Rama I, 1782–1809*, trs. Greeley Stahl, University of Arizona Press for Association for Asian Studies.
West, J. M. and E. J. Baker 1988, 'The 1987 Constitutional Reforms in South Korea: Electoral Processes and Judicial Independence', *Harvard Human Rights Yearbook* 1, 135.
White, Gordon 1996, 'Corruption and the Transition from Socialism in China', *Journal of Law and Society* 23(1), 149–69.
Wijetillake, O. 1988, 'Integrating the Judicial System and Reviewing the Administration of Justice in Papua New Guinea', *Melanesian Law Journal* 16.
Wright, Joseph J. 1991, *The Balancing Act: A History of Modern Thailand*, Asia Books, USA.
Wurfel, D. 1962, 'The Philippine Elections: Support for Democracy', *Asian Survey* 2(3), May.
Wyatt, David 1982, *Thailand: A Short History*, Yale University Press and Trasvin Publications, New Haven, London, Chiang Mai.
Xu Chongde 1995, 'China', in Saunders and Hassall, *Asia–Pacific Constitutional Yearbook 1993*, 14–21.
Yoon, D. K. 1988, 'Constitutional Amendment in Korea', *Korean Journal of Comparative Law* 16, 1.
Yoon, D. Y. 1992, *Law and Political Authority in South Korea*, Westview Press, Boulder.
Yoon, Dae-Kyu 1990, *Law and Political Authority in South Korea*, Kyungnam University Press, Seoul, and Westview Press, Boulder.
Zakaria, Haji Ahmad 1989, 'Malaysia: Quasi Democracy in a Divided Society', in Diamond et al., *Democracy in Developing Countries*, 347–81.
Zimmerman, Robert 1974, 'Student "Revolution" in Thailand: The End of the Thai Bureaucratic Polity?', *Asian Survey* 14(6), June.
Zolo, Danilo 1992, *Democracy and Complexity: A Realist Approach*, trs. David McKie, Polity Press, Cambridge.
Zweigert, K. and H. Kötz 1987, *An Introduction to Comparative Law*, Clarendon Press, Oxford.

Index

Abas, T.M.S. 54
Abas, Salleh bin 189
Abdulgani, Roeslan 65, 146
Abdullah, S. 75
Abueva, J.V. 57, 146
accountability of government 78, 130, 132, 217, 244, 246
Aceh province, Indonesia 226, 243
Adas, M. 26
adat law, Indonesia 174
Adhikari, Manmohan 83
administrative courts 182–3
Agpalo, R.E. 34
Ahmed, Chief Justice Shahabuddin 184
American Samoa 25, 42; constitutional reform 145; customary law 40; judicial system 173; party system 102
Amet, Chief Justice Arnold 85, 187
Anderson, B. 5
Ang Duong, King (Laos) 120
Angelo, A.H. 173
Anglim, J. 60
Anti-Defection Law, India 112
Aoba 19, 26
Aquino, Corazon 132, 158, 229
Ariki, House of (Cook Islands) 41
Asia, federalism in 223–30
Aung San, General 148, 224
Aung San Suu Kyi 148, 150
Australia, and Papua New Guinea 22, 25, 61, 235
authoritarianism 4–5, 34, 210, 215
authority, traditional 19, 39–42, 122, 241
autochthony 61–2, 241
Awami League 79
Ayasha, J. 209

Banaba Island 68, 76
Bangladesh: accountability of government 79; constituent assemblies 56–7, 145; Constitution (Second Amendment) Act 201; Election Commission 110; federalism 223; form of government 141; gender equality 102; head of state 125–6; Jatiya Party 112; judicial system 172, 184; martial law 201, 210; no-confidence motions 83; party system 103, 112; state of emergency 201, 206, 207, 208, 209; vote-buying 113
Banharn Silpa-archa 83, 88, 154
Bantam 14
Barisan National Front, Malaysia 98
Barisian Socialis party, Singapore 112
Barommatrailokanat, King, Thailand 16
Basic Act on the Judiciary, Indonesia 171, 184
Basic Law of Hong Kong, China 226
Basic Law of Macau, China 226
Basic Law on Judicial Powers, Indonesia 171, 177
Basic Principles on the Independence of the Judiciary, UN 191
Baxi, U. 42
Bayne, P.J. 173
Beijing Statement on judicial independence 191
Bharatiya Janata Party (BJP), India 83, 155
Bhargava, G.S. 209, 211
Bhumibol Adulyade, King 154
Bhutto, Benazir 134
bills of rights 29, 31, 35
Birenda, King 83, 121
Bisson, Sir Gordon 187
Biswas, President Abdur Rahman 79
Blaustein, A.H. 158
Bogra, Prime Minister 211
Bonifacio, Andres 5, 21
Bougainville 22, 67–8, 85, 232, 235–6, 243
Bougainville Interim Government 236
Bougainville People's Congress 236
Bougainville Revolutionary Army 204, 236
British Borneo 20

301

British colonisation 19–20, 22–4, 26, 39, 176–7, 243
Brunei 14
Buchanan, J.M. 242
Buddhist law 15
'Buddhist Socialism', Cambodia 5
bureaucratic regulation, China 16
Burma: and British colonisation 20; Burma Socialist Programme Party (BSPP) 37, 103, 202; Communist Party 224; constituent assemblies 56, 145, 147; constitutional reform 37, 147–51; coup d'etat, constitutional 202; Dhammathat (traditional law) 15; Election Commission 148; ethnic groups 224; federalism 223–4; kingship and authority 14; Lahu National Development Party 148; military authorities, involvement in operation of the state 45, 57, 148, 202; multi-party system 148; National Convention 148–51; National Convention Convening Work Committee 149–50; National League for Democracy 148, 150–1; party system 103–4; State Law and Order Restoration Council (SLORC) 104, 148, 151, 202, 244; state of emergency 208; suspension of constitutional powers 201; Tatmadaw (armed forces, Burma) 45, 57, 148, 202
Burma Socialist Programme Party 37, 103, 202
Buxbaum, D.C. 169

Cakebau, Chief 24
Cambodia 4; accountability of government 78–9; Cambodian Communist Party 38; Citizenship Law 101, 109; Constitutional Council 179; constitutional reform 38, 147; electoral commission 110; Electoral Law 109; judicial system 179, 185; kingship and authority 14, 16, 120, 147; military force 244; monitoring of elections 109; Parliamentary Law 109; Political Parties Law 109; proportional representation 95; suffrage in 101; Supreme Council of Magistracy Law 179, 185
campaigns, election 107–8
Caroline Islands 22–3
Casey, Sir Maurice 187
Catholic Bishops Conference 132
Center for Aceh Referendum (SIRA) 226
Central Election Management Committee, South Korea 108, 111

Centre for the Independence of Judges and Lawyers 189
Chakri dynasty, Thailand 46
Chalmers, D.R.C. 174
Chan, Sir Julius 84–5, 189, 236
Chaudhury government, Fiji 205
Chem Snguon 186
Chen, A.H.Y. 16
Chiba, M. 141
chiefs, Fijian 24, 30, 40–1, 159
chiefs, traditional 40, 42, 54
China, People's Republic of 35; Basic Law of Hong Kong 226; Basic Law of Macau 226; Confucian principles 16, 43; constitutional reform 36–7; 'constitutional supervision' 188; constitutions 3; and Hong Kong 175, 226–7; legal tradition 16; martial law 203; National People's Congress 37, 206; party system 103; state of emergency 206; Tiananmen Square 244
Chowdhury, S.R. 200
Christian tradition 43
Chua Kin Yeow 127
Chuan government, Thailand 182
Chulalongkorn the Great 16
Chun regime, South Korea 47
Citizens Constitutional Forum (CCF), Fiji 160
citizens, equality before the law 46
citizenship 46, 54, 92, 101, 241
Citizenship Law, Cambodia 101, 109
civil-law tradition 33, 183
civil society 8, 38, 242, 245; education in principles of 46, 48
coalitions 82–7, 98
Code of Manu 15
Coleman, Governor 145
colonial rule, legacy of 8, 55, 230, 243
colonisation 13–28, 54, 241; and the judiciary 172–3; in the Pacific Islands 21–6; in Southeast Asia 19–21
Commission on Elections, Philippines 132
Commission on Self-Determination, Guam 25
committee system in parliamentary government 76
Committee for Democratic Development, Thailand 153
common-law tradition 33, 173–4, 183, 188
Communist Party of Burma 37, 224
Communist Party, Philippines 38
communist states 35, 103
Community Development Councils, Singapore 96

Index   303

Compact of Free Association (COFA) 59–60, 223
complexity, recognition of 247
Conference of Rulers, Malaysia 129, 133, 135–6, 184, 225
conflict, constitutional 66–7, 245–6
Confucian principles 16, 43
Congress of Micronesia 63
consensus (*mufakat*), in Indonesia 77, 146
consociation 39, 98
constituencies 96–9; appointed members 100; and ethnicity 98–9; geographic basis of 97–8; functional 99; and suffrage 101; and women 101–2
constituent assemblies 56–8, 59–65, 145, 161
constitution 2, 29–53, 246–8; writing 54–71
Constitution (Amendment) Act 1994, Malaysia 137
Constitution (Amendment) Bill 1993, Malaysia 136
Constitution Drafting Assembly (CDA), Thailand 154
constitution, post-modern 246–8
Constitution Review Commission (CRC), Fiji 159–60
Constitution (Second Amendment) Act, Bangladesh 201
Constitutional Amendment (Elections) Law, Papua New Guinea 94
'Constitutional Authoritarianism', Philippines 4, 215
Constitutional Commission Act, Papua New Guinea 156
Constitutional Commission, Philippines 146, 158
Constitutional Committee, South Korea 178
Constitutional Convention, Kiribati 144
Constitutional Convention, Philippines 213
Constitutional Convention, Tonga 144
Constitutional Council, Cambodia 179
Constitutional Court, South Korea 183
Constitutional Development Commission, Papua New Guinea 109, 158
Constitutional Planning Committee, Papua New Guinea 45, 62, 232
constitutional powers, suspension of 198–221
Constitutional Review Commission, Papua New Guinea 156–7
Constitutional Review Committee, Solomon Islands 143
constitutional revision 36, 141–65, 244; by constituent assemblies 145–55; by expert commissions 142, 156–61; by parliaments 155–6; post-independence 142–61
constitutional studies 3, 5–6, 242
Constitutional Tribunal, Thailand 178–9
constitutionalism 42–3, 241–9; approaches to 33; in the Asia Pacific 1–2, 50; and democracy 75, 242–5; and emergency powers 198–9, 216–17; essence of 6, 55; global 247; in Melanesia 2; paradigm of 4; successful 3, 133; in Thailand 152; and values 42–3; viability of 44
constitutions 29–53; declared 55, 65–6; independence 13, 19, 56–66, 68, 143; interpretation of 170; modern 142, 241; negotiated 55, 56–65; sites of power 31–4; and state of emergency 208
Cook Islands: constitutional reform 145; Court of Appeal 176; customary law 40–1; judicial system 176; and New Zealand 25, 60, 145; Privy Council appeal 176
Cook, Sir Robin 187
Cordillera Administrative Region, Philippines 229
corporatism 66, 88
corruption: government 233; party 113–14
Corte's, I.R. 57, 146
Council of Chiefs, New Caledonia 40
Council of Chiefs, Vanuatu 42
Council of Grand Justices, Taiwan 170
Council of State, Vietnam 156
Council of States (Rajya Sabha), India 99
Court of Appeal, Samoa 187
Court of Appeal, Vanuatu 187
courts 33, 169–97; administrative 182–3; civil-law tradition 33; common-law tradition 33; constitutional 177–9; and emergency powers 210–14; establishment and dis-establishment of 174–83; regional appeals 186–7; religious 179–82; Syariah 179
Covenant on Civil and Political Rights, UN 67
covenants, international 215–16
Cultural Revolution 37
customary law 40, 50, 54, 141, 169, 173–4, 241

Das, B.C. 214
de Silva, H.L. 227
decentralisation 223, 230
Decentralization and Local Government Regulations Act, Vanuatu 231
Declaration for Referendum in Aceh 226
decolonisation 59–60

Defensor-Santiago, Mirian 132
Deklin, T. 45
democracy 4, 7, 91, 114, 132, 246, 247; constitutional 75, 242–4; and education 46–7; institutions of 8, 75, 77; majoritarian 82, 88, 243; multi-party 103, 148; obstacles to 46, 88
Democracy Development Committee, Thailand 153
democratic processes 154, 246
democratic values 30–1
Deve Gowda, H.D. 83
development, and law 48–9
devolution of powers 222–40
Dhammathat (traditional Burmese law) 15
Diamond, L. 31
Diem, Ngo Nhu 5
d'Iméecourt, Charles Vaudin 187, 190–1
Diro, E. 123
dispute resolution 109, 169, 174, 189–91, 246
doi moi (open door) policy, Vietnam 36, 103
due process 29, 210
Dutch colonisation 19, 49, 66, 143, 171, 243

East Asia, suspension of constitutional powers in 203–4
East Timor 226, 244
Easter Island 25
education of electorates 46–7, 107, 113, 142, 245
Election Commission, Bangladesh 110
Election Commission, Burma 148
Election Commission, Thailand 154
Election Symbols (Reservation and Allotment) Order 1968, India 109
elections 91–2, 102–11, 113, 245
Electoral Amendment Act, Western Samoa 187
Electoral Commission, India 109–10
Electoral Commission, Papua New Guinea 94, 96, 110–11
electoral commissions 108, 110–11, 154
Electoral Law, Cambodia 109
electoral laws 109–10
Electoral Review Committee, Solomon Islands 109
electoral systems 92–3; administration 108; laws 109–110; multi-member systems 96; overview of 93–6; proportional 94–5; simple plurality 93–4
elites 55, 68, 142, 143, 241
Ellice Island 61
emergency 199–200, 214–15

Emergency (Essential Powers) Ordinance 1969, Malaysia 210, 214
emergency powers 38, 198–221; characteristics of 205–10; constitutional provisions regarding 216–17; and courts 210–14; de facto 214–15; and international covenants 215–16; and international law 215–16; monitoring of 217; review of 208–9, 217; revocation of 209; use of 205–10
emergency, state of 199; declaration of 205–8; duration of 207–8; revocation of 209–10
equity 241, 244
Eri, Sir Seri 123
Establishment of Administrative Court and Administrative Procedure Bill, Thailand 182
ethnic groups 26, 67, 98–9, 160–1, 224, 241, 243
ethnicity 30, 39, 81, 98–9
ethno-nationalist state 39–42
Etpison, President Ngiratkel 60, 93
executive power 32, 33, 43, 44, 76–80, 82, 217
expert commission 58, 61, 142–3, 156, 161
experts, constitutional 142–3, 156–61

fairness 42, 241
Fatherland Front, Vietnam 103
federalism 222; in Asia 223–30
Federated States of Micronesia 59, 222; customary law 40; federalism 230; referendum 92 ; state of emergency 205
Federation of Malaya 20
Fiji 68; British colonisation 23–4; Citizens Constitutional forum (CCF) 160; civil coup 205; constituencies 97; constitution 61; constitutional reform 143, 156, 158–61; Constitution Review Commission 159–60; courts 205; customary law 40–1, 49; electoral system 92, 130, 159; ethnic groups 26, 98–9, 160–1; Great Council of Chiefs 40–1, 80, 159–60, 161; head of state 127, 130; independence 59; judicial system 187; legislature 76; military coup 204–5; Native Lands Act 101; Native Lands Commission 101; no-confidence motions 87; Parliamentary Select Committee on the Constitutution 159–60; Privy Council appeal 176; Reeves report 159, 160–1; Soqosoqo ni Vakavulewa ni Taukei (SVT) 160–1;

Index   305

state of emergency 205, 206, 207; suffrage in 101; Supreme Court 187
Fijian Nationalist Party 49
Fijian Political Party 49
Fitzpatrick, J. 199
FLNKS, New Caledonia 245
Flosse, Gaston 231
franchise 91, 98, 101
freedom 29, 54, 132, 157, 216; *see also* rights
French colonisation 20, 23–4, 26, 64, 231, 243
French Indochina 143
French Overseas Territories 64, 98, 231–2
French Polynesia 24, 64, 98, 123, 231
Frenkel, M. 222
Fukayama, F. 246

Galapagos Islands 25
Ganilau, Ratu Penaia 40, 127
Gandhi, Indira 183–4, 213
Gandhi–Jayawardene Accord 227
Garcia, Carlos 128, 132
gender equality 101–2
geography and constituencies 97–8
German colonisation 22
Ghai, Y. 143
Giddens, Anthony 29
Gilbert and Ellice Islands Colony 26, 60–1, 68
Gilbertese Constitutional Convention 61
globalisation 1, 50, 242
Golongan Karya (Golkar), Indonesia 105–6
governance 112, 244
government: accountability 78, 130, 132, 217, 244, 246; operation of 248; stability 82–8, 114–15, 146, 244–5; structure of 54; limits of 29, 31
governors-general 122–4
Great Council of Chiefs, Fiji 40–1, 80, 159–60, 161
Group Representational Constituencies (GRCs), Singapore 96
Grover, Justice 184
Guam: Commission on Self-Determination 25; independence 63; and US colonisation 24–5
Guatama 172
Guided Democracy, Indonesia 4, 99, 146, 171, 202
Guidelines of State Policy, Indonesia 125

habeas corpus 198, 203, 210, 213–14
Habermas, Jurgen 4, 46, 244, 247
Habibie, Bacharuddin Jusuf 129–30
Hahalis Welfare Society 68
Harmoko 130, 182

Hartono 76
Hasnan, H. 45
Hawaii 63–4, 122
head of state 119–40; college election of 129–31; direct election 119, 127–8; dismissal of 131; eligibility for office 126–7; immunity 135–7; monarchical 120–2; parliamentary election of 128; powers of 119, 123, 128, 133–5; presidential 124–6; reserve powers 124; roles and responsibilities of 137; selection of 126–31; term of office 131–2
Hedge, Justice 183
Hesingut report 236
Hilly, Francis Billy 123, 134
Hindu law 15
history, constitutional 13
Ho Chi Minh 5
Hong Kong 20, 175, 223, 226–7; Court of Final Appeal 175–6; electoral college 130; federalism 226–7; functional constituencies 99; head of state 130; judicial system 175–6; Legislative Assembly 175
Hong Kong Act 1985, Britain 226
Honiara Declaration 236
Hooker, M.B. 14, 16
human rights 210, 213, 242, 245, 247
human rights law 35, 48, 50, 54
Hun Sen 147
Huxley, A. 151

independence 54–5, 142, 241; judicial 188–92
Independence of Malaya Party (IMP) 20
independent candidates for election 108
Independent Election Monitoring Committee (KIPP), Indonesia 109
India: appointed members of parliament 99; communist parties 38; conflict over Kashmir 243; constituencies 96–7, 98; constituent assemblies 56; constitutional development 200; constitutional reform 155, 200; Council of States 99; courts 170; Election Symbols (Reservation and Allotment) Order 1969 109; Electoral Commission 109–10; electoral system 108, 109–110; emergency powers 215; federalism 223; gender equality 102; head of state 124, 126, 128–9, 131–3; independence constitution 56; judicial system 44, 170, 183–4; Law Commission 112; legal tradition 15; no-confidence motions 83; nominations for parliamentary seats 107; party defections 112; party

India (cont.)
    system 103; Representation of the People Act 1951 108, 114; state of emergency 200, 206, 207, 213–14; Supreme Court 44; violence, electoral 114
Indian National Congress, Malaysia 98
individual, rights of 7, 29, 34–5, 198–99, 241–2
Indonesia 5; accountability of government 130; Aceh province 226, 243; adat law 174; Administrative Court 182; appointed members of parliament 99; authoritarian rule 171; banning of *Tempo* news magazine 182; Basic Act 14/1970 on the Judiciary 171, 184; Basic Law on Judicial Powers 171, 177; communist activity 38; consensus (*mufakat*) 77, 146; constituencies 97, 99; constituent assemblies 56, 145; constitutional reform 145–6; constitutions 55, 58, 65–6, 200; and East Timor 244; electoral system 95, 107, 109, 115; federalism 223, 226; functional constituencies 99; Guided Democracy 4, 99, 146, 171, 202; Guidelines of State Policy 125; head of state 119, 125, 129, 131–2; House of Representatives (Dewan Perwakilan Rakyat) 75–7, 171; Independent Election Monitoring Committee (KIPP) 109; Indonesian Election Committee (PPI) 95; Investigating Committee for the Preparation of Independence 65; Islamic law 179–80; Islamic movements 43, 105; judicial system 170, 171–2, 177–8, 184, 188; *keluaga*, division of labour among government branches 188; Law of the National Planning Board 99; martial law 212; military authorities, involvement in operation of the state 45; military force 244; mutual co-operation (*gotong royong*) 146; National Election Commission (KPU) 96; New Order government 105, 130, 146; Pancasila 36, 55, 65–6, 105, 188; Partai Demokrasi Indonesia (PDI) 105; Partai Persatuan Pembangunan (United Development Party) 105; party system 103, 104–6, 109; People's Consultative Assembly (MPR) 125, 129, 130–1, 171, 188; Provisional People's Consultative Assembly (MPRS) 131; regional autonomy 226; sovereignty 244; suffrage in 101; state of emergency 202; Supreme Court 178; unitary state 226; violence, electoral 114
instability 8, 103, 114, 146, 158, 208–9, 244–5
institutions, democratic 8, 75, 77
Internal Security Act, Malaysia 214
Internal Security Act, Singapore 124
international agreements 215–16, 247
International Commission of Jurists 172, 199, 213, 226
International Covenant on Civil and Political Rights 215–16, 242
International Covenant on Economic, Social and Cultural Rights 242
International Law Association 199, 215
Investigating Committee for the Preparation of Independence, Indonesia 65
Irian Jaya 243
Islamic law 16, 174, 180, 225
Islamic movements 43, 105
Italia Taamale and Taamale Toelau v. Attorney General 187
Iyer, T.K.K. 211

Japan 23, 96, 119
Jatiya Party, Bangladesh 112
Java 14, 15, 146
Jeyaretnam, Joshua 127
Jimmy, Willy 86, 190
Joint Declaration between Britain and China 226
judges, expatriate 186–7, 190
Judicature Act, South Korea 171
judicial systems 169–97; impact of colonial experience 171–2; judicial activism and quietism 170–1; judicial appointments 189; judicial commissions 185; judicial independence 29, 44, 188–92; judicial institutions 44; judicial promotion 189; judicial review 169, 171, 198, 210
Judicial Committee (Repeal) Act, Singapore 177
Judicial Service Act, Thailand 185
Judicial Services Commission, Thailand 185
Judicial Services Commission, Vanuatu 191
judiciary 33, 169–97; and constitutions 183–92; independence of 188–92
Juridical Council, Thailand 182
justice 7–8, 29, 241–2

Kabua, Amata 127, 132
Kalpokas government, Vanuatu 144, 190
Kanaks 24, 231–2, 245
Kapi, Sir Mari 173

keluaga, division of labour among government branches, Indonesia 188
Kent, Robert 187
Kershaw, Anthony 60
Khaleda Zia 79, 83
Khmer Rouge 38
Khmer traditions of kingship 16
Khunkitti, Suvit 179
Kidu, Sir Biri 187
Kilage Committee 61
Kim Il Sung, President 36
Kim Jong Il, President 36
Kim Young Sam 47
Kinika, Benedict 86
Kiribati 26, 68; Constitutional Convention 144; ethnic constituencies 99; head of state 123, 128, 131–2; independence 59; judicial system 187; legislature (Maneaba Ni Maungatabu) 76; party system 102
Kittikachorn, Field Marshall Thanom 152
Korman, Maxime Carlot 86, 144, 187, 190
Kosrae 63
Kraprayoon, General Suchinda 81, 179
Kumaratunga government, Sri Lanka 58, 227, 228

Lahu National Development Party, Burma 148
Lal, Brij 159
Lao Issara (Free Lao) 143
Laos: constitutional reform 37–8; French colonisation 20–1; gender equality 102; judicial appointments 186; Lao Issara (Free Lao) 143; monarchy 120; National Assembly 79–80; party system 103; People's Supreme Courts 186
law 29, 54, 141, 174, 241, 246; and values 42–3, 50; Buddhist 15; Burmese 15; colonial 49; common-law 33, 173–4, 183, 188; constitutional 247; customary 40, 50, 54, 141, 169, 173–4, 241; Hindu 15; international 67–8, 215–16; positive 246; pre-colonial 14–15
Law Commission, India 112
Law of the National Planning Board, Indonesia 99
Law of the Three Great Seals, Thailand 15
Law Reform Commission, Papua New Guinea 157
laws: anti-subversion 214; electoral 109–10; internal security 214
Lawson, Stephanie 30
Le Code, Vietnam 17
Le Tagaloa Pita 187

League of Nations 21–3
Lederman, Dr 62
Lee Kuan Yew 5
Lee Teng-hui 48, 127
Leekpai government, Thailand 152
Legal Code of Rama I, Thailand 15
legal tradition 4, 15–18, 141
Leghari, Farooq 134
legislative processes 75–7, 82
legislature 31, 75–90; bicameral 80–2; and the executive 77–80
legitimacy 4, 6–7, 29, 34, 43, 78–9, 244
Lev, D.S. 188
Leye, President Jean-Marie 85, 123, 131, 144, 191
liberal-democratic state 34–5
Lili'uokalani, Queen (Hawaii) 64
Lim Yew Hock 58
Lini, Walter 124, 144, 187, 190
Local Administration Act and Coup Announcement, Thailand 228
loi Cadre (Framework Law), New Caledonia 231–2
Loughlin, M. 4
Lunabeck, Vincent 191

Macapagal, President Diosdado 26, 127–8, 132
Macassar 14
Macau 20, 99, 223, 226
Magsaysay, Ramon 132
Mahathir, Prime Minister 135, 189, 214
Majapahit 15
majority rule 29, 78, 82, 95
Malacca 14
Malalos Constitution, Philippines 55
Malayan Communist Party 38
Malayan Union 38
Malays, preferential treatment of 39, 98
Malaysia 39; appointed members of parliament 99; communist activity 38; Conference of Rulers 129, 133, 135–6, 184, 225; Constitution (Amendment) Act 1994 137; Constitution (Amendment) Bill 1993 136; constitutional reform 155, 202; electoral system 93, 98, 109; Emergency (Essential Powers) Ordinance 1969 210, 214; ethnic constituencies 93; executive 224; federalism 58, 223–5; head of state 135–6; House of Representatives (Dewan Perwakilan Rakyat) 125, 171, 224; Indian National Congress 98; Internal Security Act 214; Islamic law 43, 180, 225; Islamic movements 43; judicial system 176, 180, 184, 189; legislature 80, 224; monarchy 120,

Malaysia (cont.)
  122, 129, 133, 135–6; party defections 112; Privy Council appeal 176–7; Proclamation of Constitutional Principles 135; racial violence 155; single-party domination 103; state of emergency 202, 206, 207, 208, 209, 210; United Malays National Organisation (UMNO) 189, 225
Malaysian Chinese Association 98
Mamaloni, Solomon 86, 102, 134, 143
Mara, Ratu Sir Kamisese 40, 49, 61, 87, 127, 205
Marcos, Ferdinand: 'Constitutional Authoritarianism' 4, 215; dictatorship 44, 128; martial law 91, 131–2, 146–7, 203, 209, 212–13; removal from office 109, 158
Mariana Islands 22, 59, 205; *see also* Northern Mariana Islands
Marianas Political State Commission 59
Marquesas 24
Marshall Islands: constituencies 97; customary law 40; head of state 123, 127, 132; independence 63; Japanese occupation 23; judicial system 187; no-confidence motions 87; parliamentary government 59; referendum 92; state of emergency 205, 206, 207; and US colonisation 24
martial law 210; *see also* state of emergency
Martin, Chief Justice Geoffrey 187
Mataitoga, Isikeli 30
Mataskelekele, Judge Kalkot 191
Matignon Accord 64, 92, 232
Melanesia, legal tradition in 17
Members of Parliament (Vacation of Seats) Act 33, Vanuatu 113
Micah Bipartisan Committee Report on provincial government, Papua New Guinea 234–5
Micronesian Constitutional Convention 63–4
Mindanao autonomous region, Philippines 180–2, 230, 243
minorities, ethnic 67, 224, 241
minorities 30, 81–2, 94, 247
modernity 29–30, 34, 48, 241, 246
Mohammad, Governor-General Ghulam 211
Mollok, Bernard 157
Momis, John 61, 67–8
Mon Kingdom 15
monarchies 119, 120–2, 126, 133
Moonesinghe Select Committee, Sri Lanka 228

Morauta, Sir Mekere 85
Morling, Judge Trevor 187
mufakat (consensus), Indonesia 77, 146
Muhammad Ridwan Indra 76–7
Munir, Chief Justice Mohammad 211
Muslims, Santri 43
mutual co-operation (gotong-royong), in Indonesia 146
Myanmar, Union of 57; constituent assemblies 147; military authorities, involvement in operation of the state 104; Ministry of Foreign Affairs 149; party system 104
Myo Nyunt, Lt. Gen. 150

Nagriamel movement, Vanuatu 55
Nakamura, Kuniwo 93, 145
Namaliu, Rabbie 84
Namfres, Philippines 109
Narasimha Rao, P.V. 83
Nasioi people, Panguna 236
Natapei, Edward 190
National Action Party (NAP), Thailand 83
National Assembly, Vietnam 155–6
National Convention, Burma 148–51
National Convention Convening Work Committee, Burma 149–50
National Election Commission (KPU), Indonesia 95, 96, 107
National Executive Council, Papua New Guinea 204
National Goals and Directive Principles, Papua New Guinea 173
National League for Democracy (NLD), Burma 148, 150–1
National Peace-Keeping Council (NPKC), Thailand 152, 179, 203
National People's Congress, China 206
National Security Law, Taiwan 214
nationalism 5, 40, 65, 69, 143, 200
Native Lands Act, Fiji 101
Native Lands Commission, Fiji 101
Nauru: constituencies 97; head of state 123; independence 59; party system 103; trusteeship 22
Ne Win, General 37, 104, 148, 201–2, 224
Nehru, Jawaharlal 83
Nepal: communist parties 38; federalism 223; form of government 141; monarchy 120–1; no-confidence motions 83; nominations for parliamentary seats 107; party system 103
New Aspiration Party, Thailand 229
New Caledonia 24, 245; constituencies 98; Council of Chiefs 40; customary

Index   309

law 40; devolution of powers 231–2;
FLNKS 245; independence 64; *loi
Cadre* (Framework Law) 231–2;
Matignon Accord 64, 92, 232
'New Confucianism', Singapore 5
New Guinea 22, 23
New Hebrides Condominium 23
'New Order' government, Indonesia 105,
130, 146
'New Society', Philippines 4
New Zealand 25, 60, 145, 176
Niue 25, 60
no-confidence motions 82–7, 245
nominations for parliamentary seats 107
non-Strategic Trusts, UN 22
Norodom, King (Laos) 120
North Java 14
North Korea 35–6, 103
North Solomons Province 232, 235–6
North Solomons Provincial Government 235
Northern Mariana Islands,
Commonwealth of (CNMI) 59, 97, 145
Noumea Accord 232

Oda, H. 188
Office of Hawaiian Affairs 63
Omar, Abdul Hamid 189
Ong Teng Cheong 127
Ongkarn Borihan Suan Tambon, Thailand 228
Onn, President Dato 20
Organic Act for the Autonomous Region in Muslim Mindanao, Philippines 230
Organic Act for the Creation of an Autonomous Cordillera Region, Philippines 229
Organic Law on Local and Provincial Level Government, Papua New Guinea 45, 156, 204, 233–5
Organic Law on Provincial (Government) Elections, Papua New Guinea 94
Organic Law on the Integrity of Political Parties and Candidates, Papua New Guinea 157

Pacific Islands: colonisation in the 21–6;
devolution of powers 231–7;
federalism 222, 230–1; no-confidence motions 84–5, 86–7; suspension of constitutional powers 204–5;
traditional states in 17–19
Pacific Islands Law Officers Meeting (PILOM) 187
Pacific Judicial Council 187
Pakistan: conflict over Kashmir 243;
constituent assemblies 57; federalism 223; form of government 141; head of state 124, 134; instability 209; Islamic people 179; judiciary 211; martial law 208, 211; party system 103, 113; state of emergency 200, 206, 207, 208, 209, 211
Palau: constitutional reform 145;
customary law 40; electoral system 93; head of state 119, 123, 127;
independence 63; Japanese occupation 23; self-determination 60;
state of emergency 205
Paliwala, A.H. 174
Pan Malayan Council of Joint Action 20
Pancasila, Indonesia 36, 55, 65–6, 105, 188
Pangu Party, Papua New Guinea 102
Panguna copper mine, Bougainville 204, 235–6
Panyarachun, Anand 203
Papua and New Guinea Act of 1949, Australia 25
Papua Besena 68
Papua New Guinea: accountability of government 78; and Australia 22, 25, 61, 235; and Bougainville 67, 235–6, 243; constituencies 93–4, 96;
constitution 61–2, 173; Constitutional Commission Act 156; Constitutional Development Commission 109, 158;
Constitutional Planning Committee 45, 62, 232; constitutional reform 143, 156–8; Constitutional Review Commission 156–7; Constitutional (Second Amendment) Act 201;
corruption 233; customary law 50, 173–4; devolution of powers 222, 232–6; Electoral Commission 94, 96, 110–11; electoral system 93, 108, 109;
executive power 45; expert commission 61; federalism 230, 232;
head of state 119, 123, 127–8;
independence 25, 59; instability 158;
judicial system 187, 189; Law Reform Commission 157; legislature 45, 76;
National Executive Council 204;
National Goals and Directive Principles 173; no-confidence motions 84–5; nominations for parliamentary seats 107; Organic Law on Local and Provincial Level Government 156;
Organic Law on Local and Provincial Level Government 204, 233, 235;
Organic Law on Provincial Governments 235; Organic Law on Provincial (Government) Elections 94;
Organic Law on the Integrity of

Papua New Guinea (*cont.*)
  Political Parties 157; Organic Law on the Integrity of Political Parties and Candidates 157; organic laws 109; Pangu Party 102; party system 102, 112, 158; provincial government system 61, 232–5; Public Services Structure Review Committee Report 61; Report on Central–Provincial Government Relations 61; state of emergency 204; violence, electoral 114
Papua New Guinea Act, Australia 62
Paris Minimum Standards of Rights Norms in a State of Emergency 199
parliament 31–2, 92, 99, 155; *see also* legislature
Parliamentary Elections (Amendment) Act 1991, Singapore 99
parliamentary government 33, 56, 59, 75–7, 88, 141
Parliamentary Law, Cambodia 109
Parliamentary Select Committee on Constitutional Change, Sri Lanka 228
Parliamentary Select Committee on the Constitution, Fiji 159–60
Partai Demokrasi Indonesia (PDI) 105–6
Partai Persatuan Pembangunan (United Development Party, PPP), Indonesia 105–6
participation: in constitution-writing 56, 58, 68; in constitutional reform 142, 161; in decision-making processes 92, 216
parties, political 30, 102–11, 109, 113–14, 189, 244–5; anti-defection measures 111–13, 115; party-hopping 111–13, 115, 158
Party-List System Act, Philippines 99
party system: campaigns 107–8; and elections 102–11, 111–14, 246; independent candidates 108; nominations 107; single-party domination 103–6; stability of 82; Westminster 78, 87
patron–client relations 46, 48, 244
Payoyo, P.B. 215
Peace of Nanking 20
Peiris, G.L. 228
people, defining 66–9
People's Action Party, Singapore 99
People's Consultative Assembly (MPR), Indonesia 125, 129–31, 171, 188
People's Initiative for Reform, Modernization and Action (Pirma), Philippines 132
People's Supreme Courts, Laos 186

'Personalism', Vietnam 5
Petition Committee of the Office of the Juridical Council (Thailand) 121
petitions 92, 121
Philippine Independence Act, US 57
Philippines 4–5, 14, 38; accountability of government 78; autonomous regions 229, 230, 243; colonial history 21; Commission on Elections 132; constitutionalism 212; constituencies 97, 99; constituent assemblies 57, 145–6; Constitution 55, 92; 'Constitutional Authoritarianism' 4, 215; Constitutional Commission 146, 158; Constitutional Convention 57, 213; constitutional reform 132, 146–7, 156, 158; Cordillera Administrative Region 229; devolution of powers 223, 229–30; executive power in 44; federalism 229–30; *habeas corpus*, suspension of 203, 210, 213; head of state 125, 127–8, 131–2; Islamic law 179–80; judicial system 172, 180–2, 191; legal tradition 16; martial law 212–13, 215; Mindanao autonomous region 230, 243; monitoring of elections 109; Namfres 109; 'New Society' 4; Organic Act for the Autonomous Region in Muslim Mindanao 230; Organic Act for the Creation of an Autonomous Cordillera Region 229; Party-List System Act 99; party system 103; People's Initiative for Reform, Modernization and Action (Pirma) 132; presidential system 119; proportional representation 95; Shari'ah Appellate 180; state of emergency 203, 206, 207, 208
Phillips, E. 199, 211
Pitcairn Island 25
Planas v. Comelec 213
plurality, simple 93–4
Pohnpei, independence 63
Pokrong Thontee Act of BE 2457, Thailand 228
Political Parties Law, Cambodia 109
Political Status Commission, Micronesia 63
Pollwatch, Thailand 109
Polynesia, legal tradition in 17
Portuguese colonisation 19–20
postmodernism 246–7
power: chiefly 243; civilian 29; constitutional 31–3, 198–221; constitution as 244; devolution of 222–40; executive 76; limitation of 36;

political 188; state 31–6; traditional 18–19, 243
powers, emergency 38, 198–221; characteristics of 205–10; constitutional provisions regarding 216–17; and constitutionalism 216–17; and courts 210–14; and international covenants 215–16; and international law 215–16; review of 208–9; revocation of 209; use of 205–10
powers, metropolitan 59, 66, 142
powers, residual 119
Powles, G. 76
Pra Thammasat, Thailand 15–16
Prasada Rao, P.L. 75
Presidential Elections Committee, Singapore 127
presidential systems 32–3, 56, 59, 119, 124–6, 133, 141
Prevention of Discrimination and the Protection of Minorities, UN sub-commission on 189
Privy Council 121–2, 176–7
Privy Council Court of Appeal, Tonga 176
Prizzia, Ross 152
Proclamation of Constitutional Principles, Malaysia 135
proportional representation 93–5, 112
prosperity 8, 48–9, 241
Provincial Councils Act 42 of 1987, Sri Lanka 227
Provincial Government Act, Solomon Islands 237
Public Services Structure Review Committee, Papua New Guinea 61

Quirino, Elpidio 132

Rabuka, Sitiveni 49, 87, 159, 161, 204
Rahman, Tunku Abdul 20
Rama V, King, Thailand 16
Ramos, Fidel 132, 191
Ratanakosin Kingdom, Thailand 16
Ray, Justice A.N. 183
Reeves report 160–1
Reeves, Sir Paul 159
regional appeals courts 186–7
religious courts 179–82
Religious Harmony Act, Singapore 124
religious traditions 43, 48, 50, 54, 120
Report on Central-Provincial Government Relations, Papua New Guinea 61
Representation of the People Act 1951, India 108, 114
representation, quality of 245
representative government 29, 54, 80, 91–118, 243–4, 246

representatives, appointed 75–6, 100, 243
Republic of the United States of Indonesia 66
Rhee, President (South Korea) 178
Riggs, Fred 152
rights 48, 242; fundamental 35, 216; individual 29, 34–5, 241–2; protection of 7, 198–9
Rizal J. 5
Robillard, Roger de 190
Rodman, W.L. 26, 230
Roh Tae Woo 47
Rotuma 68, 159–60
Roxas, Manuel 127
RPCR, New Caledonia 245
Rudini 130
rule of law 29, 34, 42, 154, 198, 210, 244–5

Sabah 225
Sahardjo, Dr 172
Samoa: colonial history of 22; Court of Appeal 187; customary law 41; ethnic groups 26; nominations for parliamentary seats 107; state of emergency 208
Samudavanija, Chai-anan 154
Sandline International 236
Santri Muslims 43
Sarawak 225
Savang Vatthana, King (Laos) 120
Saw Maung, General 148
SCAORA 184
Sciulli, David 3
self-determination 67, 243–4
separation of power 30, 39, 44–5, 188, 245
separatist movements 67–8
Shah, Rajah Tun Azlan 122
Shariah law 16
Shari'ah Appellate, Philippines 180–1
Sharif, Nawaz 134
Shelat, Justice 183
Sihanouk, King 4, 120, 147, 186
Sikri, Chief Justice 183
Singapore 20, 58; Barisian Socialis party 112; communist activity 38; Community Development Councils 96; electoral system 96, 99, 103; federalism 223; Group Representational Constituencies (GRCs) 96; head of state 119, 124, 126–7, 132–3; Internal Security Act 124; Islamic law 43, 180; Judicial Committee (Repeal) Act 177; legal system 180; martial law 214; Parliamentary Elections (Amendment) Act 1991 99; party

Singapore (*cont.*)
  defections 112; Presidential Elections Committee 127; Privy Council appeal 177; referendum 92; Religious Harmony Act 124
'Singapore School' 5
Singirok, Brigadier-General Jerry 85, 236
Sinhala people, Sri Lanka 227
Sisowath, King (Laos) 120
Skate, Bill 85, 236
Sklar, R.L. 31
socialist-democratic state 35–9, 79–80
societies: agrarian 14; class 18, 98; colonial 45, 142; Melanesian 17–18; multi-ethnic 223; plural 82, 222, 241; Polynesian 17–18; sea-based 14; traditional 45, 48
Soeharto 131, 171; approach to Pancasila 66; downfall of 109; 'New Order' 130, 146
Soeharto government 38, 44, 125, 172; and parliament 76, 106; party system 105–6
Soekarno 49, 58, 129, 146, 170, 171; and Communist Party 38; *Confrontasi* 20; and courts 44, 172; downfall of 131; 'Guided Democracy' 4, 202; martial law 91, 212; Pancasila 65; and parliament 76; party system 104
Sokomanu, Ati George 123
Solomon Islands 68, 243; British protectorate 23; colonial history of 22, 25; constitutional development 62; constitutional reform 143; Constitutional Review Committee 143; devolution of powers 223, 237; Electoral Review Committee 109; electoral system 94, 109; federalism 230; head of state 123, 134; independence 59; judicial system 187; no-confidence motions 86; party system 102; Provincial Government Act 237; state of emergency 205
Soluta, J.A. 200
Somare, Michael 62, 84, 102
Son Sann 147
Sope, Barak 190
Soqosoqo ni Vakavulewa ni Taukei (SVT), Fiji 160–1
Soulbury Commission 58
South Asia, suspension of constitutional powers 200–1
South Korea: accountability of government 78; Central Election Management Committee 108, 111; Constitutional Committee 178; Constitutional Court 178, 183; electoral system 108, 110–11; form of government 141; head of state 125, 127, 131–2; Judicature Act 171; judicial system 170–1, 172, 178; military authorities, involvement in operation of the state 47; party system 103; State Indemnity Act 171; state of emergency 203–4, 206–7, 209
Southeast Asia: colonisation in 19–21; suspension of constitutional powers 201–3; traditional states in 14–17
sovereignty, national 217, 243
sovereignty of the people 29, 43, 66–8, 129, 241
Spanish colonisation 21
Speight, George 41
Sri Lanka: constitutional reform 227; devolution of powers 227; federalism 227–8; form of government 141; head of state 125, 127, 132; independence constitution 58, 201; Parliamentary Select Committee on Constitutional Change 228; party system 103; statte of emergency 201; United National Party (UNP) 227–8
Sri Lanka Freedom Party 228
Sriwijaya 14
stability of government 82–8, 114–15, 244–5
state: constitutional 33–4; ethno-nationalist 39–42; liberal-democratic 34–5; socialist-democratic 35–9; traditional 13–28; unitary 222, 226, 228
State Indemnity Act, South Korea 171
State Law and Order Restoration Council (SLORC), Burma 57, 104, 148, 151, 202, 244
state of emergency: declaration of 205–8; duration of 207–8; revocation of 209–10
Stephen, Sir Ninian 79
Straits Settlements 20
Strategic Trusts, UN 22
Subekti 177–8
Sudharmono 130
suffrage 91, 98, 101
Sukarnoputri, Megawati 106, 129
Sukhothai period, Thailand 15–16
Sun Yat Sen 5
Supreme Council of Magistracy Law, Cambodia 179, 185
Supreme Court, Fiji 187
Supreme Court, Indonesia 178
Supreme Court, Vanuatu 190
Suriyamongkol, Pisan 152
Surjadi 106
suspension of constitutional powers 198–221
Sutrisno, General Try 130

Index   313

Tabai, Ieremia 132
Tahiti 24, 122
Taivaiqia, Ratu Sir Josaia 40
Taiwan: constitution 5; constitutional change 47–8; Council of Grand Justices 170; democracy 47; gender equality 102; head of state 119, 127; judicial system 170, 172; martial law 208, 214; National Security Law 214; party system 103, 104; proportional representation 95; state of emergency 203, 208; suffrage in 101
Tambon Council and Tambon Administration Act, Thailand 228
Tamil separatists, Sri Lanka 227
Tamizuddin, Maulvi 211–12
Tan Soo Phuan 127
Tatmadaw (armed forces, Burma) 57, 148, 202
Taufa'ahau Tupou IV (Tonga) 122
Taukei movement 49
Teh Cheng Poh v. Public Prosecutor 209–10
Tempo, banning of in Indonesia 182
Teosin, John 68
Thailand: Administrative Court 182; appointed members of parliament 99; coalition government 88; Committee for Democratic Development 153; communist activity 38; constituent assemblies 151; Constitution Drafting Assembly (CDA) 154; constitutional reform 141, 151–5; Constitutional Tribunal 178–9; constitutionalism 55, 152; constitutions 54, 202–3; Council of Ministers 81; and democracy 46–7, 152; Democracy Development Committee 153; devolution of powers 228–9; Election Commission 154; electoral system 95, 96, 110, 154, 109; elite control 152; Establishment of Administrative Court and Administrative Procedure Bill 182; federalism 228–9; Judicial Service Act 185; Judicial Services Commission 185; judicial system 172, 178, 182–3, 185, 188; Juridical Council 182; legal tradition 15–16; Local Administration Act and Coup Announcement 228; military authorities, involvement in operation of the state 81; monarchy 120–1, 133; National Action Party (NAP) 83; National Assembly (Rathasatha) 81; National Peace-Keeping Council (NPKC) 152, 179, 203; New Aspiration Party 229; no-confidence motions 83; Ongkarn Borihan Suan Tambon 228; organic laws 154; party system 103; Petition Committee of the Office of the Juridical Council 121; petitions 121–2; Pokrong Thontee Act 228; Pollwatch 109; Pra Thammasat 15–16; Privy Council 121–2; proportional representation 95; state of emergency 202, 203; Tambon Council and Tambon Administration Act 228; unitary state 228; vote-buying 113
Thanarat, Field Marshall Sarit 152
Thapa, Prime Minister Surya Bahadur 121
Tiananmen Square 244
Timakata, Fred 124, 130
Tioulong, Chakrei Nhiek 179
Tmetuchel, Roman 93
Tokelau 60, 173
Tonga: appointed members of parliament 99; British protectorate 23; class society 18, 98; constitution 59, 144; Constitutional Convention 144; Court of Appeal 176; customary law 40; ethnic constituencies 98; independence 59; monarchy 18, 122; no-confidence motions 86; parliamentary government 76; Privy Council Court of Appeal 176; pro-democracy movement 144; state of emergency 205–6; suffrage in 101
Tonga Pro-Democracy Movement 144
Tordoff, Professor 61
Toribong, Johnson 93
traditional states 13–28
Treaty of Friendship, Britain and Tonga 23
tribal courts, Philippines 181–2
Tripoli Agreement 230
Truk 23, 63
trusteeship, United Nations 22
Tui Tonga 18
Tung Chee-hwa 130
Tupou I, Tonga 59
Tuvalu 26, 68; constitutional monarchy 61; constitutional reform 143; head of state 123, 132; independence 59; legislature 76; party system 102–3; state of emergency 205–7
Tydings-McDuffie Act 21

U Aung Toe 150
U Nu 201
UN Charter 67
UN Trusteeship Council 59, 67
Union of Malaya 20
Union of Moderate Parties (UMP), Vanuatu 85–6

United Front coalition, India 83
United Malays National Organisation (UNMO) 20, 98, 189, 225
United National Party (UNP), Sri Lanka 227-8
United Nations 22, 67-8, 243; Basic Principles on the Independence of the Judiciary 191; and Cambodia 147; Covenant on Civil and Political Rights 67; Strategic and non-Strategic Trusts 22; sub-commission on Prevention of Discrimination and the Protection of Minorities 189; Universal Declaration of Human Rights 1, 242
United States of America: colonisation 21, 24, 63-4; Compacts of Free Association (COFA) 59-60, 223; territories, representation in Congress 98; US Trust Territory of Micronesia 59, 63-4, 68; USA-Spanish Treaty of Paris 21
Unity Front, Vanuatu 85
Universal Declaration of Human Rights, UN 1, 242

Vajpayee, Atal Behari 83, 155
Vakatora, Tomasi 159
values 29, 50, 246; constitutional 241, 244; democratic 30-1; global 242, 248; and law 42-3; traditional 141, 242
Vanberg, V.J. 142
Vanua'aku Pati 86, 190
Vanuatu 23; colonial history of 25; constitution 55, 144; Council of Chiefs 42; Court of Appeal 187; customary law 40, 42; Decentralization and Local Government Regulations Act 231; electoral college 130; federalism 230; head of state 123-4, 130; independence 59; Judicial Services Commission 191; judicial system 177, 187, 189, 191; legal tradition in 18; Members of Parliament (Vacation of Seats) Act 33 113; no-confidence motions 85-6; party defections 112-13; proportional representation 95; state of emergency 205-6; Supreme Court 190
Verma, Justice J.S. 184
Vietnam 35; Committtee of the National Assembly 80; constitutional reform 36-7, 155-6; Council of State 156; *doi moi* (open door) policy 36, 103; Fatherland Front 103; head of state 128; judicial system 176, 186; *Le Code* 17; National Assembly 155-6; party system 103
Vietnam Lawyers Association 176
violence, electoral 114
Vohor, Prime Minister Serge 85-6, 123, 190
Vola ni Kawa Bula, Fiji 101
Vorachat, Chalard 153
vote-buying 113-14
voter registration 101, 108
voting 91, 98, 101

Wahid, Abdurrahman 58, 129
Wajed, Sheikh Hasina 79
Wallis and Futuna Islands 40, 98
Ward, Chief Justice Gordon 23, 187
Wasi, Prawasi 153
Watt, Prof 61-2
Weisbrot, D. 173
West New Guinea 243
Western Breakaway Movement 68
Western Samoa 23; constitutional reform 145; customary law 40-1; Electoral Amendment Act 187; independence 59; judicial system 187; monarchy 122; and NZ colonisation 25; state of emergency 205-6; suffrage in 101
Westminster models 33, 56, 102, 245; difficulties of 77, 81-2, 87
Wingti, Paias 84-5, 189
women 101-2

Yap, indpendence 63
Yo E La 148
Yongchaiyudh, Chavalit 83, 229
Yus, M. 226

Zakaria, H.A. 39
Zia, Khaleda 184

For EU product safety concerns, contact us at Calle de José Abascal, 56–1°, 28003 Madrid, Spain or eugpsr@cambridge.org.

www.ingramcontent.com/pod-product-compliance
Ingram Content Group UK Ltd.
Pitfield, Milton Keynes, MK11 3LW, UK
UKHW020353060825
461487UK00008B/641